What went wrong with Britain?

An audit of Tory failure

Edited by Steven Kettell, Peter Kerr and Daniela Tepe

MANCHESTER UNIVERSITY PRESS

Copyright © Manchester University Press 2025

While copyright in the volume as a whole is vested in Manchester University Press, copyright in individual chapters belongs to their respective authors, and no chapter may be reproduced wholly or in part without the express permission in writing of both author and publisher.

Published by Manchester University Press
Oxford Road, Manchester, M13 9PL

www.manchesteruniversitypress.co.uk

British Library Cataloguing-in-Publication Data
A catalogue record for this book is available from the British Library

ISBN   978 1 5261 7039 2   hardback
ISBN   978 1 5261 7037 8   paperback

First published 2025

The publisher has no responsibility for the persistence or accuracy of URLs for any external or third-party internet websites referred to in this book, and does not guarantee that any content on such websites is, or will remain, accurate or appropriate.

EU authorised representative for GPSR:
Easy Access System Europe, Mustamäe tee 50, 10621 Tallinn, Estonia
gpsr.requests@easproject.com

The editors and publisher recognise that Northern Ireland is part of the UK, not Britain. However, the book contains references to Northern Ireland, so for this reason the decision was made to include it in the cover design.

Typeset
by New Best-set Typesetters Ltd

Contents

Introduction: What went wrong with Britain?
– Steven Kettell, Peter Kerr and Daniela Tepe   *page* 1

1. Talking the country up, talking the country down: Modern conservatism's politics of division – Matthew Watson   14
2. Missing the crisis? The denial of structural poverty in the 'cost of living' debate – James Morrison   32
3. Covid, Brexit and the emergence of national populism – Owen Worth   53
4. The UK's chronic territorial condition: The politics of constitutional debate after devolution – Jonathan Bradbury   77
5. The crisis in our NHS pre- and post-Covid – Allyson M. Pollock, James Lancaster and Louisa Harding-Edgar   102
6. Who cares about care? The carelessness of adult social care policy – Juanita Elias, Ruth Pearson and Shirin M. Rai   122
7. Social care or social harm? The chaotic organisation of support for Looked After Children in England – Tamsin Bowers-Brown, Andrew Brierley and Alexander Nunn   141
8. Cracks in the food system: Food poverty, food aid and dietary health inequalities – Claire Thompson, Dianna Smith and Laura Hamilton   163

Contents

9	What happened to all the anti-racists? – John Narayan	181
10	Gender, austerity and crisis in an age of catastrophe – Frankie Rogan and Emma Foster	199
11	The Conservatives and the climate crisis: Ambition trumping delivery – Neil Carter	222
12	The politics of debt and perpetual crisis – Johnna Montgomerie	247
13	Brexit and the crisis of British democracy – Jonathan Hopkin	266
14	Fighting back? Britain's shifting capitalism and its discontents – David J. Bailey	288
15	Security in Britain today – Lee Jarvis and Michael Lister	310
16	What went wrong with Britain and what did Britain have to do with it? – Colin Hay	329

List of contributors	342
List of acronyms	349
Index	351

Introduction: What went wrong with Britain?

Steven Kettell, Peter Kerr and Daniela Tepe

How did this book come about?

This book was borne out of a general feeling of frustration and despair amongst the three editors. It started less as an idea for a book than as three academic friends sharing their collective sense of dismay at the enduringly crisis-ridden and seemingly deteriorating state of the country. We began by simply chatting about our shared despondency at watching inequality and poverty in the UK become ever more prevalent and visible. We shared stories, of how our towns and city centres are becoming populated by increasing numbers of rough sleepers, our experiences of being unwell and not being offered the levels of access to care the NHS once promised (while noting the relatively quick access to private health for those who can afford it), of hearing from our kids and other parents about increasing numbers of kids turning up to school hungry because they don't have enough food at home.

We talked about the explosion in demand for food banks and warm banks up and down the country, about friends working in unsafe environments in insecure jobs, about the quality of our roads and transport systems deteriorating whilst our rivers fill up with damaging levels of raw sewage and other pollutants, about one of us being made to feel at the border that they don't really belong in Britain, and about the growing mental health crisis and uncertainty over their futures many of our students face. Our strong sense was that these stories were considerably worse than the stories we would have shared even a decade ago. In addition to this, we each shared a conviction that these problems have all been exacerbated by the dismal record and misguided political choices of recent governments.

Admittedly, as both politically engaged citizens and critical social scientists, we're prone to complaining about the state of the world around us. We have lived through, and at times written or taught our students about, Blairite Britain, the financial crisis of 2008 and the years of austerity that followed, and we have always found ways to criticise the status quo. Yet, our shared conviction is that the general condition of our politics, public services, economy and quality of life in the UK has, in so many ways, become measurably worse than at any point in our collective living memories.

When, in the summer of 2023, one of the most prominent German news outlets ran with the headline 'Destitute Brits' (Heuser and Schindler, 2023) and highlighted their astonishment at the seeming acceptance in the UK of countrywide food, warm and baby bank use, and the widespread squalor of the living conditions of an increasing number of British citizens, this resonated with us. We, too, feel alarmed at how normalised this state of affairs, and alongside it, Britain's seemingly perpetual state of crisis, has become. As such, we were no less surprised at the lack of public or media outcry when, towards the end of the same year, Olivier De Schutter, the UN's special rapporteur on extreme poverty and human rights, warned the UK that its poverty levels were so low as to be in violation of international human rights (Booth, 2023), or when recent reports indicated that such levels of poverty were partly contributing towards an increase in 'Victorian era' diseases such as rickets and scurvy (Honigsbaum, 2024).

It is against this background that we decided to put this edited collection together. To us, it seemed a necessity to stop and ask ourselves what had gone wrong with Britain. So urgent was this task that our initial idea was to call the book *WTF is Wrong with Britain?* as a means of trying to

Introduction

convey the strength of our shared exasperation at the current direction of travel in which the country appears to be heading. Perhaps wisely, our publisher advised us to drop the expletive. Nevertheless, this book has been compiled in the spirit of three colleagues asking, what is effectively, a WTF?-style question.

Is this the right question to ask?

There are undoubtedly many people who will object to us asking this question in the first place – with or without the expletive. There are many, particularly on the right of the political spectrum, who believe that left-leaning academics like ourselves are invariably too quick to criticise the UK. This feeling was neatly encapsulated by Boris Johnson when, speaking in the context of the bitter divisions caused by the Brexit withdrawal process, he used his first speech as prime minister in 2019 to directly challenge 'the doubters, the doomsters, the gloomsters' – those critics 'who bet against Britain' (Johnson, 2019). Johnson famously sought to revive a sense of optimism amongst British voters with his so-called 'boosterism' – a style of leadership that was pitched against those who he and his allies viewed as 'talking Britain down'. As such, Johnson's speeches over the past few years are littered with his pleas for greater confidence and optimism. For instance, when speaking about Brexit, he described the UK's withdrawal from the European Union as 'a heroic act of national self-belief', taken by people who have 'the guts to believe in Britain'. In Johnson's view, 'with a bit of gumption and a bit of positive energy, there is no limit to what we can achieve' (*Hansard*, 11 July 2017, Cl.138).

Johnson, and others like him, are certainly right to point out that there are many good reasons to be positive about Britain. After all, the UK has the sixth largest economy in the world. We are lucky to live in a picturesque, temperate country with a peaceful and stable democracy, a strong tradition of liberal beliefs, an influential and respected presence on the global stage, a (relatively) solid record on human rights and a free national health service, which has until recently been viewed as one of the best health services in the world. We undeniably have a lot to feel very grateful for. In light of all this, perhaps Johnson is right that we are just being 'doubters' and 'gloomsters'. Yet, this is not our own sense at all. As will become all too clear to most readers, the evidence that this book throws up suggests that there are many compelling reasons to feel both doubtful and gloomy about the current trajectory of the UK.

A very different take on why this book might not be asking the right question is provided by Colin Hay in the concluding chapter to this volume. Although not challenging our choice of title, Hay astutely points to two potential pitfalls in asking the question 'what went wrong with Britain?' The first is that it conveys an implicit assumption that what has gone wrong is somehow unique to Britain. Clearly, many of the problems highlighted in this book – such as rising levels of poverty and inequality and creaking public services – are endemic to the majority of advanced democracies. With this in mind then, surely the question 'what went wrong with Britain?' can only be answered properly through a detailed comparative analysis with other countries; something this book admittedly doesn't provide.

Moreover, Hay also points out that a second problem with our question is the implicit suggestion that the things that have gone wrong with Britain are somehow Britain's fault. He makes a very good point here. Many of the chapters that follow highlight a series of poor judgements, strategic errors and political failings amongst our political elites. A problem with an analysis that places too much emphasis on these types of failings is that it can overly 'responsibilise' certain individuals for a series of problems that are, in fact, both structural and globally widespread. This is a point that we, as editors, are sensitive towards. Each of us is acutely aware of the wider structural and historical challenges that the UK faces. Amongst these we might include: the UK's relative decline from its former hegemonic position in the global economy; the constraints that neoliberal globalisation have placed on UK policymakers' capacity to manage that decline; and the negative impact that the UK has recently experienced from a series of external shocks, such as the Great Financial Crisis, the COVID-19 pandemic, the war in Ukraine and the ensuing global energy crisis. It

Introduction

is undoubtedly the case that the UK, as with most other countries, has had to endure a series of challenges, turbulent events and crises that have largely been beyond its control.

However, what is interesting to us as editors is that the contributors to this volume – all of whom are aware of these wider challenges, and all of whom are recognised scholars in their respective fields – have generally chosen to place the weight of their analyses on the overall failure of Britain's political elites to navigate these challenges well. Indeed, as the reader makes their way through each of the chapters (please take regular breaks, for it is not a happy experience) it becomes abundantly clear that the contributors to this volume all share our own sense of dismay at just how incredibly poorly recent governments have performed across nearly all areas of public policy. Indeed, there is a collective consensus throughout this volume that not only have recent governments failed to stem the flow of Britain's accelerating decline into a seemingly chronic state of permacrisis, but many of their decisions have made these crises considerably worse.

What, then, went wrong with Britain?

When we started to think about how to put this volume together, we quickly scribbled down a list of topics and themes that exceeded the scope of the book. The areas that have made it into the final version are therefore not exhaustive but hopefully provide sufficient scope for a reasonably detailed picture of the state of the country. The choice of chapters was in part due to the areas and themes we judged to be most relevant, and partly due to the availability of expert authors. As editors, we made the decision to only give a minimal amount of direction to each of the authors, aside from asking each to reflect on the question of 'What went wrong with Britain?' in relation to each of their respective areas of expertise. What has come out of this project is, as Hay eloquently describes in his concluding chapter: 'a detailed, delineated and above all disaggregated domain-by-domain mapping and description of the condition – the plight, the plights – afflicting Britain socially, politically, economically and culturally'.

What went wrong with Britain?

Yet despite this detailed mapping, the reader will be disappointed if they expect the volume to throw up any simple, formulaic answer to the question. There are, nevertheless, a handful of recurring themes that infuse the entire volume. In particular, the authors repeatedly point towards: the overwhelmingly negative impact that a decade of austerity has had on the UK's public services, levels of welfare security and social wellbeing; the damaging effects of Brexit; the persistence of growing levels of inequality and poverty; and the fact that the UK was ill-equipped to deal with the challenges of the COVID-19 pandemic. Given the amount of times these recurring themes pop up throughout the volume, it seems clear to us that there are two very broad conclusions we can posit in response the question 'What went wrong with Britain?'

The first is that a great many of the things which are wrong have become substantially worse over the course of the past decade and a half. Productivity, investment and trade have all been negatively hit by the impact of Brexit, inequalities of wealth and life chances have continued to widen, disparities of health have grown, public services are crumbling, parts of the coast have been turned into an open sewer, the trains are perpetually late or cancelled, the roads are full of pot holes, and … well, you get the picture. The second and related conclusion is that successive UK governments can be considered, at least in part, culpable for many of those problems. Here it is worth returning to Boris Johnson's retort against the gloomsters on the steps of Downing Street. 'The people who bet against Britain', he declared, 'are going to lose their shirts because we are going to restore trust in our democracy … no ifs or buts' (Johnson, 2019). There is a certain degree of irony in this statement, given the damage caused to voter trust by Johnson's short-lived premiership, which became swiftly embroiled in scandals and serial mendacity. Arguably, Johnson's stint in high office exemplifies one of the most conspicuous features of UK politics over the past decade or so; namely, the tendency for a considerable element of Britain's political establishment to proclaim an enduring patriotism and optimism for the country whilst presiding over a period of precipitous decline, falling levels of confidence in Britain's institutions, a deterioration of Britain's standing on the global stage, diminishing standards of living, crumbling infrastructure and a heightening of regional divisions which threaten the future integrity of the union itself.

The new Labour government faces a challenge unlike that of any administration since 1945. Across almost every measure, Britain as a country has been seriously depleted by fourteen years of Conservative misrule. If Labour are to succeed in their stated aim of ushering in a new era of national renewal, they will need to confront the full spectrum of crises affecting the nation. Although the election result offers a glimmer of hope for a new direction, it is far too early to draw any conclusions about the prospects of lasting change. The scale of the task is immense, the economic constraints are formidable, and only time will tell whether Labour can reverse the tide of decline.

The structure of the book

Following on from this last point, it is perhaps apt that our first chapter begins with an examination of the legacy of Johnson's premiership. Here, Matthew Watson argues that the Johnson Government ruled through mood manipulation and routine fabrication to promote a distorted and 'exceptionalist' view of British history and identity. In so doing, he (and others) conflated Britishness with claims of superiority, celebrating a 'Whig-Tory' version of history that worked to conceal many of the complexities and negative aspects of both Britain's past and present condition. This misplaced idea of British exceptionalism, Watson contends, was given fuel by the Brexit referendum, but continues to shape Conservative party politics, and is used to sow divisions, with critics regularly denounced as unpatriotic.

In chapter two, James Morrison outlines the shocking state of poverty and inequality in the UK, and highlights the failure of the British media to give adequate coverage to these issues. The chapter shows that wealth gaps are widening and that many jobs no longer provide a living wage, but that poverty is rarely portrayed as a crisis in the media. While recognition of inequality briefly hit the political agenda during the COVID-19 crisis, media narratives quickly reverted to type, emphasising a divide between taxpayers and 'scroungers' and continuing to normalise negative portrayals of welfare recipients rather than focusing on the root causes of poverty.

In chapter three, Owen Worth highlights the damaging increase in nationalism and populism in mainstream UK politics and the risk it poses to the overall stability of the union. Worth argues that Boris Johnson utilised populist tropes to push through Brexit and rally support during the pandemic, but that this approach lacked any underlying ideology or coherent sense of strategy. He goes on to argue that Liz Truss similarly pursued an aggressive neoliberal form of populism leading up to her disastrous mini budget in September 2022, which had a severe impact on the UK economy and put a huge dent in her (and others') hopes of a post-Brexit deregulated economy.

Chapter four, by Jonathan Bradbury, examines the territorial condition of the UK following devolution, Brexit and the pandemic. It discusses the ongoing debates around Scottish independence, Welsh nationalism and the political dynamics in Northern Ireland. The chapter also covers the development of regional governance in England and the question of English nationalism. The overall picture here remains unclear, with plausible prognoses for both the survival and disintegration of the UK. While there are pressures for constitutional change, nowhere does the case for breaking up the UK command a clear majority of public support.

Chapter five, by Allyson M. Pollock, James Lancaster and Louisa Harding-Edgar, discusses the ongoing crisis in the NHS and social care sector. It outlines how decades of underfunding and successive reorganisations weakened communicable disease control at the local level, and shows how bed capacity in hospitals had been drastically cut, leaving the country unprepared for a surge in patients during the pandemic. Social care provision is also shown to be chronically inadequate. Taken together, a lack of capacity and expertise, along with the absence of a properly funded public health system, led to a lethally poor response to the COVID-19 pandemic.

In chapter six, Juanita Elias, Ruth Pearson and Shirin M. Rai continue this theme by examining the crisis in the UK's social care system. The

Introduction

authors highlight how the pandemic exposed severe vulnerabilities caused by decades of underfunding combined with an ageing population. The chapter also highlights the extensive pressures faced by the social care workforce, showing how staff are overworked and undervalued whilst suffering from low pay, high levels of stress and poor working conditions. Successive governments have promised much and delivered little, leaving the UK's social care provision in a perilous state and over-reliant on unpaid labour from family members.

Chapter seven, by Tamsin Bowers-Brown, Andrew Brierley and Alexander Nunn, continues with the subject of care and discusses the social harm experienced by children in the state care system. It outlines how underfunding, poverty and disciplinary social policies have had a negative impact on the lives of children in care, highlighting placement instability, separation from siblings and poor mental health outcomes as major issues. Overall, the chapter argues that the current system prioritises short-term cost cutting over compassion, affecting the longer-term life-chances of vulnerable children and inflicting social harm on both individuals and society.

The following chapter, by Claire Thompson, Dianna Smith and Laura Hamilton, highlights the shocking state of food poverty in the UK. With successive governments having failed to get a grip on the issue, the country now faces a series of endemic problems and worsening health inequalities. Charities are filling the gaps in welfare left by austerity policies whilst the pandemic has exacerbated food insecurity. In the midst of this overall failure to protect vulnerable children, schools are increasingly being relied upon to provide meals, while rates of hunger, obesity and poor mental health are all on the rise due to the inability of many people to afford nutritious diets.

In chapter nine, John Narayan turns our attention to the persistent problem of racism in the UK. While the Black Lives Matter movement was successful at bringing this issue to the forefront of public debate in 2020, the UK government's response has been inadequate, leading to denials that institutional racism is a problem and attempts by the state to promote a form of multiculturalism focused on increasing representation rather than initiating underlying structural change. Historically, anti-racist campaigners have exposed the links that exist between racism and the broader dynamics of capitalism and imperialism. This approach holds greater potential for addressing institutional racism, especially in the current economic situation as the cost of living crisis sees growing alliances across social groups to challenge and dismantle oppressive institutions.

Chapter ten, by Frankie Rogan and Emma Foster, discusses the changing landscape of gender politics in Britain since the 1990s, when there was a resurgence of optimism for a postfeminist future. The authors highlight how this postfeminist promise has been undermined by the damaging impact of austerity policies since 2010, which have disproportionately affected women, and the negative effects of a right-wing populism that promotes conservative gender values. These trends have been exacerbated by the pandemic and the current cost of living crisis, which further reveal the gendered nature of insecurity and inequality in Britain today.

Chapter eleven, by Neil Carter, examines the UK's response to the growing climate crisis. Unsurprisingly, the record is not a good one. Successive governments have struggled to implement effective policies, while crises like Brexit, COVID-19 and the war in Ukraine have distracted from a focus on climate action. The chapter notes progress in certain areas (such as decarbonising electricity), but significant policy gaps remain regarding buildings, transport, agriculture and land use. Overall, the government's ambition has far outpaced delivery, and the capacity for future UK governments to tackle climate change remains in question due to vested interests and persistent governance problems.

The following chapter, from Johnna Montgomerie, looks at the politics of debt in the UK and highlights the failure of successive governments to adequately tackle the problem. Analysing the government's response to economic crises, as well as the effects of Brexit and the pandemic, the chapter shows how levels of debt in both the public and private sectors have substantially increased. Monetary policy has consistently favoured bailing out financial markets while fiscal policy has failed to bring meaningful relief to households. In that context, inequality has grown as

Introduction

interventions have disproportionately benefited the wealthy. Continuing economic instability and falling standards of living demonstrate the failure of neoliberal policies to resolve the problem of growing inequality and rising private debt levels.

In a similar vein, chapter thirteen, by Jonathan Hopkin, highlights how these underlying structural problems within the British economy have been exacerbated by Brexit. Here, Hopkin persuasively shows how the decision to leave the EU has failed to address the types of concerns and underlying economic issues which led a majority of voters to vote Leave. Instead, Brexit has created the conditions for a resurgence of the political right in Britain, many of whom favour limited state intervention. Implementing Brexit has highlighted the weaknesses of the UK's centralised political system in addressing complex policy issues, and the pandemic has further exposed long-running underinvestment in public services.

Staying with this theme, the next chapter, by David J. Bailey, focuses on Britain's model of capitalism and the politics of resistance. The chapter shows how British capitalism has shifted significantly towards neoliberal policies since the 1980s, leading to rising inequality and precarious employment. Yet, these developments are facing a significant amount of resistance from below. Highlighting the variety of strikes and protests against austerity, rising inflation and stagnant wages, Bailey shows how movements like UK Uncut, Black Lives Matter and renewed trade union activism have the potential to wrest meaningful concessions from government and employers.

Our penultimate chapter in this volume comes from Lee Jarvis and Michael Lister and addresses the topic of security. The authors argue that the UK's security policy suffers from a number of failings. Dogged by issues of short-termism, cronyism and a lack of diversity in the national security community, the authors argue that Britain's security policy focuses too much on external threats rather than more common internal dangers. This prioritises military security at the expense of more immediate threats such as pandemics or domestic violence. The chapter also argues that minority groups disproportionately bear the costs of security policies through measures like counter-terrorism profiling and austerity cuts. As a result, Britain's security policy is often wasteful, counterproductive and detached from the needs of the most vulnerable.

Last, but by no means least, is our concluding chapter by Colin Hay. This takes on the altogether tricky task of closing the volume by summarising the key themes and findings of our contributors. In doing so, Hay astutely points out some of the limitations of the book, two of which – its lack of comparative context and its tendency to place an over-emphasis on agency – we have already highlighted above. Beyond this though, Hay also very helpfully extrapolates from our varied collection of chapters and findings some overarching problems that can help to shed light on how the UK has managed to get itself into such a mess. Primary amongst these is the persistence of an attachment to an Anglo-liberal version of neoliberalism. This has had the effect, Hay argues, of depoliticising and individualising poverty, to the extent that widening inequality levels require no real public outcry or meaningful government action since responsibility for being poor is placed almost entirely at the hands of the individual.

In addition to the persistence of neoliberalism, Hay points out that Boris Johnson's premiership encapsulated another key problem of British governance in recent years – the tendency to overlap neoliberal ideas with a nationalistic brand of populism. This style of politics, which was chiefly galvanised by the Brexit referendum, has helped to promote an approach to governance which encourages governments to take short-termist oppositional and divisive positions on key issues rather than a longer-term, professional, competence-based and expert-driven approach.

Overall, we want to end here by saying that we hope you enjoy the book; though we're acutely aware that 'enjoy' is not quite the appropriate word to use in this context. As should already be clear, the chapters that follow tell a fairly bleak story about the multiple problems Britain faces. We would like to think that bringing them together can potentially provoke some wider discussions about how to put (or at least to start putting) some of these problems right.

Introduction

References

Booth, R. (2023) 'UK "in violation of international law" over poverty levels, says UN envoy', *Guardian*, 5 November, www.theguardian.com/society/2023/nov/05/uk-poverty-levels-simply-not-acceptable-says-un-envoy-olivier-de-schutter

Heuser, O. and Schindler, J. (2023) 'Bettelarme Briten', *Spiegel*, 10 June, www.spiegel.de/ausland/grossbritannien-armut-und-niedergang-in-uk-podcast-a-67fb7a9d-89e3-45e1-9b33-5658e0939635

Honigsbaum, M. (2024) '"It is shameful": Why the return of Victorian-era diseases to the UK alarms health experts', *Observer*, 18 February, www.theguardian.com/society/2024/feb/18/return-of-victorian-era-diseases-to-the-uk-scabies-measles-rickets-scurvy

Johnson, B. (2019) 'Boris Johnson's first speech as Prime Minister', Gov.UK, 24 July, www.gov.uk/government/speeches/boris-johnsons-first-speech-as-prime-minister-24-july-2019

1
Talking the country up, talking the country down: Modern conservatism's politics of division

Matthew Watson

Introduction

In the end, Boris Johnson resigned as he had led: remaining silent on manifold personal indiscretions while shouting loudly about non-existent successes. More so than any of his predecessors, he sought to govern through mood manipulation. Also, more so than any other former premier, he sought to govern through fabrication. Rishi Sunak ultimately gave a much more self-aware and magnanimous resignation speech, but only after he had attempted to mimic the Johnson strategy. He consistently bluffed about the strength of the economy during a cost of living crisis, while trying to whip up antagonism towards public sector workers, human rights lawyers, international courts, climate protesters, anti-racist activists, cyclists, the trans community, economists, epidemiologists, anti-poverty think tanks and anyone who stood up for the autonomy of public institutions. From the start of Johnson's premiership to the end of Sunak's, the Conservative Party managed to cut itself adrift from anything other than its dwindling band of core voters, having no governing project of which to speak but leaving endless examples of a decaying public realm, for which constant culture-war posturing proved no antidote.

Johnson's likely political epitaph will be that he ushered in the rot that ultimately undermined the most recent period of Conservative electoral dominance, with Sunak being unwilling to break free of his legacy. Johnson showed no interest in being judged on outcomes, appearing immune to shame in his government's performance as he bounced between crises and scandals on a path littered with U-turns. It was as if the country had been plunged head-first into an experiment in what might be called sociopathocracy. Through all its countless mistakes, dishonourable conduct and conspicuous law-breaking, the Johnson Government created the illusion of successful performance indicators through a combination of bluster, dissimulation, boastfulness, misdirection, exaggeration and plain old lies. No degree of corrective interventions from independent fact-checkers or even the government's own statistical agencies ever appeared enough to elicit contrition, an apology or a retraction of the offending claim, let alone a change of course. Nothing, it seemed, could be allowed to stand in the way of the Johnson Government reminding the British public how lucky they were to live in the greatest country on earth and to have politicians like them who were happy to say as much. His petty, self-absorbed and unrepentant Downing Street resignation speech was cut from precisely such a cloth.

Liz Truss also resigned as she had led. She repeatedly refused to acknowledge the chaos of her seven-week premiership, insisting that her economic experiment had been the right one for everyone except an expert class that was less patriotic than her. Even the chastening nature of defeat in her previously rock solidly Conservative constituency of South West Norfolk did not elicit a change of heart. She chose to walk out of a BBC interview on the night she burnt through a 26,000 majority rather than engage with the question of whether Trussonomics was a contributing factor to the 2024 election defeat.

Sunak initially tried to position himself as a break from the immediate past, signalling his intention to restore to the prime ministerial office both competence and integrity. Yet he became merely the latest to try to convince the public to believe things that were not true and to disbelieve things that were. The most notable claims of his first one hundred days in office were (i) to itemise the tax bill that would fall on every family to compensate for conceding to striking public sector workers' pay claims and (ii) to trumpet the UK's gains in trade following its new sovereign status post-Brexit. However, the former £1,000 figure was quickly shown by independent fact-checkers to bear no resemblance to the pay claims that unions had actually submitted, and the latter £800 billion figure was challenged for its wilfully misleading nature by the UK Office for Statistics Regulation, the government's own watchdog. Like Johnson before him, Sunak always appeared relaxed about his ministers continuing to push such easily debunked claims within the public realm, at the same time as requiring that they dismiss every analysis of the ever-accelerating economic costs of Brexit. During the 2024 general election campaign, for instance, the Conservatives repeatedly insisted that Labour's manifesto contained a hidden £2,000 tax bill for each family in the face of equally full-throated insistence from the Office for Statistics Regulation that it did not. This was while insisting that economic successes that existed nowhere other than in their own boasts were enough to pay for tax cuts that dwarfed the size of Labour's spending plans.

The Johnson Government may only have had a three-year lifespan, but its effect on how the Conservative Party conducts its politics has clearly outlived its brief term. Their defeat in the 2024 general election revealed just how significant a distance the Conservatives would need to travel to convince the public that the country they have created works as they say it does. Their party has been almost systematically remade in the image of Vote Leave's successful articulation in 2016 of a politics of grievance disconnected from any obviously implied governing project. But this has left them constantly searching for the next convenient scapegoat they can accuse of preventing the country from fulfilling its historical destiny. As the 2019–24 parliament progressed, the Conservatives fell into the pattern of complaining angrily from the sidelines about the accumulation of crisis symptoms afflicting the country, more intent on identifying enemies within who had always been Brexit naysayers than concentrating on the fact that they were elected because they had convinced the public that they alone knew how to make Brexit work.

A prime example is the difference between the Johnson Government's bungled COVID-19 response and the story his ministers came to tell about it. In the earliest days of the pandemic, when Johnson could not even be bothered to chair Civil Contingencies Committee meetings about the looming threat, he reached for the rhetorical conceits of manifest destiny to suggest that all the country needed to do to ride out COVID-19 unscathed was to reach inside itself, access its reserves of national character, assert that all would be well and carry on as normal (Johnson, 2020a). This can be seen in retrospect as both the rhetorical high-water mark of Brexitism and the moment when the impossibility of translating that rhetoric into a workable governing project became crystal clear. Even when epidemiological reality and Johnson's own near-death experience exploded the initial account of British exceptionalism, the crowing did not stop. When the country needed to be governed well, it was instead subjected to gaslighting as a political strategy. Britain, we were told, was engaged in a world-leading pandemic response (untrue except as an anti-brag), helped by an early start to the vaccination programme (partly true, but whose advantages rapidly dissipated), which itself was only made possible by Brexit (patently untrue). This allowed England to be the first country to remove all its remaining COVID-19 protections (true, but contrary to scientific advice), with no further need to worry about infection rates and the toll they were taking on both lives and livelihoods (in equal part untrue and absurd).

To explain what went wrong with Britain, then, requires a focus on what the Conservatives would allow the very notion of Britain to signify. The Johnson Government appropriated Vote Leave's entirely delusional image of British exceptionalism and treated it as synonymous with the idea of the national people it sought to govern. Anyone who questioned whether exceptionalist assumptions were really justified or who pointed out that other countries might have better social, economic, welfare and health outcomes was immediately jumped on by Conservative politicians and their outriders in the right-wing press for harbouring anti-British sentiments. The Johnson Government's stock response to criticism of any form was to accuse the critics of talking the country down. It conflated expressions of British superiority with its underlying conception of Britishness: to be British, in this view, is to believe that Britain must always be right and always be best.

How, though, did this particular mood-making practice materialise? Where do we see it most obviously imprinted in the turn to wilful fabrication? I attempt to answer these questions by investigating how Johnson's ministers came to speak for a particular conception of Britain and for whom that conception resonates. I show that government through mood manipulation and government through fabrication combined in the Johnson years to create government through division. The post-Johnson Conservative Party has yet to show any obvious signs of even wanting to escape such a self-made trap.

The Johnson Government's view of speaking for Britain

Speaking for Britain has two distinct dimensions, which often rub against one another in uncomfortable ways. One aspect exists in the realm of political imagination, a largely untethered space in which flights of fancy might combine with soaring rhetoric to etch on the public consciousness an image of what the country might become. The other exists in the realm of political reality, a much more clearly demarcated space in which constitutional norms and statutory obligations limit what might be promised. British politicians, conscious of the need to be judged on outcomes, have typically tried to strike a balance between the two. This is a central feature of what Jane Mansbridge (2003) calls 'anticipatory representation', the process of scaling back any promise that the electorate is likely to see as unfeasibly optimistic. However, Johnson seemed to be temperamentally incapable of dialling down his rhetoric if this placed limits on acting as his own cheerleader. For him, speaking for Britain rested solely in the realm of political imagination, where the ability to say what he wanted remained unconstrained by the shame he might otherwise have been expected to experience for the legion of untruths with which his premiership was marked. Mood manipulation is all that matters in the Britain he spoke for. The realm of political reality requires respect for the facts and a commitment to truthfulness that Johnson found difficult to reconcile with his preferred approach to public speaking (Oborne, 2021). It can therefore have had little role in how he chose to speak for Britain. Bragging and maintaining pretences is therefore all he appeared to have left.

This was demonstrated all too vividly in Johnson's frequent appearances at Downing Street press conferences at the height of the pandemic. The choreography of events took on the same familiar awkwardness. Johnson would begin by trying to stick to the script that his advisors had prepared for him, even though doing so in the guise of the 'Boris' character that became his signature political act made him sound less than sincere. Having become a victim of his own focus groups that found his relentless good-time-Charlie persona struck a chord with many voters, delivering grave updates on the development of the pandemic required an emotional repertoire that 'Boris' did not possess. For the most serious announcements, he was accompanied by his Chief Medical and Scientific Officers, Chris Whitty and Patrick Vallance. According to the political sketch-writer John Crace (2020), they were used as 'a human shield', their presence at the event a mere prop to prove that the Prime Minister was taking the public health threat seriously, their message of caution a remedy to his destructive Panglossian tendencies.

Yet still, when it came to fielding questions from journalists, Johnson would revert to type, no longer bound by a pre-prepared script and willing to overlook epidemiological evidence in search of good news headlines in the lockdown-sceptical (and sometimes even Covid-sceptical) conservative press. The faces of the scientific advisors would reveal their dismay at crucial public health messages being undermined. But still Johnson would make a series of improbable promises – about how easy it would be to 'squash the sombrero' of the infections curve (Johnson, 2020b), about twelve weeks being all it would take to 'send coronavirus packing in this country' (Johnson, 2020c) – designed to lighten the national mood by positioning Britain out in front of the chasing pack in its successful COVID-19 containment. The choreography was completed when the leaders of the devolved nations held their own press conferences almost immediately after Johnson's to remind their populations that, contrary to his assertions, the Prime Minister of the United Kingdom had no authority over public health policies in their jurisdictions and that what he had just said at most held only for England. They would then reiterate their preference for a more cautious approach to the cycle of locking down and opening back up, consistent with the views of the scientific advisors. If Johnson was temperamentally incapable of reining in the chutzpah, he also seemed politically incapable of grasping even the basic structure of the devolution settlement.

For his whole approach to governing, reality was only allowed to intercede at the last moment, once the preceding claim had been exposed as a hollow boast of national one-upmanship, but also once the overtly patriotic part of the population had been allowed to revel in the image of their country being the best of all. Everything, it seemed, had to be described as 'world-beating', even when it palpably was not. This was evident at an exorbitant cost in excess deaths in the early stages of the pandemic, when the only way to successfully track the trajectory of the virus was to engage in the mass testing that would identify the pattern of transmission chains. Many countries in East Asia relied on the public health infrastructure they had developed when containing SARS to operate what was, in effect, a zero-Covid policy. Meanwhile, the Johnson Government chose initially to abandon testing and refused to properly fund community health officials skilled in the task of contact tracing. Instead, it gambled on a technological solution that the Commons Public Accounts Committee ultimately described as the biggest white elephant at which a UK government had ever thrown unlimited public money (House of Commons Committee of Public Accounts, 2021; see also National Audit Office, 2021). Private sector management consultants earned staggeringly high fees only to demonstrate that they did not know what they were doing. But still ministers insisted on repeating Johnson's well-worn line that the British people were witnessing a world-beating system in operation, even as UK COVID-19 deaths surged towards the top of the one global league table nobody wanted to lead.

The same pattern of bluster and dissembling was repeated consistently beyond the politics of the pandemic. It was evident in the claims that ministers made about the UK being the most generous country in Europe for resettling refugees as millions fled Ukraine following Russia's 2022 invasion. In reality, the very opposite was closer to the truth, as the Home Office placed multiple obstacles on fleeing civilians being able to reach the UK through routes it designated 'legal'. A whistleblower working on the Homes for Ukraine scheme, through which Britons invited Ukrainian refugees to live with them, said that the scheme had been deliberately set up to fail (Townsend, 2022). The same features of wilful misdirection were also evident in the deal struck with the Rwandan government to transport all 'unauthorised' migrants to be settled outside the UK. The policy was criticised for its immorality, its inordinate expense, its likely contravention of international asylum law, and the fact that it would not solve whatever problem the government thought it was tackling. But still it had the label 'world-beating' attached to it. The same exact pattern was also evident in the government's protracted dealings over the Northern Ireland protocol of the Brexit Withdrawal Agreement. Johnson's repeated assurances that this would not create a trade border between Northern Ireland and Great Britain was always a self-interested reading of the treaty he had signed. It was designed to ensure he could pat himself on the back for having delivered a solution that represented the best of all worlds to everyone. On each occasion, it seemed to take him by surprise that simply saying that something was world-beating did not on its own make it so.

All of these policies were subjected to sustained critique at the time. However, such challenges came either from those who were susceptible to Johnson's depiction of them as Islington Remoaners or from professional experts who were quickly repositioned as anti-government activists. The policies all seem to have been designed consciously to sow division. The Vote Leave tactic of carving up the electorate into incommensurable camps before deliberately outraging one of them was never far from Johnson Government strategising. It invited disapproval so that condemnation could be repurposed as an educated establishment elite looking down their noses at ordinary people. Islington Remoaners are those who can never forgive the Brexit wing of the Conservative Party for having taken the UK out of the European Union, and professional experts were those who repeatedly said that this leap into the unknown could never end well. They were increasingly presented in potent political terms as unpatriotic people who refused to see the good in their own country. Minsters' shameless attachment of the label 'world-beating' to whatever scheme they cooked up next acted as a political trap. Those policies were not designed to function as advertised, because their inbuilt propensity towards failure served as bait. Anyone who pointed out likely contradictions that would prevent policies of supposedly unparalleled foresight from being even moderately functional was said to be willing the country to fail.

Throughout his adult life, Johnson has been an ardent devotee of the 'great man' theory of history, and he was always eager as Prime Minister to scale up this way of thinking to declare Britain to be a 'great nation'. Celebrating Britishness from this perspective is to take whatever opportunity presents itself to claim that the country can do things that no other country can simply because of who it is. Only small steps are required from here to the claim that just because the UK is doing something then it must be doing it better than anyone else could conceivably do. No degree of Brexit-inflicted harm to the economy has been sufficient to beat a retreat from the positive mood manipulation occasioned by trumpeting the advantages of reclaimed sovereignty. No degree of pandemic mismanagement has been sufficient to stop the bragging about how well everything is going now that the UK has broken free of the European Union. The Sunak Government was clearly continuity-Johnson in this regard. For both, policy performance seemed always to be a secondary consideration to the ability to create the aura of national self-congratulation. With the idea of British exceptionalism treated as synonymous with the idea of Britain itself, anyone who wished to puncture the vanity of the exceptionalism thesis ran the risk of being portrayed as anti-British.

Take those instances in which the external reality (which has a nasty habit of intervening) came in the form of international law. Johnson's Cabinet consistently refused to alter its preferred policy course out of respect for Britain's status as signatory of that law, prompting resignations from both government officials and junior ministers. It was only when it considered transgressions of international law to be inexpedient to the political task of mood manipulation – in other words, only when its bluff was well and truly called – that it chose to fall into line with what its legal advisors recommended. At all other times, the attitude was encapsulated in then Minister for Brexit Opportunities Jacob Rees-Mogg's insistence that the government had a right to treat its international obligations as purely voluntary: 'We can do what we want, ultimately' (cited in O'Carroll, 2022). International law is just another external actor, like the European Union before it, from whose grip the UK must release itself if it is to fulfil its destiny. From this perspective, pre-eminence is a British birthright, allowing UK governments to contravene international law on a whim.

Sunak's change of heart on the Rwanda deportation plan is highly instructive as an example of how this commitment to British exceptionalism outlasted Johnson. When he was Johnson's Chancellor of the Exchequer, Sunak rubbished the Rwanda scheme as an unconscionable waste of money, but as Prime Minister he made it the flagship policy of his attempts to play to nativist opinions by stopping the small-boat crossings of the English Channel. He exhibited no shame in saying that he would allow the UK to follow Russia and Belarus in revoking its membership of the European Convention on Human Rights if this proved critical to stopping a 'foreign court' from influencing British asylum policy. But from where might such a view of innate national superiority have arisen? In the following section, I suggest that it originates in a particular account of British history, one that has always found favour within the Conservative Party but has been pushed especially aggressively since its return to power in 2010.

The Johnson Government's view of British history

Professional historians today might struggle to locate the most suitable subject matter for their studies of Britain. Should they be writing a history of the centralised UK political structure, or a history of the UK's four constituent nations? Should they recognise that Britain was an empire-state long before it became a nation state and consequently think of their subject matter globally? Should British history be written from above as a history *of* the state, or from below as a history of protest and struggle *against* the state? Should it be a history of the way that the people have been governed, or a history of the way in which the very notion of a

What went wrong with Britain?

national people has materialised through the granting of political, social and economic rights? Who, in short, are the Britons to whom the history of Britain must be familiar? The broadening of professional historians' gaze since the end of the Second World War means that there is no straightforward answer to these questions, even if such developments appear to have completely bypassed the Conservative Party.

The Thatcher Government of the 1980s introduced a national curriculum for English schools to reclaim the right from local education authorities to determine what should be learnt. That power was placed in the hands of the Secretary of State for Education. Running directly contrary to the more expansive approach of professional historians, successive Conservative Secretaries of State have sought to narrow the curriculum in favour of something more reassuring to their own political mindset (Brocklehurst, 2015). The history of rights won, often in struggles with Conservative administrations, gives way to the history of military battles won, events in which the British character is said to have come to the fore. The history of how the British people became what they are today is sacrificed for a history of how their ascent would have been much more difficult in the absence of prescient, benevolent and overwhelmingly successful rulers. Children are told how fortunate they are to be born in such a special country by removing from the curriculum all intimations of its ordinariness. Rhetorical embellishment and factual dishonesty are merely more extreme versions of such a telling of events.

Modern Conservatism's preferred version of British history is a curious combination of what Herbert Butterfield (1950 [1931]) described as the Tory approach and the Whig approach. The Tory approach emphasises the British character, which it treats as a reflection of the dominant personalities of any given age. Monarchs, prime ministers and generals take centre stage, with British history being reduced to tales of successful territorial acquisitions. Monarchs are remembered primarily for the size of the empire they ruled over, prime ministers for the strength of the imperial spirit they instilled in loyal subjects, and generals for the lands they handed over as new crown possessions. Meanwhile, the Whig approach emphasises British ideals, which it believes are embedded in the essence of state institutions. Appeal is made to the Whig totems of Magna Carta (1215), Habeas Corpus (1679), the Bill of Rights (1689) and the Act of Settlement (1701), which are collectively depicted as links in an 800-year chain that continues to provide for individual liberty protected by parliamentary democracy. The Conservative Party's preferred version of national history focuses on the way in which Britain was the first to guarantee personal rights of free assembly, free association, free conscience and free speech, and it uses this to explain how the British royal family came to rule over the biggest Empire the world has ever known.

As Butterfield warned, such accounts are sanitised versions of what, in practice, was a much messier history. They represent national nostalgia moods, fictionalised accounts that allow the collective 'us' to feel better about our national inheritance. It is history told for a self-serving purpose, and as such it will licence no perspective other than that which supports the opinion that Britain has always been the first or the best at everything it makes a national mission. The Johnson Government was almost certainly out on its own in the extent to which it made exaggeration and dissimulation the primary symbols of its governing ethos. Yet its wilful conflation of British exceptionalism with the very idea of Britain was entirely consistent with how, since the 1980s, Conservatives have insisted British history is taught in English schools. It differed only in the degree to which it was willing to push the argument that anything other than a celebratory history of Britain is equivalent to the anti-patriotic practice of talking the country down. Once again, it spied political opportunities for entrapping its opponents by inviting objections to its chauvinistic tone, and it hoped to be rewarded electorally having first divided the country into patriotic and anti-patriotic camps.

The extended gaze of professional historians over the last seventy years therefore occupies a curious double position relative to modern Conservatism's preferred version of Britain. On one side, it enabled the Johnson Government to profit from sowing division. Professional historians were enlisted in such a ploy, having their reputations traduced for daring to think differently to how ministers wished UK children to imagine their country. They placed themselves outside the Johnson Government's chosen nostalgia moods through their dismissal of both the Tory and the Whig approach to British history and their refusal to say that everything in the national past was great, glorious, honourable and decent. This made them susceptible to right-wing culture war attacks for trying to make people feel bad about their country. Yet such attacks came thick and fast only because professional historians' conception of British history represented a significant threat to how the Johnson Government wished to present the inheritances of achievement, conduct and character from the national past. Very few professionals involved in either the researching or the teaching of British history are willing to endorse the self-congratulatory version that Conservative Secretaries of State have stipulated since the rewriting of the national curriculum in 2013. The organisation representing those professionals, the Historical Association, polled its members following the release of then Secretary of State Michael Gove's personally approved draft curriculum. Only 4 per cent could find anything positive to say about Gove's requirement that history be taught to a prescribed list of accomplishments through which the nation had proved itself to be either the first or the best (Historical Association, 2013).

Culture war attacks were perhaps the only option available to ministers who found themselves having to argue that they knew more than professional historians about the professional historians' specialist area of expertise. Political considerations persuaded David Cameron first to instruct Gove to backtrack from some of the most egregious excesses of his draft history curriculum and ultimately to remove him from the Education ministry altogether. However, it would be difficult to say that this was reality intervening as anything other than short-term electoral calculations concerning Gove's plummeting popularity. The teaching of history remained central to the Johnson Government's attempts to govern through mood manipulation and fabrication.

The self-styled Common Sense Group of Conservative MPs now routinely argues for disbarring historians from accessing public funding if their research projects are deemed to be insufficiently patriotic. This prompted an open letter from the Royal Historical Society (2021) to ask then Culture Secretary, Oliver Dowden, to clarify whether the government had now abandoned the Haldane principle that ministers must play no role in influencing individual academic funding decisions. Nothing much has changed – unless it is for the worse – since Gove responded to the Historical Association's rejection of his curriculum by dismissing history teachers, academics and educationalists as 'the Blob'. Professional experts were sneered at for being 'Enemies of Promise' and inhabitants of a 'Red Planet' (Gove, 2013a). They were accused of 'standing in the way of progress' (Gove, 2013b) for no reason other than not sharing the Secretary of State's conception of what counts as British history. The Common Sense Group now acts as Gove's outraged outriders at the very suggestion that the purpose of history is to understand rather than to extol. Contributing to its manifesto, *Conservative Thinking for a Post-Liberal Age*, the MP James Sunderland and lead writer for the *Daily Express* David Maddox complained of a 'year zero approach to history and a belief that what was in the past was wrong and should be condemned' (Sunderland and Maddox 2021: 30). From this perspective, history is not something that evolves in the writing, but something that has to be conserved for fear that it might be diminished.

This chimes with Gove's vision for how schools should teach history: children sitting silently behind desks set up in rows, trying to memorise the names and dates of kings, queens, politicians and famous battles. He assumed that this would help them to understand national history as a chronology, rather than as a series of episodes connected by theme as opposed to date. Yet his case for chronology was only ever a fig leaf for imposing his chosen content. It is possible to teach as a chronology the history of resistance, the history of protest or the history of marginalised groups claiming rights against a state embodying the principles of a reactionary conservative establishment. Gove, though, never had any intention of permitting such focal points into his curriculum. Chronology for him could only ever mean stitching together carefully selected events that could be interpreted through a combined Tory–Whig approach as a celebratory account of national history capable of putting the 'great' into Great Britain (Watson, 2020). Dissenters were to be shouted down in *ad hominem* attacks against members of the Blob for selling the country's children short by refusing to let them hear 'inspiring stories' from the nation's past (Gove, 2010).

The hallmarks of Johnson's style of government – governing through mood manipulation and governing through fabrication – were clearly in evidence when Gove's curriculum wars were at their most rabid in 2013. They were in evidence again when numerous Vote Leave alumni – Johnson, Jacob Rees-Mogg, Daniel Hannan and Andrea Leadsom amongst them – used big but obviously fanciful claims to promote the now much mocked 'sunlit uplands' of regained national independence. There should consequently have been no surprise in 2019 that Johnson won a commanding parliamentary majority by consistently invoking a different reality to the one in which the election was actually being fought (Brown, 2019). The self-styled natural party of government now appears to govern as it campaigns, in both instances channelling its view of Britain as something to be applauded rather than considered, vaunted rather than pondered, embellished rather than understood. However, the 2024 general election, set against the backdrop of a cost of living crisis and a widespread perception that public institutions had deliberately been allowed to wither on the vine, exposed the political limits of such an approach.

Conclusion

Gove studied English at Lady Margaret Hall, Oxford, but still felt able to declare that he knew more about how history should be taught than those who had been responsible for doing so their whole careers. He was aware that they considered British history to be much more diverse than the sycophantic story he wanted told but pressed ahead anyway. He has been joined in this regard by other illuminati of the Oxford Union debating society. Johnson (Classics, Balliol) and Rees-Mogg (History, Trinity) had first honed their public characters at Eton. For their younger selves, as it was throughout their parliamentary careers, it is not what you say that matters, and certainly not how close what you say is to the truth, but perfecting an effortless superiority in how you say it (Kuper, 2022). Johnson and Rees-Mogg have each published historical works, Johnson (2014) a hagiography of Churchill festooned with easily corrected factual inaccuracies, Rees-Mogg (2019) a series of sketches of eminent Victorians that its reviewers thought was most notable for the lack of research effort underpinning its content. Both books were widely panned for their self-serving subject matter, their fundamental unseriousness as historical texts and the liberty they took with the facts.

Misplaced claims, historical inventions and a departure from the record were never a cause for concern for Gove during his tenure as Secretary of State for Education. Neither were they for Johnson and Rees-Mogg during their moonlighting stints as wannabe historians. They all went as far as to wear the scorn of professional experts as a badge of honour. Their only crime, they said, was to refuse to be drawn into the game of talking their country down. They addressed the patriotic part of the population and asked to be rewarded politically for emphasising good news stories about what they believe remains the greatest country on earth. They sought to turn into a governing mantra a peculiar conception of Britishness that refuses to accept even the possibility that the UK is an ordinary, middle-power European country. It was a deliberate tactic to conflate the very idea of Britishness with claims of British exceptionalism, but one which now appears to have run out of road electorally.

To preserve an unrelentingly positive national mood in the face of the accumulation of so much contrary evidence requires retreat into a parallel universe that very few people can recognise from their own experiences. It is no wonder just how important conspicuous fabrication became to the way in which the UK was governed during the 2019–24 parliament. Johnson, Gove and Rees-Mogg may not be as prominent in the phase of modern conservatism we are now entering, but the party they steered onto the electoral rocks has yet to show any signs that it wants to genuinely change course. If the Conservatives remain locked into tilting at windmills rather than trying to reconnect with the public, this might look like a political gift to the new Labour Government. Yet it still has to deal with a public that has been deliberately divided since 2016 in an environment in which trust in politicians has reached an all-time low. The context for governing is hardly propitious if what it takes to govern well in the near future is to persuade people who felt genuinely comforted by Johnson's eulogies to exceptionalism that he was deceiving them all along.

References

Brocklehurst, H. (2015) 'Educating Britain? Political literacy and the construction of national history', *Journal of Common Market Studies*, 53(1): 52–70.

Brown, F. (2019) 'Investigation finds "88% of Tory ads misleading compared to 0% for Labour"', *Metro*, 10 December, https://metro.co.uk/2019/12/10/investigation-finds-88-tory-ads-misleading-compared-0-labour-11651802/

Butterfield, H. (1950 [1931]) *The Whig Interpretation of History*, Cambridge University Press, Cambridge.

Crace, J. (2020) 'Tired of being Boris Johnson's patsy, Patrick Vallance fights back', *Guardian*, 16 July, www.theguardian.com/politics/2020/jul/16/tired-of-being-boris-johnsons-patsy-patrick-vallance-fights-back

Gove, M. (2010) 'All pupils will learn our island story', Speech to the Conservative Party Conference, Birmingham, 5 October.

Gove, M. (2013a) 'I refuse to surrender to the Marxist teachers hell-bent on destroying our schools', *Daily Mail*, 23 March, www.dailymail.co.uk/debate/article-2298146/I-refuse-surrender-Marxist-teachers-hell-bent-destroying-schools-Education-Secretary-berates-new-enemies-promise-opposing-plans.html#ixzz2OTOslXOB

Gove, M. (2013b) Excerpts from speech to Conservative Party Conference, *Guardian*, 1 October, www.theguardian.com/politics/2013/oct/01/michael-gove-militant-teaching-unions

Historical Association (2013) 'You spoke. We listened. Our response to the History Consultation 2013', www.history.org.uk/ha-news/news/1779/you-spoke-we-listened-our-response-to-the-histor

House of Commons Committee of Public Accounts (2021) *Test and Trace Update: Twenty-Third Report of Session 2021–22*, HMSO, London.

Johnson, B. (2014) *The Churchill Factor: How One Man Made History*, Hodder and Stoughton, London.

Johnson, B. (2020a) 'PM speech in Greenwich: 3 February 2020', Gov.UK, www.gov.uk/government/speeches/pm-speech-in-greenwich-3-february-2020

Johnson, B. (2020b) 'PM comments at daily coronavirus press briefing', 12 March, *Guardian*, https://www.theguardian.com/politics/live/2020/mar/12/trumps-travel-ban-wont-have-much-impact-on-spread-of-coronavirus-says-rishi-sunak-live-news

Johnson, B. (2020c) 'PM comments at daily coronavirus press briefing', 19 March, *Guardian*, https://www.theguardian.com/world/2020/mar/19/boris-johnson-uk-can-turn-tide-of-coronavirus-in-12-weeks

Kuper, S. (2022) *Chums: How a Tiny Caste of Oxford Tories Took Over the UK*, Profile, London.

Mansbridge, J. (2003) 'Rethinking representation', *American Political Science Review*, 97(4): 515–528.

National Audit Office (2021) *Test and Trace in England – Progress Update*, NAO, London.

Oborne, P. (2021) *The Assault on Truth: Boris Johnson, Donald Trump and the Emergence of a New Moral Barbarism*, Simon and Schuster, London.

O'Carroll, L. (2022) 'Johnson preparing to "fix" Northern Ireland Brexit deal', *Guardian*, 22 April, www.theguardian.com/politics/2022/apr/22/johnson-preparing-to-fix-northern-ireland-brexit-deal

Rees-Mogg, J. (2019) *The Victorians: Twelve Titans Who Forged Britain*, W.H. Allen, London.

Royal Historical Society (2021) 'RHS asks government to clarify its position on historical research', 21 March, https://royalhistsoc.org/rhs-asks-government-to-clarify-its-position-on-historical-research

Sunderland, J. and Maddox, D. (2021) 'The Conservative case for media reform', in The Common Sense Group, *Common Sense: Conservative Thinking for a Post-Liberal Age*, Common Sense Group, London.

Townsend, M. (2022) 'Homes for Ukraine whistleblower says UK refugee scheme is "designed to fail"', *Guardian*, 23 April, www.theguardian.com/world/2022/apr/23/homes-for-ukraine-whistleblower-says-uk-refugee-scheme-is-designed-to-fail

Watson, M. (2020) 'Michael Gove's war on professional historical expertise: Conservative curriculum reform, extreme Whig history and the place of imperial heroes in modern multicultural Britain', *British Politics*, 15(3): 271–290.

2
Missing the crisis? The denial of structural poverty in the 'cost of living' debate
James Morrison

Introduction

Britain is riven by economic inequality: wealth and income gaps have never been wider; many paid jobs barely pay; and serious long-term health conditions are most prevalent among people from the poorest communities. This is especially true of those living in multigenerational households and working in historically undervalued sectors, such as social care – rhetorically re-framed as 'essential' by politicians and journalists only until the COVID-19 panic subsided (and, with it, any pretence of seriously starting to value them).

As if levels of disadvantage pre-dating the pandemic were not acute enough, millions of people have emerged from it even poorer, with worsening inequalities of health, education and income. But where is the media coverage of the depth and scale of this human catastrophe? In an age when almost all issues of popular concern (however short-lived) are framed as 'crises' – from winter beds shortages in the NHS to disputes over exam grades to Britain's national finances – poverty scarcely moves the dial as public outrage fails to materialise and, in its absence, the media looks the other way.

This chapter considers how early optimism about the contribution media discourse might make in forging a post-COVID social settlement

– or 'new normal' – faded as news agendas and narratives reverted to type. It argues that, far from embracing a more inclusive diagnosis of Britain's economic inequality problem, the media continues to downplay poverty as the deep-seated, structurally rooted issue it is – instead painting the unfolding 'cost of living crisis' as both a decontextualised, *externally* imposed event and a form of 'leveller' that supposedly caught almost everyone (bar the super-rich) in its impoverishing embrace. As incomes stagnated, energy and grocery prices soared, and economic inequalities continued to widen in the wake of the pandemic, there was always another act of God or aberrant bogeyman to blame for these escalating pressures – from Vladimir Putin disrupting fuel prices by invading Ukraine to short-lived Prime Minister Liz Truss's notorious 'mini Budget', which plunged sterling into free fall by spooking overseas investors with its blizzard of uncosted tax cuts.

At the root of the country's inequality problem is its addiction to moralising neoliberal narratives that individualise responsibility for poverty and reserve collective outrage (and action) only for crises that are seen to affect us *all* – from Covid to escalating heating bills. In the early days of Covid, then Chancellor Rishi Sunak revived talk of social security 'safety nets' and the need for governments to be 'judged by their compassion' as he unveiled a multi-billion-pound package to pay the wages of millions of workers forced to stay at home, and a short-term boost to Universal Credit (the main working-age benefit) to help those losing their jobs (Sunak, 2020a). But as soon as the pandemic was over the Tories went back to their old ways – launching a 'Way to Work' drive to force those unemployed for four weeks or more to accept any job offer or lose their benefits, and rebooting the anti-welfare rhetoric of the Coalition years. By the time Sunak himself was installed in 10 Downing Street, concerns about rising levels of 'economic inactivity' – people out of work and not actively seeking it, usually due to disability, illness and/or caring responsibilities – saw the Tories and press cheerleaders framing young people with work-limiting mental health conditions as carriers of a 'British disease' of 'laziness' (Denham, 2024). Now, with Labour back in power – and already warning of tough fiscal decisions ahead around 'welfare' – it remains to be seen how far, or how fast, it will move to reset 'work-shy' narratives, let alone whether it will decisively address inequality through policy. While Work and Pensions Secretary Liz Kendall has pointedly condemned the Tories' 'strivers versus scroungers' rhetoric, she has also warned that there will be 'no option of a life on benefits' under Keir Starmer's 'changed Labour Party' (Kendall, 2024a).

Crisis, what crisis? The culture of poverty denial

What would it take to wake up the UK news media – and public – to the extent of the mounting poverty emergency? How close do we need to be to the despair and destitution endured by one in five Britons and three in ten children (Joseph Rowntree Foundation, 2025) to appreciate the misery of what it means to lack food, fuel and other basic essentials?

At the start of the COVID-19 pandemic hopes were high that, if one positive emerged, it was likely to be a heightened public awareness – and concern – about deep-rooted inequalities that had hitherto been widely denied. Day by day it became clearer that both COVID-19 itself and lockdown restrictions were disproportionately impacting already economically disadvantaged groups, especially many BAME people, those living in high-density housing, multigenerational households and/or workers in low-paid frontline jobs it was impossible to do from home – from cleaners to shelf-stackers. Moreover, society's sudden dependency on supermarkets and delivery services finally spotlighted 'essential workers' who had long been exploited in poorly paid, precarious sectors of the economy. With businesses mothballed, millions furloughed and still more forced into the arms of an unwelcoming welfare state – a highly conditional £335-a-month Universal Credit payment suddenly their only source of income – the six degrees of separation previously insulating most people from Britain's meagre benefits system were sharply reduced. If there was ever a time to reset attitudes to 'welfare', surely this was it?

Since the panic around COVID-19 faded there have been plenty of other newsworthy reasons for poverty and benefits to remain in the spotlight. From the slow-burn recognition that rising wholesale costs and collapsing supply chains owe as much to Brexit as coronavirus, to the exacerbating impact the war in Ukraine and Liz Truss's 'kamikaze Budget', the least well-off (as ever) have continued to suffer most (Hourston, 2022).

Yet, when it comes to debating poverty, national outrage remains in stubbornly short supply. While the 'cost of living crisis' has sparked incessant coverage of hard-pressed household budgets, instead of focusing on struggling unemployed or disabled people journalists have obsessed over its impact on those less used to counting their pennies, such as the 'squeezed middle' (Antonucci et al., 2017) – as food poverty campaigner Jack Monroe and others have noted (Edwards, 2022). More broadly, sympathy for 'the poor' is once more reserved for the most manifestly 'deserving' groups, notably pensioners and low-waged 'working people', or discrete forms of hardship that most insult basic notions of human dignity – from 'child' to 'funeral poverty'. All the while, concerned politicians, pundits and even campaigners continue to performatively qualify their concerns, reassuring sceptical publics that they are championing only the worthiest causes. As ever, this enables those with ideological aversions to 'welfare' to continue peddling long-standing diagnoses of the causes of poverty that blame it on individual pathologies and behavioural defects instead of what it is: an avoidable symptom of structural economic failings bequeathed by decades of neoliberal dogma.

For a brief moment in 2020, discourses – and attitudes – had finally seemed to be shifting. When Emily Maitlis, anchor of BBC2's *Newsnight*, delivered her celebrated monologue debunking the 'myth' that the pandemic was 'a great leveller' – highlighting the plight of 'lower paid members of our workforce' and 'those who live in tower blocks'– the social media reception suggested a high level of public cut-through (Maitlis, 2020). Perhaps more remarkable was the fact that Maitlis' broadcast coincided with an even starker discursive turn at the heart of government. Addressing one of a series of press conferences announcing rescue packages for anxious households forcibly laid off by Britain's frozen economy, then Conservative Chancellor Rishi Sunak promised:

What went wrong with Britain?

> When you need it, when you fall on hard times, we will all, as one society, be there for you – to take care of you, until you are, once again, ready to take care of yourself and others. (Sunak, 2020b)

This was a statement prioritising society over individuals that channelled the spirit of the 1948 address in which Labour Prime Minister Clement Attlee had launched his 'new Social Services': the melange of contributory and non-contributory protections for pensioners, low-waged workers, unemployed and disabled people that later governments would repeatedly undermine. In unveiling his collectivist vision of this post-war 'welfare state', Attlee had aligned it to 'the new principle' that we 'combine together to meet contingencies with which we cannot cope as individual citizens' (Attlee, 1948).

Sunak's revival of this rhetoric was of a piece with a renewed spirit of 'Covid-era' solidarity that was even (briefly) evident in reliably welfare-sceptic reaches of the media. On the date of an earlier address, in which he had pledged to 'help pay people's wages' through his unprecedented furlough scheme (Sunak, 2020a), ex-*Telegraph* editor Charles Moore hailed his intervention as 'the right big gesture' (Moore, 2020), while television presenter-turned-tabloid columnist Carole Malone – a conservative commentator with form for baiting benefit recipients – confessed she had 'wept' when Ministers 'effectively nationalised the economy' to 'protect those in greatest need' (Malone, 2020). Even Alex Brummer, city editor of the pathologically anti-statist *Daily Mail*, praised 'the vision of what is being done', dubbing it 'every bit as far reaching' as Attlee's 'bold promise of protecting people from cradle to grave' (Brummer, 2020).

In truth, though, the new collectivism was only ever likely to last so long – and stretch so far. Even at the time, a closer reading of political speeches and comment pieces exposed early hints of a creeping (but all-too-familiar) demarcation between a virtuous and respectable in-group – encompassing *most* of society, especially the pensioners and 'hardworking' households hallowed by mainstream politicians (Cameron, 2013) – and a discursively absent out-group of 'unmentionables'. In drawing pointed rhetorical oppositions between the valorised imaginary of 'working people' and an alternately shamed and ignored minority dismissively categorised as 'workless', almost all the major parties and mainstream newspapers were culpable in (to quote Gerbner) the 'symbolic annihilation' of anyone who *remained* out of work once enforced furloughs and lockdowns ended (Gerbner, 1972). For all its surface generosity, Sunak's furlough was trained on protecting those who had hitherto been respectably employed, so that these virtuous 'workers' could 'retain' their jobs post-pandemic (Sunak, 2020a). Its embrace was therefore reserved for people rendered *temporarily* unemployed *by* the pandemic, not those already out of work beforehand. Moreover, his primary mechanism – a temporary £1,000-a-year rise in Universal Credit – barely repaired one-fifth of the real-terms cut in the value of benefits endured by long-standing recipients during the preceding decade of Tory austerity (Brewer and Handscomb, 2021).

Likewise, in praising Sunak for protecting 'those in greatest need', media sympathy was reserved for the 'millions' worried about losing 'their jobs and their homes' (Malone, 2020) and finding themselves 'on the verge of unemployment' *for the first time* (Moore, 2020). As so often happens, us-versus-them discourses were implicitly mobilised to build false oppositions between contributors and non-contributors, 'working' and 'workless' poor, the visible 'virtuous' and invisible, annihilated 'unmentionables': an intrinsically neoliberal dichotomy between 'deserving' and 'undeserving' poverty rooted in commodified notions of virtue and effort.

With 'cost of living' replacing 'Covid' as the crisis shorthand of the moment, the lives of Britain's poorest citizens once more came under siege: both minimum wage rates and average earnings fell ever further behind living costs; an 'inflation-proofed' benefits and pensions uprating failed to keep pace with inflation; new schemes once more strong-armed unemployed and disabled people into any jobs available (however ill-suited and demeaning); and ministers rebooted earlier drives to tackle benefit fraud (Department for Work and Pensions, 2022). The stage was therefore set for a post-pandemic settlement every bit as immiserating as the austerity-ravaged decade preceding it. More recently, despite early moves by Labour to address some of these inequities – notably by strengthening trade union rights, raising the minimum wage and agreeing to a series of public-sector wage demands designed to make up for years of precarity and stagnation – the deification of 'working people', and symbolic annihilation of those dubbed 'workless', looks set to continue.

The coming sections aim to open a conversation about the role the media has played in promoting a reversion to the 'old normal' in post-pandemic Britain – by pathologising poverty and problematising welfare. Following an overview of the sociopolitical and media context predating the pandemic, they go on to show how early discursive turns towards promoting a new collectivism are receding from the public agenda as rapidly as COVID-19 itself – by excluding from their rhetorical embrace social 'unmentionables' such as the long-term unemployed. Conversely, as the spirit of Covid-era solidarity recedes, familiar folk devils are re-emerging in the public sphere – notably the pervasive figure of the 'scrounger'. In the closing sections I demonstrate how, as in the pre-pandemic period, allusions to such tropes are in danger of becoming so taken for granted that they are insinuating themselves into contexts and conversations to which discussion of benefits or poverty have little or no relevance. In this way, the re-embedding of 'welfare common-sense' (Jensen, 2014) allows the 'scrounger' trope to achieve such a level of public recognition – and semiotic fluidity – that it can be separated from its usual contexts (e.g., discussions about work, poverty or the benefits system) with little loss of meaning through decontextualised discursive practices that might be conceptualised as normative 'scrounger-bashing' (Morrison, 2021).

Austerity, deepening structural poverty and other 'old normals'

By any standards, the United Kingdom is a wealthy country. Based on the typical measure used to calculate national wealth, gross domestic product (GDP), it was the world's fifth richest in 2022 – with a value of $2.83 trillion USD(World Population Review, 2022). Immediately before the pandemic, the picture was much the same: in 2019 and 2020 respectively, it ranked sixth (behind India) and fifth (just ahead of India), most league tables measuring the size of its economy with values of $2.83 trillion slipping to $2.7 trillion as COVID-19 struck (World Bank, 2021).

Yet the UK is a grossly unequal society. According to a 2022 Institute for Fiscal Studies (IFS) report focusing on living standards and inequality, overall measures of 'relative' child poverty (defined as a household income worth less than 60 per cent of the median) rose in the years leading up to the pandemic, while a quarter of families with children were in 'absolute' poverty – existing on less than 60 per cent of the median as it had stood in 2011 (Crib et al., 2022). Although overall absolute poverty rates fell by 1 percentage point between 2019–20 and 2020–21 to 17 per cent, this was solely because of the temporary uplift in Universal Credit during Covid – and both relative and absolute poverty began rising again as Universal Credit fell back from 2021–22. Moreover, around four in ten adults in 'workless' households had remained relatively poor throughout this time, compared to one in ten of those in which at least one adult was in paid work (Francis-Devine, 2024). Relative *child* poverty rose in those eight years to 2019–20 thanks to sustained social security cuts initiated by the Coalition.

Economic disadvantage is also an increasingly intersectional problem, as certain minority ethnic groups and people with disabilities and long-term illnesses are disproportionately likely to be poor. For all the recent media and political emphasis on white working-class 'left-behind' communities, by 2019–20 poverty rates were highest for households headed by people from Bangladeshi or Pakistani backgrounds and lowest for those from white ethnic groups (Francis-Devine, 2024). More than a quarter of families in which someone was disabled were relatively poor, compared to 15 per cent of those in which no one had a disability (Francis-Devine, 2024). Given all these statistics, it is hardly surprising that reliance on food banks (a term barely heard until the 2010s) has increased exponentially over the past decade, with the number of food parcels distributed each year multiplying 100 times over between the financial crash and the pandemic (Clark, 2024).

In many ways, this picture marks a logical end point for an era that commenced with the Conservative-led Coalition's sustained and systematic rhetorical assault on unemployed and disabled people, underpinned by a 'doxa' of 'welfare commonsense' dishonestly pitting 'strivers' against 'skivers' (Jensen, 2014). By 2020, absolute poverty had largely been confined to working-aged people, with families disproportionately penalised – including (presumably unintentionally) those in which all adults were working. Moreover, by the end of the pandemic, growing numbers of young men and older women had become statistically invisible – by 'opting out' of both the workforce and unemployment claimant count. According to a 2021 Resolution Foundation report, the pandemic saw sharp rises in the number of men under 45 as well as 55 to 64-year-olds becoming voluntarily 'economically inactive' – i.e., 'not working or looking for work' – and therefore vanishing from official measures of both employment *and* unemployment (Brewer et al., 2021: 8). Far from being work-shy, many of these people were likely to be what the Organisation for Economic Co-operation and Development (OECD) defines as 'discouraged workers': people who, 'while willing and able to engage in a job, are not seeking work or have ceased to seek work because they believe there are no suitable available jobs' (OECD, 2003). Others constitute what the Resolution Foundation (2018) calls the 'forgotten unemployed': those 'falling through the cracks and not getting the financial support that they need and are entitled to', often because they are put off by the complexity and conditionality of the benefits system.

One of the main forces driving Britain's descent into ever-deepening economic inequality is that, for all the country's affluence, it has developed an ideological blind-spot around the desirable extent of using tax-and-spend policies to alleviate poverty – and, despite promising early gestures by Starmer's Government (principally the formation of a dedicated new Child Poverty Unit), at time of writing there was little hard evidence to suggest this decades-long myopia was about to end. Even during the initial 1970s/1980s neoliberal turn, historical trends show that fiscal policy was used more liberally to redistribute through benefits – though this was partly explained by steep rises in unemployment caused by deindustrialisation (Clark and Dilnot, 2002: 9–10). It also disguised the fact that society had been much more equal during the post-war period, when there was near full employment for long periods; fewer working-aged people had to claim benefits; and those who did experienced 'significant increases in benefit *levels*' (Clark and Dilnot, 2002: 9–10, added emphasis). Today, pensioners are by far the biggest beneficiaries of the welfare state – accounting for around half the total £299 billion social security bill in 2023–24 (Gov.uk, 2024). This remained well in excess of the cost of working-aged benefits, even at a time of hysterical headlines about rising 'inactivity' rates (Mackley *et al.*, 2022).

Indeed, for all the superficial uptick in the trajectory of social security spending in the Thatcher years, the past 50 years have witnessed repeated retrenchments in the scope and generosity of working-aged 'welfare', underpinned by a growing ideological shift away from 'big-state' solutions towards a combination of market-style interventions and, latterly, an effective revival of historical approaches to social protection based around principles of conditionality, individual self-help and charity-led voluntarism. Where the Georgians used 'the workhouse test' to force those needing poor relief into unwaged slavery, the Coalition introduced sanctions-based workfare for unemployed people. For the forerunners of today's food banks, soup kitchens and night shelters for people experiencing homelessness, we might delve further back in history – to parish-level 'outdoor' and 'indoor relief' offered by medieval alms-houses and formalised in the Poor Law of 1601 (Health Foundation, 2022). In the past decade alone, the story of 'welfare reform' has been one of cutbacks and coercion for claimants: a toxic cocktail of household benefit caps; bedroom taxes; two-child limits; and year-on-year freezes to once annually uprated incomes. And, while recent surveys suggest there is at last an appetite for a return to more generous social protections – notably the removal of the egregious two-child benefit cap – it remains to be seen if Labour will accede to these calls, given the self-imposed current-account straitjacket imposed by Chancellor Rachel Reeves.

Given this backdrop, it is hardly surprising that, while levels of UK poverty have worsened, so too has the wealth and income gap between rich and poor. In the words of an authority no less drily apolitical than the Office for National Statistics, 'the rise in inequality of household income after taxes and benefits' since 2010 is 'largely down to the diminishing effectiveness of cash benefits to redistribute income from the richest to the poorest, coinciding with the freezing of many cash benefits at their financial year ending (FYE) 2016 values' (O'Neill, 2021). Immediately prior to the pandemic, the incomes of the richest one-fifth of the population were 12 times higher than those of the poorest fifth (at £107,800 on average, compared to £8,500) – the former rising, over the decade to 2020, by an average of 0.9 per cent, while the latter *fell* by 0.3 per cent (O'Neill, 2021).

From media discourse to public attitudes and back again

What, then, has been the position of the media and the public as this picture of ever-worsening inequality has unfolded? A consistent feature of the ways in which poverty and social security have been deliberated in the political public sphere is how both media and politicians routinely frame 'work' as the 'solution' to poverty, and social security – or 'welfare' – as a last resort for a tiny minority of deserving people genuinely unable to lift themselves out of it. Others, such as the long-term unemployed, are either demonised as *undeserving* or marginalised (if not annihilated altogether) from the national conversation.

The prevalence of negative narratives about the long-term unemployed and disabled has inspired extensive research since Golding and Middleton (1982) popularised the term 'scroungerphobia': a moral panic casting them as deviants inimical to the civilised values of mainstream British society. This and later studies explored the historical evolution of conceptions of poverty, with many pointing to a centuries-old continuum of discourses othering the 'undeserving poor' (Golding and Middleton, 1982; Welshman, 2013; Morrison, 2019). Such overviews demonstrate the durability of long-standing ideas that poverty is an inherited behavioural trait, not an economic condition. More recently, attention has turned to examining how such media–political archetypes insinuate themselves into popular culture, particularly 'poverty porn' reality shows (Jensen, 2014).

Research has also increasingly examined how the public itself contributes to popular discourses, on newspaper comment threads and social media (Brooker et al., 2015; Morrison, 2019). Moreover, in analysing the *triggers* for such discourses, many studies situate moral panics around 'scroungers' in the context of periods of severe societal upheaval, unease and insecurity (e.g., Golding and Middleton, 1982; Morrison, 2019): phases much like the present, as we emerge from a decade of post-crash austerity and economic instability, latterly exacerbated by COVID-19, Brexit, Russia–Ukraine, Truss and the ongoing 'cost of living crisis'.

While in-depth research into public attitudes is limited, surveys demonstrate a consistent increase in suspicions about the fraudulent behaviour and fecklessness of working-aged benefit recipients – barring a periodic softening of opinion since the early 2010s, when the Coalition's anti-welfare rhetoric peaked (e.g., Taylor-Gooby and Taylor, 2015). Alongside more quantitative barometers of public opinion like the annual British Social Attitudes survey, the few qualitative studies suggest such perspectives are shaped, at least partly, by media and political agenda-setters. In their 'Talking about Poverty' initiative, the Joseph Rowntree Foundation and Frameworks Institute identified media-political framing as a key factor influencing public perceptions of benefit recipients, pointing to an ingrained belief that 'individuals rather than society' were to blame for economic inequality and that '"real" poverty' was a 'problem of the past' (Taylor-Gooby and Taylor, 2015: 3).

Post-pandemic scrounger discourse? The limits of the new collectivism

How, then, has any of this changed since Covid, the advent of Boris Johnson's short-lived promises to deliver 'Levelling Up' and the more recent social and economic jolts delivered by Brexit, the Ukraine–Russia conflict and the Truss Government? While the pandemic might initially have led us to expect a more marked and enduring softening of attitudes towards benefit recipients, as more people were forced to engage with the welfare state during the pandemic, all indications are that the pendulum has since largely swung back. In their longitudinal project 'Welfare at a Social Distance', de Vries et al. (2021) revealed how, despite initially becoming more sympathetic towards those experiencing poverty during Covid, the public later reverted to a judgmental position. They also exposed a stark distinction in attitudes towards people made unemployed *by* Covid and those already out of work *beforehand* – strongly echoing the 'deserving/undeserving' binary implicit in ministerial (and media) rhetoric justifying the limits of emergency social security interventions discussed previously.

But while all this work paints a picture redolent of pre-Covid *attitudes* towards poverty and welfare, little analytical attention has been paid, to date, to the question of how media and political *discourses* began to evolve in the early stages of Britain's post-pandemic recovery. To what extent (and how soon) did the news media and its key sources on such matters – politicians and pundits – begin to revert to the common sense anti-welfarism of old? Although it is impossible to provide definitive answers to this question in such a short chapter, we can make some preliminary observations about the direction of travel of welfare discourses, based on an exploratory analysis of selected mediated events during the 'late-Covid' and early 'post-Covid' periods. This final section considers three 'discourse events' (Fairclough, 1992) symbolising the subtle, at times near-subliminal, normalisation of tropes that perpetuate associations between working-aged 'welfare' and 'undeserving' poverty. These were:

- An August 2021 *Sky News* interview in which then Prime Minister Boris Johnson justified removing the temporary £1,000-a-year Covid 'uplift' in Universal Credit by arguing that claimants should 'rely on their own efforts' to avoid poverty (Plummer, 2021).
- An October 2021 discussion on Channel 5's *Jeremy Vine* current affairs talk show about comments by entrepreneur (and Conservative Party donor) Charlie Mullins likening people opting to work from home post-pandemic to 'dole scroungers' (Mullins, 2021).
- A May 2022 intervention by the IFS think tank in the ensuing 'cost of living' debate warning of tensions between working-aged benefit recipients offered targeted support by government and families 'on modest incomes' exempted from such help (Adam *et al.*, 2022).

Missing the crisis?

Low-paid workers as scroungers

In a *Sky News* interview on 26 August 2021, Boris Johnson responded to a question asking him to justify the government's then impending removal of a £20-a-week uplift in Universal Credit introduced to limit the financial impact of lockdown restrictions on low-income households with an answer incorporating these widely reported remarks:

> My strong preference is for people to see their wages rise through their efforts rather than through taxation of other people put into their pay packets, rather than welfare. (Eardley and Wilson, 2021)

Though brief, Johnson's comment – reported by numerous outlets, including the BBC, the *Independent*, the *Huffington Post* and *Big Issue* – was loaded with familiar anti-scrounger connotations. In juxtaposing Universal Credit recipients with the 'other people' who 'put into their pay packets' through taxation, he explicitly revived a long-standing (and misleading) opposition between 'working people' (contributors) and those on 'welfare' (takers). This denied two inconvenient facts confirmed by the government's own statisticians: that 42 per cent of Universal Credit recipients are actually in work (Gov.uk, 2022) and anyone earning more than £12,570 a year but still entitled to this benefit would have been paying both National Insurance and income tax, often at a disproportionately higher marginal rate than most other taxpayers (Reuben, 2021). In other words, at least four out of ten of the people Johnson framed as inactive, by associating them with 'welfare' – a passive term consistently misused as a cue to trigger negative associations with working-aged benefits (see Jensen, 2014; Morrison, 2019) – were already using 'their efforts' (his words) to contribute.

While Johnson did tacitly acknowledge that some Universal Credit recipients were employed, by referring to 'pay packets', his juxtaposition displaced responsibility onto individuals to lift *themselves* out of poverty – reviving the long-standing neoliberal narrative that people are poor because of personal failings. By suggesting they had the power to raise their wages by their own 'efforts', he further denied the truth that many Universal Credit recipients already worked full time and/or faced barriers to undertaking longer hours such as lack of childcare.

What went wrong with Britain?

Homeworking scroungers

On 25 October 2021, Channel 5's *Jeremy Vine* talk show broadcast a live discussion with Charlie Mullins, millionaire founder of the company Pimlico Plumbers, prompted by a newspaper interview in which he had likened employees still working from home during the later stages of the pandemic to 'dole scroungers'. Mullins had argued that homeworking led to a situation where 'people don't want to go to work, thinking they're entitled to stay home' – warning that 'when youths leave school now they're never going to go and work in their life because the culture is, "well my mum or dad work from home that's what I'll do"' (Lawson, 2021). By adding that 'you've got to break the cycle', he interdiscursively invoked the decades-old neoliberal narrative that poverty (and benefit dependency) are forms of deviancy passed intergenerationally through what Sir Keith Joseph (the architect of Thatcherism) saw as a socialised 'cycle of deprivation' (Welshman, 2007). Pressed on his opinions by *Jeremy Vine* presenter Claudia-Liza Vanderpuije, Mullins doubled down – arguing that homeworking was 'equivalent to drawing benefits when you should be going to work' (Mullins, 2021).

Significantly, while Mullins' remarks were presented to viewers as problematic, it was the nature of the *problematisation* – not his overtly prejudiced views – which revealed most about the extent to which scrounger discourse had been normalised. Far from contesting the existence of 'dole scroungers', Vanderpuije instead queried whether it was fair to compare homeworkers to them – asking *Daily Telegraph* journalist Angela Epstein whether she thought she was 'as bad as a dole scrounger'. The discussion therefore reflected what Jensen (2014) terms the 'doxa' of 'welfare commonsense' – by implicitly *accepting* Mullins' premise that scroungers existed. More significantly, it presaged angry public reactions to Mullins' comments subsequently reported in several other outlets, which focused not on the unfairness of terms like 'scrounger' but on people's indignation that the term might be used to describe *them* (e.g., Bolton, 2021). In other words, implicit to the *Jeremy Vine* discussion and the wider debate it sparked was the same underlying opposition Johnson had mobilised in his *Sky News* remarks two months earlier: a binary distinction between hardworking taxpayers (the virtuous 'us') and freeloading scroungers (the deviant 'them').

Competing claims for 'deservingness': Low earners versus the squeezed middle

In May 2022, as the 'cost of living crisis' unfolded, then Chancellor Sunak unveiled a new package of emergency financial support specifically targeted at the poorest households – primarily those receiving Universal Credit and other income-replacement benefits. While broadly welcoming the intervention, the IFS – which had previously identified those 'most in need' as 'the out-of-work group' and urged Sunak to raise their benefits (Johnson, 2022) – responded with this comment by its director, Paul Johnson:

> There are inevitably going to be families on modest incomes, who are just out of reach of the means tested benefit system, who will feel hard done by relative to the generous treatment of those families not so different from them who are receiving benefits. (Adam *et al.*, 2022)

Johnson's comments were noteworthy in several respects. On the one hand, they drew a pointed contrast with those of his namesake, Boris, by spelling out how, for all the us-versus-them divisiveness of dominant anti-welfare rhetoric, low-income households receiving Universal Credit were 'not so different from' those 'just out of reach' of benefits. Undermining this message, however (in what became a much-clipped soundbite), was his warning about resentments that might be sparked by prioritising the very poorest over the 'squeezed middle'. In other words, by highlighting the plight of people with *relatively* declining incomes in the same breath as describing 'the generous treatment' of those in *absolutely* precarious positions – individuals 'receiving benefits' – Johnson risked triggering a resentful reaction towards 'scroungers' from struggling households not claiming social security.

Conclusion

As Britain's cost of living crisis grinds on, there seems to be, at best, only qualified hope of any rapid revival of the new collectivism that fleetingly asserted itself during Covid – even despite the recent election of the first Labour government since 2010. While the Tories expected those at the bottom to give thanks for the return of inflation-linked benefit rises, undermined by ever-tougher conditionality for those out of work, the onus is now on that party to redefine the terms of debate around poverty and 'welfare'. One way of doing so would be to mobilise mounting discontent at soaring food and fuel bills and creaking public services to unite people on middle and lower incomes in a common cause: that of rebalancing the economy and establishing a more equitable social settlement. When faced with the 'welfare question', Labour has form for dissembling: at best, shiftily changing the subject or, at worst, implicitly buying into 'scrounger' discourse by engaging with the terms of debate dictated by Tories and tabloids. Boxed into a corner by then BBC political editor Nick Robinson in the early stages of the Coalition's war on 'shirkers', then Labour leader Ed Miliband conceded there was 'a minority in many communities who can work and aren't doing so' (BBC, 2010). Even today, the party often reserves its outrage at the societal fractures wrought by the Tories for the plight of 'working people' – implicitly disregarding 'undeserving' and/or 'unmentionable' groups, such as the long-term unemployed and those too sick or disabled to work (Pring, 2022). Moreover, when it *does* acknowledge the plight of those groups, it tends to revert to tropes about 'workless' people languishing in a 'life on benefits' (Kendall, 2024a) while buying into cliches about the 'dignity', 'pride' and 'purpose' of (by implication, *all*) work (Kendall, 2024b) – despite the ever-growing evidence base exposing many of today's jobs as over-regimented, and physically and emotionally degrading (see Weeks, 2011; Frayne, 2022).

Nonetheless, there may be some cause for optimism in more progressive policy ideas recently floated by ministers – including a new child poverty strategy and potential rights for employees to negotiate compressed

Missing the crisis?

('four-day') working weeks and/or 'term-time' hours to fit around family commitments. The test now is whether the scope of any newly rediscovered compassion dares extend beyond more manifestly 'deserving' groups, such as those already in work or seeking jobs to replace ones lost during Covid – and, more importantly, whether it can take media and public opinion with it.

References

Adam, S., Emmerson, C., Johnson, P., Joyce, R. and Karjalainen, H. (2022) 'IFS response to government cost of living support package', Institute for Fiscal Studies, 26 May, https://ifs.org.uk/publications/16066

Antonucci, L., Horvath, L., Kutiyski, Y. and Krouwel, A. (2017) 'The malaise of the squeezed middle: Challenging the narrative of the "left behind" Brexiter', *Competition & Change*, 21(3): 211–229.

Attlee, C. (1948) 'PM Clement Attlee – new social services and the citizen (the beginning of NHS) – 4 July 1948', www.youtube.com/watch?v=9rqyzWzDONQ

BBC (2010) 'Labour failed on welfare reform – Ed Miliband', BBC News, 25 November, www.bbc.co.uk/news/uk-politics-11842711

Bolton, J. (2021) 'Channel 5 Jeremy Vine viewers outraged as guest says home-workers "as bad as dole scroungers"', MyLondon, 25 October, www.mylondon.news/news/uk-world-news/channel-5-jeremy-vine-viewers-21964878

Brewer, M. and Handscomb, K. (2021) 'Half measures: The Chancellor's options for Universal Credit in the Budget', 19 February. Resolution Foundation, London, https://www.resolutionfoundation.org/publications/half-measures/ [resolutionfoundation.org].

Brewer, M., McCurdy, C. and Slaughter, H. (2021) *Begin Again? Assessing the Permanent Implications of COVID-19 for the UK's Labour Market*, Resolution Foundation, London.

Brooker, P., Vines, J., Sutton, S., Barnett, J., Feltwell, T. and Lawson, S. (2015) 'Debating poverty porn on Twitter: Social media as a place for everyday socio-political talk', *Proceedings of the 33rd Annual ACM Conference on Human Factors in Computing Systems*, https://dl.acm.org/doi/10.1145/2702123.2702291

Brummer, A. (2020) 'Boris Johnson's government is going for broke to fight coronavirus – now let's hope it works', *Daily Mail*, 21 March, www.dailymail.co.uk/columnists/article-8136963/ALEX-BRUMMER-Boris-Johnsons-Government-going-broke-fight-coronavirus.html

Cameron, D. (2013) 'David Cameron's speech – in full', *The Telegraph*, 2 October, www.telegraph.co.uk/news/politics/david-cameron/10349831/David-Camerons-speech-in-full.html

Clark, D. (2024) 'Number of people receiving emergency food parcels from Trussell Trust food banks in the United Kingdom from 2008/09 to 2023/24', Statista, www.statista.com/statistics/382695/uk-foodbank-users/#statisticContainer

Clark, T. and Dilnot, A. (2002) *Long-term Trends in British Taxation and Spending*, Institute for Fiscal Studies, London, https://ifs.org.uk/sites/default/files/output_url_files/bn25.pdf [ifs.org.uk]

Crib, J., Waters, T., Wernham, T. and Xu, X. (2022) *Living Standards, Poverty and Inequality in the UK: 2022*, Institute for Fiscal Studies, London.

de Vries, R., Geiger, B., Scullion, L., Summers, K., Edmiston, D., Ingold, J., Robertshaw, D. and Young, D. (2021) 'Solidary in a crisis? Trends in attitudes to benefits during COVID-19', https://salford-repository.worktribe.com/output/1335315/solidarity-in-a-crisis-trends-in-attitudes-to-benefits-during-covid-19

Denham, A. (2024) 'Laziness has become the new British disease', *The Telegraph*, 24 July, www.telegraph.co.uk/news/2024/07/24/laziness-has-become-the-new-british-disease/#:~:text=How%20did%20Britain%20get%20here,is%3A%20gradually%20%E2%80%93%20then%20suddenly

Department for Work and Pensions (2022), 'New benefit counter-fraud plan set to save taxpayer £2 billion', Gov.UK, 19 May, www.gov.uk/government/news/new-benefit-counter-fraud-plan-set-to-save-taxpayer-2-billion

Eardley, N. and Wilson, S., (2021), 'Make Universal Credit top-up permanent – Tory MPs', BBC News, 26 August, www.bbc.co.uk/news/uk-politics-58331179

Edwards, C. (2022) 'How can journalists report responsibly on the cost of living crisis?', Journalism.co.uk, 17 August, www.journalism.co.uk/news/how-can-journalists-report-responsibly-on-the-cost-of-living-crisis-/s2/a956327/

Fairclough, N. (1992) 'Discourse and text: Linguistic and intertextual analysis within discourse analysis', *Discourse & Society*, 3(2): 193–217.

Francis-Devine, B. (2024) 'Poverty in the UK: Statistics', House of Commons Library, 8 April, https://commonslibrary.parliament.uk/research-briefings/sn07096/

Frayne, D. (2022) *The Refusal of Work: The Theory and Practice of the Resistance to Work*, Zed Books, London.

Gerbner, G. (1972) 'Violence in television drama: Trends and symbolic functions', in G.A. Comstock and E.A. Rubinstein (eds) *Television and Social Behaviour*, Vol. 1, US Department of Health, Education and Welfare, Washington, DC.

Golding, P. and Middleton, S. (1982) *Images of Welfare: Press and Public Attitudes to Poverty*, Martin Robertson, Oxford.

Gov.uk (2022) 'Universal Credit statistics, 29 April 2013 to 13 January 2022', 15 February, www.gov.uk/government/statistics/universal-credit-statistics-29-april-2013-to-13-january-2022/universal-credit-statistics-29-april-2013-to-13-january-2022

Gov.uk (2024) 'Public spending statistics: July 2024', 30 August, www.gov.uk/government/statistics/public-spending-statistics-release-july-2024/public-spending-statistics-july-2024

Health Foundation, The (2022) 'The Poor Law 1601', https://navigator.health.org.uk/theme/poor-law-1601

Hourston, P. (2022) 'Cost of living crisis', Institute for Government, 7 February, www.instituteforgovernment.org.uk/explainers/cost-living-crisis

Jensen, T. (2014) 'Welfare commonsense, poverty porn and doxosophy', *Sociological Research Online*, 19(3): 277–283.

Johnson, P. (2022) 'Helping the poor is easy, Chancellor, everyone else may just have to suffer', Institute for Fiscal Studies, 31 January, https://ifs.org.uk/publications/15924

Joseph Rowntree Foundation (2025) 'UK poverty 2025', 29 January, https://www.jrf.org.uk/uk-poverty-2025-the-essential-guide-to-understanding-poverty-in-the-uk

Kendall, L. (2024a) 'Liz Kendall full speech: "How we'll get Britain working again, and follow in the footsteps of Attlee, Wilson and Blair"', LabourList, 4 March, https://labourlist.org/2024/03/labour-party-work-budget-2024-workers-unemployed-young-people-plan-benefit-work/

Kendall, L. (2024b) 'Getting Britain working', Gov.uk, 23 July, www.gov.uk/government/speeches/getting-britain-working

Lawson, A. (2021) '"They're as bad as dole scroungers": Pimlico Plumbers founder Charlie Mullins claims parents who work from home are as bad a benefits cheats – and says it "sends the wrong message" to children', *Daily Mail*, 23 October, www.dailymail.co.uk/news/article-10123897/Business-tycoon-claims-parents-work-home-bad-benefits-cheats.html

Mackley, A., Kirk-Wade, E., Hobson, F., Harker, R. and Kennedy, S. (2022) 'An introduction to social security in the UK', House of Commons Library, 1 June, https://commonslibrary.parliament.uk/research-briefings/cbp-9535/

Maitlis, E. (2020) 'Coronavirus: They tell us it's a great leveller … it's not | Emily Maitlis | @BBCNewsnightonline – BBC', www.youtube.com/watch?v=L6wIcpdJyCI

Malone, C. (2020) 'Don't listen to Twitter morons – Boris and Rishi are playing a blinder, says Carole Malone', *Daily Express*, 21 March, www.express.co.uk/comment/expresscomment/1258258/coronavirus-rishi-sunak-boris-johnson-pub-lockdown-mortgage-help

Moore, C. (2020) 'With stakes as high as these, Rishi Sunak has made the right big gesture', *Daily Telegraph*, 20 March, www.telegraph.co.uk/news/2020/03/20/stakes-high-rishi-sunak-has-made-right-big-gesture/

Morrison, J. (2019) *Scroungers: Moral Panics and Media Myths*, Bloomsbury, London.

Morrison, J. (2021) 'Scrounger-bashing as national pastime: The prevalence and ferocity of anti-welfare ideology on niche-interest online forums', *Social Semiotics*, 31(3): 383–401.

Mullins, C. (2021) 'Charlie Mullins compares work from home staff to "benefit scroungers" | Jeremy Vine on 5', 25 October, www.youtube.com/watch?v=YAmiKGgMcwM

OECD (2003) *OECD Glossary of Statistical Terms*, OECD Publishing, Paris.

O'Neill, J. (2021) 'Effects of taxes and benefits on UK household income: Financial year ending 2020', Office for National Statistics, 28 May, https://www.ons.gov.uk/peoplepopulationandcommunity/personalandhouseholdfinances/incomeandwealth/bulletins/theeffectsoftaxesandbenefitsonhouseholdincome/financialyearending2020#:~:text=The%20rise%20in%20inequality%20of, ending%20(FYE)%202016%20values

Plummer, K. (2021) 'Boris Johnson said Brits shouldn't rely on handouts – and everyone had the same takedown', indy100, 27 August, https://www.indy100.com/politics/boris-johnson-handouts-mocked-reaction-b1909727

Pring, J. (2022) 'Labour conference: Anger at Starmer's "divisive" pledge to back "working people"', Disability News Service, 29 September, www.disabilitynewsservice.com/labour-conference-anger-at-starmers-divisive-pledge-to-back-working-people/

Reuben, A. (2021) 'Why some parents effectively pay a 71% tax rate', BBC News, 24 November, www.bbc.co.uk/news/58870012

Resolution Foundation (2018) '300,000 "forgotten unemployed" people aren't accessing the state support to which they are entitled', 2 January, www.resolutionfoundation.org/press-releases/300000-forgotten-unemployed-people-arent-accessing-the-state-support-to-which-they-are-entitled/

Sunak, R. (2020a) 'The Chancellor Rishi Sunak provides an updated statement on coronavirus', Gov.uk, 20 March, www.gov.uk/government/speeches/the-chancellor-rishi-sunak-provides-an-updated-statement-on-coronavirus

Sunak, R. (2020b) 'Chancellor's statement on coronavirus (COVID-19): 8 April 2020', https://www.youtube.com/watch?v=fAYoHd7wdsU

Taylor-Gooby, P. and Taylor, E. (2015) 'Benefits and welfare: Long-term trends or short-term reactions?', in J. Curtice and R. Ormston (eds) British Social Attitudes 32, https://natcen.ac.uk/publications/british-social-attitudes-32

Weeks, K. (2011) The Problem with Work: Feminism, Marxism, Antiwork Politics, and Postwork Imaginaries, Duke University Press, Durham, NC.

Welshman, J. (2007) From Transmitted Deprivation to Social Exclusion: Policy, Poverty and Parenting, Policy Press, Bristol.

Welshman, J. (2013) Underclass: A History of the Excluded: 1880–2000, Hambledon Continuum, London.

World Bank (2021) 'GDP per capita (current US$)', https://data.worldbank.org/indicator/NY.GDP.PCAP.CD

World Population Review (2022) '2022 world population by country', https://worldpopulationreview.com/

3
Covid, Brexit and the emergence of national populism
Owen Worth

Introduction

One of the more noticeable symptoms of malaise within British political society can be seen in the increase of populism and populist content within national politics. Whilst the birth of the tabloid and the wider 'Murdochisation'[1] of the popular media saw an emergent culture of populism from the 1970s, populism in party politics was generally marginalised within Westminster. In addition, whilst leaders such as Margaret Thatcher engaged in forms of populism, this was usually placed within a wider strategic context geared towards building a distinct political programme (Hall, 1988). Yet, populism has become a central feature of British politics within the last decade or so, being increasingly prominent during and after the Brexit referendum. Indeed, as a series of crises gripped the UK in the years following Brexit, populist measures appeared to be the go-to position of Conservative governments as a means of survival. However, the inability of Sunak to engage adequately with this populism, amidst the collapse of the Conservative Party, saw the Reform Party take over 14 per cent of the vote at the 2024 general election and gain five MPs, with Nigel Farage finally gaining a seat in Westminster. As such, populism maintains a significant position within the opposition bench. In government however, the reliance on populism peaked during the

Johnson administration and was utilised during the British withdrawal from the European Union and throughout the COVID-19 pandemic. Yet, the sensationalism that saw the fall of Boris Johnson coupled with the collapse of the Liz Truss premiership has shown the limits of reliance on populism and indeed reveals a far bigger problem at the heart of Britain.

This chapter shows how populism, and in particular a right-wing form of English nationalism, has become mainstream within political society since the Brexit vote. Whilst this phenomenon might have occurred at the centre of government, Johnson himself looked to tap into a wider collection of reactionary right-wing forces that had been unleashed during the Brexit referendum. Brexit might have instigated an era of populism, but Johnson found that the COVID-19 epidemic could be yoked to his own unique brand of populism to maximum effect. The perceived winning of the vaccine war, coupled with weekly broadcasts to the nation where Johnson played up his own near-death experience of catching the virus, built upon this brand. Whilst COVID-19 also went some way in masking the problems associated with Brexit and increasing issues around inequality and poverty, its events precipitated Johnson's downfall. In addition, the contrasting non-populist styles of governance of the pandemic provided by the then First Ministers of Scotland and Wales, Nicola Sturgeon and Mark Drakeford, proved to be more successful, and as such furthered the loosening of the bonds between Westminster and Edinburgh and Cardiff, respectively.

The turn to populism in Britain has followed the wider development that has emerged across Europe, the Americas and beyond since the global financial crisis, and which has been discussed across the political and social sciences (Mudde, 2007; Moffitt, 2016; Mondon and Winter, 2020). Britain saw itself move from a peripheral figure to the forefront of the populist wave, as a previously marginalised collection of social forces entered the mainstream with the Brexit vote and its aftermath. This has been unique within British political discourse. Much had previously been made of how forms of nationalist and reactionary populism had floundered due to the stability of the party system within Britain, with any potential right-wing radicalism being unable to make any breakthrough politically or rhetorically

(Cronin, 1996; Eatwell, 2000). Whilst the British National Party (BNP) had made greater strides than any other party on the far right to date in the early part of the century, it was the rise of the UK Independence Party (UKIP) that would trigger the populist explosion. Starting out as a single-issue party, UKIP had been transformed under the leadership of Nigel Farage into a confrontational political entity, keen to attack multiculturalism, immigration and Islam alongside its Euroscepticism. The significant increase of support for UKIP in the opinion polls during the time of the Conservative–Liberal Democrat Coalition led to a concern within the Conservative Party that UKIP might significantly eat into their vote share and gain several seats in the forthcoming general election in 2015. As such, the Prime Minister, David Cameron, made the fatal error of including an in/out EU referendum in the Conservative Party manifesto. Whilst Cameron was never convinced that the Conservative Party would gain an outright majority (Glencross, 2016), the over-estimation of the extent of UKIP support, coupled with the poor performance of the Labour Party and the collapse of the Liberal Democrats, saw the Conservatives gain a surprise majority.

It can be suggested that the Brexit referendum, which allowed for the explosion of the right-wing forces that UKIP was developing, was at best a gamble that backfired and at worst an accident. What followed has led to an unprecedented period of British politics, where any form of parliamentary consensus has been difficult to reach. Before 2019, the significant splits in the two main political parties were evident. Jeremy Corbyn's left-wing opposition never gained parliamentary legitimacy due to the opposition from the Parliamentary Labour Party. At the same time the splits over Brexit within the Conservative Party saw Johnson take highly confrontational steps when in office, such as expelling long-standing members and proroguing Parliament. Whilst the majority gained at the 2019 election provided Johnson with enough votes to push through legislation, it also produced a new era of populist Conservative MPs that led to a fresh period of unpredictability. Boris Johnson's own leadership fallacies have been discussed and dissected, but his form of 'empty' populism did serve to cover up the ideological cracks below the surface of the Party.

As we will see here, the post-Johnson era has left a series of ongoing populist soundbites regarding the nature of post-Brexit politics (from both main parties) amidst a United Kingdom that is increasingly losing its legitimacy as an entity. It also led to the collapse of the Conservative Party, as the populist myths that Johnson's period in office relied upon came crumbling down, leading to the worst parliamentary election result in the Party's history and the revival of the pre-Brexit UKIP Party in the form of the Reform Party.

Right-wing populism, strategic populism and empty populism

The study of populism has dominated the social sciences in the last decade or two. It is not the place in this chapter to discuss the nature of such debates but rather to acknowledge that populism has been understood as a collective of anti-elitist movements that have mobilised against established political practices (Brennan, 2017; Mudde, 2004; Muller, 2017; Judis, 2016). Whilst discussed as both a left-wing strategy and as a potential vehicle for organic mobilisation, it has often largely been associated with the radical right, particularly since the end of the Cold War (Mudde, 2007). In Britain, populism would become prominently associated with the rise of UKIP, particularly under the leadership of Nigel Farage, with strong mobilisation in both Conservative-shire areas (such as the South of England) and in the post-industrial 'left-behind' areas, often associated with the North of England (Goodwin and Milazzo, 2015). Yet, the victory of Jeremy Corbyn as leader of the Labour Party saw a mobilisation of left-wing populism similar to that which occurred in Greece and Spain with Syriza and Podemos, respectively (Worth, 2019a). To a degree, the post-Brexit landscape in British politics would briefly resemble a forum where competing types of populism would spar, condemned by a confrontational form of centrism that rejected both in equal measure. This was particularly evident after the 2017 general election that saw the forces of Corbynism make significant political advances. However, the election of Boris Johnson, coupled with his general election success in 2019, saw the form of right-wing populism associated with Brexit re-strengthen its supremacy.

As I have already suggested, the Brexit referendum was the focal point for the explosion of right-wing populism. Previously, right-wing reactionary campaigns on anti-immigration, anti-multiculturalism and British nativism had been located within far-right parties such as the National Front and the BNP, or in fringe elements of the Conservative Party, such as the Monday Club.[2] These had successfully been marginalised, yet the surge in support for the BNP under the leadership of Nick Griffin in the early part of the twenty-first century contributed towards the disruption to mainstream parties in certain post-industrial areas of England, prior to the rise of UKIP. UKIPs own high point was at the 2014 local and European elections, where it returned over 160 councillors across the UK (all but three in England) and comfortably topped the poll in the EU elections. The anti-immigration rhetoric that had been aired by the BNP had created an environment for UKIP to tap into, and it became a key part of their own programme alongside its long-standing Euroscepticism (Evans and Menon, 2018). The Brexit referendum allowed this to appear in the mainstream, as UKIP populists merged with prominent Conservative politicians in mobilising the Brexit vote (Worth, 2022).

The populism that marked the Brexit vote was aided by two separate campaigns that appeared to compete for publicity. Vote Leave was the official campaign and became synonymous with high-profile actors such as Dominic Cummings, Boris Johnson and Michael Gove. Leave.EU was the rival set-up, associated with Nigel Farage and Arron Banks, and was keener to push populist material in the spirit of UKIP. Whilst Cummings, as director of Vote Leave, looked to distance himself from the nativist populism and anti-immigration rhetoric that was emerging from Leave. EU, Vote Leave became increasingly confrontational as the campaign developed, making a series of anti-Turkish declarations in response to Leave.EU's notorious 'breaking point' poster.[3] At the same time, Michael Gove sought to follow a classic populist trail by leading a series of attacks on political and economic experts. The populist legacy left by the referendum has been evident in every government since the vote.

The type of populism espoused by the victors of the Brexit referendum retained the language and confrontational appearance from that campaign but appeared increasingly strategic in its expression. The disastrous Theresa May Government was fraught with splits over the form that Brexit would take, and whist May herself attempted to play the nationalist card by rejecting European Economic Area (EEA) membership (which would have promoted a 'softer' form of Brexit) this appeared to underline a distinct commitment towards a post-Brexit Union and to a new settlement for the UK (Favell, 2019; Atkins, 2022). Yet, her approach alienated both the 'Remainers' that favoured a softer Brexit as well as hard-line Brexiteers. The appointment of Boris Johnson as Foreign Secretary in 2016 provided an opportunity for Johnson to build upon his reputation by embarking upon a set of bizarre populist stunts that included using jingoistic names to refer to several countries he was visiting and citing Rudyard Kipling's colonial poem 'Mandalay' whilst attending a sacred temple in Myanmar. These continued, with an increase in Islamophobic and nationalist articles written for the popular press (Johnson, 2018; Johnson and Hunt, 2018). May's refusal to dismiss Johnson allowed him to garner the support of the hard-line Brexiters in the Tory Party, vote down her Brexit bills and ultimately replace her as Prime Minister.

Within the first few months of Johnson's leadership he demanded a renegotiation of the Brexit deal under the threat of a no deal, prorogued parliament to limit the time in which it could block such a no deal Brexit, and then dismissed twenty-one MPs from the Conservative Party for not supporting his plans. The subsequent 2019 election success saw the party increase its numbers and win a substantial majority in the House of Commons. At the same time Conservatives themselves lost their own position as a broad-church party as moderate MPs (ever increasing numbers left the party or refused to stand at the election) were effectively replaced by individuals firmly rooted in this new culture of populist nationalism. Despite this, such a strategy still left Johnson with significant problems, particularly in the long term. Contained within the Conservatives was a contradictory mix of free market Brexiters, who had demanded a new era of deregulation and a radical programme of tariff reduction, and new 'red-wall' MPs and supporters from traditional Labour voting constituencies, who had joined the party attracted to the notion of 'levelling up' and who favoured the nativist policies that the ending of freedom of movement would offer (Worth, 2022). Rather than provide any solutions Johnson appeared to embody a collection of ad hoc ideas, inhabiting forms of 'empty' populism that failed to achieve any aim or wider ideological goal.

The term 'empty populism' has provided great depth to those in the fields of political communications and political representation (Jagers and Walgrave, 2007; Laclau, 2005; Mofitt and Tormey, 2014). In this sense it can facilitate a very real significance in forging a link between the 'political' and the 'people'. Yet, it can also refer to a practice that, if lacking an end to a means, becomes highly problematic in its execution. For example, as Stuart Hall classically illustrated, the utilisation of populism by Thatcher and the new right in the 1980s served a distinct purpose (Hall, 1988). Hall showed how a form of authoritarian populism emerged out of the organic crisis in the 1970s with the collapse of the so-called post-war Keynesian-inspired consensus (Hall, 1979). This populism was used strategically to build what we now understand as a hegemonic neoliberal project within Britain (Hall, 1988). In this way, Thatcher engaged with some campaigns that were being endorsed by groups such as the National Front and the Monday Club in order to co-opt them into her wider free market strategy. In doing so, far-right groups and movements became marginalised. Under Johnson, it can be argued that such reactionary positions were engaged merely for effect (Worth, 2022). Rather than place them within a wider form of mobilisation, the forms of nativist nationalism and jingoism were used in an empty manner by Johnson, often as a stop gap to make up for the lack of such a wider plan. In doing so, the contradiction between the free-marketers and the nativist protectionist positions expanded.

Despite this, whilst Johnson's populism appeared ideologically contractionary and empty in essence, it did succeed in winning a decisive election in 2019 and in formerly withdrawing Britain from the EU with what many at the time felt was a Brexit that was 'hard' enough to satisfy hard-line Brexiteers.[4] He also utilised populism in a way that would win popular support and increase his own personal ratings. For example, his use of populist language in dealing with both Brexit and the Covid crisis served to mobilise voters to his cause. The winning of the 2021 Hartlepool by-election, which seemed to both consolidate and increase Johnson's support in the 'red wall' areas was testament to this and showed that in terms of results it was effective. However, his uneven use of populism opened wounds which he became increasingly unable to address. Whilst many of the principal arch-Brexiters came from the Thatcherite/free market/ hyper-liberal economic wing of the Conservative Party (and indeed many of the key players of UKIP)[5] the reality is that those who voted for Brexit were evenly split between the Tory heartlands and post-industrial traditional Labour areas that favoured far greater intervention in the economy (Worth, 2017). Johnson did not appear to address these inconsistencies in office, instead favouring an empty populism that sustained his popularity. The fallacies of this were made stark when Liz Truss's pursuit of a neoliberal populism failed so badly. However, as the UK left the EU and almost immediately entered its Covid period, Johnson's uneven use of populism would both sustain him and bring him down.

Covid

The pandemic created a fresh set of challenges for Johnson and a collection of populist narratives that were often opposed to him. Accompanying this was a jingoism around vaccine nationalism that would provide another populist stop gap in the dispute with the EU (Foster and Feldman, 2021). Johnson's initial response to COVID-19 was notoriously dismissive. His stunts of shaking hands with hospital staff as a way of showing that the pandemic was harmless was comparable to similar responses by Donald Trump and Jair Bolsonaro. As such the UK was one of the last countries to enter a lockdown and incurred one of the worst rates of death during the first wave of the pandemic (Sasson, 2021). Johnson would then become significantly ill with the virus, which he would later use to full media effect to enhance his leadership. Indeed, one of the more noticeable allies of Johnson throughout his period as leader was the popular print media, which provided him with significant support. Having been effectively 'one of them' in an earlier incarnation as a journalist and columnist, Johnson received the kind of backing from the right-wing press that had not even been seen during the Thatcher years.[6] Covid and his own experience of the illness would see such outlets build a collection of narratives to further enhance his image of being a true representative of the people. At the same time however, many of his Brexit supporters were embarking on an anti-lockdown populism that sought to plant the seeds of an opposition that would continue to grow as the pandemic developed (Bergsen, 2020). Much has been made of the right-wing populist foundations of the anti-lockdown movements, with detailed arguments around their form and content, and what they mean for the changing nature of populism (Bratich, 2021; Brubaker, 2021; Gerbaudo, 2020; Russell, 2022; Vieten, 2020). In the UK, anti-lockdown discourses ranged from those that placed them within a wider conspiratorial framework of the sort typified by the extreme right (for example, see Worth, 2019a), to those that insisted that their opposition was drawn from libertarian concerns. Both, however, appeared populist in their expression and there was some convergence around their depiction of Covid policy as being authoritarian as opposed to protective. In Britain, many of Boris Johnson's backbench supporters who enabled his accession to Conservative Party leader and subsequently Prime Minister criticised his position on lockdowns and mask wearing. In particular they were opposed to the concession of decision-making power given to the Scientific Advisory Group for Emergencies (SAGE) that was advising the government throughout the crisis. By the end of 2020, the COVID Recovery Group was set up by Tory backbenchers to oppose any prolonged extension to future lockdowns. These included arch-Brexiteer Steve Baker and the former head of the 1922 Committee Graham Brady, arguably two of the most prominent voices in maintaining support on the Tory backbenches.

Boris Johnson's first Covid scandal, later leading to a snowballing of further scandals that saw his downfall, was with his chief adviser, Dominic Cummings. At the height of lockdown, Cummings was seen travelling without reason to the North East of England whilst experiencing Covid symptoms. This led to over forty members of the Conservative Parliamentary Party demanding (without success) his resignation. More importantly however was the fact that Johnson's Covid policy sowed the first seeds of opposition in a parliamentary party that had previously provided unwavering support. This was unimaginable after the 2019 election when Johnson had effectively sidelined all previous Conservative Party traditions in favour of his narrow form of Brexit populism. Yet, in following the advice taken by SAGE, Johnson came up against this same populist resistance that he had done so much to develop and utilise. Whilst not representative of the protest movements that were growing at the political fringes to the wider lockdown strategies, the opposition developed within the House of Commons did find like-minded criticisms with the many popular media outlets that had backed Johnson's leadership (Gerbaudo, 2020).

The vaccine race helped Johnson's brand of populism get back on course and saw Johnson move to shore up support from those that were critical of his position on the lockdown. Vaccine nationalism had become a feature of Covid politics, with advanced economies looking to competitive state-led initiatives to gain a lead in the race to vaccinate their populations. The process led to an uneven distribution of the vaccine and did not adequately deal with the spread of the virus internationally as new variants emerged from countries that had not had the same access to the vaccine as the populations of the developed world (Zhou, 2021). For Johnson, this race had an extra incentive as it provided a ready-made example of how the UK would not just benefit from Brexit but appear superior to the entire EU system (Catterall, 2021; Mylonas and Whalley, 2022). In offering the first vaccines for public consumption in December 2020, Johnson managed to push his popular form of nationalism to the forefront at a time when studies were increasingly showing a strong correlation between nationalism and the vaccine race in England (Vanderslott *et al.*, 2021). The much-heralded vaccine 'success' saw Johnson reach a post-2019 peak in his popularity, the last time that the public appeared more positive than negative over Brexit (YouGov, 2021; Statista, 2022).

Covid, Brexit and national populism

The 'Partygate' incident that would eventually bring down Johnson did not emerge until November 2021 when the *Daily Mirror*, the one popular tabloid that was hostile to Johnson, published a set of allegations that a series of indoor gatherings and parties had occurred within Downing Street during the winter of 2020–21 in breach of the lockdown laws that were in effect at the time (Crerar, 2021). This led to a series of subsequent claims and counterclaims which suggested that such gatherings were frequent, culminating in the involvement of the police, the issuing of fines for participants (including Johnson and the Chancellor Rishi Sunak), and to the publication of the Sue Grey report that was highly critical of Downing Street behaviour at the time. As before, Johnson managed to find another form of populist endeavour to use as a means of deflecting attention from 'Partygate' by embarking upon a full-frontal campaign to support Ukraine after the Russian invasion. As with Brexit previously, the move from one piece of showmanship to another had more to do with political survival and empty or spontaneous populism rather than anything that could be seen as strategic.

English nationalism

One of the most significant characteristics of the post-Brexit populism to have emerged from the right is one that has been distinctly 'English' in its orientation. In the many subsequent commentaries since the Brexit referendum, the notion of 'Englishness' has appeared as being one of the significant characteristics behind the vote (Wellings, 2020; Kenny, 2020; Henderson and Wyn Jones, 2021, Galent, 2022). At one level, this is an empirical observation: Scotland voted against Brexit; in Northern Ireland, the Brexit vote was overwhelmingly favoured by Unionists, and likewise in Wales, those who identified with being Welsh as opposed to British or English were far more likely to vote remain (Dorling, 2018; Wyn Jones, 2019). At the same time, and paradoxically within England itself, those who identified with being more British than English were more likely to vote Labour and to reject Johnson's vision of a post-Brexit Britain than those who identified more with Englishness. This tended to reinforce the idea that the Britain that the Conservative Party was constructing post-Brexit was one that was overwhelmingly English-centric, with its British expression being one that was at odds with Celtic or indeed multicultural inclusion (Opinium, 2020). The Englishness that emerged was geared around an imperialist nostalgia that placed the Anglosphere at the forefront of its worldview (Wellings, 2020). Perhaps more than any individual other than Nigel Farage, Johnson embodied this English jingoism to the full and used it as a vehicle to attack the EU as well as wider bodies based upon international law, and as part of the wider culture wars that were emerging within civil society. In doing so, the United Kingdom has looked more prone to collapse that it has at any time since the Irish War of Independence in the early 1920s.

In Scotland the Brexit vote has been enough for the forces of separatism to demand a second referendum. Both Johnson and May's governments did nothing to address these concerns by looking for a more inclusive Brexit or by engaging more widely with the different parts of the Union, and instead merely dismissed Scotland's vote in the Brexit referendum and claims for a second independence vote. The subsequent electoral dominance of the Scottish National Party (SNP) coupled with the general hostility between Westminster and the Scottish Parliament (Holyrood) has precluded any efforts to forge a future inclusive union (McEwan, 2018; McCrone and Keating, 2021). As such, discussions have taken place on what type of Scotland would emerge from a victory in such a referendum, despite Westminster itself pledging to block this move (Beasley, and Kaarbo, 2018; Manley, 2019).

The government in Wales adopted a more circumspect approach to the Covid crisis, providing an antithesis to Johnson's populism, which led to greater discussion of separatism (Goodwin-Hawkins, 2020). Whilst groups such as Yes Cymru have emerged in recent years in support of Welsh independence, and while support has reached numbers that Scotland was achieving just two years before the referendum in 2014, in Wales' case, the dominant Labour Party hasn't so readily dismissed the notion of independence as the Scottish Labour Party has (Paun and Hall, 2021). The then First Minister of Wales, Mark Drakeford, did not rule out the possibility of Welsh independence, and stressed the need for substantial reform for the Union to survive (Drakeford, 2021).

Finally, the adoption of a type of Russian roulette policy over the Northern Ireland protocol has threatened to create huge tensions between communities in the six counties, instabilities within the island of Ireland, and conflict between Ireland and the UK government as well as between the UK and the EU (Duparc-Portier and Figus, 2021; Murphy, 2021). The protocol allowed for EU standardisation to occur within Northern Ireland, effectively creating a customs border across the Irish Sea. This protocol was supposed to be flexible enough to manage the fragile condition of the governance and society within Northern Ireland yet had been cobbled together by Johnson at the last-minute to push Brexit through (Hayward and Komarova, 2022). The threats and soundbites from Johnson in the last few months of his leadership again reflected the spontaneous nature of his populism, without further consideration to what scrapping the protocol might do to the Good Friday Agreement and to the management of a borderless Ireland (Murphy and Evershed, 2021). As it is, Rishi Sunak's move towards the permanent Windsor Framework, which provides the compromise of a 'Stormont brake' in the form of a UK veto to EU laws to Northern Ireland, and which splits goods going from Britain to the six counties and those going to the Republic, appeared as an attempt to reach a post-Brexit solution and to bring the chaos of Johnson's populism to an end. Certainly, the Windsor Framework was overwhelmingly supported in the House of Commons and met with enthusiasm in the EU and the US, yet it remains opposed by many Unionist parties, included the largest – the DUP – in Northern Ireland.

In the cases of Scotland, Wales and Northern Ireland, the post-Brexit Conservative governments responded to problems such as these by re-articulating their narrow perception of Englishness. As opposed to those that aligned with the Celtic identity in Scotland, Wales or Northern Ireland (or indeed those in England who favoured a more multicultural view of Britain), the Englishness that the Conservative governments have pursued since 2016 has been overwhelmingly associated with the core of the Vote Leave/Leave.EU campaigns at the Brexit referendum. The anti-immigration,

What went wrong with Britain?

Empire-nostalgic, jingoistic populism that Cummings, Gove and Johnson from Vote Leave and Banks and Farage from Leave.EU sought to construct at the referendum – often in competition with each other – has been used as a template for post-Brexit Britain. In doing so, it antagonises all groups that do not fit into this narrow form of English identity. Within England itself, this has set the scene for the playing out within civil society of the so-called 'culture wars' whereby those that appear antagonistic to this narrative can be reduced and dismissed as being 'woke', 'Marxist' or 'post-modern'. In Scotland, Wales and Northern Ireland it serves to exacerbate an increasing fracturing of the Union itself.

After Boris: Populism contained or untamed?

On 7 July 2022, the last act of Boris Johnson's premiership occurred when the Government Deputy Chief Whip, Chris Pincher, resigned after an alleged sexual assault following a night out. It was subsequently revealed that Pincher had a long history of similar behaviour which Johnson at first claimed not to know about before conceding that he did. It appeared to be the straw that broke the camel's back, leaving Johnson to resign as his Cabinet deserted him. In June 2023, Johnson resigned as an MP altogether, citing a mob-rule mentality plotting against him, after the Commons Privileges Committee found that Johnson had misled the house on numerous occasions in light of the 'Partygate' affair.

This brings us to the question of how populism will continue to play out in the aftermath of Johnson and whether populism has run its course with his downfall or whether it will continue to hinder the British state in years to come. As mentioned above, the short-lived Truss premiership might suggest that populism had indeed reached as far as it could go as a national strategy. Liz Truss's own leadership campaign rested upon a populism that was very much geared around the rubric of a low tax economy. In addition, her position on the Union, Northern Ireland and Brexit appeared to be as, if not more, confrontational than Johnson's. Her period in office saw her adopt an aggressive form of neoliberal populism that instigated a tax-reducing mini budget of the sort that the ultra-free market Brexiters had been calling for. It was also met with great enthusiasm from leading proponents of the 'Singapore-on-Thames' model, with Farage himself hailing it as the 'best Conservative budget since 1986' and others proclaiming it as the first step towards realising the benefits of a post-Brexit Britain (Daily Mail, 2022; Heath, 2022). However, and perhaps ironically given its ideological focus, the markets reacted negatively to the budget announcement, plunging the pound into crisis. The fallout led to Chancellor Kwasi Kwarteng being sacked before Truss herself resigned within fifty days of assuming office (Kutllovci, 2022; Bale, 2023).

The fallout of the brief Truss administration led to two developments. The first is that support for the Conservative Party fell to levels not seen since the 1990s (Keate, 2024). Even during Johnson's final days he was still only trailing Labour leader, Keir Starmer, marginally, yet Starmer maintained a consistent 15–20 per cent lead in the polls over Rishi Sunak in the run up to the 2024 election. Whilst Sunak's own personal popularity remained broadly on a par with Starmer's, he did not manage to revive the Conservative Party's fortunes and the party collapsed at the said 2024 election. Secondly, Truss's doomed budget firmly signalled the death knell for any post-Brexit El Dorado. If Johnson's attempt to argue for both a deregulated free market and a protectionist future worked in the 2019 general election alongside the rhetoric of 'getting Brexit done', then the pursuit of the former by Truss had seemingly been exhausted. Whilst Sunak's government might have attempted to appear more statesmanlike and less populist, national populism remained integral during his period in office. Thus, while the ideological fervour towards a free market populism might have withered, the commitment towards a national populism that appeals to the red wall areas and focuses on the culture wars and immigration has remained.

Whilst some of those that symbolised the Johnson era, such as the Home Secretary, Priti Patel, and the former leader of the Commons, Jacob Rees-Mogg, have followed Johnson onto the fringes – and in the case of the latter, out of parliament post-election – others emerged under Sunak and continued to deploy reactionary language and campaigns. Suella Braverman replaced Patel as Home Secretary and embarked upon Patel's controversial pledge to deport refugees with far more vigour and using a more confrontational approach than her predecessor. Like Patel (and indeed Sunak), Braverman comes from a family of Indian heritage who gained prominence during the British Empire and has long been situated to the right of the political spectrum. Her constant use of 'cultural Marxism', a term adopted by Nesta Webster after World War I and used by Hitler as *Kulturbolschewismus* in *Mein Kampf*, and which refers to a far-right antisemitic conspiracy theory, has drawn consistent criticisms but is a term that she maintained as a reference in the 'culture wars' (Manavis, 2018; Worth, 2019a). Her confrontational approach was aided by Kemi Badenoch, a right-winger of Nigerian ethnicity who has been quick to use her ethnicity to attack equality groups such as Black Lives Matter and similarly utilised the culture wars, with attacks on the teaching of Critical Race Studies, the negative portrayal of the British Empire, and stirring up divisions over the debate on transgender rights.

Yet, Sunak found it difficult to contain such populism. Braverman was eventually sacked for attacking the Metropolitan Police for displaying bias to left-leaning protests, whilst the outspoken red-wall MP Lee Anderson, who Sunak appointed as vice chair of the party, defected to Reform after being suspended by the Conservative Party for Islamophobia. In the run up to the general election, Nigel Farage announced he would stand for Reform in Clacton. In doing so, Reform gathered momentum in the run up to the election, and took much of the political space that Johnson had taken from the Labour Party in 2019. As a result, the Conservative Party suffered a more significant loss than it would have if such populism was contained (if it was at all possible to contain it). The Conservative's Party's vote fell to 23.7 per cent, making it the lowest percentage for a second party since 1922. Sunak might have looked to stem the chaos of the Johnson years, but his lack of any vision for a post-Brexit strategy for the UK at large and his inability to stem the reliance on populism led to its catastrophic defeat.

The landslide Labour election victory might suggest that populism would be on the wane at the centre of British politics. Labour's acceptance of Brexit, the Labour/Conservative convergence around the Windsor

Framework, and the commitment towards ending the confrontation with the EU that dominated the Johnson administration might also suggest that a post-Brexit consensus might emerge, with populism increasingly located in the Reform Party and with the said Reform Party taking the space as the UK's radical right party in line with many other European countries. However, a closer look at both the election and the direction that the Conservatives have gone in since suggest that populism remains as prevalent. The leadership battle to replace Sunak certainly placed populist campaigning at the forefront of the Party. From the outset, candidates seemed to be concerned with engaging with the ideas and campaigns of the Reform Party in order to re-engage with voters, with Badenoch, arguably the most right-wing candidate in the campaign, winning the final contest in November 2024. As a result, confrontations with the EU have been replaced with confrontations around international law over the management of refugees and withdrawal from the European Court of Human Rights, whilst the wider populist position against 'woke' culture has been reinforced. The growth of right-wing broadcast media outlets such as GB News and Talk Radio has seen a previously unprecedented move that has put right-wing populist commentary at the centre of a new medium, despite the various breaches of the UK's broadcasting impartiality law, allowing populist language to maintain prominence.

Labour's landslide election victory result also appears remarkable in that, whilst the result was decisive, the extraordinary manner in how it was achieved arguably leaves the UK in a more fragile position. Whilst large Labour gains in Scotland alongside the Windsor Framework in Northern Ireland might provide an opportunity for the Labour Party to rebuild the Union, the failure to find a substantive position on Brexit, the economy and indeed on the future of the UK has left little hint as to what Labour in government might look like in the long term. The first 100 days of his administration saw Starmer fall to an approval rate lower than that of Sunak (Keate, 2024). Yet, a closer look at the election result makes this appear less astonishing as it might otherwise. The 32 per cent of the vote achieved by Labour was the lowest winning percentage of any single-party majority since universal suffrage, despite being the second highest majority since World War II. The number of votes gained were half a million less than those received by Corbyn in 2019 and three million less than he received in 2017 (where the Party polled 40 per cent). Perhaps the main consistency in Starmer's leadership has been to maintain a frontal assault on his predecessor. His period as leader has been marked by aggressive tactics towards his own party members, including summary expulsions and a war upon the Corbyn 'cultism'. In doing so, Starmer has alienated a large chunk of younger voters (the so-called 'youthquake') that were politicised by Corbyn in 2017 (Worth, 2019a). At the same time, his dismissal of rejoining the single market and/or customs union has likewise served to alienate a large chunk of remain voters that now – due to population change and demographic shifts since 2016 – make up most of the electorate.

Labour's victory was thus tempered by a significant reduction in votes in areas where they previously were strong (Starmer saw his own majority halved), with both the Greens and Independent candidates, including the expelled former leader Jeremy Corbyn, gaining seats from them. Starmer also further suspended seven left-wing MPs within weeks of coming into power for voting against the reduction of fuel allowances to pensioners. Starmer's landslide thus appears both brittle and open to attacks from not just the continued populist surge from the right but also from an internationalist left, whose grievances with Starmer include a dismissal of all pledges made during his leadership campaign, the rejection of a radical economic alternative to the prevailing neoliberal model, the clampdown of any left-wing opposition from within the party and the reluctance to condemn Israeli aggression in the Middle East. At present, it thus seems unlikely that Labour's position under Stamer is likely to forge a new form of political normality capable of keeping such populism at bay.

Conclusion

The last decade or so in British politics has been unprecedented. Whilst a significant opposition was building to EU membership and was accompanied by a rise in reactionary campaigns, David Cameron's gamble to proceed with a binary referendum on membership backfired with significant long-term effects. What has occurred since the Brexit vote has been the noticeable reliance on nationalist forms of populism within the political mainstream. Whilst this arguably played off against left-wing populism in terms of the rise of Corbyn during the aftermath of the referendum and the leadership of Theresa May, it took centre stage with Boris Johnson. What has become increasingly apparent is that, since Johnson's marginalisation of opposition within the Conservative Party over Brexit, the form of national populism that he developed (however empty or otherwise it might have been) became central to his leadership.

Johnson was unique in terms of contemporary British politics. Rather than offer a strategic vision of a post-Brexit Britain, he embarked upon a collection of populist campaigns that were highly contradictory in nature. Whilst his ability to argue for both a deregulated free market and a protectionist future worked in the 2019 general election alongside the rhetoric of 'getting Brexit done', his premiership was marked by similar stunts that did not promote any longevity. Within this environment, Covid became a double-edged sword. On one level it allowed him to continue his many promises by insisting that the COVID-19 emergency had changed the goalposts in terms of policy commitments. On another level his adoption of the measures that SAGE had suggested during Covid saw him antagonise many on the right wing of the party whom he had wooed previously with his populist antics. The final act of his premiership seemed to end in farce, with this directionless populism seemingly running its course.

The aftermath of Johnson was followed by the short-lived leadership of Liz Truss, which effectively ended the ideological vision of a pure market post-Brexit system that had long been cherished within Conservative circles. The subsequent Sunak Government appeared to take a more pragmatic approach to politics, yet its reliance on populism was still evident. Ultimately, the failure to deliver the post-Brexit El Dorado that Johnson seemed to promise through his brand of populism cost the Conservatives their worst electoral defeat in history. Yet, despite the landslide that Labour achieved in 2024, it appears at present that the Labour Party under Starmer is making similar mistakes to those of his Conservative predecessors. By failing to address the continued economic fallout from Brexit and instead focusing on balancing the books, as opposed to configuring a new form of post-Brexit economics, the current government will merely continue to produce wider instability. The narrow centrist position held by the Government also seems content to continue encouraging an alienation with the new left within civil society that emerged during the Corbyn era (Worth, 2019a). This will not only potentially enhance greater instabilities within wider society, which have appeared camouflaged by the inflated result of the landslide election victory, but will also allow right-wing populism greater impetus as an oppositional force.

At present the Labour government seem content to sit on its large majority and manage Britain's post-Brexit decline through prudency. However, without a substantial economic and political strategy that offers an alternative to the empty populism of neoliberal continuity the Johnson era appeared to endorse, it risks creating even deeper instabilities than have hitherto existed. The rapid emergence of Reform alongside a newly created right-wing opposition led by the 'culture warrior' Kemi Badenoch threatens to unleash a collection of reactionary forces potentially more damaging than the opportunism of the Johnson leadership.

Notes

1 This is not referring to the domination of Rupert Murdoch as such but rather the trend towards populism within the popular press that began with the takeover of news media outlets by individuals such as Rupert Murdoch and Robert Maxwell and which has continued a culture of populist news consumption.
2 The Monday Club was set up in 1961 as a group within the Conservative Party that opposed decolonisation. It became notorious for supporting apartheid South Africa and was strongly opposed to immigration. The Parliament Conservative Party maintained a high membership of the Monday Club, until links were finally severed in 2001.
3 Leave.EU attracted a great deal of criticism by displaying posters that depicted a crowded queue of immigrants under the title 'breaking point'. Vote Leave responded with a number of similar alarmist claims that suggested Turkey would join the EU and 'flood' Britain through immigration.

4 One that kept out of both EEA membership and any form of customs union. Hard-line Brexiters adopted the phase BRINO ('Brexit In Name Only') to refer to those who sought membership of certain EU institutions. Indeed, the term continues to be used today by those that campaign against any form of involvement of European Courts and for leaving the European Court of Human Rights.
5 As Arron Banks commented in his Brexit 'memoirs', the main potential of Brexit was that it could build a 'Singapore on Acid' (Banks, 2017).
6 By the right-wing press I am referring to the tabloid newspapers *The Sun* and *The Daily Mail*, the two largest selling daily newspapers in the UK, and the ultra-Eurosceptic *Daily Express*, as well as the traditional right-wing Conservative broadsheet, *The Daily Telegraph*, which Johnson worked for and contributed to from the 1990s onwards. Others, such as *The Times*, were highly sympathetic towards him, especially in the 2019 election, but did not provide the same unwavering support.

References

Atkins, J. (2022) 'Rhetoric and audience reception: An analysis of Teresa May's vision of Britain and Britishness after Brexit', *Politics* 42 (4): 216–230.
Bale, T. (2023) *The Conservative Party After Brexit: Turmoil and Transformation*, Polity, Cambridge.
Banks, A. (2017) *The Bad Books of Brexit*, Biteback, London.
Beasley, R. and Kaarbo, J. (2018) 'Casting for a sovereign role: Socialising an aspirant state in the Scottish independence referendum', *European Journal of International Relations*, 24(1): 8–32.
Bergsen, P. (2020) 'Why the pandemic and populism still work together', Chatham House, 10 March, www.chathamhouse.org/2020/11/why-pandemic-and-populism-still-work-together
Bratich, J. (2021) 'Give me liberty or give me Covid! Anti-lockdown protests as necropopulist downsurgency', *Cultural Studies*, 35(2-3): 257–265.
Brennan, J. (2017) *Against Democracy*, Princeton University Press, Princeton, NJ.
Brubaker, R. (2021) 'Paradoxes of populism during the pandemic', *Thesis Eleven*, 164(1): 73–87.
Catterall, P. (2021) '"Greed, my friends": Has Boris Johnson finally revealed his political "philosophy"?', LSE, 29 March, https://blogs.lse.ac.uk/politicsandpolicy/greed-my-friends/
Crerar, P. (2021) 'Boris Johnson broke "Covid lockdown rules" with Downing Street Party at Xmas', *Daily Mirror*, 30 November.
Cronin, M. (ed.) (1996) *The Failure of British Fascism*, Palgrave, London.
Daily Mail (2022) 'At last! A true Tory budget', 23 September.
Dorling, D. (2018) 'Brexit and Britain's radical right', *Political Insight*, 9(4): 36–39.

Drakeford, M. (2021) 'Speech on the launch of the Independent Commission on the Constitutional Future of Wales', Welsh Government, 14 January, https://www.gov.wales/wales-first-minister-welcomes-new-report-calling-for-reform-of-the-uks-constitution-on-radical-federalist-lines

Duparc-Portier, G. and Figus, G. (2021) 'The impact of the new Northern Ireland protocol: Can Northern Ireland enjoy best of both worlds?', *Regional Studies*, 56(8): 1404–1417.

Eatwell, R. (2000) 'The extreme right and British exceptionalism: The primacy of politics', in P. Hainsworth (ed.) *The Extreme Right in Western Europe*, Routledge, London.

Evans, G. and Menon, A. (2018) *Brexit and British Politics*, Polity, Cambridge.

Favell, A. (2019), 'Brexit: A requiem for the post-national society', *Global Discourse* 9 (1): 157–168.

Foster, R. and Feldman, M. (2021) 'From "Brexhaustion" to "Covidiots": The United Kingdom and the populist future', *Journal of Contemporary European Research*, 17(2): 117–127.

Galent, M. (2022) 'English nationalism and its role in building support for Brexit', in J. Sondel-Cedarmas and F. Berti (eds) *The Right-Wing Critique of Europe*, Routledge, London.

Gerbaudo, P. (2020) 'The pandemic crowd: Protest in the time of COVID-19', *Journal of International Affairs*, 73(2): 61–76.

Glencross, A. (2016) *Why the UK Voted for Brexit: David Cameron's Great Miscalculation*, Palgrave, London.

Goodwin, M. and Milazzo, C. (2015) *UKIP: Inside the Campaign to Redraw the Map of British Politics*, Oxford University Press, Oxford.

Goodwin-Hawkins, B. (2020) 'The intimate borders of epidemiological nationalism', *Anthropology in Action*, 27(3): 67–70.

Hall, S. (1979) 'The Great Moving Right Show', *Marxism Today*, January 14–20.

Hall, S. (1988) *The Hard Road to Renewal*, Verso, London.

Hayward, K. and Komarova, M. (2022) 'The protocol on Ireland/Northern Ireland: Past, present and future precariousness', *Global Policy* 13(S2): 128–137.

Heath, A. (2022) 'Britain back at its boldest: Budget adds up to greatest I have even seen', *Daily Telegraph*, 24 September.

Henderson, A. and Wyn Jones, R. (2021) *Englishness*, Oxford University Press, Oxford.

Jagers, J. and Walgrave, S. (2007) 'Populism as political communication style: An empirical study of political parties' discourse in Belgium', *European Journal of Political Research*, 46(3): 319–345.

Johnson, B. (2018) 'Denmark got it wrong. Yes, the Burka is oppressive and ridiculous – but that's still no reason to ban it', *Daily Telegraph*, 5 August.

Johnson, B. and Hunt, J (2018) 'Cheques debate', *Mail on Sunday*, 9 September.

Judis, J.-B. (2016) *The Populist Explosion: How the Great Recession Transformed American and European Politics*, Global Reports, Columbia.

Keate, N. (2024) 'Keir Starmer now more unpopular than Nigel Farage – poll', *Politico*, 8 October, www.politico.eu/article/keir-starmer-more-unpopular-nigel-farage-poll/

Kenny, M. (2020) 'English nationalism, the 2019 election and the future of the British state', *Political Insight*, 11(1): 24–27.

Kutllovci, L. (2022) 'Hardwired to self-destruct: The (un)remarkable prime ministership of Liz Truss', *European View*, 21(2): 223–224.

Laclau, E. (2005) *On Populist Reason*, London, Verso.

Manavis, S. (2018) 'What is cultural Marxism? The alt-right meme in Suella Braverman's speech in Westminster', *New Stateman*, 22 October.

Manley, G. (2019) 'Scotland's post-referenda future', *Anthropology Today*, 35(4): 13017.

McCrone, D. and Keating, M. (2021) 'Questions of sovereignty: Redefining politics in Scotland', *Political Quarterly*, 92(1): 14–22.

McEwan, N. (2018) 'Brexit and Scotland: Between two unions', *British Politics*, 13: 65–78.

Moffit, B. (2016) *The Global Rise of Populism: Performance, Political Style and Representation*, Stanford University Press, Stanford.

Moffit, B. and Tormey, S. (2014) 'Rethinking populism: Politics, mediaisation and political style', *Political Studies*, 62(3): 381–397.

Mondon, A. and Winter, A. (2020) *Reactionary Democracy: How Racism and the Populist Far Right Became Mainstream*, Verso, London.

Mudde, C. (2004) 'The populist zeitgeist', *Government and Opposition*, 39(4): 541–563.

Mudde, C. (2007) *Populist Radical Right Parties in Europe*, Cambridge University Press, Cambridge.

Muller, J.-W. (2017) *What is Populism?* Penguin, London.

Murphy, M. (2021) 'Northern Ireland and Brexit: Where sovereignty and stability collide', *Journal of Contemporary European Studies*, 29(3): 405–418.

Murphy, M. and Evershed, J. (2021) 'Contesting sovereignty and borders: Northern Ireland, devolution and the Union', *Territory, Politics, Governance*, 5: 661–677.

Mylonas, H. and Walley, N. (2022) 'Pandemic nationalism', *Nationalities Papers*, 50(1): 3–22.

Opinium (2020) 'UK: National identity in Britain', 9 March, www.opinium.com/resource-center/national-identity-in-britain/

Paun, A. and Hall, D. (2021) 'Why is Welsh independence on the agenda?', Institute For Government, 22 April www.instituteforgovernment.org.uk/explainers/welsh-independence

Russell, F. (2022) 'Pox populi: Anti-vaxx, anti-politics', *Journal of Sociology*, 59(3): 699–715.

Sasson, I. (2021) 'Age and Covid-19 mortality: A comparison of Gompertz doubling time across countries and causes of death', *Demographic Research*, 44(16): 379–396.

Statista (2022) 'In hindsight do you think Britain was right or wrong to leave the European Union?', www.statista.com/statistics/987347/brexit-opinion-poll/

Vanderslott, S., Emary, K., te Water Naude, R., English, M., Thomas, T., Patrick-Smith, M., Henry, J., Douglas, N., Moore, M., Stuart, A., Hodgson, S. and

Pollard, A. (2021) 'Vaccine nationalism and internationalism: Perspectives of COVID-19 vaccine trial participants in the United Kingdom', *BMJ Global Health*, 6(10): 1–11.

Vieten, U. M. (2020) 'The "new normal" and "pandemic populism": The COVID-19 crisis and anti-hygienic mobilisation of the far-right', *Social Sciences*, 9(9): 165.

Wellings, B. (2020) *English Nationalism: Brexit and the Anglophone Sphere*, Manchester University Press, Manchester.

Worth, O. (2017) 'Reviving Hayek's dream', *Globalizations*, 14(1): 104–109.

Worth, O. (2019a) *Morbid Symptoms: The Global Rise of the Far Right*, Zed Books, London.

Worth, O. (2022) 'The great moving Boris show: Brexit and the mainstreaming of the far right in Britain', *Globalizations*, 20(5): 814–828.

Wyn Jones, R. (2019) 'Why the future of Welsh politics is likely to be much more fractured and divided than its past', Nation.Cymru, 24 September, https://nation.cymru/opinion/richard-wyn-jones-brexit-wales-identity/

YouGov (2021) 'Voting intentions', 28 May, https://yougov.co.uk/politics/articles/36177-voting-intention-con-43-lab-29-27-28-may

Zhou, R. (2021) 'Vaccine nationalism: Contested relationships between COVID-19 and globalization', *Globalizations*, 19(3): 450–465.

4

The UK's chronic territorial condition: The politics of constitutional debate after devolution

Jonathan Bradbury

Introduction

This chapter addresses the question: what has happened to the UK's territorial condition following devolution, Brexit, COVID-19 and fourteen years of Conservative governments? In so doing, it finds an unclear picture. Whilst there has been a temptation for those taking the temperature of the UK's territorial condition to look for a revivified Union or, more commonly, its imminent demise, the reality is that while there has been new territorial contestation it appears to co-exist with a difficult but operational political stability in most parts of the state. Welsh Labour, the SNP and Sinn Féin have all promoted distinct and divergent political projects at the devolved level, but there appear to have been few clear transformative pay-offs for public policy to underpin new predominant loyalties to Scotland, Wales and Ireland in public attitudes. Polls on public attitudes throughout the period of Conservative Government have suggested the importance of support for Scottish and Welsh independence and Irish reunification but there has been no clear winner between cases for the long-term survival of the UK or its break up. With the advent of the new Labour Government in 2024 there remains equally plausible prognoses in favour either of disintegration or a revived Union. Years of relative Conservative failure in territorial management has bequeathed a state where devolution has thus far not provided a decisive route to restabilising the Union. Their legacy instead is a chronic territorial condition of continued contestation but not an acute one of imminent break-up. This is still a legacy that poses considerable challenges for an incoming Labour Government, though in the immediate aftermath of the 2024 election they appear to be setting a course focused on stability.

Scotland

In Scotland, the devolution of extensive legislative and tax raising powers has made the Scottish Parliament one of the strongest sub-state legislatures in the world. Despite this, during the last ten years the pro-independence movement has maintained considerable momentum for further change. First, the extent of devolution has continued to be disputed with the SNP government arguing that in the aftermath of the 2014 independence referendum a consensus had formed for a far more extensive devolution of welfare state powers than was provided by the eventual 2016 Scotland Act. The lack of comprehensive welfare powers to mitigate against UK Conservative government spending cuts gave the SNP administration further political capital on this point.

Second, the case for another independence referendum has been made very rapidly. The lack of an immediate mandate for a further referendum after the 2014 defeat was originally accepted, as it had been framed as a once in a generation event. Nevertheless, Nicola Sturgeon, as SNP Leader and First Minister from 2014, said that this situation only applied as long as the material conditions that had held during the referendum did not change. A key argument made by the Better Together campaign in 2014 had been that independence could threaten Scotland's place in the European Union, so when the UK left the EU following the vote for Brexit, Nicola Sturgeon could say that the material conditions had changed and that Scotland had been taken out of the EU against her will (Keating, 2019).

After 2016, successive Conservative prime ministers said that they would not grant a second referendum, prompting some in the SNP to call for confrontational responses, including a Catalonia-style unofficial referendum or a strategy of sequenced SNP elected member resignations to create by-elections where independence would be made the key issue. However, Nicola Sturgeon stuck to a rigorously constitutional strategy, believing it essential to build a national consensus around the case for independence so as to ensure that, when it happened, it was popularly accepted as legitimate. Following a strong performance by the pro-independence parties (the SNP and Scottish Greens) in the 2021 Scottish parliament elections, Sturgeon announced that they would hold a second referendum in October 2023, and challenged the UK government to stop them.

The Conservative government's implementation of Brexit threw further coal on the fire. First, the EU Withdrawal Bill originally proposed in 2017 sought to transfer repatriated EU powers in all areas, including those within the devolved responsibilities, to the UK Parliament in the first instance. The Scottish government legislated to repatriate EU powers in devolved areas, in direct contradiction to the UK legislative process. However, in the Miller Judgement in 2017 the UK Supreme Court upheld Westminster's right to decide on these matters without the need for consent from devolved parliaments. The 2020 Internal Market Act then set the rules for the post-Brexit UK economy on the basis of the two key market access principles of mutual recognition and non-discrimination. The application of these rules meant that, in effect, no economic actor in the UK economy would be bound by Scottish legislation when operating in the Scottish market. Given the Miller Judgement, the Scottish government had little choice but to accept the Act. It had to do the same in November 2022 when the Supreme Court also ruled that it was the UK Parliament's decision as to whether Scotland could hold a second independence referendum.

In this context, the COVID-19 pandemic provided a countervailing challenge for the UK and Scottish governments to work together. In many ways they did, with the Scottish government broadly following the same strategy as that applied across the UK, adopting policies of lockdowns, track and trace interventions, and population health monitoring allied to a range of policies including the use of face masks. In hindsight, the

Scottish government made many of the same mistakes – for example, discharging older patients back to care homes without testing – resulting in similar rates of infection.

At the same time, however, the Johnson Government's political management of the pandemic left much to be desired. In contrast, Nicola Sturgeon, through regular press conferences, cut a figure of moral rectitude in her single-minded commitment to serving the people. She often stood accused of cynically announcing approaches in Scotland ahead of a UK government announcement for political advantage after private UK-wide talks. But within Scotland, Sturgeon and her government appeared to the public to be taking the initiative and demonstrating the benefits of devolution.

In response to this unfolding political story, what has been the state of public opinion on Scotland's constitutional status? In the September 2014 referendum 55 per cent of voters voted No to independence with 45 per cent in favour. In the period between then and the pandemic, polls on a forced Yes or No to independence question suggested strong support for both Yes and No votes, with a norm of each recording over 40 per cent of the vote. The sustained rise in support for independence to compete with support for the Union was a clear legacy of the referendum (Henderson et al., 2022). Overall, though, polls continued to record consistent, albeit small, No majorities, apart from in a few polls immediately after the 2016 EU referendum. During the pandemic, opinion polls again largely recorded No majorities, but there were polls that suggested consistent Yes majorities between June 2020 and January 2021 and then again between March and April 2021, and October and December 2022. Since the end of the pandemic, polls recording a No majority again have generally outweighed those recording a Yes majority, but the latter are more regular than before the pandemic.

What is interesting about this is that Brexit did not appear to drive public opinion towards a Yes vote. Instead, it was perceptions of Scottish and UK governance of the pandemic that appeared to have had the main effect on pushing up the Yes vote and making it more regularly competitive in polls. Demonstration of the autonomy of Scottish governance has been more important than grievance at departing the EU. Nevertheless, No remains generally ahead. Equally, when those polled are able to express a view on the full range of constitutional preferences, the plurality of support generally focuses on more powers for the Scottish Parliament. A Survation poll in July 2023 found that independence was supported by 23 per cent of those polled while support for more powers stood at 28 per cent. Less than a third of those polled entertained a weaker parliament, abolition or didn't know. This sustains the argument that Scotland has definitely embraced a strong form of devolution but the basis for consensus may well lie in strengthening the Parliament rather than independence.

Since 2022 the momentum behind the case for independence has receded. The SNP has experienced a police inquiry into the party's administration of funds donated for independence campaigning against a backdrop of questions over levels of party membership and the state of the party's finances as a whole. Drops in party membership were linked to the SNP government's legislation on gender recognition, which had at its heart the acceptance of self-identification for transgender people. This proved to be controversial, especially with those holding religious views. In February 2023 Nicola Sturgeon resigned as party leader and first minister to be succeeded by the Health Minister, Humza Yousaf.

Party problems continued, though, as Sturgeon went on to be interviewed by the police over the party's management of its internal financial affairs. These problems served to provide new impetus to those who had criticised the SNP's performance in government. In some areas of policy there had been notable successes, for example self-sustainability in renewable energy. However, there were mounting criticisms of the record both on health care and education performance, and the creation of a nationwide police force had been accompanied by a number of controversies over its handling of individual cases. Things got worse when Humza Yousaf's government declared its 2030 net zero targets unachievable, leading to the collapse of its power sharing agreement with the Scottish Greens. Yousaf resigned as First Minister and party leader in May 2024 to be replaced by John Swinney. During this period the SNP slipped from its long-held ascendancy in the polls, with Labour as the main beneficiary.

What went wrong with Britain?

At the 2024 UK general election Labour became the biggest party in Scotland as its vote share rose by 16.7 per cent to 35.3 per cent and the party went from one seat to thirty-seven. Meanwhile the SNP vote share went down 15 per cent to 30 per cent and their number of seats from 49 to 9. It was a bad night for the Conservatives as well as their share of the vote halved to 12.7 per cent and went from 6 to 5 seats.

Despite the SNP's problems, the likely Yes vote in a possible independence referendum remained generally over 40 per cent in polls both before and after the 2024 general election. Demographic change may also point to its growth, as independence is more popular among younger voters. Having said that, the period since 2007 has provided unusually fertile ground for the growth of an independence vote as Westminster has struggled to cope with a succession of economic, strategic and health crises. One might ask, if the case for independence has not taken a decisive lead in such circumstances then what prospects are there of this happening in the near future? In response the new Labour Government has not adopted a strategy of devolving more powers, the option that polls indicate is the most popular if voters are given a full choice. But its focus on economic growth and social reform, including reform of workers' rights, may well prove popular. In the October 2024 budget Labour significantly raised social policy expenditure with consequential rises in block grant funding for health and education in Scotland. If Labour is able to maintain the focus on economic and social policy issues and strongly challenge the SNP at the 2026 Scottish Parliament elections, a reduction in focus on the constitutional debate remains equally plausible.

Wales

In Wales, devolution has been significantly extended from its original settlement in 1998. Under the 2006 Government of Wales Act (GOWA) and following a Yes majority in a referendum in 2011, the National Assembly for Wales gained primary legislative powers. Under the 2014 GOWA it gained income tax varying powers as well as some smaller tax powers. Under the 2017 GOWA, the model of devolution changed from the conferred powers model to the reserved powers model. Welsh devolution now more closely resembles Scottish devolution and since 2020 the Assembly has been renamed the Welsh Parliament/Senedd Cymru. The principal difference remains, though – the extent of devolved powers. Since 2017, the Welsh Labour government has focused on requesting the devolution of policing and criminal justice powers to gain equity with Scotland and Northern Ireland. UK Conservative governments up to 2024 resisted these demands, saying that a period of stability and consolidation is needed. There was no appetite at the centre for more devolution in Wales (Bradbury, 2021b).

The period from 2016 also saw an increased interest in the option of independence. In contrast to Scotland, support in polls had historically been below 20 per cent but consideration of independence was promoted afresh by the emergence of a new grassroots movement, Yes Cymru, which held several marches with numbers in the thousands and led to a new social media phenomenon of indycuriosity. Yes Cymru's emergence was mainly borne out of frustration with Plaid Cymru's lack of progress and attracted people supportive of independence but not necessarily of Plaid Cymru. Plaid Cymru responded under the leadership of Adam Price by establishing a party commission, which reported in 2020 with an extensive set of proposals on how independence might be achieved (Plaid Cymru, 2020).

Brexit also had implications for Welsh constitutional debate. The Welsh Labour government took a similar view to the SNP administration in Scotland, asserting the need for their consent to be given for the UK government to legislate in devolved areas and developing their own legislation on repatriating EU powers in devolved areas directly to Wales. The Welsh government responded somewhat differently to the Miller Judgement in 2017 and sought to negotiate a compromise with Westminster. This proved to be relatively successful and was key to ensuring that the eventual 2018 EU Withdrawal Act did indeed devolve the bulk of EU powers in devolved areas (such as agriculture and fisheries) to the devolved parliaments. While the SNP government maintained a confrontational stand-off during these discussions, they ultimately shared in the benefits of this deal

(Paun *et al.*, 2019). There could be no such amelioration though of the potential effects of the 2020 Internal Market Act. The Welsh Labour government strongly opposed both the market access rules and the new concurrent powers the UK government gave itself to spend in policy areas such as transport, which had been devolved. Both threatened to undermine devolution (Wyn Jones and Morgan, 2023).

In the wake of these developments, the Welsh Labour government under First Minister Mark Drakeford updated its constitutional position. Government policy statements adopted the language of the UK being a voluntary association of nations, where popular sovereignty replaced the primacy of UK parliamentary sovereignty, meaning it was Wales' right to consider its constitutional future on its own terms. In this context, Welsh Labour again argued for the devolution of policing and criminal justice powers but also argued for structures through which the Welsh government could influence UK governance as a whole. Welsh Labour called this policy radical federalism (Welsh Government, 2019). In part, this reflected a genuine development in intellectual thought; in part, it was a statement of defiance against any repetition of the approach taken by the UK government during Brexit; but also politically it gave Labour a defence against the Yes Cymru-inspired push for independence.

When the pandemic struck, Labour were struggling in the Welsh opinion polls against challenges both from the Conservatives and Plaid Cymru, and Mark Drakeford had very low public recognition and approval levels. The Welsh government also broadly fell in line with a UK-wide approach to responding to the pandemic, with differences being more of degree than principle. They also made the same mistakes and in January 2021 when the UK was assessed as having the highest Covid death rate in the world, Wales had the highest death rate among the UK nations. Yet his perceived handling of the pandemic was the political making of Mark Drakeford's tenure as First Minister. His intellectual capacity for understanding the issues and the calmness with which he explained and asserted public health responses won him much public praise. From a constitutional perspective, Drakeford pointed out the fiscal advantages of Treasury economic support during the pandemic, thus highlighting what he saw as the economic Achilles heel of independence. However, he also complained of a lack of Conservative government consultation during the crisis, highlighting the need for a new respect for devolution as part of seeing the UK as a voluntary consensual union.

In response to these unfolding events, there have been headline grabbing polls suggesting 30 per cent or more support independence. Typically, these have involved the asking of non-standard questions or have reflected spikes of opinion on particular issues. Analysis of regular polls asking the same question reveals more sobering trends. Undoubtedly, as shown in Table 4.1 there has been some movement towards independence. On a forced choice vote, however, there remains a clear majority in favour of No. Polls considering the full range of constitutional preferences (see Tables 4.2 and 4.3) also show some rise in support for independence but they also show a decline in support for the 'more powers' and 'existing powers' options, and slight rises in support for 'less powers' and 'abolition'. More of those polled say that they are undecided, not going to vote or refused to answer. This suggests a possible move to a more polarised electorate caused by the focus of the public debate being on independence. As support for independence increases, a substantial number of those polled who may have supported more powers for a Senedd within the UK may no longer see this as a safe option and the numbers in favour of less powers or abolition grows. In comparing with Scotland, it appears that the movement towards independence has also grown in the wake of Brexit and the pandemic, but it is still only a limited move and it appears to have stimulated more caution among those voters definitely not wishing to entertain independence.

As Wales approached the 2021 Welsh Parliament elections, the expectation was that the option of independence would be central to debate. In practice, Plaid Cymru failed to stimulate interest in the issue, Labour increased their seat tally and Mark Drakeford was widely seen as winning the election on the basis of perceived competence in dealing with the pandemic. Plaid Cymru again did not break through and, subsequently, the pressure for independence has subsided. Internal differences in Yes

Table 4.1: YouGov polls on public responses to the question: Do you want Wales to be an independent country?

	Yes (%)	No (%)	Undecided/not-voting/refused (%)
4–7 Dec 2023	22	56	22
3–7 February 2023	22	54	24
25 Feb–March 2022	21	53	26
20–26 Jan 2021	21	56	23
20–26 Jan 2020	21	56	23
30 June–July 2016	15	65	20
8–11 Sept 2014	17	70	14

Sources: YouGov, 'Should Wales be an independent country?', https://docs.cdn.yougov.com/ew9dwj6qt6/YG%20Trackers%20-%20Wales%20-%20Indy%20ref.pdf, accessed on 20 November 2020; and YG Trackers - Wales - Indy Ref W.pdf (yougov.com), accessed 2 April 2024.

Table 4.2: YouGov polls on public attitudes to constitutional preferences for the Welsh Parliament/Senedd Cymru

	Independence (%)	More powers (%)	Existing powers (%)	Less powers (%)	Abolition (%)	Undecided/Refused (%)
May 2023	13	21	20	7	20	16
Feb 2023	15	20	21	7	20	16
Sept 2022	17	19	21	7	19	15
June 2020	16	20	24	5	22	14
Jan 2020	14	18	24	8	17	19

Source: https://blogs.cardiff.ac.uk/electionsinwales/ accessed on 20 November 2020 and Survey Report (yougov.com), accessed 2 April 2024.

Cymru have made it a much less potent pressure group, and Price resigned from the leadership of Plaid Cymru in 2023 following an internal party report that detailed complaints about sexual harassment and bullying, as well as his subsequent inability to command the united support of his party to continue as leader. He has been succeeded by Rhun ap Iorwerth who has adopted a more cautious approach and talk of independence is

Table 4.3: St David's Day (1 March) BBC ICM polls on public attitudes to constitutional preferences for the Welsh Parliament/Senedd Cymru, formerly National Assembly for Wales

	Independence (%)	More powers (%)	Existing Powers (%)	Less Powers (%)	Abolition (%)	Undecided (%)
2021	14	35	27	3	15	6
2020	11	43	25	2	14	3
2019	7	46	27	3	13	2
2018	7	44	28	4	12	4
2016	6	43	30	3	13	4
2014	5	37	28	3	23	5
2012	7	36	29	2	22	4
2010	11	40	13	18	13	4

Source: www.icmunlimited.com/our-work/bbc-wales-st-davids-day-poll-2020/ accessed on 20 November 2020 and Voting attitudes and Senedd powers quizzed in poll for BBC Wales – BBC News, accessed on 2 April 2024.

now lower in the mix. An independent commission appointed by the Welsh government on the future of devolution outlined the options of entrenched devolved powers, federalism and independence in its final report in 2024 without firmly recommending any option (Welsh Government, 2024). Pro-independence campaigners appear to be back to encouraging a conversation about independence as one of the options, in a situation rather akin to where the SNP was in 2007 when it encouraged a national conversation on independence as a prelude to a focused debate when the time was more propitious.

In developing that conversation, there are pressures that may yet favour more support for independence in Wales as a result of changing party fortunes. In the 2024 UK general election, Plaid Cymru saw their vote share rise by 4.9 per cent to 14.8 per cent and increased their seat share to four out of thirty-two constituencies. The expected reform of the electoral system (on the basis of a ninety-six seat d'Hondt list system based on sixteen multi-member constituencies) is expected to make it easier for Plaid Cymru to have a regular platform in coalition administrations following the 2026 Senedd elections. Labour continue to be the dominant party. In the 2024 UK general election, Labour won 37 per cent of the vote and twenty-seven of the thirty-two constituencies. They remain in government in Cardiff Bay. However, the UK election performance actually involved a 3.9 per cent reduction in vote share, and at the devolved level Labour has seen a turnover of leaders as rapid as that seen in Scotland. In 2024, Drakeford was succeeded as First Minister by Vaughan Gething, but his leadership unravelled after criticisms of his decisions over donations to his leadership campaign and his authorisation of deletion of ministers' WhatsApp messages during the COVID-19 pandemic. Following a Senedd vote of no confidence and ministerial resignations, he stood down to be replaced by Eluned Morgan. Such turmoil has heightened the pressure on Labour, where in a manner similar to the SNP's position, there is criticism of under-performance on the economy, health and education.

Having said that, the immediate impact of a UK Labour Government appears to have been to reduce the focus on constitutional debate. UK Labour ministers have ruled out devolving any further powers, saying the key focus is on economic and social policy. Instead, UK and Welsh Labour ministers have embarked on an unusually high level of co-operation in developing a policy agenda designed to help Welsh Labour get into a strong position for the 2026 Senedd elections. Meanwhile, it is just as possible that the beneficiaries of any Labour failure may well be Reform UK rather than Plaid Cymru. In the 2024 UK general election, Reform UK saw its vote share go up in Wales by 11.5 per cent to 16.9 per cent, largely at the expense of the Conservatives. A YouGov poll in September 2024 suggested 24 per cent support for independence, 46 per cent for the current devolved Senedd, and 31 per cent for abolition. Even a majority of Plaid Cymru supporters support a Senedd with more powers rather than independence. Consequently, while Plaid Cymru offer a plausible political challenge, the independence debate remains live, and though Labour are under considerable pressure, pressures for further constitutional change remain far from overwhelming and, indeed, strongly contested from the right.

The UK's chronic territorial condition

Northern Ireland

In Northern Ireland, the future of devolution has been considered primarily in existential terms. Sinn Féin, the dominant nationalist-republican party, have seen it as a stepping stone to a united Ireland. Their strategy has been to win power in both the Republic and in Northern Ireland, and from those platforms persuade the electorates both sides of the border of the value of unification, prior to calling a border poll. Conversely, the Democratic Unionist Party (DUP), the dominant Protestant-Unionist party, has seen participation in devolved government as essential to denying Sinn Féin that platform in the North, and to normalising devolution in Northern Ireland as equivalent to that in Wales and Scotland as a part of the modern governance of the UK. In the short-term, everyone holds their noses and participates in power-sharing government while seeking to legitimise their long-term goals. Both parties have been susceptible to dissent and outflanking – Sinn Féin from the Real IRA and Continuity IRA, who have believed that the ballot box strategy traps them in the UK; the DUP from many of its own members and rejectionist Unionists who continue to hate sharing power with people they consider to be former terrorists.

From 2007 to 2017 it appeared that the DUP held the upper hand in this relationship, as it dominated the Unionist party bloc in Northern Ireland elections and held the first ministership. But these years saw continued competition between the DUP and Sinn Féin over the long-term future of Northern Ireland, and the Coalition and Conservative UK governments appeared less engaged with managing this competition than the previous Labour governments (Todd, 2017). In 2017, Sinn Féin refused to support the re-nomination of Arlene Foster as the DUP First Minister following the Renewable Heat Incentive scandal – a scheme introduced by Foster but which had hugely run over budget. Sinn Féin demanded an alternative DUP candidate, the DUP refused to backdown and so the power-sharing administration could not be formed, leaving government to be conducted by officials strictly within pre-existing policies. The 2019 UK general election proved that this impasse was damaging to both Sinn Féin and the DUP, as the electorate registered their frustration at not having devolved government at all by supporting a surge for the non-sectarian Alliance Party. In January 2020, power-sharing government was restored with Foster again as First Minister, a post she held until being succeeded by Paul Givan in June 2021.

Sinn Féin's position during this period was boosted by the historic outcome of the 2020 Irish general election. Sinn Féin broke the traditional two-party dominance of Fianna Fáil and Fine Gael by taking the most first preference votes and thirty-seven seats against Fianna Fáil's thirty-eight and Fine Gael's thirty-five The latter two parties had refused to govern with Sinn Féin so buried their own differences by agreeing a coalition along with the Green Party. Sinn Féin's position in the North was then transformed by their historic victory in the 2022 Northern Ireland Assembly elections. Sinn Féin's position in being the leading party in the nationalist-republican bloc did not change; rather the key change was the fall in support for the DUP as the Unionist vote divided across the DUP, Traditional Unionist Voice as well as the Ulster Unionist Party. For the first time, Sinn Féin had the right to nominate their leader, Michelle O'Neill, to the post of First Minister while the DUP would have to settle for the Deputy role. In both the Republic and the North, Sinn Féin's discipline in establishing themselves as the leading democratic voice of republicanism and Irish reunification appeared to be paying off.

Brexit gave considerable impetus to nationalist-republican gains during this period (Teague, 2019). This was because Ireland was able to influence the EU's negotiating position on the new EU–UK trade agreement, which would replace UK membership of the EU to prevent a hard economic border being established between Northern Ireland and the Republic and so sustain one of the key planks of the 1998 Belfast Agreement. The Northern Ireland protocol provided for the continued application of EU customs union and single market rules in Northern Ireland, meaning that trade could continue to flow uninterrupted and a wide range of policy matters could still be dealt with across the whole island of Ireland. This was a key dimension of the dynamic of normalising an all-Ireland government. At the same time, the very negotiation of the protocol represented a significant undermining of the Unionist position as it effectively created an economic

The UK's chronic territorial condition

border, involving customs checks, between Northern Ireland and the rest of the UK. Boris Johnson had previously gone to Northern Ireland and courted Unionist support by saying he would defend their interests in any Brexit deal and yet as Prime Minister he negotiated the protocol as a necessary feature of getting a deal. The negotiation of the protocol, which came into force in January 2021, made it very difficult for the DUP to stay in devolved government while also trying to manage Unionist opinion. In February 2022, Paul Givan stood down as First Minister and when the 2022 Northern Ireland elections took place devolved government was suspended again. It was the Unionist backlash over the Northern Ireland protocol and the DUP's failure to defend Unionist interests that contributed substantially to the fracturing of the Unionist vote that let Sinn Féin become the largest party overall.

In contrast, the handling of the pandemic in Northern Ireland was not especially significant in influencing the nationalist-Unionist political dynamic. The power sharing administrations of Foster and Givan presided over the administrative response in a manner that again followed broader UK strategy. When it came to the elections of 2022 it was Brexit that was seen as the game changer in influencing Northern Irish electoral opinion and not the handling of the pandemic. The DUP refused to rejoin power sharing government until the Northern Ireland protocol was readdressed, leading to a further period of government by officials. Ultimately this pressured both the EU and the UK government to reconsider the protocol and led to the negotiation of the Windsor Framework in 2023. This reduced the customs checks on goods coming from the UK into Northern Ireland, gave the UK government more control over VAT rates, and established a mechanism for Northern Irish and UK governments to have a say over any new single European Market law that might affect Northern Ireland. After much internal discussion the DUP Leader, Jeffrey Donaldson, persuaded his party to return to power sharing, with Michelle O'Neil becoming the first Sinn Féin First Minister.

What, then, were the implications of these developments? Table 4.4 gives a summary of polls conducted between 2016 and early 2024 on attitudes to a border poll on the future of Northern Ireland. They show

Table 4.4: Polls on public responses in Northern Ireland to the question: How would you vote in a border poll on the future of Northern Ireland?

	Remain in the UK (%)	Join a reunited Ireland (%)	Undecided/ not-voting/ refused (%)
Feb 2024 (Lucid Talk)	49	39	12
Dec 2023 (IPSOS)	51	30	20
Dec 2022 (IPSOS)	50	27	23
Aug 2022 (Lucid Talk)	48	41	11
May 2022 (NILTS)	48	34	18
Dec 2021 (Ashcroft)	49	41	10
May 2021 (Kantor)	44	35	21
Jan 2021 (LucidTalk)	47	42	11
Sept 2019 (Ashcroft)	45	46	9
Sept 2016 (IPSOS)	63	22	15

Northern Ireland Border Poll 2016 | Ipsos, accessed on 2 April 2024.

a fall in support for remaining in the UK and a rise in support for a united Ireland in the years after the EU Referendum vote in 2016. This has given a big boost to Irish republican hopes, with a 2019 poll conducted by Lord Ashcroft indicating a one-point lead for a united Ireland. Having said that, the story remains one of trendless fluctuation, with marked variations depending on the pollster. Overall, support for remaining in the UK is still generally ahead and support for a United Ireland remains some way off the 60 per cent figure widely seen to be needed in polls to build pressure on the UK secretary of state for Northern Ireland to call a border poll. Why is this the case? Largely, it is because while virtually all Protestant voters support remaining in the UK, around a quarter of Catholics still support remaining in the UK. An increasing minority of Northern Irish voters also do not see themselves as naturally aligned to the nationalist–Unionist divide, and have developed a politics of loyalty specific to Northern Ireland that underpins support for the non-sectarian Alliance party.

Since the restoration of power-sharing government in early 2024, Sinn Féin have had a significant opportunity to make their case for the benefits of a united Ireland. In the 2024 UK general election, the vote in Northern Ireland appeared to confirm their ascendancy as they were the largest party (with 27 per cent of the vote), taking seven of the eighteen seats. Meanwhile, Traditional Unionist Voice emerged as a new voice for hardline unionism, the DUP's vote share fell by 8.5 per cent and the unionist vote became further fragmented. The fact that Sinn Féin's electoral position appeared to strengthen in opinion polls in the Republic for much of 2023 and early 2024 served to further underpin the apparent cogency of the Sinn Féin rise both sides of the border (Hayward, 2024). Several structural factors also appear to be on their side. Demographic change means that the proportion of the population identifying as Catholic is now higher than Protestant and this is expected to grow. Following Brexit, living standards are now higher in the Republic than in Northern Ireland and if the UK does not see an economic upturn in the years ahead voters may see it as economically beneficial to support a united Ireland. The DUP are clearly divided about returning to power-sharing government while the Northern Ireland protocol is still in place, albeit revised in its practice by the Windsor Framework. Refusenik unionism could yet leave Sinn Féin on their own to negotiate with the UK government, a position they have always wanted. Michelle O'Neil is being cautious but she expects there to be a border poll within ten years.

On the other hand, while Unionism is on the back foot there remains a long way to go for the case for a border poll to be made. In the June 2024 Republic of Ireland local elections, following public opposition to an apparent inflow of migrants from the North as a result of the UK Government's Rwanda policy and disapproval of Sinn Féin's pro-immigration response, Sinn Féin actually polled very badly. They achieved just 11.79 per cent first preference votes and 102 seats out of 949. Both Fine Gael and Fianna Fáil achieved twice that proportion of first preference votes and took 493 seats between them. This shows the fluidity of voting behaviour in the South. Meanwhile in the North a crucial issue will be whether unionism can regroup and, specifically, whether the DUP can re-consolidate unionist support and reclaim the First Minister position following the next Assembly elections due by May 2027. Electoral preferences expressed since the 2019 UK general election also appear to point to a frustration at deficiencies in basic governance; that the everyday issues that voters face are not being given sufficient attention by the parties, and that long-term problems have not been addressed. The growing third category of loyalty to Northern Ireland and how well it is governed suggests that there will be strong challenges for a Sinn Féin First Minister in getting the timing right for the case for a border poll.

England

In England, the focus has been on developing regional governance to complement local government in addressing policy performance problems rather than integration issues associated with regional identity. London has simply developed on the regional local government model already provided by the Elected Mayor and the Greater London Authority. In the rest of England, the Conservative–Liberal Democrat Coalition initially introduced local enterprise partnerships with stronger private sector leadership. Subsequently, Conservative governments developed a city region capacity of combined authorities and combined county authorities under the 2009 Local Democracy, Economic Development and Construction Act and the 2023 Levelling Up and Regeneration Act. Under this legislation, local councils have been able to seek combined authority status, and by 2023 England had nine city region combined authority bodies, including Greater Manchester, the Liverpool City Region, West Midlands, the North East, South and West Yorkshire, and western England. In addition, the presence of elected metro mayors has given them some direct public accountability. The attraction of seeking such status has been the offer of so-called devolution deals from central government, by which the combined authorities have been able to constitute themselves as integrated transport authorities and economic prosperity boards, and receive central funding under contract, borrow on a limited basis, and levy their constituent authorities to address regional infrastructure and regeneration needs.

The Conservative Government's appetite for economic regionalism expanded in 2021 to include nine freeports on the English coastline, from the Thames and Solent in the South to the Humber and Teesside in the North. These were to be economic areas where tax breaks were offered to encourage new economic activity and customs rules did not apply until goods left their boundaries. In 2023, then Chancellor Jeremy Hunt introduced what he called trailblazer deals for Greater Manchester and West Midlands combined authorities, under which they gained multi-year single settlements rather than single year prescribed individual policy settlements. By 2024, England was due to have three further combined authorities with mayors as well as other non-mayoral devolution deals, and established authorities sought similar additional trailblazer powers (Sandford, 2023). At the same time, city region devolution deals without elected metro mayors were sought and offered in Wales and in Scotland, and both Wales and Scotland had freeports designated by the UK Conservative government. This approach offered some challenge to economic models being developed under devolution, though in Scotland the SNP government embraced freeports as greenports, adding aims for net zero and fair work outcomes to accompany those for regeneration. These developments were accompanied by some nascent political movements in England that echoed the former campaign for a Northern Assembly. None of these movements, though, have led to concerted campaigns for elected regional parliaments in England.

Pressures around England as a political construct have also had some significance, though rather more on the basis of developing correctives to the implications of devolution elsewhere in the UK than developing any new, explicitly English, nation-building project. From 1998 onwards there were perceived resentments against contemporary versions of the West Lothian Question, which highlighted the unfairness of Scottish MPs in the House of Commons being able to vote on matters that related to England that in Scotland were devolved and could not be voted on by

English MPs. A campaign for an English Parliament was established in 1998 and lobbied for a referendum to bring constitutional parity with the rest of the UK. During the 2000s, the Conservative party internally debated whether and how to address this issue. Ultimately, David Cameron as Conservative Prime Minister judged the moment had come in 2014 following the Scottish independence referendum. The result was the introduction of the English Votes for English Laws procedure in the House of Commons to shore up public faith in the existing UK Parliament's ability to allow English MPs to have ultimate say over matters pertaining just to England.

Survey research in England has found evidence of public resentments regarding the operation of the Union. It has suggested that a key driver of support for Brexit in England was an English nationalist concern about sovereignty rather than a British one. Many pro-Brexit English identifiers also are devo-sceptical. This has provided the context for Conservative election campaigns that have sought to weaponise English resentments against Scotland, notably the 2015 general election, when Labour Leader Ed Miliband was portrayed as being in the pocket of the then SNP Leader, Alex Salmond (Kenny, 2014; Henderson and Wyn Jones, 2021). In contrast, Boris Johnson in his very successful 2019 campaign displayed a much more subtle understanding of how to attract public support in each part of Britain without resorting to such tactics. His politics of levelling up appealed to sentiments across the UK. Subsequently, the experience of the pandemic did not appear to give any particular momentum to English sentiment, and as a result the Campaign for an English Parliament has still not achieved lift-off, and no major political party has committed to creating one.

In the light of these political developments, what has happened to public views on the future governance of England? YouGov polling over the last twenty-five years has tended to suggest stronger support for an English Parliament among those with an opinion than those against. In February 2024, a YouGov poll indicated 9 per cent strongly support and 20 per cent tending to support an English Parliament with 9 per cent strongly opposed and 15 per cent tending to oppose. Meanwhile, 47 per

Table 4.5: *British Social Attitudes polling preferences on options for future governance of England*

	Governed as it is now (%)	England has own Parliament (%)	Each region has own assembly (%)	Don't know/ won't vote (%)
2020	55	22	20	3
2015	50	20	23	7
2010	53	23	13	11
2005	54	18	20	8
2000	54	19	18	9
1999	62	18	15	5

Source: British Social Attitudes survey data.

cent of those polled didn't know how they would vote. Such polling suggests a significant lack of public knowledge on the issue and that the issue is one of low political importance. Table 4.5 shows British Social Attitudes survey data on a range of current, Parliament or regional assembly options. This suggests that there was some immediate movement between 1999 and 2000 towards greater support for England having its own Parliament or regional assemblies but that the dispersal of opinion has remained fairly constant ever since. Polling suggests majority support for England being governed as it is now. Such data suggests that we should be sceptical as to whether the English dog is really showing strong signs of being ready to bark.

In the years ahead there may be grounds for further momentum in the rise of English consciousness as a result of Brexit, culture wars and responses to devolution in the rest of the UK. The case for an English Parliament may grow as a perceived necessary defence of English interests in a more formally federalised UK, or in the development of confederal British-wide arrangements if the UK broke up. Having said that, the sovereigntist impetus behind Brexit appears to be receding while concerns about economic benefits are rising, and polls consistently show a majority in favour of returning to the EU. Instead, directly elected regional assemblies may become a necessary democratic accompaniment to metro mayors if their powers grow and accountability deficits become politically significant. Nevertheless, much of the focus among local and regional elites in England has remained on the economic and social disparities between London and the rest of England. The accompanying policy performance problems and the perceived remedy of levelling up policies remain highly significant, probably more so than issues of identity and debates on the extent to which England or its regions are politically integrated or not with the rest of the UK.

This policy emphasis appears to be reflected in both recent Conservative and current Labour Government priorities. The reform of English governance is not treated as a constitutional issue; rather it is instrumental to policy needs. While the Sunak Government actually played down the commitments to levelling up amidst the manifestly low levels of public spending devoted to it, Labour recommitted to it ahead of the 2024 UK general election as something the public clearly wanted to happen. While Labour dropped the specific term 'levelling up', Keir Starmer met the now twelve regional mayors within days of the election to assure them of their importance to Labour's plans to grow the economy. The Autumn Budget affirmed Labour's commitment to introducing integrated funding settlements that give the combined authorities more autonomy in developing longer term spending plans.

Conclusion

The period since devolution has not wiped away the centuries of national striving for recognition and rights among the UK's stateless nations. The Blair government never expected that it would; in the main they simply hoped that devolution would make the operation of the UK state seem fairer in Scotland, Wales and Northern Ireland without inflaming an English backlash and bring about a greater relative political stability (Bradbury, 2021a). As we can see in the preceding sections, cases for more devolved power as well as national separation in Scotland, Wales and Northern Ireland have continued to be made, and positions of elected power for nationalist parties or parties seeking to compete with them in devolved administrations have provided potent platforms for trying to persuade electorates of the need for further change. The needs of England have also had to be addressed. At the same time though, bottom-up pressures are never quite as strong as territorial elites hope and countervailing pressures make promoting change difficult.

It has been tempting to portray UK central government as inept and/or centralist in its responses, exemplified by portrayals of the moves to recentralise the state following Brexit (Keating, 2021). Such portrayals miss the point: that it is perfectly to be expected that both central and territorial political elites will fight for what they feel is right and, in the process, get things wrong and be open to critical interpretation. By and large UK central government prior to Brexit was remarkably non-interventionist and arguably has only been interventionist during the period of Brexit to reset the basic rules of the UK economy before likely retreating again from displays of overt centralism in the future. That said, the period since 2007 has seen some huge challenges of financial crisis, EU withdrawal and the pandemic, which have all provided opportunities for territorial movements to find the UK wanting. Conservative governments, particularly under Boris Johnson in the development of Brexit legislation, have suggested a lack of respect for devolution, which has provoked responses.

In this context we have seen that everywhere across the UK there is significant popular support for constitutional change. The UK as a state looks vulnerable. Crucially though, nowhere does the case for breaking up the UK command a majority of public support. Perhaps more importantly, it remains some way off gaining clear majorities of 60 per cent plus in polls that might create the pressure for UK government to concede further referenda. In each part of the UK we can predict factors that may sustain growth in dissent, but equally there are factors that could play the other way.

The battle for the future of the UK will be based on political learning. It is clear that between the 1970s and 1990s a generation of politicians in Scotland and Wales learned a lot from the failures of devolution and independence movements in the 1960s and 1970s, and in Northern Ireland from the limited gains of armed struggle. New strategies for change were developed and much was achieved and had to be accepted at the UK centre. Territorial change campaigners by and large have been hoping for a transformational push in the wake of Brexit, which has not happened. They will undoubtedly press on and develop revised strategies for realising their aims. In Scotland and Northern Ireland, parties intent on breaking up the UK are in prime places of government office.

Nevertheless, we may now see the gradual emergence of a generation of politicians at both the centre and across the UK that comes to terms with devolution and regional reform as intrinsic features of the UK state and more successfully develops strategies for renewed state territorial integration. This has not been apparent in the post-Brexit Conservative governments: they have pursued little more than a defiant policy of saying there will be no more devolution and trying to find short-term fixes to political clashes with devolved administrations amidst a highly limited implementation of levelling up ambitions. Nevertheless, during the period of Conservative government there were a wide range of parliamentary inquiries that reflected this search for understanding and ways forward, to which the Labour party added their own in-depth inquiry under the chairmanship of former Prime Minister, Gordon Brown (Labour Party, 2022). On entering government, Keir Starmer immediately introduced a council for the regions and nations as a body designed to symbolise respect for devolution in all its forms, and to provide a basis for discussion of issues of mutual interest. It met for the first time in Scotland in October 2024. Contestation about the essential location of the demos will continue, but this is not uncommon in territorially complex populations. It is also possible to find stable accommodations and better government and policy outcomes that are accepted as fair and help the state function better if the mechanisms can be found to make this work.

References

Bradbury, J. (2021a) *Constitutional Policy and Territorial Politics in the UK, Union and Devolution, 1997–2007*, Bristol University Press, Bristol.

Bradbury, J. (2021b) 'Welsh devolution and the Union: Reform debates after Brexit' *Political Quarterly*, 92(1): 125–131.

Hayward, K. (2024) 'A new dispensation? What changes of government in London and Dublin could mean for Northern Ireland', *Political Insight*, March, 29–31.

Henderson, A. and Wyn Jones, R. (2021) *Englishness: The Political Force Transforming Britain*, Oxford University Press, Oxford.

Henderson, A. Johns, R., Larner, J. and Carman, C. (2022) *The Referendum that Changed a Nation: Scottish Voting Behaviour 2014–2019*, Palgrave, Basingstoke.

Keating, M. (2019), 'Brexit and the nations', *Political Quarterly*, 90(S2): 167–176.

Keating, M. (2021) *State and Nation in the United Kingdom*, Oxford University Press, Oxford.

Kenny, M. (2014) 'The return of Englishness in British political culture', *Journal of Common Market Studies*, 53(1): 35–51.

Labour Party (2022) 'A new Britain: Renewing our democracy and rebuilding our economy', Report of the Commission on the UK's Future, accessed 9 April 2024, https://labour.org.uk/wp-content/uploads/2022/12/Commission-on-the-UKs-Future.pdf

Paun, A., Cheung, A. and Valsamidis, L. (2019) 'Devolution at 20', Institute for Government, accessed 1 April 2025.

Plaid Cymru (2020) *Towards an Independent Wales*, Report of the Independence Commission, Y Lolfa, Aberystwyth.

Sandford, M. (2023), 'English devolution deals in the 2023 Autumn Statement', House of Commons Library, 30 November, accessed 9 April 2024, https://commonslibrary.parliament.uk/english-devolution-deals-in-the-2023-autumn-statement/

Teague, P. (2019) 'Brexit, the Belfast Agreement and Northern Ireland: Imperilling a fragile political bargain', *Political Quarterly*, 90(4): 690–704.

Todd, J. (2017) 'Contested constitutionalism? Northern Ireland and the British–Irish relationship since 2010', *Parliamentary Affairs*, 70: 301–321

Welsh Government (2019) Reforming our Union: Shared Governance in the UK, Welsh Government, Cardiff, accessed 28 November 2020, https://gov.wales/sites/default/files/publications/2019-10/reforming-our-union-shared-governance-in-the-uk.pdf

Welsh Government (2024) *Final Report of the Independent Commission on the Constitutional Future of Wales*, Welsh Government, Cardiff, accessed 9 April 2024, https://www.gov.wales/sites/default/files/publications/2024-07/independent-commission-on-the-constitutional-future-of-wales-final-report.pdf

Wyn Jones, R. and Morgan, K. (2023) 'Brexit and the death of devolution', *Political Quarterly*, 94(4): 625–633.

5

The crisis in our NHS pre- and post-Covid

Allyson M. Pollock, James Lancaster and Louisa Harding-Edgar

Introduction

Evidence to the COVID-19 public inquiry has rekindled anger over the lack of preparedness in the UK's systems and services for managing communicable diseases: no lessons were learned from the Infected Blood Inquiry scandal. The reports of the recent public inquiry reveal the weaknesses in the system resulting from the priority given to commissioning clinical services over the communicable disease system; the abolition of the Public Health Laboratory Service; a loss of public health expertise; and the fragmentation and part privatisation of services. The systematic dismantling and destruction of services and the system for communicable disease control over more than two decades is laid out clearly in many of the reports to the public inquiry.

The public inquiry has yet to examine the system for communicable disease control at the time of Covid – and it has shown no signs of having read the reports into the Infected Blood Inquiry. Nevertheless, it is clear that the impact of Covid was exacerbated by depleted health services and political mismanagement such that these systems and services failed spectacularly. The science and the lack of evidence underpinning public health policies that enforced prolonged lockdowns on a global scale are also being questioned. The early evidence from the World

Health Organization (WHO) on China in February 2020 told us that COVID-19 was a disease that spared the young and killed vulnerable older people. Normally, it is the job of adults to protect the young and of the NHS to protect the sick. Yet children were being told they had to stay at home to protect their teachers and 'granny', and the public were told to stay at home to protect the NHS and save lives. The economic and public harms of prolonged lockdowns and the loss of schooling and socialising were not fully considered or debated in Parliament or by the mainstream media, especially their impact on the health of young people and children and, specifically, the poorest and most disadvantaged in society.

Government messaging centred on fear and enforcement. Young people and children were accused of being asymptomatic spreaders and 'vectors' of disease. Moreover, any questioning of evidence behind policies that rode roughshod over human rights was attacked. Political polarisation over the responses to Covid became a global phenomenon, as did the censorship, with social media magnifying rather than illuminating the divisions. One example of this was the scientific divide between the John Snow Memorandum and the Great Barrington Declaration where scientists set out and stood behind their opposing views. Hiding behind the precautionary principle, proponents of strict lockdowns and mass masking and mass testing, for the most part, ignored the question of needing to consider short-, medium- and long-term harms and costs. Instead, all 'public health' interventions were weighed equally and treated with the same reverence, often in the absence of evidence, ignoring the need to draw a distinction between evidence and uncertainty and unknowns.

After herd immunity was abandoned in the UK, zero Covid was advocated and countries such as China were cited as successful models of the approach, although subsequently this has been abandoned or redefined (Escandón *et al.*, 2021; Nabavi and Dobson, 2021). Covid is now the stuff of myths and legends. The real challenges, though, are not to relive and retell the pandemic, but to understand the ways in which successive parliaments and governments have progressively and systematically defunded and dismantled the systems for public health and communicable disease control across the NHS and social care sector. Covid laid bare their shortcomings and failings. Rising waiting lists, long waits in accident and emergency, ambulance failures, bed and staff shortages, an increased use of the private sector and strikes by nurses, ambulance workers and doctors all signal an NHS in crisis. From there the next challenge is to look forward to ensure that our Parliament commits to rebuilding and reinstating services to safeguard the public health against future pandemics. However, the incoming Labour government have given us little cause for hope. A first step would have been to introduce a Bill in Parliament reinstating the duty of the Secretary of State for Health to secure and provide key health services throughout England. This duty, in place with the founding of the NHS in 1948 and delegated to health bodies, was abolished in 2012 in England. Instead, the current Secretary of State for Health, Wes Streeting, is carrying on the policies of previous governments, continuing the drive to privatising and breaking up the NHS and shrinking its services. Settling the junior doctors strike in the first few weeks was simply buying the silence and tacit agreement of the BMA, or as Bevan put it, stuffing the doctors' mouths with gold.

Hospital bed capacity

Few can forget the scenes in February 2020 in Italy, the first European country hit by the pandemic, when hospitals ran out of beds to treat people (BBC News, 2020). The UK had been closing NHS beds for decades and average bed occupancy had consistently been more than 85 per cent above the recommended limit for safe care, making it very poorly placed to deal with a pandemic (OECD and European Union, 2022). There was no surge capacity.

At the outset of the pandemic in 2020, England had only 7.3 critical care beds per hundred thousand people (OECD, 2021). This is fewer than many European countries, including Germany, which had four times as many critical care beds per head of population. Total bed capacity is also much lower in the UK than most European countries. There were 2.4

The crisis in our NHS pre- and post-Covid

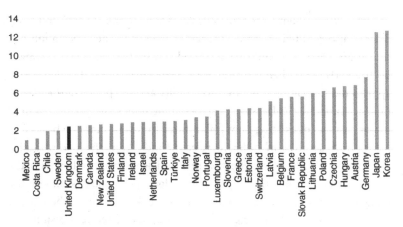

Figure 5.1 Hospital beds, total per 1000 inhabitants, 2021
Source: OECD, 2023

beds per thousand people in 2021 compared to 5.7 in France, and 7.8 in Germany (Figure 5.1; OECD, 2023).

Drivers for bed closures

NHS bed closures have been ongoing since the inception of the NHS. More than 300,000 NHS beds have closed (100,000 in the last fifteen years alone) and today the NHS has a quarter of the beds that it had at its outset in 1948 (Triggle, 2018). Radical changes in treatment and the availability of treatments for communicable diseases and mental health enabled shorter lengths of stay and treatment at home, as well as the closure of tuberculosis sanitoria, infectious disease hospitals and mental illness hospitals. The policy of de-institutionalisation of care for older people and people with learning difficulties was more complicated. For older people this policy was more one of re-institutionalisation, with beds opening in the private sector following NHS closures and a shift in responsibility for funding care to individuals and then to local authorities when those individuals became too poor to pay. In the acute hospital sector, new treatments for acute conditions including surgery and heart disease also resulted in reduced lengths of stay and the expectation was that more efficiency could be squeezed out by bed closures. However, by the early 1990s bed closures were being driven not by changes in approaches to treatment but by affordability and the policy of the private finance initiative (PFI). New hospitals built under the policy required major closures of existing ones (often three for every new one built) and community services in order to release funds from the sale of buildings and land. PFI is, in effect, a sale and lease back policy, and the annual charge payable from operating budgets puts a huge strain on the budgets of hospitals. Politicians and policymakers justified the closure of hospitals and beds, saying that centralisation of services resulted in better outcomes of care. The evidence base for this was always weak at best and efficiencies that were claimed for the policy never materialised. Nevertheless, PFI policy drove bed and other service closures; NHS bed occupancy was always running above safe levels throughout the year. A lack of surge capacity, especially in winter, resulted in inefficiencies in the rest of the system with surgical beds, for example, being blocked by medical cases (outliers or delayed discharges of people), contributing to waiting lists.

When the pandemic hit, the government responded to NHS bed shortages by spending £220 million on building Nightingale hospitals and awarding thousands of contracts worth up to £2 billion to private healthcare companies to provide additional capacity (Ryan et al., 2021). In the event, the Nightingale hospitals could not be staffed and most of the private hospital capacity was never used for Covid patients. Decommissioning Nightingale hospitals has increased their total cost further – now forecast to be £532 million (Bethell, 2021).

Social care provision

In response to the pandemic, in March 2020, NHS England and NHS Improvement issued a letter to NHS trusts instructing them to clear the beds and discharge older people waiting for care in the community (Stevens and Pritchard, 2020). Managers boasted that the pandemic had enabled them to clear hospital beds of older people needing to be discharged. They failed to realise that people with Covid were being discharged back to care homes where the disease spread to other residents and staff.

Data from across the world shows that deaths from Covid mainly occurred among older people (Verity et al., 2020). By the end of 2022, England recorded 177,180 deaths from COVID-19 within 28 days of a positive test result – 82 per cent of deaths were in those aged 70 and over, who account for about 15 per cent of the population (UK Health Security Agency, 2023a).

Social services in the UK are among the most privatised and fragmented in the western world. The majority of long-stay beds in the UK are under the ownership and control of multinationals. The adult social care market in England was worth around £16.5 billion in 2019, with around 430,000 adults living in care homes (National Audit Office, 2021a). NHS long-stay beds have been in decline since the 1970s (Figure 5.2), with 84 per

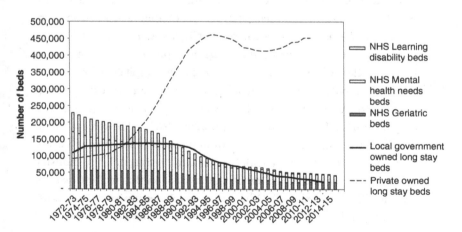

Figure 5.2 Average daily number of NHS geriatric, mental health needs and learning disability needs beds and number of available long-stay beds by provider, 1972–2016
Source: Sutaria et al., 2017. Figure reproduced by permission of the *BMJ*

cent of care home beds now owned by for-profit companies (Naylor and Magnusson, 2019). The remainder are provided by the NHS, councils and not-for-profit organisations such as charities. Sheltered housing and warden-controlled homes are important alternatives to residential care, but data on these are not collected.

Local government net expenditure fell by 20 per cent in real terms between 2010/11 and 2022/23, but over the same period, local authority net expenditure on adult social care increased by 42 per cent, from £14.4 billion to £20.5 billion (Foster, 2024). The Health Foundation has estimated that when the increase in the UK's ageing population is considered, spending per person on adult social care services fell by around 12 per cent in real terms between 2010/11 and 2018/19. Reduced funding has been accompanied by further privatisation and the shifting of responsibility for funding to individuals, as well as the tightening of NHS and local authority eligibility criteria. Those who fund their own care subsidise the care of those who are paid for by local authorities: in 2017 it was estimated that self-funders were paying an additional £8,000 per year for residential care, compared to the cost paid by local authorities (Plimmer, 2017). Often, there have been long delays in assessing eligibility for care funding, and an inconsistent and inequitable application of criteria (Public Accounts Committee, 2018).

Throughout the pandemic, the government poured billions of pounds into the pockets of multinational owners of private hospitals and residential care homes, but it spectacularly failed to reinvest and sort out the low and inadequate staffing levels that resulted in poor quality care during the pandemic and in poor outcomes, including death. Although £54 billion flows into the long-term care sector from the state and individuals every year (Office for National Statistics, 2022a), the residential care industry expects an 11 per cent return on capital invested in this sector (Burns *et al.*, 2016). The National Audit Office (2021a) quotes estimates by LaingBuisson that spend on self-funded care amounts to around £8.3 billion across England.

From US data, we can see that for-profit companies generally have the lowest staffing and poorest quality as they seek to maximise profits for investors (Harrington *et al.*, 2017). Care services in England employ roughly

1.6 million care staff, of which 85 per cent are employed by the independent sector. The sector is 165,000 workers short (Skills for Care, 2022), which results in inadequate care, while the use of agency staff moving from one home to another during the pandemic increased the risk of disease transmission. In 2022, 16 per cent of care homes inspected were found to be inadequate or in need of improvement by the Care Quality Commission (2022).

The social care workforce is generally poorly paid, with poor terms of service and high staff turnover. In total, 30 per cent of 'direct care' workers in England were employed on a zero-hours contract in 2021–22 (Skills for Care, 2022) and 21 per cent of care workers are paid less than the real living wage (Resolution Foundation, 2023). Many will have a heavy daily schedule – providing brief but intimate care for a large number of people. Staff on zero-hours contracts do not receive sick pay and may therefore feel pressured to go to work when sick. The average age of staff is 44 years, with more than a quarter of staff being aged 55 or over. There is a high turnover of staff (29 per cent in 2021/22) with a reduced number of new starters to replace leaving staff in the same year. Spend on agency staff increased from 9 to 13 per cent of the total spend on staff between 2020 and 2022 (Care Quality Commission, 2022).

The emergency legislation in the UK (The Coronavirus Act, 2020) severely curtailed the legal rights to social care services of older people, ill and disabled people living at home and in residential settings. The Disability Law Service concluded that the action was contrary to international law – constituting 'regressive' social care legislation targeting those least able to cope – and made no strategic sense. It argued that a rational response to the emergency would have been to 'radically redress the care and support deficits of the past decade, rather than take the action that is mandated by the 2020 Act' (Disability Law Service and Clements, 2020). Downgrading service provision for the most vulnerable and the lack of access to essential social care and other vital services, such as speech therapy, physiotherapy, mental health therapy and routine NHS services, has led to more health crises, more hospital admissions and more pressure on carers. In the health survey of England 2019, 17 per cent of people aged 16 and over reported providing unpaid care (NHS Digital, 2020), and estimates of the value of this care can be more than £100 billion (National Audit Office, 2020a and 2021a).

Dismantling the communicable disease control system

When the pandemic struck, the UK's system for control of communicable diseases failed spectacularly. Measures such as quarantine and travel restrictions were not implemented to begin with. There was limited capacity for contact tracing, and the UK government had to abandon it in March 2020, two weeks before lockdown (Roderick, Pollock and Macfarlane, 2020). The poor response to the pandemic was because governments have defunded the system, closed services for infectious diseases and public health laboratories, and degraded and downgraded public health, with unclear accountability between local authorities and the NHS (Infected Blood Inquiry, 2022). Instead of rebuilding that public health capacity in the face of the pandemic, the government created a parallel privatised system, awarding billions of pounds in contracts through a fast-track system, with disastrous consequences (Thompson, 2023; National Audit Office, 2020a and 2021a).

In the UK, responsibility for outbreak control had, since the nineteenth century, been with local authorities, remaining there with the creation of the NHS in 1948. This is the level at which people are best placed to respond and manage it, because those carrying out patient care and contact tracing need to understand their local communities and have their trust. In the first fifty years or so of the NHS, communicable disease control began with the patient and the doctor and the identification of cases; it linked to local laboratory reports and tests, and if the disease was included in a statutory reporting mechanism and was notifiable, the reports were passed to the proper officers in local public health departments, which issued advice and undertook contact tracing and surveillance. They ensured that information flowed to the centre to be used locally and centrally to monitor the disease, and could request further advice and support from the centre as needed. However, legal and organisational developments in the system since the introduction of the internal market in 1990 and the creation in 2003 of the Health Protection Agency (HPA) have resulted in the centralisation and defunding of communicable disease control systems, the dismantling and eventual abolition of local laboratories and public health departments, and the loss of vital local expertise and workforce capacity (Lancaster and Pollock, 2022).

The shift from health protection to health promotion

From the 1970s onwards, policymakers came to believe that communicable diseases had decreased in importance (Department of Health and Social Security, 1976). The 1990s would see a shift in the practice of public health from clinical epidemiology, communicable disease control and medical administration to a growing emphasis on lifestyle, health education and health promotion. This also reflected a political shift from collective state responsibility to individual responsibility for health and health promotion interventions, to which 'lifestyle' diseases were well suited.

Between 1988 and 2021, the numbers of clinical public health consultants per capita fell by almost half. Although the 1988 report of the Chief Medical Officer, Donald Acheson, into the future of the public health function recommended an expansion of the number of public health physician consultants from 11.4 to 15.8 per million population by 1998 (Acheson, 1988), by 2021 the numbers of clinical public health consultants had reached just 7.2 public health physicians in service per million population in England (Edbrooke-Hyson, 2022).

In 2003 the requirement for a medical education and clinical training was removed for the consultant-led public health workforce and entry to the specialism was widened. These changes resulted in a disciplinary and organisational split between the medical and non-medical workforce. Over half (53 per cent) of the clinically trained public health workforce are located in the NHS, the Department of Health and Social Care or its executive agency, the UK Health Security Agency (UKHSA) (Edbrooke-Hyson, 2022) and are thus under political control, mainly involved in health protection and communicable disease control activities. In contrast, the majority of the non-medical specialist public health workforce are located within local authorities where the focus is on health promotion activities. When Covid hit there was little or no expertise in outbreak control within local authorities; only 18 per cent of directors of public health in 2021 had medical training (see Milsom et al., 2019).

The Public Health Laboratory Service

Shortly after the outbreak of Covid the director of WHO urged countries to 'test, test, test'. But tests there were none in the UK. For many months, only patients admitted to hospital could be tested. Laboratories found they didn't have the equipment or materials needed for the PCR tests, and university research laboratories were called upon late in the day to join the effort, but the response was chaotic and poorly coordinated. The system and network of peripheral laboratories known as the Public Health Laboratory Service (PHLS), which could have provided this service, had been dismantled in 2003 with the creation of the Health Protection Agency.

The PHLS was established in the NHS Act 1946. It ran a national (England and Wales) network of laboratories, as well as at its Colindale headquarters (the Central Public Health Laboratory), which included specialist and reference laboratories to provide expert advice on specific pathogens (Acheson, 1988; Galbraith, 1981). This network of regional and area laboratories (fifty-two in the 1970s and 1980s) was mostly based in hospitals and run jointly with the NHS hospital laboratories. Although, like the other 300 or so microbiological laboratories in NHS hospitals in England and Wales, these public health laboratories provided diagnostic and other services to hospitals and health authorities, they had an additional public health function. Their data were sent to the PHLS' 'pivotal centre', the Centre for Communicable Disease Control, set up in 1977 following the 1973 smallpox outbreak in London, so as to provide a national picture of infectious disease and give country-wide support to local authority and health authority medical officers (Galbraith, 1981; Department of Health and Social Security, 1980).

In this way, an effective national surveillance system, key to the detection and control of all diseases and monitoring the risk of disease, was developed. In the 1980s and 1990s, PHLS considered that its sophisticated surveillance system meant that England was the only country in Europe to pick up Europe-wide outbreaks of food-poisoning (Smith, 1992).

In 1990 Margaret Thatcher's government created an internal market in the NHS, fragmenting services that had previously been integrated into and under the direct management of area bodies. The internal market created the purchaser–provider split where area bodies became purchasers, and providers such as hospitals would now compete for revenue through contracts. PHLS laboratories also had to sell their services to health authorities and trusts. However, health authorities under pressure to make savings prioritised care of their patients and those of local GPs – public health functions and surveillance, including the funding of PHLS laboratories, was not a priority.

By 2003, concerns were being expressed that NHS laboratories had no incentive to rise to the public health challenge, such as the surveillance of sexually transmitted infections, and that health protection was being harmed by having to compete with other clinical services for resources (Department of Health, 2003). The creation of the HPA in 2003 only made things worse by making communication and coordination between the different organisations involved in communicable disease control even more complex and unclear. At the HPA's creation, PHLS was abolished and its network of thirty-eight laboratories was broken up and transferred mostly to NHS trusts and NHS foundation trusts, with only a small core of eight laboratories and the Colindale campus moving to the HPA itself. There was no consultation with PHLS on its abolition.

Budgetary cuts and the discontinuation in 2005 of ringfenced funding for the laboratories meant that trusts were unable to take on the support of microbiology laboratories. Over time, many were closed or dispersed, and neither the HPA nor the trusts were again able to act in a coordinated manner to deliver effective surveillance and to provide surge capacity in the event of large outbreaks of infectious disease (Duerden, 2005).

What went wrong with Britain?

After the laboratories were transferred to Public Health England (PHE), there were six regional laboratories in 2016. In 2022, UKHSA reported that there were just five (Public Health England, 2016; UK Health Security Agency, 2023b). PHE and UKHSA do not report on the number of collaborating laboratories.

Developments after the abolition of the HPA

The HPA was abolished by the Health and Social Care Act 2012, which fundamentally reorganised the NHS in England and changed yet again the institutional arrangements for public health. It established PHE as a non-statutory executive agency of the Department of Health to carry out the secretary of state's duty to protect the health of the public. Local authorities were given the duty of improving the health of the people in their area and were required to appoint a director of public health. This post, however, had no health protection functions (other than in an emergency) and the focus was on health improvement.

The public health grant allocations to local authorities in England were cut by 24 per cent in real terms per capita between 2015–16 and 2021–22 (Finch, Marshall and Sunbury, 2021), and surveys of public health highlight how local authorities were decommissioning services and using ringfenced public health money for other purposes (Iacobucci, 2014). Most of PHE's expenditure went to local authorities for health improvement, for example in 2019–20 this amounted to £2.9 billion of the £3.8 billion total net expenditure (Public Health England, 2022).

In August 2020, in the midst of the pandemic, the UK government announced that a new executive agency would be established, bringing together PHE, NHS Test and Trace and the Joint Biosecurity Centre, which had been established in May 2020 to collate and analyse data relevant to Covid. In the event, PHE's health protection tasks were transferred to a new executive agency, UKHSA, and health improvement and other public health functions to the Office for Health Improvement and Disparities (within the Department of Health and Social Care), NHS England and NHS Digital. UKHSA is now responsible for protecting every member of every community from the impact of infectious diseases, chemical, biological, radiological and nuclear incidents, and other health threats. It describes itself as providing 'intellectual, scientific, and operational leadership at national and local level, as well as on the global stage, to make the nation's health secure' (UK Health Security Agency, 2023c). However, it makes little information publicly available about what it does. Moreover, its website only refers to England. The important thing to note is it remains under ministerial control and has no independence.

Following their removal from the NHS in 2012, directors of public health (now in local authorities) lost access to health and clinical data at a local level as information and support functions for commissioning were relocated in non-statutory commissioning support units divorced from public health, which could be run by the private sector. Their responsibilities were for health improvement. This legislative and organisational shift, together with the widening of the speciality to non-medics, means that not only are most directors of public health neither medically qualified nor familiar with clinical medicine, but they also have little or no experience of health services administration. Since 2003, health protection functions have been centralised, and over time the clinical workforce has moved to the centre under political control. The effect is a profound loss of expertise and knowledge in local communicable disease control. The implications of this loss of expertise and knowledge would play out in many ways and especially in the billions of pounds diverted to unevidenced and expensive mass testing, especially in Liverpool, which became the case study for waste and ineffective testing policies in the asymptomatic population (Raffle and Gill, 2021).

The government response to a lack of local laboratory capacity for tests and overall local public health capacity, however, was not to rebuild the system for communicable disease control and expand NHS laboratory capacity and contact tracing services in England but was, instead, to continue the policy of centralisation and privatisation, handing out large contracts to put in place a parallel system of centralised, privatised call handling centres run by Serco and Sitel. In England, the contracts for

Serco and Sitel, who provided call handlers for test and trace, were worth over £700 million (National Audit Office, 2020a). In total, £28.5 billion was spent on test and trace (National Audit Office, 2021b).

With a lack of microbiology testing facilities, from April 2020 onwards ten new 'lighthouse laboratories' were opened by NHS Test and Trace for large-scale rapid COVID-19 testing, some in public-private partnerships with industry, including AstraZeneca and GSK. Regional sites to collect samples from the public were provided by Sodexo and Boots, and some operated by Deloitte. Serco, G4S and Levy provided facilities management, while Randox provided home testing kits, the logistics for which were provided by Amazon (Roderick *et al.*, 2020). From March 2022, a 'demobilisation' of the laboratories began, and the only laboratory currently referred to on the UKHSA website is the Rosalind Franklin 'megalab' at Leamington Spa (UK Health Security Agency, 2021).

Crucially the loss of expertise and lack of science and evidence guiding policy has resulted in billions of pounds being wasted – lining the pockets of start-up companies and cronies of politicians. When tests became available in their hundreds of millions and were given to the public, this was done with little thought and at great cost to the public purse. Tests were misused, misapplied and misreported, and all because the experts in testing at the UK national screening committee were not consulted. Testing or screening is extremely complex. It appears that the significance of a test being positive or negative was not understood by the policymakers and scientific advisers. Test reporting was chaotic and nonsensical. But by then tests and testing, like PPE and masks, had become big business and extremely lucrative, especially for those with close links to politicians. As with extended lockdowns and school closures, science was ignored and billions of pounds wasted.

Conclusion

Covid has demonstrated just how incredibly expensive it is when the public health system for communicable disease control fails and when science is ignored. The billions being pumped into the NHS and private providers are but a small fraction of the sums that are now required to shore up the UK economy.

Public health services in the UK have been the target of several major reorganisations in the last fifty years, which have been associated with budgetary cuts, closures and loss of staff and expertise. The sheer number and scale of reorganisations has been extremely disruptive, first weakening and then removing communicable disease control at the local level and, from 1990, increasing marketisation and outsourcing. The overall effect has been to further fragment public health services for communicable disease control, reducing the number of specialists, particularly those with medical training, and reducing the overall expertise of the workforce.

The impact of Covid provides the most compelling case possible for a national care service free at the point of delivery with all the elements of sheltered housing, community and home support, and residential care integrated. A national care service would require legislation but since many of the private providers funded by the state are in significant financial difficulty the net cost of bringing these directly under local authority control is likely to be small. According to a 2019 Institute for Public Policy Research paper, 'Social Care: Free at the Point of Need', the cost would be 1 per cent of total government expenditure (Quilter-Pinner and Hochlaf, 2019). In so doing it would go a long way to ensuring that we have a resilient and well-resourced system that not only frees up NHS resources for acute care but is also able to cope with the next epidemic.

The real threat to safety today comes not from viruses. The threat is that our healthcare, social services, and public health services for communicable disease control and handling local outbreaks are underprepared and unable to deal with pandemics. And that threat is rooted in the campaign *against* our safety, operating in the name of market freedom. This campaign is being waged though the media and is one our political class barely talks about. The NHS is being progressively dismantled and privatised and destroyed. A new campaign is needed to legislate for the founding vision, a vision and belief that is as strong as ever in in the public's mind, and to reinstate the NHS. There is little sign of this happening with the new government, who like previous Labour governments are simply implementing what their predecessors put in place – a system designed to leach money from the NHS to private profit and shareholders. The institutional memory of how an NHS could and should be organised has almost completely disappeared. Meanwhile, inequalities in wealth and health are continuing to grow as the great divide between rich and poor and the haves and the have-nots deepens.

References

Acheson, D. (1988) *Public Health in England: The Report of the Committee of Inquiry into the Future Development of the Public Health Function*, HMSO, London.

Bethell, Lord (2021) 'Coronavirus: Hospitals', UK Parliament: Written answer, 11 January, UIN HL11662, https://questions-statements.parliament.uk/written-questions/detail/2020-12-30/hl11662

BBC News (2020) 'Coronavirus: Italian patients treated in tents and warehouse', 13 March, www.bbc.com/news/av/world-europe-51883589

Burns, D., Cowie, L., Early, J., Folkman, P., Froud, J., Hyde, P., Johal, S., Rees Jones, I., Killett, A. and Williams, K. (2016) *Where Does the Money Go? Financialised Chains and the Crisis in Residential Care*, CRESC Public Interest Report, Centre for Research on Socio-Cultural Change, http://hummedia.manchester.ac.uk/institutes/cresc/research/WDTMG%20FINAL%20-01-3-2016.pdf

Care Quality Commission (2022) 'The state of health care and adult social care in England 2021/22', www.cqc.org.uk/publication/state-care-202122

Department of Health (2003) *The Government Response to 'Fighting Infection', Fourth Report of the House of Lords Select Committee on Science and Technology 2002–2003*, HMSO, London, https://webarchive.nationalarchives.gov.uk/ukgwa/20130107105354/www.dh.gov.uk/assetRoot/04/06/97/68/04069768.pdf

Department of Health and Social Security (1976) *Prevention and Health: Everybody's Business: A Reassessment of Public and Personal Health*, HMSO, London https://archive.org/details/b32219957/page/n1/mode/2up?ref=ol&view=theater

Department of Health and Social Security (1980) 'Co-ordination of epidemiological services for communicable diseases and food poisoning: Communicable disease surveillance centre', Health Circular HC (802)2.

Disability Law Service, and Clements, L. (2020) 'Coronavirus Act threatens care for disabled people: A position statement', 3 April, www.lukeclements.co.uk/coronavirus-act-threatens-care-for-disabled-people/

Duerden, B. (2005) 'Twenty-first-century medical microbiology services in the UK', *Nature Reviews Microbiology*, 3(12): 979–83.

Edbrooke-Hyson, V. (2022) 'A capacity review – public health specialists in 2021', Health Education England, www.hee.nhs.uk/sites/default/files/documents/Public%20Health%20Capacity%20Review%20-%202021%20v26.pdf

Escandón, K., Rasmussen, A.L., Bogoch, I. I., Murray, E. J., Escandón, K. and Popescu, S. V. (2021) 'COVID-19 false dichotomies and a comprehensive review of the evidence regarding public health, COVID-19 symptomatology, SARS-CoV-2 transmission, mask wearing, and reinfection', *BMC Infectious Diseases*, 21(1): 710.

Finch, D., Marshall, L. and Sunbury, S. (2021) 'Why greater investment in the public health grant should be a priority', The Health Foundation, 5 October, www.health.org.uk/news-and-comment/charts-and-infographics/why-greater-investment-in-the-public-health-grant-should-be-a-priority

Foster, D. (2024) 'Funding for adult social care in England', House of Commons Library, https://researchbriefings.files.parliament.uk/documents/CBP-7903/CBP-7903.pdf

Galbraith, N. S. (1981) 'A national public health service', *Journal of the Royal Society of Medicine*, 74:16–21.

Harrington, C., Jacobsen, F. F., Panos, J., Pollock, A., Sutaria, S. and Szebehely, M. (2017) 'Marketization in long-term care: A cross-country comparison of large for-profit nursing home chains', *Health Services Insights*, 10.

Iacobucci, G. (2014) 'Raiding the public health budget', *BMJ*, 348.

Infected Blood Inquiry (2022) 'Expert report to the Infected Blood Inquiry: Public health and administration', www.infectedbloodinquiry.org.uk/evidence/expert-report-infected-blood-inquiry-public-health-and-administration

Lancaster, J. and Pollock, A. (2022) 'A supplementary report for the Infected Blood Inquiry into structures and funding of the communicable disease control system in England', Infected Blood Inquiry, https://allysonpollock.com/wp-content/uploads/2022/12/IBI_2022_Lancaster_Supplementary.pdf

Milsom, R., Liu, D., Chappel, D. and Sasiak, A. (2019) 'A capacity review – public health specialists in 2019', Health Education England, www.hee.nhs.uk/sites/default/files/documents/Public%20Health%20Capacity%20Review%20-%20 2019%20FINAL.pdf

Nabavi, N. and J. Dobson (2021) 'Zero Covid—known unknowns', *BMJ Opinion*, 22 March, https://blogs.bmj.com/bmj/2021/03/22/zero-covid-known-unknowns/

National Audit Office (2020a) 'Investigation into government procurement during the COVID-19 pandemic', www.nao.org.uk/reports/government-procurement-during-the-covid-19-pandemic/

National Audit Office (2020b) 'The Government's approach to test and trace in England – interim report', www.nao.org.uk/wp-content/uploads/2020/12/The-governments-approach-to-test-and-trace-in-England-interim-report.pdf

National Audit Office (2021a) 'The adult social care market in England', www.nao.org.uk/reports/adult-social-care-markets/

National Audit Office (2021b) 'Test and trace in England – progress update', www.nao.org.uk/wp-content/uploads/2021/06/Test-and-trace-in-England-progress-update.pdf

Naylor, A. and J. Magnusson (2019) *Data That Cares*, Future Care Capital, London, https://futurecarecapital.org.uk/wp-content/uploads/2020/03/Data-that-cares-full-report-single.pdf

NHS Digital (2020) 'Health survey for England 2019', https://digital.nhs.uk/data-and-information/publications/statistical/health-survey-for-england/2019

OECD (2021) *Health at a Glance 2021: OECD Indicators*, OECD Publishing, Paris, https://doi.org/10.1787/ae3016b9-en

OECD (2023) 'Hospital beds (indicator)', https://doi:10.1787/0191328e-en

OECD and European Union (2022) *Health at a Glance: Europe 2022: State of Health in the EU Cycle*, OECD Publishing, Paris, https://doi.org/10.1787/507433b0-en

Office for National Statistics (2022a) 'Healthcare expenditure, UK Health Accounts: 2020', www.ons.gov.uk/peoplepopulationandcommunity/healthandsocialcare/healthcaresystem/bulletins/ukhealthaccounts/2020

Plimmer, G. (2017) 'Self-funding care home residents subsidise council places', *Financial Times*, 16 February, www.ft.com/content/6c61fa30-f1dc-11e6-8758-687615182126

Public Accounts Committee (2018) 'NHS continuing healthcare funding: Thirteenth report of session 2017–2019', https://publications.parliament.uk/pa/cm201719/cmselect/cmpubacc/455/455.pdf

Public Health England (2016) 'Annual report and accounts 2015/16', www.gov.uk/government/publications/phe-annual-report-and-accounts-2015-to-2016

Public Health England (2022) 'Annual report and accounts 2020/21', www.gov.uk/government/publications/phe-annual-report-and-accounts-2020-to-2021

Quilter-Pinner, H. and Hochlaf, D. (2019) *Social Care: Free at the Point of Need: The Case for Free Personal Care in England*, Institute for Public Policy Research, London, www.ippr.org/research/publications/social-care-free-at-the-point-of-need

Raffle, A. E. and Gill, M. (2021) 'Mass screening for asymptomatic SARS-CoV-2 infection', *BMJ*, 373.

Resolution Foundation (2023) 'Who cares? The experience of social care workers and enforcement of employment rights in the sector', www.resolutionfoundation.org/app/uploads/2023/01/Who-cares.pdf

Roderick, P., Pollock, A. and Macfarlane, A. (2020) 'Getting back on track: Control of Covid-19 outbreaks in the community', *BMJ*, 369.

Ryan, S., Rowland, D., McCoy, D. and Leys, C. (2021) *For Whose Benefit? NHS England's Contract with the Private Hospital Sector in the First Year of the Pandemic*, Centre for Health and the Public Interest, London, https://www.chpi.org.uk/reports/for-whose-benefit?rq=ryan

Skills for Care (2022) 'The state of the adult social care sector and workforce in England', www.skillsforcare.org.uk/stateof

Smith, J. (1992) 'The role of PHLS in the EEC', Proposal for a European Community Centre for Communicable Disease Control, 10 March, The National Archives, JA 397/96.
Stevens, S. and Pritchard, A. (2020) 'Letter to: Chief executives of all NHS trusts and foundation trusts; CCG Accountable Officers; GP practices and Primary Care Networks; providers of community health services. Important and urgent – next steps on NHS response to COVID-19', 17 March, www.england.nhs.uk/coronavirus/wp-content/uploads/sites/52/2020/03/urgent-next-steps-on-nhs-response-to-covid-19-letter-simon-stevens.pdf
Sutaria, S., Roderick, P. and Pollock, A. (2017) 'Are radical changes to health and social care paving the way for fewer services and new user charges?', *BMJ*, j4279.
Thompson, H. (2023) 'Latest updates on UK Government COVID-19 contracts and spending', Tussell, 15 March, www.tussell.com/insights/covid
Triggle, N. (2018) 'The history of the NHS in charts', BBC News, 24 June, www.bbc.co.uk/news/health-44560590
UK Health Security Agency (2021) 'Rosalind Franklin Laboratory', Gov.UK, 8 December, www.gov.uk/guidance/nhs-test-and-trace-rosalind-franklin-laboratory
UK Health Security Agency (2023a) 'COVID-19 confirmed deaths in England (to 31 December 2022): Report', https://www.gov.uk/government/publications/covid-19-reported-sars-cov-2-deaths-in-england/covid-19-confirmed-deaths-in-england-to-31-december-2022-report
UK Health Security Agency (2023b) *Specialised Microbiology Network Public Health Laboratory, Yorkshire and the Humber: Public Health Microbiology Services User Handbook*, https://assets.publishing.service.gov.uk/government/uploads/system/uploads/attachment_data/file/1080010/PHL_London_user_manual.pdf
UK Health Security Agency (2023c) 'UKHSA annual business plan: 2023 to 2024', https://www.gov.uk/government/organisations/uk-health-security-agency.
Verity, R., Okell, L. C., Dorigatti, I., Winskill, P., Whittaker, C., Imai, N., *et al.* (2020) 'Estimates of the severity of coronavirus disease 2019: a model-based analysis', *The Lancet Infectious Diseases*, 20(6): 669–77.

6
Who cares about care? The carelessness of adult social care policy

Juanita Elias, Ruth Pearson and Shirin M. Rai

Introduction

Adult social care – that is, the set of practices, institutions and governance structures that enable individuals and their families to access support for their care needs, especially in old age – is never far from the political spotlight in UK politics. In the context of an ageing population and widespread funding cuts under the post-financial crisis austerity policies of the previous Conservative government, the sector has been hobbling from one crisis to the next. Even with the recent change of government, politicians continually promise that they have plans to solve the social care problem but fail to acknowledge that the broken system is the inevitable result of decades of underfunding and the failures of privatised and financialised 'solutions' to public service provisioning.

On assuming office in July 2019, Prime Minister Boris Johnson boldly proclaimed his ambition to 'fix the crisis in social care once and for all' (cited in Foster, 2021). These comments need to be understood in relation to the manifesto U-turns around care in old age that had marked Theresa May's 2017 election campaign (see below), as well as the reshaping of the electoral map in 2019 with 'red wall' Conservatives now representing seats in the North of England that had suffered some of the worst effects of austerity on social care provisioning. But rather than heralding a 'levelling up' for the sector, such a promise in fact followed a familiar pattern. As Needham and Hall (2022) suggest, what is striking about social care is that '[w]hilst government inaction on social issues is not unusual, a feature here is the frequency with which governments themselves say something must be done'. This failure to address one of the UK's most pressing policy issues can be characterised as a form of 'policy drift' in which, in the face of financial, political and bureaucratic challenges, piecemeal initiatives are preferred over major policy re-design.

We build upon this perspective, suggesting that at the heart of the social care crisis lies a wider societal failure to properly recognise and value the work of caring for others; a lack of value assigned to the work of care, which is highly gendered, *enables* policy drift. The failure to address the challenges and problems facing the social care sector – which include financial issues (who pays for care and how are care systems funded?) and workforce challenges (recruitment, retention, endemic low pay and poor conditions of work) – in many respects stem from the fact that issues relating to the place of care in society and social care needs *can* go unaddressed. As we argue in this chapter, at the core of policy decisions relating to the social care of an ageing population lies the assumption that there is always someone, usually a female family member, who can step in and pick up the pieces (Elias *et al,*, 2016). Unpaid carers, are estimated to be made up of between 4.2 and 6.5 million people and dominated by women, generate savings to the country of around £132 billion a year (Andrews [Hansard], 2023). This poses a major challenge to a new Labour government who seem unwilling to address deep seated social inequities in the context of ongoing commitments to fiscal constraint. In this chapter, we contest the idea that care for older people can easily and straightforwardly be taken on by family members, pointing to the depletive consequences of care labour for individuals and society, and how the inability to access adequate care in old age reproduces class, racial and gender inequalities.

What went wrong with Britain?

Exposing vulnerabilities

Successive government plans to fix the social care sector are, in reality, not even sticking plasters. Just eight months after Johnson's commitment to 'fix' social care, the extent and depth of the problems in the sector were catastrophically revealed during the first wave of the COVID-19 pandemic. The pandemic underlined the long-standing policy neglect and underfunding of the care sector, as well as a wider policy failure to not ascribe importance to older lives (Adult Social Care Committee, 2022). Regardless of how many senior government ministers sought to ensure that they were being seen to perform the weekly 'clap for carers' during the Covid period, it was a care*lessness* that characterised the government's approach to social care; subjecting the sector to more than mere policy drift but a 'wilful structural disregard' (Kaur and Rai, 2021). Patients were released from NHS hospitals into care homes without being tested for the virus, care homes and domiciliary care providers lacked access to adequate PPE supplies and, locked out of NHS supply chains, faced significantly higher costs for PPE. On top of this, there was inadequate sick pay and protections in place for a workforce earning poverty wages that could not afford to self-isolate, with care workers experiencing declining physical and mental health (Bottery, 2020; Jameson, 2020; Nyashanu *et al.*, 2022). A 2023 Nuffield report underlined these problems, noting the lack of understanding of the social care sector by those tasked with leading the response (Curry *et al.*, 2023)

Under such conditions, excess deaths of the cared for and their carers were inevitable. At the peak of the first wave of the pandemic, excess deaths in care homes in England and Wales were 6,331 for the single week ending 24 April (Scobie, 2021), and between 20 March 2020 and 21 January 2021 16.7 per cent of deaths due to COVID-19 were in care homes (Office for National Statistics, 2022). A low-paid social care workforce also bore the brunt of the pandemic as social care workers – especially domiciliary and home care workers – were one of the groups at highest risk of COVID-19 mortality (Hodgson *et al.*, 2020). The pandemic also revealed the deep-rooted nature of racial inequalities in the UK (Platt, 2021), and these too played out in social care settings, not least because of the disproportionately high levels of employment of ethnic minority workers in the care sector (especially in lower paying roles), as a consequence of which minoritised groups were disproportionately represented in the COVID-19 death lists (Equality and Human Rights Commission, 2022). Finally, as always, government policy on COVID-19 revealed deep gender inequalities – women became the shock absorbers of the crisis, taking on the extra social reproductive labour necessitated by lockdown policies and being disproportionately represented in the frontline of health and care workers and vulnerable to the consequences of neglect and underfunding of the NHS systems (Women's Budget Group, 2020b; Herten-Crabb and Wenham, 2022).

Social care, unlike the NHS, is a means-tested service in which non-state care providers (private providers and non-profits/charities) dominate – with many of the largest providers backed by private equity. Social care services are the statutory responsibility of local governments, who since 2010, under conditions of austerity, have been denied the necessary funding to invest in the sector, let alone to ensure that the care needs of citizens are adequately met. Between 2010 and 2020 central government funding for local authorities fell by 55 per cent, resulting in declining spending on social care and further rationing of access to social care – with families facing huge financial uncertainty over the cost of care. In 2022, following the disastrous Truss 'mini budget', the then new Chancellor of the Exchequer, Jeremy Hunt, sought to ease the financial pressure of social care provision on English local councils by granting them additional flexibility in the setting of council tax and increased grant funding, with further funding directed towards the sector in 2024 (Department for Levelling Up, 2024). But in the context of high inflation, the aftermath of the COVID-19 pandemic and the growing crisis in local authority financing, increased funding for social care proved insufficient – serving simply to stave off crisis rather than addressing its structural causes.

One issue that has been inadequately addressed is the workforce crisis in the sector, in which difficulties in recruiting and retaining staff impact the delivery and quality of services. Between 2020/21 and 2021/22 this situation became particularly acute as the vacancy rates in this sector rose abruptly from 7 per cent to 10.7 per cent and the number of vacancies rose from 110,000 to 165,000 (Bottery and Mallorie, 2023: 25). The staffing crisis was compounded by two factors: low pay and the exclusion of care workers from the post-Brexit shortage occupation list. As the local government social care ombudsman reported in 2022, the upshot of this was that social care is an 'under-resourced system unable to consistently meet the needs of those it is designed to serve' (cited by Bottery and Mallorie, 2023: 7). Labour force challenges in social care did eventually lead to the opening of skilled migration routes for overseas care workers. By the end of 2023, 57,700 visas for senior care workers/care workers had been issued – constituting 33 per cent of all skilled migration into the UK, with most migrants coming from outside the EU (India, Zimbabwe and Nigeria were the top three countries that workers migrated from) (Sumption and Strain-Fajth, 2023). However, whilst migration has helped to address the skills gaps and labour needs of the sector, significant concerns have been raised about the labour abuses that systems designed to support care worker migration into the UK have enabled. This includes corrupt practices by migration agents and recruiters, failures to place workers in employment, and how the precarity of migrant worker visas creates opportunities for abuse and exploitation by employers (Stacey, 2024).

Even with funding and workforce changes, analysis from Age UK suggests that we have in place a social care system that is 'unprepared for population ageing' (AgeUK 2024). Two million people aged over 65 in England are now living with unmet care needs, with implications not only for those in need of care, but also the high numbers of unpaid carers whose own health and wellbeing suffers as a result of taking on additional care labour (AgeUK, 2024).

Over the last two decades, efforts to fix social care have largely focused on the financial sustainability of the sector, and the policy debate has centred on the concerns of middle-income voters in relation to how to pay for social care in old age. The Johnson Government's plans for social care, for example, were framed almost exclusively in relation to discussions of enabling 'ordinary' homeowning older people to avoid the 'catastrophic cost' of having to sell their homes to fund their social care needs. In the period 2022–24, Conservative policy continued to frame the care crisis in terms of the costs to individual homeowning households – promising to bring in a cap on total care costs by 2025 (a policy first proposed in 2014, see below). Consistently missing from this policy framing, however, are issues of quality of care for older people, the poor pay and conditions of the social care workforce, the unsustainable reliance on unpaid and informal carers to plug the gaps in social care provision, and the physical and emotional depletion, and worsening financial insecurity, of those who do the work of care and those that they care for.

Building back better?

In March 2022, the Conservative government launched its policy paper 'Build Back Better: Our Plan For Health and Social Care' (UK Government, 2022). In many ways the plan was a reworking of earlier plans and initiatives that had focused on the issue of *who pays* for social care. The headline was that no one would have to pay more than £86,000 on care in their lifetime (although in reality the figure would be higher since this was just for 'personal care' and not for wider costs associated with social care – for example, accommodation and food in care homes). A 1.25 per cent levy on National Insurance came into effect in April 2022 to fund these changes, only later to be scrapped by the post-Johnson (Truss and Sunak) governments. The proposed reforms were just the latest manifestation of various social care proposals that emerged out of the 2011 review of social care funding undertaken by Andrew Dilnot. The resulting 'Fairer Care Funding' report set out the case for a lifetime care cap (albeit a much lower 'cap' of somewhere between £25,000 and £50,000) (Dilnot, 2011). The Coalition government suggested that it would implement the Dilnot Review, albeit in a moderated form with a proposed cap closer to £75,000, but this has not happened. The lack of a plan or clear political consensus as to how the state's contribution to adult social care would be funded contributed to a lack of progress on Dilnot's recommendations. Dilnot had suggested that pensioners could start paying National Insurance to meet the £2 billion a year costs to the state – earning the policy the title of 'granny tax' (Beattie, 2011).

As this example of media reporting shows, social care is an issue that can generate high levels of negative media coverage, leading to a situation in which politicians would rather not talk about it at all. For example, over 2013–14, Labour considered and ultimately rejected proposals for an estates tax of up to 15 per cent. The policy was dropped in advance of the 2015 general election after it was branded a 'death tax' (Swinford, 2015). In 2017, Theresa May's government faced an electoral drubbing when her proposal to put in place a £100,000 care cap was dubbed a 'dementia tax' (Inman, 2017). Finding a sustainable and fair solution to the funding of adult social care has been compounded by years of austerity, particularly at local government level. As a result, successive governments have endlessly kicked the can down the road when it comes to the issue of social care funding. It would appear that very similar tendencies have emerged within the current Labour government, who moved to scrap plans for a care cap and yet have given few other indications about how best to manage the crisis in social care provision for older people. Policy draft, inaction and unpaid carers picking up the pieces remains the 'policy template' for the sector (Bottery, 2024).

The result is that key trends in social care provision are incredibly worrying – and even more so in the context of rising inflation and declining wages (the so-called 'cost of living crisis'). As the King's Fund (2023) reported in a briefing to the House of Lords, government policy in this area lacks 'credibility'. Demand for care is rising but access to services provided through local authorities has narrowed. Despite record high requests for social care funding, the numbers receiving care from local authorities is 58,000 lower than it was in 2015/16. Part of the reason for this is that the means-tested upper threshold for accessing support has not increased with inflation. At the same time, the failure to implement the cap on care costs means that one in seven people over 65 face care costs of £100,000 upwards. The inflationary pressures have also led to increases in the cost of care provision, alongside the ongoing impact of the rising costs associated with infection control measures that the sector has experienced since the pandemic. Even though the amount that local authorities pay for care services has increased significantly since 2015/16, most pay well below the sustainable rate for these services. The unpaid workforce of 'carers' that sustain the sector also receive far less government support in the form of direct payments or respite care – this is despite the ambition of the 2014 Care Act to better support unpaid carers.

Issues relating to the funding of social care may well be politically toxic, but addressing the issue of who pays for care is an important part of developing long-term solutions that meet the needs of those requiring care, their families and the social care workforce. 'Funding crisis' narratives abound in the social care sector. These have included the so-called 'Barnet graph of doom' (in which social care was predicted to account for almost the entirety of local authority spending) (Brindle, 2012). In 2015, local authorities were permitted to raise council tax by up to 3 per cent (the 'adult social care precept') to increase funding for the sector, but this has proven insufficient and the trend towards ever more 'meaner' means tests to access social care continues. Social care has seen widespread privatisation, entangling the sector within wider financialised practices and networks, whilst working conditions and pay in the sector have faltered and even worsened.

Private and non-profit (charitable) providers have long played an important role in the delivery of care services, but some of the largest providers of social care are private equity backed – exposing a sector focused on providing welfare services to some of society's most vulnerable to the risky financial engineering practices such as leveraged buyouts that characterise private equity investment. This was witnessed most dramatically in 2011 when the private equity-backed Southern Cross group collapsed, impacting 31,000 care home residents. In domiciliary care, austerity pushed many local authorities to commission care services from ever larger corporate providers of social and welfare services. Concerns have been raised, therefore, that any increases in funding for social care would be syphoned off by the large corporate actors in the sector (Burns et al., 2016).

Crisis talk pervades discussions of adult social care – and understandably so. An inability to afford care in old age, care providers facing the risk of financial collapse, local authorities unable to deliver key welfare services and low-quality care arrangements – marked by 15-minute visits, or poor conditions in care homes, along with an exhausted social care workforce facing severe issues of recruitment and retention – are certainly signs of a sector in crisis. However, because of the nature of care and caregiving, it seems that a 'tipping point' is never quite reached. Even at the cost of mass deaths in care homes, such as we saw during Covid, social care reform is something that politicians would rather not deal with. As both scholars and activists have been emphasising, this is largely because there is always someone – usually women – around to pick up the pieces. 'Fixing care' in reality is about asking families to do more and squeezing paid care workers in an ever more privatised and financialised care sector (Horton, 2022). In the context of an ageing population and the withdrawal of the state from funding care services and social protection, the ability of households to deliver care has been progressively undermined at precisely the time that they are being extolled by political leaders to take on more and more care labour. For example, then Health Secretary Sajid Javid said in his Conservative Party conference speech that health and social care 'begins at home', suggesting that citizens 'have to take some responsibility' (Javid, 2021; see also, Akhter *et al.*, 2022: 1125). As Emma Dowling (2021) writes, this results in a fundamentally flawed 'care fix' that offloads care work onto the family, and it is women in particular who are more likely to take on unpaid care labour. This is made possible because care work is work that cannot not be done – someone *has* to take on this work (Elson, 2002; Pearson, 2019). Not to care for an older family member is something that many people simply cannot imagine. Increased burdens of care labour are therefore tied to the affective dimensions of care –we care for others because we care about them – and this can be used for political purposes. As Dowling writes: 'the emotions, feelings and relationships involved [in caring] play an important role in enabling the restructuring of care, where people's sense of compassion and responsibility are mobilized in attempts to compensate for or cope with the care crisis' (2021: 6).

Depletion and care

Rai *et al.* (2013) have suggested that the depletion of individuals, households and communities engaged in activities such as caring occurs when the inputs into their lives (recognition, health, rest, leisure and food) fall short of the outputs (care work, paid work, responsibility for managing care) that they have to produce. They adopt the phrase 'depletion through social reproduction' to capture this dynamic, with the term 'social reproduction' being used here to denote the everyday work involved in ensuring that people and communities can survive and reproduce themselves. In this sense, care labour is a crucial component of social reproduction. We introduce these more theoretical concepts at this point because we want to emphasise that asking individuals to take on more and more unpaid care work and undervaluing care labour, even when it is paid for, is not without cost. These costs are borne by individuals, but also by communities and society more broadly. The depletion of the individual can be physical as well as mental. For unpaid and underpaid care workers this includes experiencing tiredness, sleeplessness, reduced self-worth, insufficient time for oneself, the enjoyment of friendships and participation in community life. As Hussein (2017) notes in her study of the paid care workforce, care workers often experience high levels of psychological work stress. In 2015–16, we ran a small survey of care workers (n=189) to collect evidence for the Political Studies Association's Commission on Care (see Elias *et al.*, 2016). Our findings provide some important context for understanding why workers in the sector are experiencing depletion through social reproduction. The precariousness of jobs – not just zero-hour contracts but also irregular work patterns (45 per cent of survey respondents had irregular work patterns) and work in multiple locations that can lead to greater travel (30 per cent of survey respondents worked in more than five locations and 10 per cent in two to five locations) – adversely affects the wellbeing of care workers. Long travel times can lead to the extension of the working day, greater tiredness and vulnerability to illness. In the survey, 60 per cent of respondents worked more than eight hours a day. Work-based stress is a major reason for workers resigning from their jobs (Hussein, 2017; see also Lingham *et al.*, forthcoming).

A 2023 House of Lords debate also drew attention to the situation facing unpaid care workers who are recipients of the lowest of all means-tested state benefits: 'It is no wonder they are worried sick about heating and food bills, and that they do not manage to stay in work – and when they do, the support they get is significantly less than that offered by other countries' (Andrews [Hansard], 2023). The physical and mental health issues that unpaid carers face are significant. Carers UK, for example, have reported that carers experience declining physical and mental health relative to the rest of the population, the direct result of the pressures of the role – which include fifty hours of care each week. Public Health England now see caring as a social determinant of health (Carers UK, 2021).

Delivering care to older people in England is an urgent task that is being carried out under extremely stressful conditions – the ensuing depletion through social reproduction not only impacts individual wellbeing but has wider consequences, impacting carers' households and communities and ultimately undermining the quality of care and threatening the sustainability of the care sector. Those delivering care in the formal sector are often faced with low pay and poor working conditions, while the growing number of unpaid carers receive no compensation at all. For paid and unpaid carers, depletion is a serious concern. But it should be a concern for society as a whole. Placing too great a burden on either paid or unpaid carers may well risk breaking the care system.

Like the labour market as a whole, care labour is also racialised and affects depletion of those in the care sector. In terms of paid care workers, racialised minorities are disproportionately represented in the sector: 14 per cent of England's working age population are from racially minoritised groups (UK Government, 2023) but in 2022 this group of adult social care workers made up 23 per cent of workers (Skills For Care, 2022) and more were on zero-hours contracts than white workers (Equality and

Human Rights Commission, 2022). The precarity of life and of employment has affected racially minoritised workers badly and has contributed to their depletion. In recent research undertaken as part of the Co-POWeR consortium investigating the racialised impacts of COVID-19 in the UK,[1] we found that care workers felt that racist violence increased in their daily experience of work – from both colleagues to those who they cared for (see Lingham et al., forthcoming). Migration histories and migrant identities are important for understanding experiences of care services and caring (both paid and unpaid).During Covid, this experience was adversely affected by racism, depleting not only carers but also care receivers from migrant backgrounds, who worried for their health and end-of-life care, of funeral rituals and death away from home (Akhter et al., 2022).

Commitments to 'build back better' after the pandemic was not the experience of those dealing with gender and racialised and age-related exclusions. Build back better as rhetoric could not address the fundamental inequalities that mark the world of care and caring in the UK today.

Conclusion

As feminist political economists writing on care, we are acutely aware of the low priority afforded to the labour of unpaid carers on the policy agenda, even though some progress is being made in this regard because of the work of campaigning organisations such as the Women's Budget Group (see below). It is remarkable that yet again the issue of social care appears to be missing from the political agenda; during the 2024 election it was only the Liberal Democrats who sought to campaign on this issue – whilst both the Labour and Conservative parties maintained a deafening silence. We opened this chapter with a discussion of the Johnson Government's plans to fix social care 'once and for all', but such commitments quickly fizzled away; social care is once again 'too difficult' and 'too costly'. It was announced in April 2023, for example, that plans to increase funding by £500 million for the social care workforce initially mentioned in the 2021 Heath and Social Care White Paper would be halved (Cooney, 2023). The Starmer government's efforts to appear fiscally responsible have led to the ending of any expensive government commitments to capping individuals' care spending and widening access to means-tested care – a policy that Labour were never especially committed to.

In this chapter, we sought to bring both gender and race to the forefront of our analysis of the crisis in social care. The question that needs asking is: What are the long-term prospects for the delivery of a social care model that is both sustainably financed and delivers care without reproducing gendered and racialised inequalities and generating depletion through social reproduction? Are we able to look towards a future scenario in which an ageing population is supported? As the Labour peer Baroness Andrews stated in a 2023 House of Lords debate: 'the future is catching up with us: we will have a population of about 2 million in 10 years' time who will be ageing without care, with no family to look after them. Where are the plans for these people to get the support they need?' (Andrews [Hansard], 2023).

As things stand, it is hard to see within the newly elected Labour Government either the capacity or willingness bring about significant reforms to the sector that might end decades of policy drift. Plans for some sort of National Care Service were initiated under the Gordon Brown Government in 2010, but were rapidly dismantled following the Labour Party's electoral defeat in the same year. Since then, commitments to a National Care Service in some form have been a mainstay of Labour Party manifestos. In June 2023, a report by the Fabian Society commissioned by the then Shadow Health and Social Care Secretary Wes Streeting sought to set out a 'roadmap' towards a National Care Service that would be accessible to all; rooted in a commitment to upholding the rights of carers and the cared for; that would improve working conditions; include commitments on delivering affordable care; and stressed the need for clearer governance structures and accountability within the sector. Interestingly the report also recognises that the market for care is often marked by 'unacceptable commercial behaviours' (Cooper and Harrop, 2023: 4) and called for reforms to care commissioning practices and better financial scrutiny of the largest care providers (thus potentially dealing with the issue that any increased funding to the sector would be adsorbed by large private providers in order to pay dividends to shareholders at the expense of the workforce and end users). Many civil society organisations, think tanks, trade unions and politicians have welcomed the findings of the Fabian Society report. But it is unlikely that such a 'roadmap', however well thought through, will be delivered any time soon, especially given the current Labour government's continual prioritisation of 'fiscal credibility'. The new Health and Social Care Secretary, Streeting, has said very little of substance when it comes to Labour's plans for social care. We have seen some initial comments that a royal commission would be established to examine the challenges facing the sector – although this would appear simply to be another example of one of the tools employed by government that enables policy to drift endlessly.

As things stand the picture looks very bleak. Policy narratives need to shift – care is viewed simply as a financial and fiscal burden, but little attention is paid to the wider social and economic costs of undervaluing care (Whittome, 2023). In this regard, attempts to see care as 'social infrastructure' are important for recognising the economic and social value of investment in the care sector (Women's Budget Group, 2020a). Similarly, efforts to reframe how we talk about care in ways that demonstrate the economic and social value of care as a *collective* activity can help to challenge dominant assumptions about the private and individual nature of caring (Oxfam, 2023). Such initiatives matter in terms of highlighting the negative social and economic consequences that will result from not pressuring the government to value care.

Politicians and policymakers need to hit reset when it comes to discussions of social care. The crisis narrative that surrounds the sector has created a narrowing of the policy agenda – solutions to the care crisis were presented by successive Conservative governments purely in terms of addressing the concerns of ageing middle-income voters, an electorate mainly focused on the cost of social care to individuals. Finding sustainable financial solutions that will ensure that the care needs of an ageing population are met is certainly an important priority, but these solutions should be geared towards creating a social care system built upon principles of valuing care as a vital part of society and the economy, as well as enabling all of society to age well, and not just on the priorities of asset-owning classes. A major part of the problem is that the political focus has long been on finding politically palatable funding solutions that do not alienate key groups of voters. What has been lacking is a focus on developing a sustainable and just social care system in which the needs of carers (both paid and unpaid) and the cared for are at its centre. Policymaking has been made through a 'crisis lens' – that is, how best to deliver some minimal level of social care within conditions of 'crisis' (be it post-financial crisis austerity measures, health crises or the current cost of living crisis). The issue of adult social care for older people is often presented in terms of the 'crisis' within the NHS, with social care reform seen simply as a way of relieving pressure on the health service and cutting waiting lists. The result is a minimalist approach to social care in which the state only steps in when it is absolutely 'necessary', a policy position that fundamentally rests upon the idea that carers remain a shock absorber group allowing the carelessness of policy on care to continue.

Moreover, such minimalist thinking means that successive governments have not addressed questions about what it means to live well and with dignity in old age, or how those who do the work of care should be recognised and enabled to thrive, a claim made forcefully in the 2022 Adult Social Care committee report 'A "Gloriously Ordinary Life"'. Ageing with dignity means that we need to ensure that the social care system is accessible and navigable for all, regardless of socio-economic status, gender and race, and that individuals and their families are encouraged to access the support that they need rather than finding themselves unable to navigate constant bureaucratic obstacles. Sustainable and long-term solutions to the care crisis should not only focus on the question of 'who pays' for care but also on the workforce, the quality and conditions of care, the experiences of those who are able and unable to access care, how the sector is governed, and how failures in care provision reproduce racial and gender inequalities. In the context of the demographic shift that will see one in seven people in the UK projected to be over the age of 75 by 2040, a genuine 'fix' for the care sector is one that society as a whole stands to benefit from.

Notes

1 Undertaken under WP6 'Care, caring and carers', of the project Co-POWeR –'Consortium on practices of wellbeing and resilience in BAME families and communities', ESRC Grant Reference Number: ES/W000881/1, see https://warwick.ac.uk/fac/soc/pais/research/projects/copower

References

Adult Social Care Committee (2022) 'A "gloriously ordinary life": Spotlight on adult social care – report of session 2022–23, HL Paper 99', 8 December, https://publications.parliament.uk/pa/ld5803/ldselect/ldadultsoc/99/9902.htm

AgeUK (2024) 'State of health and care of older people in England', www.ageuk.org.uk/discover/2024/september/state-of-health-and-care-of-older-people-in-england-2024/

Akhter, S., Elias, J. and Rai, S.M. (2022) 'Being cared for in the context of crisis: Austerity, COVID-19, and racialized politics', *Social Politics*, 29(4): 1121–1143.

Andrews, Baroness (2023) 'House of Lords debate on social care', Hansard, HL Vol. 829, https://hansard.parliament.uk/Lords/2023-03-30/debates/621F2EF9-1966-40C3-8B21-2E3B0E478452/SocialCare

Beattie, J. (2011) 'Dilnot report: Pensioners warned they face £2bn granny tax to find long term care', *Daily Mirror*, 5 July, www.mirror.co.uk/news/uk-news/dilnot-report-pensioners-warned-they-face-139537

Bottery, S. (2020) 'How Covid-19 has magnified some of social care's key problems', The King's Fund, 25 August, www.kingsfund.org.uk/publications/covid-19-magnified-social-care-problems

Bottery, S. (2024) 'Labour never loved the idea of a care cap – now it must decide what to do instead', The King's Fund, 2 August, www.kingsfund.org.uk/insight-and-analysis/blogs/labour-cap-on-care-costs

Bottery S. and Mallorie, S. (2023) 'Social care 360', The King's Fund, March, www.kingsfund.org.uk/sites/default/files/2023-05/social_care-360_2023.pdf

Brindle, D. (2012) 'Graph of Doom: A bleak future for social care', *Guardian*, 15 May, www.theguardian.com/society/2012/may/15/graph-doom-social-care-services-barnet

Burns, D., Cowie, L., Earle, J., Folkman, P., Froud, J., Hyde, P., Johan, S., Rees Jones, I., Killett, A. and Williams, K. (2016) 'Where does the money go? Financialised care chains and the crisis in residential care', CRESC Public Interest Report, March, https://hummedia.manchester.ac.uk/institutes/cresc/research/WDTMG%20FINAL%20-01-3-2016.pdf

Carers UK (2021) 'Carers' health and experiences of primary care: Data from the 2021 GP Patient Survey', www.carersuk.org/media/shbb4cos/carers-uk-gp-patient-survey-report-2021-web.pdf

Cooney, C. (2023) 'Halving social care workforce funding in England an "insult", ministers told', *Guardian*, 4 April, www.theguardian.com/society/2023/apr/04/halving-social-care-workforce-funding-in-england-an-insult-ministers-told

Cooper, B. and Harrop, A. (2023) *Support Guaranteed: The Roadmap to a National Care Service*, Fabian Policy Report, Fabian Society, London.

Curry, N., Oung, C., Hemmings, N., Comas-Herrera, A. and Byrd, W. (2023) *Building a Resilient Social Care System in England*, Nuffield Trust, London, www.nuffieldtrust.org.uk/sites/default/files/2023-05/Building%20a%20resilient%20social%20care%20system%20in%20England.pdf

Department for Levelling Up (2024) 'Press release: Government announces a further £200 million boost for councils', Gov.UK, 24 January, www.gov.uk/government/news/government-announces-a-further-600-million-boost-for-councils

Dilnot, A. (2011) *Fairer Care Funding: The Report of the Commission on Funding of Care and Support*, Vol. 1, The Stationery Office, London.

Dowling, E. (2021) *The Care Crisis: What Caused it and How Can We End it?*, Verso, London.

Elias, J., Pearson, R., Phipps, B., Rai, S. M., Smethers, S. and Tepe, D. (2016) *Towards a New Deal for Care and Carers: Report of the PSA Commission on Care*, University of Warwick/PSA Commission on Care, Coventry.

Elson, D. (2002) 'The International Financial Architecture: A view from the kitchen', *Femina Polica*, 11: 26–37.

Equality and Human Rights Commission (2022) *Experiences from Health and Social Care: The Treatment of Lower-Paid Ethnic Minority Workers*, Equality and Human Rights Commission, https://equalityhumanrights.com/sites/default/files/inquiry-experiences-and-treatment-of-lower-paid-ethnic-minority-workers-in-health-and-social-care-report_0.pdf

Foster, D. (2021) 'Reform of adult social care funding: Developments since July 2019 (England)', House of Commons Library, Research Briefing, 12 May, https://commonslibrary.parliament.uk/research-briefings/cbp-8001

Herten-Crabb, A. and Wenham, C. (2022) '"I was facilitating everybody else's life. And mine had just ground to a halt": The COVID-19 pandemic and its impact on women in the United Kingdom,' *Social Politics* 29(4): 1213–1235.

Hodgson, K., Grimm, F., Vestesson, E., Brine, R. and Deeny, S. (2020) 'Briefing: Adult social care and COVID-19', The Health Foundation, 30 July, www.health.org.uk/publications/reports/adult-social-care-and-covid-19-assessing-the-impact-on-social-care-users-and-staff-in-england-so-far

Horton, A. (2022) 'Financialization and non-disposable women: Real estate, debt and labour in UK care homes', *Environment and Planning A*, 54(1): 144–159.

Hussein, S. (2017) 'The English social care workforce: The vexed question of low wages and stress', in K. Christensen and D. Pilling (eds) *The Routledge Handbook of Social Care Work around the World*, London: Routledge.

Inman, P. (2017) '"Dementia tax" and social care funding: The conservative plans explained'. *Guardian*, 18 May, www.theguardian.com/society/2017/may/18/social-care-funding-what-are-the-conservatives-proposing

Jameson, H. (2020) 'Fifth of care homes took on Covid patients, survey reveals', LocalGov, 24 August, www.localgov.co.uk/Fifth-of-care-homes-took-on-Covid-patients-survey-reveals/50979

Javid, S. (2021) 'Speech to the Conservative Party conference', 5 October, https://www.ukpol.co.uk/sajid-javid-2021-speech-to-conservative-party-conference/

Kaur, R. and Rai, S.M. (2021) 'COVID-19, care and carelessness', Countercurrents, 17 June, https://countercurrents.org/2021/06/covid-19-care-and-carelessness/

King's Fund (2023) 'Briefing: Debate in the House of Lords: The future of adult social care', 27 March, https://www.kingsfund.org.uk/insight-and-analysis/evidence-and-consultations/debate-house-lords-future-adult-social-care

Lingham, J. T., Rai, S. M. and Akhter, S. (forthcoming) 'Race, gender and class under COVID-19: Narratives of care, caring and carers', *European Journal of Politics and Gender*.

Needham, C. and Hall, P. (2022) 'Dealing with drift: Comparing social care reform in the four nations of the UK', *Social Policy and Administration*, 57(3): 287–303.

Nyashanu, M., Pfende, M. and Ekpenyong, M.S. (2022) 'Triggers of mental health problems among frontline healthcare workers during the COVID-19 pandemic in private care homes and domiciliary care agencies: Lived experiences of care workers in the Midlands region, UK', *Health and Social Care in the Community*, 30(2), doi: 10.1111/hsc.13204

Office for National Statistics (2022) 'Deaths involving COVID-19 in the care sector, England and Wales', www.ons.gov.uk/peoplepopulationandcommunity/birthsdeathsandmarriages/deaths/articles/deathsinvolvingcovid19inthecaresectorenglandandwales/deathsregisteredbetweenweekending20march2020andweekending21january2022

Oxfam (2023) 'How to talk about care in the UK: A framing toolkit', Oxfam, https://oxfamilibrary.openrepository.com/bitstream/handle/10546/621498/gd-uk-care-narratives-300523-en.pdf

Pearson, R. (2019) 'A feminist analysis of neoliberalism and austerity policies in the UK', *Soundings*, 71: 28–39.

Platt, L. (2021) 'Why ethnic minorities are bearing the brunt of COVID-19', LSE Research for the World Blog, www.lse.ac.uk/research/research-for-the-world/race-equity/why-ethnic-minorities-are-bearing-the-brunt-of-covid-19

Rai, S. M., Hoskyns, C. and Thomas, D. (2013) 'Depletion: The cost of social reproduction', *International Feminist Journal of Politics*, 16(1), 86–105.

Scobie, S. (2021) 'Covid-19 and deaths of care home residents', Nuffield Trust, 17 February, www.nuffieldtrust.org.uk/news-item/covid-19-and-the-deaths-of-care-home-residents

Skills for Care (2022) 'The state of the adult social care sector and workforce in England', www.skillsforcare.org.uk/adult-social-care-workforce-data/Workforce-intelligence/publications/national-information/The-state-of-the-adult-social-care-sector-and-workforce-in-England.aspx

Stacey, K. (2024) 'Sixfold rise in foreign care workers in UK complaining of exploitation', *Guardian*, 19 August, www.theguardian.com/society/article/2024/aug/19/sixfold-rise-in-foreign-care-workers-in-uk-complaining-of-exploitation

Sumption, M. and Strain-Fajth, Z. (2023) 'Migration and the health and care workforce', ReWage and Migration Observatory Evidence Paper, COMPAS, University of Oxford.

Swinford, S. (2015) 'Andy Burnham resurrects plans for a "death tax"', *Telegraph*, 29 May, www.telegraph.co.uk/news/politics/andy-burnham/11637026/Andy-Burnham-resurrects-plans-for-a-death-tax.html

UK Government (2022) 'Build Back Better: Our Plan for Health and Social Care', Policy Paper, www.gov.uk/government/publications/build-back-better-our-plan-for-health-and-social-care/build-back-better-our-plan-for-health-and-social-care

UK Government (2023) 'Ethnicity facts and figures: Working age population', www.ethnicity-facts-figures.service.gov.uk/uk-population-by-ethnicity/demographics/working-age-population/latest

Whittome, N. (2023) 'Care is a Gen Z issue: The compelling case for an economy with care at its heart', *New Statesman*, 7 March, www.newstatesman.com/spotlight/healthcare/2023/03/care-gen-z-issue

Women's Budget Group (2020a) 'Creating a caring economy: A call for action, report of the Commission on a Gender Equal Economy', https://wbg.org.uk/wp-content/uploads/2020/10/WBG-Report-v10.pdf

Women's Budget Group (2020b) 'Crises collide: Women and Covid-19: Examining gender and other equality issues during the Coronavirus outbreak' https://wbg.org.uk/wp-content/uploads/2020/04/FINAL.pdf

7

Social care or social harm? The chaotic organisation of support for Looked After Children in England

Tamsin Bowers-Brown, Andrew Brierley and Alexander Nunn

Introduction

The UK has become a more disciplinary society, and that discipline is deeply embedded in state institutions (Brierley, 2023; Nunn and Tepe, 2022). One of the social groups who are most negatively affected by this discipline is children who are taken into the collective care of the state after a social work intervention; so-called 'Looked After Children'.

At the outset, there are several clarifications we wish to make. First, we do not argue that all children who receive a social work intervention, including being Looked After, are harmed or that they are worse off after this intervention than they might otherwise be, and we recognise research that addresses this issue (e.g., Berridge, 2012a, 2012b). We also recognise that many well-meaning, dedicated and hardworking people work with great motivation and care, and are successful in their efforts to make a positive difference in the care system. Neither do we argue that children who are looked after are necessarily destined for negative long-term outcomes. Much remains within their own agency and, wherever possible, it is important to note and promote that agency. We also acknowledge that poor outcomes of care experienced people can often be short-lived and even those that experience hardships such as addiction, school exclusion and custody can grow to live fruitful lives (see Brierley, 2019).

However, the central argument we do make is that those children who are taken into the care of the state are currently not sufficiently supported to realise their potential, or to live full and satisfying lives. We argue that the failure of the 'care system' and a wider range of institutions, including in the education and criminal justice systems, to provide sufficient support is an example of 'social harm' – a set of negative outcomes that could be prevented by better resourced or differently designed social processes and institutions. The purpose of this chapter is to raise awareness of that harm and, through this, engage a broader range of people and stakeholders in efforts to change this, which might include microacts of kindness or support as well as more focused campaigning and activism.

During the period in which this chapter was written, the Independent Review of Children's Social Care (the Care Review) was published, having been commissioned prior to the pandemic. Their conclusion is fully in line with ours. As they put it:

> [the]... gap between what children and families need and what services offer is seen in every corner of children's social care ... problems go unaddressed, more children are unable to live with their families, and more are moved to a home that cannot meet their needs. This whirlwind of activity often ends with young people leaving care with no loving relationships to provide the foundation of a good life ... and so the spiral escalates. (Independent Review of Children's Social Care, 2022:34–35)

This chapter will juxtapose the ideals of 'social care' with the reality of 'social harm' for the children for whom it is deemed necessary to be taken into the care of the state. We argue that both state and society project harm rather than care onto these children. We highlight how policy is motivated by ill-thought through short-term neoliberalising and disciplinary motivations, rather than the prioritisation of compassion and human dignity, so much so that the strategic organisation of the 'care' system is emblematic of 'What went wrong with Britain'.

Social care or social harm?

Social harm

The concept of 'social harm', developed by a small number of criminologists, emphasises that the harms that arise from criminal activity are complex, and are often the result of a combination of harmful activities that are either opaque and unseen, or regarded as legitimate by the criminal justice system. In this view, harms include physical, economic, emotional or psychological, cultural, and environmental factors. These factors are preventable, insofar as human institutions and behaviour might be redesigned to mitigate, offset or eradicate them (Pemberton, 2016: 34). Harms are social in two distinct, yet often overlapping, respects: they are more than individual in nature, and they arise from shared institutions, processes or phenomena. *Social harms* are shared harms even if they only *appear* to manifest for particular people or social groups. This is because these harms impinge on the ability to fully partake in society and therefore our collective potential is harmed.[1] Social harms also arise from shared processes and institutions if, for example, they are caused by social structures (e.g., poverty or inequality) or institutions (e.g., state institutions or 'the market') or even norms generating harmful attitudes and behaviours (e.g., racism, sexism, violence) (Cremin and Bevington, 2017).

The genesis of this concept (see Canning and Tombs, 2021; Hillyard, 2004) came from internal debates within criminology, with critical researchers wanting to highlight that harms are not just generated in acts of individual criminality but result from broader social processes and institutions, including those superficially designed to respond to criminality. Moreover, they sought to show that criminality itself may be the result of harm and that the definition of what is legal and illegal may itself be harmful. The utility of the concept might be limited by this context and one possible criticism is that it serves mainly as a descriptive categorisation of the outcomes of processes, rather than a theory that explains why these outcomes arise. On the other hand, the major advantage of the concept is that it serves as an accessible mechanism to convey evidence about negative outcomes and to link these to social structures and institutions. It is in this way that we draw on the concept in this chapter; as a means of highlighting contradictions within a system (incorporating multiple overlapping institutions and social processes) that is superficially about extending care, but is, in many respects, harmful in its processes and outcomes.

One further comment on harm as a concept is worth making here. We regard social harm not just as a descriptor for direct negative outcomes, in this case experienced by young people in the care system, their families and social networks. Rather, we argue that a social system that generates harms of the nature discussed below is harmful indirectly to all because it hampers the ability of some members of society from playing their full part, thereby damaging the fabric of social relations. Moreover, it contributes to the reproduction of harmful structural violence in institutions (channelling resources into responsive institutions – e.g., health or criminal justice) and behaviours (people harmed will often behave in harmful ways to others). In this way, we challenge the idea that there is a distinction between individual behavioural and more structural explanations for harms.

From social care to social harm

Nationally, the referrals for child protection, assessments, the proportion of Child Protection Plans starts, Care Order applications (National Audit Office, 2019) and the numbers of children in care have risen continuously over the last decade, and the increase is replicated everywhere, at the same time as being geographically uneven. In the North East, there are now in excess of 40 per cent more children and young people in care than there were in 2015, far in excess of the national change (21 per cent). This is not just a reflection of population size; the rate of children in care (per 10,000 of the under-18 population) has also risen markedly, by nearly 12 percentage points since 2015. This rate varies widely across the country. There are more than 190 per 10,000 children in care in Blackpool (in the North-West of England), and just 26 in Merton (a London Borough). There are several causes of the change in the number and proportion of children who are 'looked after' by the state. Some are positive, such as the 'Staying Put' arrangement, which were one part of the provisions

Social care or social harm?

introduced by the Children and Families Act (2014). 'Staying Put' means that, rather than leaving care abruptly at age 18, some young people are able to stay with their carer until the age of 21. This partly recognises wider social changes over recent decades that mean many young people transition to adulthood at a later age than they did in previous generations. These provisions also make it easier for children in care to make similar transitions to other young people who are not in the care system, including attending University and being able to travel 'home' to their foster carer in university holidays. Nationally around 55–60 per cent of children who are in care on their eighteenth birthday stay with their foster carer, with this reducing to 22 per cent by the time they reach the age of 20. There are fewer children now leaving care at age 16 and 17 to live independently than there were prior to the introduction of these measures.

A further reason for the expanding population of children in care is a growth in the number of older children entering care. Growth in the over-16 population has accounted for around 40 per cent of the change in numbers since 2014. Increasing numbers of unaccompanied children who are refugees and asylum seekers is also part of the growth. In 2023, there were around 7,090 children in this category.

Poverty as a harmful pathway to care

The main recorded reason for children being taken into care remains 'abuse or neglect', though this has decreased slightly from 61 per cent in 2014 to 56 per cent in 2022, with family dysfunction and families in acute stress being the next two most significant causes. However, this data is problematic because, while other factors (such as poverty or poor education) may be related to 'abuse or neglect', official data does not record these contextual factors. Less than 1 per cent of Care Orders are recorded as responses to 'low income'. Nevertheless, the reality is that 'most families where a child is taken into care will be experiencing multiple forms of need' (Benaton et al., 2020: 338).

The correlation between poverty and care is clear. Child poverty has been on the rise over the last decade and now around a third of children in the UK are living in poverty (Rae and Carruthers, 2022), with this being substantially higher for certain ethnic minority groups, children of lone parents and children in larger families (Department for Work and Pensions, 2023). Bywaters and colleagues' research shows that the more deprived an area, the higher the rate of Child Protection Plans and Care Orders (Bywaters, 2020; Bennett *et al.*, 2022). Children in the most deprived 10 per cent of areas are over ten times more likely to be in care or subject to a Child Protection Plan than those in the least deprived 10 per cent. The prevalence of Care Orders increases in proportion with every decile in the national indices of deprivation. Simply put, there is a strong relation between poverty and care proceedings.

There are at least four aspects to the pathway between poverty and 'care'. First, poverty itself has a direct impact on children's wellbeing. The reality in the UK is that child poverty has become a matter of international concern (Alston, 2019). During the pandemic, for the first time in seventy years, the United Nations helped to fund food parcels for children in England, and it took campaigning by celebrity footballers to force the government to provide emergency food relief for families unable to adequately feed their children during school holidays. In December 2022, Shelter recorded that 120,710 children in England were homeless and living in temporary accommodation – 1 in every 100 children (Shelter, 2022). Despite the indicative evidence that families experiencing homelessness or poor quality housing have these experiences, there is a lack of data collection to fully explore the issue. Failure to provide housing (for example, to some migrant families and those who are notionally 'intentionally homeless') or adequate and appropriate housing (for example, when families with children are placed in temporary accommodation) is part of the explanation for increased child welfare concerns. Aside from family and parental homelessness being a pathway into the care system, young people who have been in care are also much more likely to become homeless when they leave care. For example, the All-Party Parliamentary Group for Ending Homelessness estimated that around a third of care leavers become homeless in the first two years after they leave care and a quarter of people experiencing homelessness have been in care at some point (Greaves, 2017).

Second, a wide range of authors identify an ongoing (and intensifying) theme in social policy and rhetoric associated with blaming and disciplining poorer families and parents for their own poverty (Crossley and Lambert, 2017). A process of 'responsibilisation' (Murray and Barnes, 2010) has blamed poorer sections of the population for their own inability to compete, and families in particular are deemed to generate intergenerational problems associated with their children lacking the capacity or willingness to do so (MacDonald et al., 2014). Politicians and civil servants have sought to emphasise family responsibility in this way (Gove, 2013; Wilshaw in OFSTED, 2016) and focus disciplinary social policy on disadvantaged families who are accused of causing 'trouble' (McKendrick and Finch, 2017).

Third, in a context of austerity, supportive state services have been increasingly withdrawn or watered-down, generating concern about the support available to families and children (Bennett et al., 2020; National Audit Office, 2019). Local Authorities have seen increasing pressures on their budgets since the financial crisis of 2008 (and fiscal pressures associated with significant bailouts for financial institutions) including reductions in family support services (Action for Children, 2020; Action for Children et al., 2019; ADCS, 2017; Smith et al., 2018). Financial constraints and negative rhetoric have been particularly targeted at social work departments, affecting service quality and preventative family support (Ferguson, 2016; Parton, 2014). The result may have been to generate increased use of services of last resort such as Care Orders (Stalford, 2019, p. 395). The combination of welfare and service retrenchment with increased need means there is a growing gap between social needs and the ability of the state and local authorities to respond to it, even before COVID-19 or the current 'cost of living crisis' (Action for Children et al., 2019).

Fourth, these social conditions (poverty plus austerity plus disciplinary politics), especially in the decade following the financial crisis, have put poorer families under considerable pressure. Inequalities and insecurity generate pressure on families to 'keep up', increasing stress inside the family, and accentuate family break-up, domestic violence and other causes of abuse and neglect. For example, Cross et al. (2022) found that homelessness, including living in temporary accommodation, increases the chances of child maltreatment, family stress and engagement with children's social care services. The social harm of poverty and inequality generates behavioural outcomes that generate further social harm.

A harmful care system

We have already discussed the general reduction in supportive services for families and the regional disparity in budget cuts that have been unevenly felt across the country, with the North East, Yorkshire and Humber and London experiencing the worst effects (Action for Children et al., 2019). Several reviews have found that central government does not understand the drivers of growth in demand for care or variation in how it is provided by top-tier local authorities, and that local authorities themselves often lack the capacity to effectively organise supply to meet this need (Narey, 2016; National Audit Office, 2019).

As the care system has grown, the vast majority of the increase has been met by private provision – in the case both of private residential homes and private fostering agencies. The Children's Commissioner (2020c) has warned that we know very little about the market as it has developed. The Commissioner also argues that increasing private provision is often out-of-locality and unregulated – the cost of these placements puts local authority budgets under even further pressure. The necessity for quick placements at awkward times and monopolised power leads to decisions that are motivated by urgency rather than what is best for those requiring a placement. While they are cautious not to make assumptions, they also highlight the growing role of private equity investors in the provision of children's care, mergers that lack transparency, and the growth of large national and international providers in the market. The Children's Commissioner does not say this, but the increasing role of private equity ought to be a particular cause for concern. Private equity investors lack transparency and typically attempt to take a time-limited stake in firms and networks of firms that have property or other assets that can be restructured and sold, reduce staff pay, make quick returns and sell on at a profit within five years or so (Morgan and Nasir, 2020).

Social care or social harm?

In addition, the Children's Commissioner, the Youth Justice Board (YJB), and children's charities (such as Become) have repeatedly pointed to instability in care placements as a cause for concern. They argue that too many children have frequent changes in care placement. The Children's Commissioner's Care Stability Index (Children's Commissioner, 2020a) drew attention to the numbers of children with multiple care placements: 25 per cent of children in care had multiple placements within two years. More recent government data shows that 22 per cent of children in care for two years or more have had three care placements or more within the last two years. While instability is more common for older children, the number of younger children experiencing instability has increased slightly, and there is a subgroup of children that experience very large degrees of instability and are more likely to be moved out of their locality and into private – and sometimes unregulated – provision. Placement instability and the ways that this can generate isolation, increase exposure to both criminality and victimhood, be detrimental to mental health and cause emotional distress (Children's Commissioner, 2019) are a driver for over-criminalisation of Looked After Children (YJB, 2015). These are social harms that result from the implementation of problematic strategic approaches. The life stories of Ben Ashcroft (*51 Moves*) and Andi Brierley (*Your Honour, Can I Tell You My Story* highlight the human story of such policy and practice (Ashcroft, 2013; Brierley, 2019).

Related to the growth in demand for care and the changing nature of the market for care provision has been the growth in unregulated provision, particularly for older children in care or for more complex cases (Children's Commissioner, 2020d). This was the subject of a *Newsnight* investigation and a subsequent Department for Education consultation in the summer of 2020. Around 6,000 young people live in 'independent' or 'semi-independent' placements, a rise of 80 per cent since 2010. A high proportion move straight into these premises or soon after entering care. More than 40 per cent of these were unaccompanied asylum seekers (Department for Education, 2020). Many of these placements are not subject to OFSTED inspection and do not meet the definition for 'providing care'. They are mostly in the private sector and their use is highly uneven across the country, with greater use in London and the East of England and less use in the North East. Children's charities such as Become (2020b) argue that all provision in the care sector should include the provision of 'care' and that unregulated provision needs to be swiftly curtailed. The Children's Commissioner points out that such placements are sometimes combined with infringements on liberty, sometimes with the approval of courts, but sometimes in arrangements of questionable legality, and that they are associated with the greater use of temporary and agency staff, instability in placements and driving up costs, with some costing as much as £5,000 per week (Children's Commissioner, 2020b). They also highlight wide variation in the quality of the care experience in these settings (Children's Commissioner, 2020d).

Children's charities continue to highlight other issues such as the 'care cliff' on leaving care and sibling separation. Despite the 'Staying Put/Close' policy, which was intended to increase the number of young people staying connected to their foster or residential placement after reaching the age of 18, this has not been fully delivered. Care leavers often report lower wellbeing, loneliness, debt problems, housing instability and homelessness (Baker et al., 2022; Centre Point, 2017). Become (2020a) continue to focus on sibling separation in the care system. A BBC campaign also drew attention to this, finding that up to 12,000 young people in care were not living with their siblings (Kenyon and Forde, 2020). Where connection and belonging are shown to contribute to wellbeing, the separation of siblings seems to be an additional blow in inflicting social harm where the opportunity for maintaining connection would be of emotional benefit.

Social harm as mental health trauma

Unsurprisingly then, given the litany of stages at which there are encounters that compound exclusion from society or enforce stigma, poor health (especially mental health) is a key mediator between the experience of being in care and these negative outcomes. Children in care are supposed to have a physical health check and complete a mental health questionnaire every year. Evidence from the latter shows that more than 42 per cent of boys in care had an emotional/psychological wellbeing score that was a cause for concern in 2023, compared to less than 10 per cent of the other children of the same age. Poor mental and emotional health seems to be most pronounced in the 9–11 age range. In a recent review, Luke *et al.* summarise evidence that 'up to 38 per cent of looked after children have symptoms that are indicative of conduct disorders; up to 12 per cent could be diagnosed with emotional disorders and up to 8 per cent have hyperkinetic symptom' (2008:19).

There is an increasing understanding that childhood trauma has a lasting impact on cognitive and emotional development, which affects behaviour, with knock-on effects on the likelihood of future negative outcomes (see Brierley, 2023). The emergent literature on adverse childhood experiences (ACEs) demonstrates these linkages conclusively (Bellis *et al.*, 2014, 2018; Hughes *et al.*, 2017). ACEs include abuse and neglect; parental conflict/domestic abuse; parental illness and death/imprisonment and material deprivation. As we have seen, many children in care have experienced several of these, in addition to separation from their family. Direct links between these experiences and physical and mental ill-health are clear, but also that they are passed through an increased tendency to adopt risky behaviours. The research shows that almost half of the population has experienced one ACE and 9% have experienced four or more, with deprivation being correlated to having experienced multiple ACEs. Where people have four or more ACEs, 'modelling suggested that 11.9% of binge drinking, 13.6% of poor diet, 22.7% of smoking, 52% of violence perpetration, 58.7% of heroin/crack cocaine use, and 37.6% of unintended teenage pregnancy prevalence nationally could be attributed to ACEs' (Bellis *et al.*, 2014). Adverse childhood experiences demonstrate that the additional care needed to increase wellbeing should be a priority, individually and collectively.

Evidence on the maltreatment of children in care shows that it has a range of effects on psychological, neurological and physiological development depending on a number of factors, such as the individual child's prior development and propensities, the timing of the experience, contextual factors and post-trauma experiences. The point being that, while these are generally negative experiences that might be expected to have significant impacts, those impacts are divergent rather than uniform in nature (Luke et al., 2018; Woolgar, 2013).

One important implication of the ACE literature in particular is to draw attention away from simplistic ideas, such as binaries between what negative outcomes might be associated with structural factors outside of the child's control and those that are impacted by their own behaviours. This evidence shows that these are not distinct but inter-related phenomena. What matters therefore is to understand that social conditions contribute to reducing the support available to families and to increased stress for families, which may harm children's development in ways that shape their long-term prospects in a range of life impacting ways. At the very least, being in the collective care of the state is not sufficient to offset these impacts and, as a consequence, children who are removed from their families by the state have more negative life chances than other children.

It is clear that these outcomes are harmful for those directly affected. They are also harmful in the broader sense. As the Care Review for England outlined, the costs of negative long-term outcomes for children who have needed a social worker is approximately £23 billion per year and more than £700,000 for each child (Independent Review of Children's Social Care, 2021). While it is not comparable to direct harm, this is a harm experienced by the whole of society. Further, every person unable to fulfil their potential because of the impact of ACEs will have at least some harmful knock-on consequences for others with whom they have (or fail to have) personal relationships. This harm is social in its origins but also in its outcomes.

Social harm through educational inequality

Across the education sector, from schooling to higher education, the opportunities for those in care and those who are care experienced are differently experienced than by their peers in the broader population: participation, exclusions, attainment and progression are all areas that demonstrate that for children in care the educational playing field is unevenly skewed against them.

Under pressure to meet their institutional targets, schools often permanently or temporarily 'exclude' individuals they determine as not performing or conforming, or undermining the ability of others to do so. School exclusions have been a controversial issue over recent years, arguably being prima facie evidence of the way that discipline is embedded deeply in state institutions. School exclusions have been rising in recent years (both permanent and fixed term): there were more than 787,000 suspensions in 2022/23, up from just over 300,000 in 2014/15 and more than 9,300 permanent school exclusions in 2022/23 (Department for Education, 2020. Suspensions are now at a rate of 9.33 for every 10,000 children, more than double that in 2015/16, and the permanent exclusion rate has risen from 0.8 to 0.11 in the same period. But more telling than this is the detail of who is excluded from school, why, and what happens to them when they are excluded. A child 'Looked After' by the state is more than 5 per cent more likely to be temporarily excluded(Paget *et al.*, 2018; Timpson, 2019). While violent behaviour is administratively recorded as an important reason for both fixed and permanent exclusions, the most prominent reason for both is disruptive behaviour. Wider research suggests that exclusion processes reflect wider inequalities and prejudices and that teachers are well informed of the need to discipline but are less clear on protective legislation like the Equality Act. Moreover, inequalities in confidence and the institutionally valued forms of social and cultural capital are identified as making some parents from lower socio-economic class groups and from some cultural and ethnic groups less likely to be heard and less effective at challenging school and Local Education Authority disciplinary decisions (Graham *et al.*, 2019). Once excluded, most children are referred to an 'alternative provision', but this can range widely in quality and effectiveness (IFF Research *et al.*, 2019). What emerges from this data and associated research is that state discipline operating through partially autonomous school behaviour policies is systematically targeting those children who are oppressed by socio-economic and political inequalities in wider society.

In addition to exclusions, children who are or have been in the care system tend also to have worse educational attainment (Jackson, 1998; Welbourne and Leeson, 2012). As an example, in 2023 the 'Attainment 8 measure at the end of Key Stage 4' (usually age 16) for all children was 46.3. The comparable figure for children who were 'Looked After' was just 19.4. There is a debate about whether these differences are caused, or more properly only partly mitigated, by the care system (e.g., Berridge, 2007, 2017; Jackson, 2007, 2010; Jackson and Höjer, 2013). For example, 'children in need' but not in care did marginally worse in the same year at 18.3, and children with longer periods in care tend to do better than those who have been in care for a shorter period. The issue here is not so much that being in care doesn't make attainment worse, but that it doesn't make any serious contribution to narrowing the gap with all other children.

Progress from compulsory to Further and Higher Education (HE) is also a noted problem and a noted gap in the literature and evidence base (Cameron *et al.*, 2012: 338). Recent research suggests that young people with care experience are much less likely than the rest of the population to go on to study at HE (Harrison, 2017; Baker, 2022). Estimates of HE participation among this group range from as low as 6 per cent to 11 per cent but are far below the overall average of more than 40 per cent. Once in HE, young people with care experience have a much harder time transitioning to university (over a quarter arrive at university on their own, rather than with a carer), staying in university, dealing with accommodation problems and holiday periods (when they should have entitlement to stay in university accommodation) (Ellis and Johnston, 2019). Around 40 per cent of care leavers are not in education, employment or training (NEET) at age 19–21.

Social harm through the criminal justice system and victimisation

In addition to care leavers being over-represented in NEET figures, they are also over-represented in the criminal justice system. Nunn *et al.* (2021)

report that children in care are 3 per cent as likely as other 16–17-year-olds to have a criminal record and 4 per cent of care leavers are in custody at age 21. Though data is problematic, the Laming Review of Looked After Children and the Criminal Justice System found that children in care who have contact with the police have a higher risk of being cautioned compared to other children, and that just under half of the children in custody or on remand in secure settings had been in care at some point. It also found that children with a care background in secure settings had a lower chance of family visits, were less likely to know where they would be living when released and were more likely to be physically restrained or feel threatened while in custody (Laming, 2016). The Ministry of Justice's survey of prisoners' family backgrounds found that around 7 per cent of their sample had been in care for the majority of their childhood, and of the rest, 24 per cent said they had been in care at some point, suggesting that children with some care background are far more likely to end up in prison than the wider population (Williams *et al.*, 2012).

In addition to being more likely to be involved in the criminal justice system, children in care are also more likely to be the victims of crime while in care, and of course this may also relate to apparent later offending behaviour. Children in care are repeatedly shown to be more likely to be targeted for sexual and criminal exploitation, especially when in residential care settings ('children's homes' as opposed to foster care with a family), where exploitation is often related to the significant numbers of children who 'go missing' from care (Shaw and Greenhow, 2020). In recent years, children in care have also been disproportionately targeted for involvement in 'county lines' gang activity (Home Office, 2018), where their victimhood is often obscured by the fact that they have engaged in criminal activity themselves while being exploited. Again, risks of this sort of exploitation are aggravated by being placed in residential care and out of authority care placements where children are placed at a greater distance from peer and family networks or familiar professionals (Howard League, 2017; Shaw and Greenhow, 2020). The YJB identified 'Young people placed in high crime and high deprivation areas' as a contributing cause of the disproportionality of care experience children in the youth justice system (YJB, 2015). Therefore, even the justice system itself recognises that the significant drivers behind this group being involved in crime are often outside the child's control and emphasises social harm, a position argued by justice practitioners with intersectional experiences of care, prison and being care leaver advocates (Brierley, 2021; Fitzpatrick et al., 2016).

Conclusion

The story for a large proportion of young people in the care system is bleak. As a society, we have demonstrated a lack of compassion, investment and prioritisation of these children and young people. Despite the best efforts of many in caring, educational and social work roles, the deeply entrenched layers of deprivation, poor wellbeing and precarity impact children taken into the care of the state in structured and structuring ways, which are systematic and ideologically driven mechanisms of social harm. The removal of supportive services, and the proliferation of pernicious policy agendas, serve to systematically suggest that some of us are disposable. Reform of the care system cannot be effective without a broader assessment of the associated societal issues that contribute to social harm. The Labour government elected in 2024 made important manifesto commitments on reducing child poverty, protecting children from exploitation and improving the care system, including the promise of a Children's Wellbeing Bill in the subsequent Kings Speech. It is too early to judge how serious or significant these reform efforts will prove, but the intent at least is welcome. Ultimately, the will to view the care of young people through a lens of moral obligation and decency seems to have been sacrificed to a harmful rather than caring system, one that neither provides children looked after by the state the opportunity to thrive nor for society to benefit from the improved social and economic outcomes that would result from this. It may be tempting to see this as purely state-imposed harm, but the state acts to place children in our collective care; it is therefore our collective responsibility to demand change.

Note

1 This is consistent with the understanding of democracy in cosmopolitan theory (see Nunn and Morgan, 2016).

References

Action for Children (2020) 'Children and young people's services: Funding and spending 2010/11 to 2018/19', https://media.actionforchildren.org.uk/documents/Joint_report_-_childrens_services_funding_2018-19_May_2020_Final.pdf

Action for Children, National Children's Bureau, NSPCC, The Children's Society and Barnardos (2019) 'Children and young people's services: Funding and spending 2010/11 to 2017/18', www.barnardos.org.uk/sites/default/files/uploads/childrens-services-funding-report.pdf

ADCS (Association of Directors of Children's Services) (2017) 'A country that works for all children', https://www.adcs.org.uk/wp-content/uploads/2024/04/ADCS_A_country_that_works_for_all_children_FINAL.pdf

Alston, P. (2019) 'Visit to the United Kingdom of Great Britain and Northern Ireland: Report of the Special Rapporteur on extreme poverty and human rights', United Nations, https://undocs.org/A/HRC/41/39/Add.1

Ashcroft, B. (2013) *51 Moves*, Waterside Press, Winchester.

Baker, C., Briheim-Crookall, L. and Selwyn, J. (2022) *The Wellbeing of Children in Care and Care Leavers – Learning from the Bright Spots Programme: Strategic Briefing*, Research in Practice, Dartington, www.researchinpractice.org.uk/children/publications/2022/september/the-wellbeing-of-children-in-care-and-care-leavers-learning-from-the-bright-spots-programme-strategic-briefing-2022/

Baker, Z. (2022) 'The phase one report for the care-experienced graduates project', National Network for the Education of Care Leavers, www.nnecl.org/articles/the-phase-one-report-for-the-care-experienced-graduates-project

Become (2020a) 'Submission to the call for written evidence for the Civil Society Submission to the UN's List of Issues Prior to Reporting', 31 August, www.becomecharity.org.uk/for-professionals/resources/submission-to-the-call-for-written-evidence-for-the-civil-society-submission-to-the-un-s-list-of-issues-prior-to-reporting-2020/

Become (2020b) 'Submission to the Department for Education's consultation on reforms to unregulated provision for children in care and care leavers', https://www.becomecharity.org.uk/media/2412/become-uncrc-civil-society-submission-to-the-un-s-list-of-issues.pdf

Bellis, M. A., Hughes, K., Ford, K., Hardcastle, K. A., Sharp, C. A., Wood, S., Homolova, L. and Davies, A. (2018) 'Adverse childhood experiences and sources of childhood resilience: A retrospective study of their combined relationships with child health and educational attendance', *BMC Public Health*, 18(1): 792.

Bellis, M. A., Hughes, K., Leckenby, N., Perkins, C. and Lowey, H. (2014) 'National household survey of adverse childhood experiences and their relationship with resilience to health-harming behaviors in England', *BMC Medicine*, 12(1): 72.

Benaton, T., Bowers-Brown, T., Dodsley, T., Manning-Jones, A., Murden, J. and Nunn, A. (2020) 'Reconciling care and justice in contesting social harm through performance and arts practice with looked after children and care leavers', *Children & Society*, 34(5): 337-353.

Bennett, D. L., Mason, K. E., Schlüter, D. K., Wickham, S., Lai, E. T., Alexiou, A., Barr, B. and Taylor-Robinson, D. (2020) 'Trends in inequalities in Children Looked After in England between 2004 and 2019: A local area ecological analysis', *BMJ Open*, 10(11): e041774.

Bennett, D.L., Schlüter, D.K., Melis, G., Bywaters, P., Alexiou, A., Barr, B., Wickham, S. and Taylor-Robinson, D. (2022) 'Child poverty and children entering care: A longitudinal ecological study at local area-level in England, 2015-2020', *The Lancet*, 7: e496-503.

Berridge, D. (2007) 'Theory and explanation in child welfare: Education and looked-after children', *Child & Family Social Work*, 12(1): 1-10.

Berridge, D. (2012a) 'Educating young people in care: What have we learned?' *Children and Youth Services Review*, 34(6): 1171-1175.

Berridge, D. (2012b) 'Reflections on child welfare research and the policy process: Virtual school heads and the education of looked after children', *The British Journal of Social Work*, 42(1): 26-41.

Berridge, D. (2017) 'The education of children in care: Agency and resilience', *Children and Youth Services Review*, 77: 86-93.

Brierley, A. (2019) *Your Honour, Can I Tell you my Story?*, Waterside Press, Winchester.

Brierley, A. (2021) *Connecting With Young People in Trouble: Risk, Relationships and Lived Experience*, Waterside Press, Winchester.

Brierley, A. (ed.) (2023) *The Good Prison Officer: Inside Perspectives*, Taylor & Francis, London.

Bywaters, P. (2020) *The Child Welfare Inequalities Project: Final Report*, University of Huddersfield, Huddersfield.

Cameron, C., Jackson, S., Hauari, H. and Hollingworth, K. (2012) 'Continuing educational participation among children in care in five countries: Some issues of social class', *Journal of Education Policy*, 27(3): 387-399.

Canning, V. and Tombs, S. (2021) *From Social Harm to Zemiology: A Critical Introduction*, Routledge, London.

Centre Point (2017) 'Policy report: From care to where? Care leavers' access to accommodation', https://centrepoint.org.uk/sites/default/files/2023-06/from-care-to-where-centrepoint-report.pdf

Children's Commissioner (2019) 'Pass the parcel: Children posted around the care system', https://www.childrenscommissioner.gov.uk/resource/pass-the-parcel-children-posted-around-the-care-system/#:~:text=%E2%80%9CI%20 feel%20like%20a%20parcel,moved%20on%20to%20somewhere%20else.%E2%80%9D&text=There%20are%20over%2030%2C000%20looked,out%20of%20area%27%20in%20England

Children's Commissioner (2020a) 'Stability index 2020', https://www.childrenscommissioner.gov.uk/resource/stability-index-2020/

Children's Commissioner (2020b) 'The children who no-one knows what to do with', https://www.childrenscommissioner.gov.uk/resource/the-children-who-no-one-knows-what-to-do-with/#:~:text=This%20paper%20summarises%20the%20findings,%27Stability%20index%202020%27

Children's Commissioner (2020c) 'Private provision in children's social care', https://assets.childrenscommissioner.gov.uk/wpuploads/2020/11/cco-private-provision-in-childrens-social-care.pdf

Children's Commissioner (2020d) 'Unregulated: Children in care living in semi-independent accommodation', https://assets.childrenscommissioner.gov.uk/wpuploads/2020/09/cco-unregulated-children-in-care-living-in-semi-independent-accommodation.pdf

Cross, S., Bywaters, P., Brown, P. and Featherstone, B. (2022) 'Housing, homelessness and children's social care: Towards an urgent research agenda', *The British Journal of Social Work*, 52(4): 1988–2007.

Crossley, S. and Lambert, M. (2017) 'Introduction: "Looking for trouble?" Critically examining the UK government's troubled families programme', *Social Policy & Society*, 16(1): 81.

Cremin, H. and Bevington, T. (2017) *Positive Peace in Schools: Tackling Conflict and Creating a Culture of Peace in the Classroom* (First ed.) Routledge, London.

Department for Education (2020) 'Looked After Children in independent or semi-independent placements', www.gov.uk/government/publications/looked-after-children-in-independent-or-semi-independent-placements

Department for Work and Pensions (2023) 'Households Below Average Income: For Financial Years Ending 1995 to 2022', www.gov.uk/government/statistics/households-below-average-income-for-financial-years-ending-1995-to-2022

Ellis, K. and Johnston, C. (2019) *Pathways to University from Care: Findings Report One*, The University of Sheffield, Sheffield, https://doi.org/10.15131/SHEF.DATA.9578930

Ferguson, H. (2016) 'Researching social work practice close up: Using ethnographic and mobile methods to understand encounters between social workers, children and families', *The British Journal of Social Work*, 46(1): 153–168.

Fitzpatrick, C., Williams, P. and Coyne, D. (2016) 'Supporting looked after children and care leavers in the criminal justice system: Emergent themes and strategies for change', *Prison Service Journal*, 226: 8–13.

Gove, M. (2013) 'Speech to the NSPCC: Getting it right for Children in Need', Gov.UK 12 November, www.gov.uk/government/speeches/getting-it-right-for-children-in-need-speech-to-the-nspcc

Graham, B., White, C. and Potter, S. (2019) 'School Exclusion: A Literature Review on the Continued Disproportionate Exclusion of Certain Children', Department for Education, https://assets.publishing.service.gov.uk/media/5cd15de640f0b63329d700e5/Timpson_review_of_school_exclusion_literature_review.pdf

Greaves, R. (2017) 'Homelessness prevention for care leavers, prison leavers and survivors of domestic violence', All-Party Parliamentary Group for Ending Homelessness. www.crisis.org.uk/media/237534/appg_for_ending_homelessness_report_2017_pdf.pdf

Harrison, N. (2017) 'Moving on up: Pathways of care leavers and care-experienced students into and through higher education', National Network for the Education of Care Leavers, https://careleaverpp.org/wp-content/uploads/2018/01/Summary-of-Moving-on-Up-report.pdf

Hillyard, P. (ed.) (2004) *Beyond Criminology: Taking Harm Seriously*, Pluto Press, London.

Home Office (2018) 'Criminal exploitation of children and vulnerable adults: County lines guidance', www.gov.uk/government/publications/criminal-exploitation-of-children-and-vulnerable-adults-county-lines

Howard League (2017) 'Ending the criminalisation of children in residential care. Briefing two: Best practice in policing', Howard League for Penal Reform, https://howardleague.org/publications/ending-the-criminalisation-of-children-in-residential-care-briefing-two-best-practice-in-policing/

Hughes, K., Bellis, M., Hardcastle, K. A., Sethi, D., Butchart, A., Mikton, C., Jones, L. and Dunne, M. (2017) 'The effect of multiple adverse childhood experiences on health: A systematic review and meta-analysis', *The Lancet Public Health*, 2(8): e356–e366.

IFF Research, Mills, M., and Thomson, P. (2019) 'Investigative research into alternative provision', Department for Education, https://assets.publishing.service.gov.uk/media/5bc611a4ed915d0b0349a64d/Investigative_research_into_alternative_provision.pdf

Independent Review of Children's Social Care (2021) 'Paying the Price'.

Independent Review of Children's Social Care (2022) 'Independent review of children's social care – Final report', https://assets.publishing.service.gov.uk/media/640a17f28fa8f5560820da4b/Independent_review_of_children_s_social_care_-_Final_report.pdf

Jackson, S. (1998) 'Educational success for looked-after children: The social worker's responsibility', *Practice*, 10(4): 47–56.

Jackson, S. (2007) 'Progress at last?', *Adoption & Fostering*, 31(1): 3–5.

Jackson, S. (2010) 'Reconnecting care and education: From the Children Act 1989 to Care Matters', *Journal of Children's Services*, 3: 48.

Jackson, S. and Höjer, I. (2013) 'Prioritising education for children looked after away from home', *European Journal of Social Work*, 16(1): 1–5.

Kenyon P. and Forde, E. (2020) 'Thousands of siblings split up in care system', BBC News, 14 January, www.bbc.com/news/uk-51095939

Laming, H. (2016) 'In care, out of trouble: How the life chances of children in care can be transformed by protecting them from unnecessary involvement in the criminal justice system', Prison Reform Trust.

Luke, N., Sinclair, I., Woolgar, M. and Sebba, J. (2018) What works in preventing and treating poor mental health in looked after children?, The Rees Centre, University of Oxford.

MacDonald, R., Shildrick, T. and Furlong, A. (2014) 'In search of "intergenerational cultures of worklessness": Hunting the Yeti and shooting zombies', Critical Social Policy, 34(2): 199–220.

McKendrick, D. and Finch, J. (2017) '"Under heavy manners?": Social work, radicalisation, troubled families and non-linear war', The British Journal of Social Work, 47(2): 308–324.

Morgan, J. A. and Nasir, M. A. (2020) 'Financialised private equity finance and the debt gamble: The case of Toys R Us', New Political Economy, 26(3): 455–471, https://doi.org/10.1080/13563467.2020.1782366

Murray, L. and Barnes, M. (2010) 'Have families been rethought? Ethic of care, family and "whole family" approaches', Social Policy and Society, 9(4): 533–544.

Narey, M. (2016) 'Residential Care in England', Department for Education, www.gov.uk/government/publications/childrens-residential-care-in-england

National Audit Office (2019) 'Pressures on children's social care', National Audit Office.

Nunn, A. and Morgan, J. (2016) 'World society and a world state in the shadow of the world market: Democracy and global political economy', in F. Offor and R. Badru (eds) Transnational Democracy, Human Rights and Race Relations, Create Space, Charleston, SC.

Nunn, A. and Tepe, D. (2022) 'Disciplinary neo-liberalisation and the new politics of inequality', The British Journal of Criminology, 62(5): 1305–1322.

Nunn, A., Turner, R., Adhikari, J. and Brooks, C. (2021) 'Derbyshire virtual school: Creative mentoring programme final report', Derbyshire County Council.

OFSTED (Office for Standards in Education, Children's Services and Skills) (2016) The Report of Her Majesty's Chief Inspector of Education, Children's Services and Skills 2016, OFSTED, London.

Paget, A., Parker, C., Heron, J., Logan, S., Henley, W., Emond, A. and Ford, T. (2018) 'Which children and young people are excluded from school? Findings from a large British birth cohort study, the Avon Longitudinal Study of Parents and Children', Child Care Health Dev, 44(2): 285–296.

Parton, N. (2014) The Politics of Child Protection: Contemporary Developments and Future Directions, Macmillan, Basingstoke.

Pemberton, S. A. (2016) Harmful Societies: Understanding Social Harm, Policy Press, Cambridge.

Rae, M. and Carruthers, J. (2022) 'Childhood poverty is rising in the UK, but the government continue to ignore it', *British Medical Journal*, Apr 1:377:0872.

Shaw, J. and Greenhow, S. (2020) 'Children in care: Exploitation, offending and the denial of victimhood in a prosecution-led culture of practice', *The British Journal of Social Work*, 50(5): 1551–1569.

Shelter (2022) '1 in every 100 children in England will wake up homeless this Christmas', Shelter England, 21 December, https://england.shelter.org.uk/media/press_release/1_in_every_100_children_in_england_will_wake_up_homeless_this_christmas#:~:text=Posted%2021%20Dec%202022%20120%2C710%20children%20in,crisis%20continues%20to%20deepen%20the%20housing%20emergency

Smith, G., Sylva, K., Smith, T., Sammons, P. and Omonigho, A. (2018) 'Stop start: Survival, decline or closure? Children's centres in England, 2018', Sutton Trust, www.suttontrust.com/wp-content/uploads/2018/04/StopStart-FINAL.pdf

Stalford, H. (2019) 'The price is rights!: Cost benefit analysis and the resourcing of children's services', *Children and Youth Services Review*, 99: 395–407.

Timpson, E. (2019) 'Timpson review of school exclusion', Department for Education.

Welbourne, P. and Leeson, C. (2012) 'The education of children in care: A research review', *Journal of Children's Services*, 2: 128, edsemr.

Williams, K., Papadopolou, V. and Booth, N. (2012) 'Prisoners' childhood and family backgrounds', Ministry of Justice, www.gov.uk/government/publications/prisoners-childhood-and-family-backgrounds

Woolgar, M. (2013) 'The practical implications of the emerging findings in the neurobiology of maltreatment for looked after and adopted children: Recognising the diversity of outcomes', *Adoption & Fostering*, 37(3): 237-252.

Youth Justice Board (2015) 'Keeping children in care out of trouble: An independent review chaired by Lord Laming Response by the Youth Justice Board for England and Wales to the call for views and evidence', https://assets.publishing.service.gov.uk/media/5a807ebce5274a2e87dba227/YJB_response_Laming_Review_keeping_children_in_care_out_of_custody.pdf

8

Cracks in the food system: Food poverty, food aid and dietary health inequalities

Claire Thompson, Dianna Smith and Laura Hamilton

Introduction

Britain's rate of food poverty is among the worst in Europe, the number of food banks continues to rise and child hunger is now such a widespread problem that schools are giving out food to struggling families. The COVID-19 pandemic, the invasion of Ukraine and the cost of living crisis are all widely cited as the most recent drivers of worsening deprivation and failures in the food system, including increasing food prices. While these recent stressors have undoubtedly worsened poverty, inequality and hunger in the UK, they are not the cause. These were already well-established problems. As we will discuss, the State has had to endure the pressures of economic upheaval and conflict before, and it has done so without letting the diets and health of low-income households become collateral damage. However, in the contemporary sociopolitical context and under the leadership of the previous Conservative Government, (food) poverty was (and might still be) on the cusp of being accepted as an unfortunate, but largely inevitable, feature of modern Britain, and one that charities and faith organisations are best placed to mitigate.

Trends and differences in food and eating habits have long been a barometer of the functioning of institutions in society and the political ideologies that shape them. The war years and post-war period, up until

1954, were characterised by conflict and economic upheaval. And yet, that era saw a very different approach to food policy and the food system than the one we have today. The aim was to distribute food 'fairly'. Rationing, price controls, provision for special groups and arrangements for communal feeding were intended to safeguard the nation nutritionally (Murcott, 2002). These policies, based on need rather than market mechanisms, were successful. Nutritional inequalities were reduced (El-Sayed *et al.*, 2012) but not eradicated. As well as being deeply pragmatic, this approach pre-empted and developed alongside *'welfare capitalism'*[1] and the establishment of the post-war welfare state. The 1940s saw a major economic slump (Supple, 1999) and in response to this, national food policy was based on redistribution and need, as was social and economic policy. This is demonstrated in the creation of a National Health Service (NHS), the extension of council housing, the introduction of workplace canteens, cheap milk, universal social security, commitment to full employment, rent controls, food subsidies (Whiteside, 1996) and the 1944 Education Act, which made school meal provision a statutory duty for local authorities (Evans and Harper, 2009).

Food systems and welfare are intricately linked. Food policy is social policy. The breakdown of the post-war consensus in the 1980s and the widening inequality that ensued has been framed by many commentators as a failure of state social policy to protect the most vulnerable and marginalised from the ravages of market forces. Further, that it was an inevitable consequence of the neoliberalism that came to dominate British economics and governments (Lavalette and Penketh, 2003) and, by extension, their approach to food systems. For example, school meals were deregulated once again, and market mechanisms were introduced to their provision via the Education Act 1980 and the Local Government Act 1988.

The political discourse of the 1980s and 1990s was broadly accepting of corporatised globalisation as it took hold (Lang, 1999). This movement allowed for the systematic moulding of taste by giant corporations and the proliferation of cheap, processed and energy dense foods (Lang, 1999). It is people living in more deprived areas, as opposed to wealthier ones, who are more likely to be exposed to advertisements for this 'junk food' and more likely to consume it (Finlay *et al.*, 2022). The effects have been marked. The UK has the highest rate of childhood obesity in Europe, with an estimated 40 per cent of children overweight or obese, an increase from 35 per cent prior to the pandemic (NHS Digital, 2021).

Hunger and obesity are interconnected. They are both symptoms of an unequal society and, by extension, a failing food system. Those on low incomes do not have the means to purchase adequate food, and the foods they can afford tend to be high in energy and low in nutrients – leaving them the unenviable choice between foods that will make them ill and overweight or no food at all.

State retreat and the rise of food banking

In 2008 we saw a financial crisis and a sharp rise in global food prices. This was compounded in 2010 by the introduction of, what turned out to be, over a decade of austerity measures in the UK. As these cuts took hold, food banks and food poverty became embedded in public and policy discourses (Thompson, 2022). Austerity policies introduced by the Conservative– Liberal Democrat Coalition Government were a systematic programme of public spending cuts and tax rises, justified as a means of reducing the budget deficit and government debt, whilst helping the country recover from the effects of the financial crisis (Fairclough, 2015). While the funding and functionality of local health and welfare provision was being destabilised by cuts, an increase in demand for services was driven by ongoing benefit reforms that worsened income and health inequalities (Bambra *et al.*, 2018). It is difficult to overstate the violence of these austerity measures and the resulting hardship and hunger they caused (Cooper and Whyte, 2017). Between 2009 and 2017 the number of people earning less than a 'living wage' rose from 3.4 to 5.5 million, whilst the number of patients admitted to hospital with malnutrition trebled (Shannahan, 2019).

Charities and social enterprises were filling the gaps created by the state retreat and funding cuts, which put these organisations and the sector as a whole under immense pressure, as they often lacked the appropriate capacity and resources to provide consistent levels of service in the long term (Weaks, 2016). Welfare pluralism and a blurring of state and charity responsibilities for responding to hardship intensified (Birrell and Gray, 2016). The state narrative around the increasing role of charities and the third sector was framed positively as the 'Big Society', a flagship policy of David Cameron's 2010 Conservative Party general election campaign, subsequently becoming Coalition government policy (Cabinet Office, 2010). These trends were amplified by the roll-out of Universal Credit, which was beset by administrative errors and delays, resulting in financial hardship for claimants (Timmins, 2016; Newbigging et al., 2017; The Trussell Trust, 2018; Thompson et al., 2020a).

Food banks were the most prominent and pervasive incarnation of charities 'filling the gap' created by funding cuts. According to Sustain, an alliance of organisations working to improve the food system and tackle food poverty, there was only one reported food bank in the UK in 2000 (Hawkes and Webster, 2000). Twenty years on, appraisals from the Independent Food Aid Network (2023) estimate that there were at least 1,172 independent food banks and 1,393 Trussell Trust food banks operating across the UK. The 'need' for food banks has been widely debated, with some commentators questioning whether people used them simply because they were there, rather than because they were experiencing genuine hardship. As Lord Freud controversially stated, 'it is difficult to know which came first, the supply or the demand' (Hansard, 2 July 2013, Cl.1072).

Critics have positioned the food bank sector as an exemplar of the nexus of state retreat, precarity and volunteerism (Briggs and Foord, 2017). For example, between 2010 and 2013 Trussell Trust food banks distributed significantly higher numbers of food parcels in local authorities with specific characteristics of material deprivation, such as greater unemployment, benefits sanctions and cuts to government spending (Loopstra et al., 2015).[2] Further, the roll-out of Universal Credit was significantly associated with an increase in food bank use (Jenkins et al., 2021). Welfare reform more generally served to heighten the need for food banks, leaving people financially worse-off (Lambie-Mumford, 2014) and at the mercy of punitive welfare regimes (Cummins, 2016). As the state cut benefit support, the food bank sector responded and, in doing so, changed the welfare landscape *and* the food environment.

The food aid environment: a postcode lottery of locational disadvantage

As current trends in food poverty and food banking continue, the diets of those on low incomes are increasingly characterised by reliance on donated food. The new government's pre-election anti-hunger strategy may prove to challenge these trends. They will need to, given that food aid outlets, and food banks in particular, are now so prolific that they must be considered part of the food environment (Thompson *et al.*, 2019). At the same time, food banks operate as a form of poverty relief, redistributing food instead of income (Smith and Thompson, 2022), meaning that they must also be considered part of the welfare landscape. In fact, this is part of the normalisation of food banks as a new alternative safety net that has developed in response to failures of the state (Beck and Gwilym, 2022).

Unfortunately, as well as being over-stretched and working beyond capacity, food aid providers and outlets are not uniformly distributed around the country. Some people have better access to donated food than others. We often hear the term 'postcode lottery' in reference to access to NHS healthcare. It is equally apt in describing access to food aid. Explained simply, support for food insecurity is patchy and reflects where there is capacity for help – it flourishes where there is space to host a service and also sufficient volunteers to deliver it. We explored this in an early paper mapping risk of food insecurity against the locations of Trussell Trust centres for distribution (because no comprehensive database of food banks is available) and found no statistically significant association with the locations of these centres and either area deprivation (measured using the 2015 Index of Multiple Deprivation) or the food insecurity risk measure (Smith *et al.*, 2018). This highlighted the potential mismatch between food aid provision geographically and 'demand'. This is even before we consider the issue of limited opening hours for much food aid (Thompson et al., 2019).

As different food aid providers have different eligibility criteria, inequalities in access are inadvertently created where one food aid provider does not strictly limit access, while another aims to restricts support to a set number of food parcels within a limited time period (independent food banks vs Trussell Trust, for example). We have seen these differences in access to food banks even in local districts, such as the New Forest where the independent Basics Bank did not restrict access, but the two affiliated with the Trussell Trust asked clients to attend only six times each year. Therefore, if someone lives in the catchment area for the independent food bank, they will have access to much more donated food than people who must use those associated with Trussell Trust (Smith et al., 2021).

Food aid has, for some time now, been moving from the traditional food bank model to formats where people have higher agency and may not require a referral to attend, such as food pantries and community fridges. Sometimes they have to pay a nominal membership fee for access. In return, they get an experience that is a little bit more like shopping – they have some limited scope to choose which foods they want. Conversely, in these settings, we hear more examples of people choosing not to attend regularly when the products available do not match their preferences, such as when there is a lack of meat available for a sustained period. While this can be considered positive in terms of avoiding food wastage, such irregular attendance can also create challenges in planning for the food aid providers, where storage of fresh or frozen items may be problematic if there is not sufficient turnover of food. This demonstrates the precarity of demand as well as provision. Ultimately, food aid is outside of formal welfare provision and people who are food insecure and in need of immediate help are at the mercy of what is close to them, what they are eligible to use and what fits around any other work or caring commitments.

The food aid sector is a volatile one (May et al., 2019). Food banks can be set up and subsequently close down, merge or change the type of service they provide before local statutory services are aware of any change.

And there is no centralised 'registration' or process for establishing a food bank in the first place (Hamilton and Dickinson, 2021). As a result, statutory service providers, such as GPs or Job Centre staff, can refer clients in good faith to much needed support from food banks that are no longer operating. This means vulnerable clients can miss out on food aid support that could prevent them from slipping into destitution because the statutory agency they are interacting with does not have a well-developed policy on referral. In either case, it is the most disadvantaged who suffer from the lack of oversight and understanding. There has long been a clear locational disadvantage at play that impacts the food aid people can access geographically, temporally and administratively.

The 'public health crisis' of food poverty

Those on low incomes are often unable to afford enough food (Griffith et al., 2013), and the food that they can afford is typically poor in quality and high in salt, fat and sugar (Dinour et al., 2007). Such diets are associated with a range of conditions including hypertension, iron deficiency and impaired liver function (Markovic and Natoli, 2009; Dinour et al., 2007). Food poverty is a social determinant of health (Raphael, 2009) with prolonged episodes of food poverty linked to poorer mental health and obesity (Dinour et al., 2007; Jones, 2017; Elgar et al., 2021). Poor mental health costs health services in England over £40 billion each year (National Mental Health Development Unit, 2011) and spending on obesity-related ill health is forecast to rise to £9.7 billion per year by 2050 (Public Health England, 2017).

Since 2010, levels of material deprivation and the prevalence of mental health conditions have increased dramatically (British Medical Association, 2016) and improvements in life expectancy have stalled (Royal Society for Public Health, 2018; Office for National Statistics, 2018; Raleigh, 2022). Provision and quality of free school meals (FSMs) in different areas is uneven, with restrictive criteria that excludes some groups (Holloway et al., 2014; Royston et al., 2012). Food banks have proliferated, and the number of food parcels handed out to families has risen dramatically. In addition, welfare support has routinely been withheld by successive UK governments as a tool for controlling immigration (O'Connell and Brannen, 2019; Hamilton *et al.*, 2022). Food poverty has become a recognised public health and social justice crisis.

As with structural inequalities and injustices more generally, the COVID-19 pandemic and lockdowns served to both exacerbate the ongoing crisis of food poverty and cement the expectation that the food aid system, rather than the state, is responsible for trying to tackle it. After years of dismantling and stripping away public services and funding, the UK was ill-equipped to keep the nation fed as the pandemic rolled-on. The uncertainty and interruptions to the economy as a result of lockdowns and mitigation measures disrupted global and local food systems and traditional supply chains, causing food shortages and anxiety amongst consumers (Hobbs, 2020). These disruptions served to limit access to fresh food, tilting the balance towards greater availability and consumption of highly processed long-life foods (Tan *et al.*, 2020). The impacts of food system issues were, and look set to continue being, more severe for those on low incomes and those living in deprived communities (Cummins *et al.*, 2021; Hamilton and Dickinson, 2021; Hamilton *et al.*, 2022). In July 2020, part one of the 'National Food Strategy' was launched in response to the COVID-19 pandemic, recommending urgent action to address dietary inequalities and food poverty for children (Dimbleby, 2020). Not enough was done or has been done since to address these problems.

The end of March 2020 (after the first lockdown was announced) saw the biggest spike in Universal Credit claims to date, with 500,000 new claimants applying in just nine days (Ball and Gye, 2020). The pandemic also drove the rise in demand for food banks to an all-time high (Beck and Gwilym, 2022). The food bank sector responded to the crisis and there was an outpouring of voluntary support for people who were struggling with food and other necessities, but it was not enough. Food banks were struggling to keep up with growing need before the pandemic and the restrictions brought all manner of new challenges with it. For example, many experienced volunteers in food banks had to stay at home to isolate due to their age (a substantial proportion of volunteers are older people) and/or health conditions because they were at greater risk from COVID-19. This made it difficult for food banks to maintain a reasonable level of staffing, reducing their capacity to respond to people's needs (Thompson et al., 2020b; Hamilton and Dickinson, 2021).

All hands on deck: wide ranging efforts to address food poverty

As the food poverty crisis rolled on and the impacts of COVID-19 and the lockdowns increased in severity, a mix of people, professionals and organisations were caught up in efforts to tackle it. Food banks obtain their food stock from a variety of sources, including public donations, other charities and retail outlets. There is competition between food aid providers for this stock. Established food banks have long had relationships with supermarkets and organisations like FareShare, so they have regular and guaranteed sources of food to distribute and are not left reliant solely on donations. When the lockdowns started, there was a groundswell of goodwill and community support, with many ad hoc groups setting up food provision in their own communities and trying to help by 'setting up their own food bank'. Never have the public been so actively involved in food aid. However, as community-driven responses, these were not always linked to a charity or an established food bank with ties to existing retail or food aid systems. Yet, they were still connecting with suppliers within these systems to obtain enough food to distribute. In doing so, they further disrupted the food system and the supply chain to food banks, diverting food from established charities and providers that those experiencing food poverty had come to rely on.

There were also concerns about the conditions within which food was being stored and distributed (e.g., from household garages) by 'pop-up' food banks (Hamilton and Dickinson, 2021). Providing food aid, at any scale, is not a straightforward or simple process. Established food banks and similar organisations have become adept at considering factors around food safety, environmental health and risk management. Although food banks started out as a temporary measure, they now operate as part of a complex and organised system of food provision. Food aid providers have had to recalibrate their networks in response to this added complexity and ensure that issues such as competition for stock and food storage concerns do not negatively impact the populations using their services.

Some local authorities went to extraordinary lengths during the pandemic to ensure that low-income families were fed (Thompson et al., 2020b). However, they simply did not always have the funds and/or infrastructure to feed the large and growing number of children and young people in the way they wanted and needed to. Food parcels as replacements for FSMs were not always adequate in quantity or quality, nor substantive enough for the child's needs, as seen by the various photographs posted on social media at the time. And whilst the vouchers were welcomed and provided families with some choice, cash-payment via child benefit or Universal Credit were preferred (Thompson et al., 2020b). Ultimately, disruptions to the food system and the disproportionate impact on those on lower incomes led to renewed calls for greater public health-led government intervention to prevent and address food poverty, and for cash-first responses to alleviate poverty (Power et al., 2020; Hamilton and Dickinson, 2021).

Hungry children

More than four million children in the UK live in households affected by food insecurity. Numbers have continued to rise throughout the pandemic and beyond (Goudie, 2022). Schools and teachers have long been involved in trying to mitigate and ameliorate food poverty for the children they teach and their families. Austerity measures resulted in widespread poverty and hardship for families which, in turn, prompted the development of a variety of child feeding initiatives in schools and community settings to combat child hunger. Increasing numbers of children simply did not have enough to eat at home, leading to schemes such as breakfast clubs and holiday hunger initiatives becoming an essential part of school and local government provision (Lambie-Mumford and Sims, 2018).

Cracks in the food system

The COVID-19 pandemic resulted in severe disruptions to food provision in schools. This was particularly significant for children eligible for FSMs, which are usually given as a hot or cold meal in school, but this was not possible due to school closures. This exacerbated existing issues with what was an already inadequate and restrictive FSM provisions (Holloway et al., 2014; Royston et al., 2012). Free school meals are not only important for the child's diet, but also for the diets of others in the household (Acheson, 1998) and are vital for the most disadvantaged children living on the lowest incomes (O'Connell et al., 2019). For some, this meal will be the *only hot meal* they eat that day (Rodrigues, 2012).

Applications for FSMs increased as the lockdowns progressed, and more families were pushed into financial hardship and had to claim Universal Credit. Across the country, local authorities, charities and schools had to arrange replacements, such as food parcels or supermarket vouchers, typically £15– £20 per week per child. These 'alternative provisions' varied and were sometimes woefully inadequate (Parnham et al., 2020). In some cases, teachers were hand-delivering vouchers and FSM food parcels to families' front doors (Kim and Asbury, 2020), whilst in others, parents were expected to pick these up in-person from the school. The national voucher scheme (run by Edenred), set-up to distribute FSM vouchers to families, was beset by administrative issues early on, albeit temporarily, leaving families without this vital benefit. Even the children of 'key workers', who were still able to attend school during lockdowns, did not always receive a hot meal (Rose et al., 2021).

The ongoing scandals around FSM provisions during the pandemic attracted a great deal of media coverage, commentary and outrage. Easily the most pertinent example of this is from the professional footballer Marcus Rashford, who was moved to establish a Child Poverty Taskforce: a coalition of charities and food businesses that successfully campaigned to expand entitlement to FSMs and to extend funding for provision into the school holidays (O'Connell and Brannen, 2020). His lobbying has made him an unexpected advocate for children experiencing food poverty. While his work, and that of other campaigners, is valuable, what is really needed is more efficient and sustainable solutions to (food) poverty, such as increases to benefits (Sinha *et al.*, 2020) or cash-first responses.

Post-lockdowns, these efficient and sustainable solutions have yet to materialise and the future for FSMs is unclear. A commitment to the policy has been abandoned in Scotland, while Wales is rolling it out. In England, the London Mayor, Sadiq Khan, has committed FSMs to all children attending state primary schools in London while he's mayor. The new Prime Minister, Kier Starmer, has yet to commit to FSMs. In the meantime, the task of addressing child hunger continues to be taken up by a range of sectors and actors, largely without central state-led coordination or acknowledgement. The cost of living crisis has amplified child hunger and, once again, widened the remit and responsibilities of schools and teachers. Hundreds of schools across the country are running their own food banks, inside schools, to make sure children and their families have enough to eat. Teachers give up their personal time, money from school budgets and sometimes food from their own homes to make this work (McRae, 2022). In a way, food banks in schools can be seen as a logical progression from breakfast clubs and holiday hunger initiatives. Schools are becoming progressively more entangled in providing poverty relief and the mitigation of state failure. It is difficult to see how this can be undone, how schools in low-income neighbourhoods will ever be able to go back to focusing on education rather than ameliorating crises.

Conclusion

Food systems are the outcome of policy and political choices; food is contested territory (Lang, 1999). The food system of pre-pandemic Britain was already under strain, with the proliferation of unhealthy diets, growing levels of food poverty and widening dietary health inequalities. COVID-19 and the resulting mitigation measures heaped yet more pressure on welfare and voluntary services and highlighted the inequities and failings of the UK food system (Dimbleby, 2020). The Conservative Government's Levelling Up agenda, vague at best, never really tackled the issue. In fact, its policies amplified the drivers of food poverty. The ongoing rise of food banks and obesity, the (arguably) poor response to the national food strategy and the impeded economic recovery from the pandemic and Brexit continue to have very real, material impacts on people's ability – or lack thereof – to have a healthy and affordable diet.

The cost of living crisis, in particular, is making things worse still for those on low incomes. Rising prices, tax increases, energy price hikes, social security cuts and stagnating wages are pushing millions of families beyond breaking point (Patrick and Pybus, 2022).

In World War Two and the post-war years, a time beset by economic problems, an interventionist approach to food policy was employed to make sure that vulnerable groups were fed. While this approach was far from perfect and could not eradicate long-standing inequalities (Murcott, 2002), it was much more comprehensive than the fragmented and multi-sector nature of contemporary responses to food poverty. The advocacy and provision efforts of the charities, communities and even celebrities that have been drawn into food poverty awareness and provision are noble and the work done is important. However, it is not a substitute for an effective safety net that protects people from the depths of (food) poverty. Nowhere is this more apparent than in relation to child hunger.

Notes

1 The era of post-World War Two capitalism characterised by a concern for the welfare of various social groupings expressed usually through social-security programs, collective-bargaining agreements, state industrial codes and other guarantees against insecurity (Esping-Anderson, 1990).
2 The analysis is only reflective of the 251 local authorities in which Trussell Trust food banks were operational in during 2013 and does not include any independent food aid outlets or food banks open, but not associated with the Trussell Trust, at the time.

References

Acheson, D. (1998) 'Independent inquiry into inequalities in health', Department of Health and Social Care, www.gov.uk/government/publications/independent-inquiry-into-inequalities-in-health-report

Ball. J. and Gye, H. (2020) 'Coronavirus latest: Universal credit claims surged after support for self-employed was announced', *iNews*, 29 March, https://inews.co.uk/news/coronavirus-universal-credit-claims-surged-support-self-employed-413417

Bambra, C., Garthwaite, K. A. and Greer Murphy, A. (2018) 'Geopolitical aspects of health: Austerity and health inequalities', in A. Bonner (ed.) *Social Determinants of Health: An Interdisciplinary Approach to Social Inequality and Wellbeing*, Policy Press, Bristol.

Beck, D. and Gwilym, H. (2022) 'The food bank: A safety-net in place of welfare security in times of austerity and the covid-19 crisis', *Social Policy and Society*, 22(3): 545–561.

Birrell, D. and Gray, A. (2016) *Delivering Social Welfare: Governance and Service Provision in the UK*, Policy Press, Bristol.

Briggs, S. and Foord, M. (2017) 'Food banks and the transformation of British social welfare', *Czech and Slovak Social Work/Sociální Práce/Sociálna Práca*, 17: 72–86.

British Medical Association (2016) 'Health in all policies: Health, austerity and welfare reform. A briefing from the board of science', www.bma.org.uk/media/2086/bos-health-in-all-policies-austerity-briefing-2016.pdf

Cabinet Office (2010) 'Building the Big Society', www.gov.uk/government/publications/building-the-big-society

Cooper, V. and Whyte, D. (2017) (eds) *The Violence of Austerity*, Pluto Press, London.

Cummins, I. (2016) 'Wacquant, urban marginality, territorial stigmatization and social work', *Aotearoa New Zealand Social Work*, 28: 75–83.

Cummins, S., Berger, N., Cornelsen, L., Eling, J., Er, V., Greener, R., Kalbus, A., Karapici, A., Law, C., Ndlovu, D. and Yau, A. (2021) 'COVID-19: Impact on the urban food retail system and dietary inequalities in the UK', *Cities and Health*, 5: S119–S122.

Dimbleby, H. E. A. (2020) 'The National Food Strategy: Part one', www.nationalfoodstrategy.org/wp-content/uploads/2020/07/NFS-Part-One-SP-CP.pdf

Dinour, L. M., Bergen, D. and Yeh, M. (2007) 'The food insecurity-obesity paradox: A review of the literature and the role food stamps may play', *Journal of the American Dietetic Association*, 107: 1952–1961.

El-Sayed, A. M., Scarborough, P. and Galea, S. (2012) 'Unevenly distributed: A systematic review of the health literature about socioeconomic inequalities in adult obesity in the United Kingdom', *BMC Public Health*, 12.

Elgar, F. J., Pickett, W., Pförtner, T. K., Gariépy, G., Gordon, D., Georgiades, K., Davison, C., Hammami, N., MacNeil, A.H., Azevedo Da Silva, M. and Melgar-Quiñonez, H.R. (2021) 'Relative food insecurity, mental health and wellbeing in 160 countries', *Social Science Medicine*, 268:113556.

Esping-Andersen, G. (1990) *The Three Worlds of Welfare Capitalism*, Princeton University Press, Princeton, NJ.

Evans, C. E. L. and Harper, C. E. (2009) 'A history and review of school meal standards in the UK', *Journal of Human Nutrition and Dietetics*, 22: 89–99.

Fairclough, I. (2015) 'Evaluating policy as argument: The public debate over the first UK austerity budget', *Critical Discourse Studies*, 13: 57–77.

Finlay, A. H., Lloyd S., Lake, A., Armstrong. T., Fishpool, M., Green, M., Moore, H. J., O'Malley, C. and Boyland, E. J. (2022) 'An analysis of food and beverage advertising on bus shelters in a deprived area of Northern England', *Public Health Nutrition*, 25(7):1989–2000.

Goudie, S. (2022) 'New data show 4 million children in households affected by food insecurity', The Food Foundation, www.foodfoundation.org.uk/publication/new-data-show-4-million-children-households-affected-food-insecurity

Griffith, R., O'Connell, M. and Smith, K. (2013) 'Food expenditure and nutritional quality over the Great Recession', Briefing Note (BN143), Institute for Fiscal Studies.

Hamilton, L. and Dickinson, A. (2021) 'Informing the Hertfordshire food poverty needs assessment: Household experiences of food poverty and support service provision in Hertfordshire. Hatfield', Centre for Research in Public Health and Community Care (CRIPACC) University of Hertfordshire, https://arc-eoe.nihr.ac.uk/sites/default/files/uploads/files/Hamilton%20%20Dickinson%202021%20-%20Informing%20the%20Hertfordshire%20Food%20Poverty%20Needs%20Assessment_0.pdf

Hamilton, L., Thompson, C. and Wills, W. (2022) 'Hostile environments: Immigration and food poverty in the UK', University of Hertfordshire, Hatfield, https://doi.org/10.18745/pb.25713

Hansard (2013) 'Food: Food banks', debated in the Lords Chamber, Vol.746, 2 July, Cl.1072, https://hansard.parliament.uk/Lords/2013-07-02/debates/13070283000459/FoodFoodBanks

Hawkes, C. and Webster, J. (2000) *Too Much and Too Little? Debates of Surplus Food Redistribution*, Sustain, London.

Hobbs, J. E. (2020) 'Food supply chains during the COVID-19 pandemic', *Canadian Journal of Agricultural Economics*, 68: 171–176.

Holloway, E., Mahony, S., Royston, S. and Mueller, D. (2014) 'At what cost? Exposing the impact of poverty on school life', The Children's Society, London, https://basw.co.uk/policy-and-practice/resources/what-cost-exposing-impact-poverty-school-life#:~:text=This%20report%20explores%20the%20impact,on%20the%20cost%20of%20school

Independent Food Aid Network (2023), 'Mapping the UK's independent food banks', www.foodaidnetwork.org.uk/independent-food-banks-map

Jenkins, R. H., Aliabadi, S., Vamos, E. P., Taylor-Robinson, D., Wickham, S., Millett, C. and Laverty, A. A. (2021) 'The relationship between austerity and food insecurity in the UK: A systematic review', *EClinicalMedicine*, 33: 100781.

Jones, A. (2017) 'Food insecurity and mental health status: A global analysis of 149 countries', *Journal of Preventative Medicine*, 53: 264–273.

Kim, L. E. and Asbury, K. (2020) '"Like a rug had been pulled from under you": The impact of COVID-19 on teachers in England during the first six weeks of the UK lockdown', *British Journal of Educational Psychology*, 90: 1062–1083.

Lambie-Mumford, H. (2014) 'Food bank provision and welfare reform in the UK', SPERI British Political Economy Brief No. 4, Sheffield Political Economy Research Institute.

Lambie-Mumford, H. F. and Sims, L. (2018) '"Feeding hungry children": The growth of charitable breakfast clubs and holiday hunger projects in the UK', *Children and Society*, 32(3): 244–254.

Lang, T. (1999) 'The complexities of globalization: The UK as a case study of tensions within the food system and the challenge to food policy', *Agriculture and Human Values*, 16: 169–185.

Lavalette, M. and Penketh, L. (2003) 'The welfare state in the United Kingdom', in C. Aspalter (ed.) *Welfare Capitalism around the World*, Casa Verde, Hong Kong.

Loopstra, R., Reeves, A., Taylor-Robinson, D., Barr, B., McKee, M. and Stuckler, D. (2015) 'Austerity, sanctions, and the rise of food banks in the UK', *BMJ*, 8:350:h1775.

Markovic, T. P. and Natoli, S. J. (2009) 'Paradoxical nutritional deficiency in overweight and obesity: The importance of nutrient density', *Medical Journal of Australia*, 190: 149–151.

May, J., Williams, A., Cloke, P. and Cherry, L. (2019) 'Welfare convergence, bureaucracy, and moral distancing at the food bank', *Antipode*, 51: 1251–1275.

McRae, I. (2022) 'Teachers are setting up food banks in schools to help families in the cost of living crisis', *Big Issue*, 12 September, www.bigissue.com/news/social-justice/teachers-are-setting-up-food-banks-in-schools-to-help-families-in-the-cost-of-living-crisis/

Murcott, A. (2002) 'Food and nutrition in post-war Britain', in P. Catterall and J. Obelkevich (eds.) *Understanding Post-War British Society*, Routledge, London.

National Mental Health Development Unit (2011) 'Factfile 3: The costs of mental ill health', Policy into Practice, London.

Newbigging, K., Mohan, J., Rees, J., Harlock, J. and Davis, A. (2017) 'Contribution of the voluntary sector to mental health crisis care in England: Protocol for a multimethod study', *BMJ Open*, 7: e019238.

NHS Digital (2021) 'National Child Measurement Programme, England 2020/21 school year', https://digital.nhs.uk/data-and-information/publications/statistical/national-child-measurement-programme/2020-21-school-year/age

O'Connell, R. and Brannen, J. (2019) 'Food poverty and the families the state has turned its back on: The case of the UK', in H. P. Gaisbauer, G. Schweiger and C. Sedmak (eds.) *Absolute Poverty in Europe: Interdisciplinary Perspectives on a Hidden Phenomenon*, Policy Press, Bristol.

O'Connell, R. and Brannen. J. (2020) 'What food-insecure children want you to know about hunger', *The Conversation*, 14 September, https://theconversation.com/what-food-insecure-children-want-you-to-know-about-hunger-146140

O'Connell, R., Knight, A. and Brannen, J. (2019) 'Living hand to mouth: Children and food in low-income families', Child Poverty Action Group, https://cpag.org.uk/news/living-hand-mouth

Office for National Statistics (2018) 'Changing trends in mortality in England and Wales: 1990 to 2018', www.ons.gov.uk/peoplepopulationandcommunity/birthsdeathsandmarriages/deaths/articles/changingtrendsinmortalityinenglandandwales1990to2017/1990to2018

Parnham, J. C., Laverty, A. A., Majeed, A. and Vamos, E. P. (2020) 'Half of children entitled to free school meals did not have access to the scheme during COVID-19 lockdown in the UK', *Public Health*, 187: 161–164.

Patrick, R. and Pybus, K. (2022) 'Cost of living crisis: We cannot ignore the human cost of living in poverty', *BMJ*, 377.

Power, M., Doherty, B., Pybus, K. J. and Pickett, K. E. (2020) 'How COVID-19 has exposed inequalities in the UK food system: The case of UK food and poverty', *Emerald Open Research*, 2.

Public Health England (2017) 'Health matters: Obesity and the food environment', www.gov.uk/government/publications/health-matters-obesity-and-the-food-environment/health-matters-obesity-and-the-food-environment-2

Raleigh, V. (2022) 'What is happening to life expectancy in England?', The King's Fund, 10 April, www.kingsfund.org.uk/publications/whats-happening-life-expectancy-england

Raphael, D. (2009) *Social Determinants of Health: Canadian Perspectives*, Canadian Scholars' Press, Toronto.

Rodrigues, L. (2012) *'Food for thought: A survey of teachers' views on school meals'*, British Association of Social Workers.

Rose, K., O'Malley, C., Brown, L., Ellis, L. J. and Lake, A. A. (2021) 'Pizza every day – why?': A survey to evaluate the impact of COVID-19 guidelines on secondary school food provision in the UK', *Nutrition Bulletin*, 46: 160–171.

Royal Society for Public Health (2018) 'RSPH deeply concerned by short-sighted cuts to public health budget', 21 September, www.rsph.org.uk/about-us/news/rsph-deeply-concerned-by-short-sighted-cuts-to-public-health-budgets.html

Royston, S., Rodrigues, L. and Hounsell, D. (2012) 'A policy report on the future of free school meals', The Children's Society, https://d3hgrlq6yacptf.cloudfront.net/5f3ecf1e68cdc/content/pages/documents/1429471607.pdf

Shannahan, C. (2019) 'The violence of poverty: Theology and activism in an 'age of austerity', *Political Theology*, 20: 243–261.

Sinha, I. P., Lee, A. R., Bennett, D., McGeehan, L., Abrams, E. M., Mayell, S. J., Harwood, R., Hawcutt, D. B., Gilchrist, F. J., Auth, M. K. and Simba, J. M. (2020) 'Child poverty, food insecurity, and respiratory health during the COVID-19 pandemic', *The Lancet Respiratory Medicine*, 88: 762–763.

Smith, D., Parker, S., Harland, K., Shelton, N. and Thompson, C. (2018) 'Identifying populations and areas at greatest risk of household food insecurity in England', *Applied Geography*, 91: 21–31.

Smith, D. and Thompson, C. (2022) *Food Deserts and Food Insecurity in the UK: Exploring Social Inequality*, Routledge, London.

Smith, D., Wilson, L., Paddon, L., (2021) 'The cost of living in the New Forest', https://newforestcab.org.uk/wp-content/uploads/2022/01/Cost-of-Living-New-Forest-Report.pdf

Supple, B. (1999) 'British economic decline since 1945', in R. Floud and D. McCloskey (eds.) *The Economic History of Britain Since 1700*, Cambridge University Press, Cambridge.

Tan, M., He, F. J. and MacGregor, G. A. (2020) 'Obesity and covid-19: The role of the food industry', *BMJ*, 369.

Thompson, C. (2022) 'The emergence of "food poverty" as a research topic', in D. Smith and C. Thompson (eds.) *Food Deserts and Food Insecurity in the UK: Exploring Social Inequality*, Routledge, London.

Thompson, C., Guise, A., Edgar, R., Solly, S. and Burrows, M. (2020a) *Universal Credit: The Health Impacts for People who are Experiencing Homelessness*, Groundswell, London.

Thompson, C., Hamilton, L., Dickinson, A., Fallaize, R., Mathie, M., Rogers, S. and Wills, W. (2020b) 'The impact of Covid-19 and the resulting mitigation measures on food and eating in the East of England: Interim Report', NIHR ARC East of England and University of Hertfordshire, Hertfordshire.

Thompson, C., Smith, D. and Cummins, S. (2019) 'Food banking and emergency food aid: Expanding the definition of local food environments and systems', *International Journal of Behavioral Nutrition and Physical Activity*, 16.

Timmins, N. (2016) 'Universal Credit: From disaster to recovery?', Institute for Government.

Trussell Trust (2018) 'Left behind: Is Universal Credit truly universal?', https://s3-eu-west-1.amazonaws.com/trusselltrust-documents/Trussell-Trust-Left-Behind-2018.pdf

Weaks, L. (2016) 'The training and development needs of the health charity sector: What 20 years' experience tells us', The King's Fund, 1 July, www.kingsfund.org.uk/blog/2016/06/training-and-development-health-charity-sector

Whiteside, N. (1996) 'Creating the welfare state in Britain, 1945–1960', *Journal of Social Policy*, 25: 83–103.

9
What happened to all the anti-racists?
John Narayan

Introduction

In two moments, 2020 seemed to reveal what British anti-racists had been telling anyone who would listen for over 60 years: Britain has a racism problem. As the COVID-19 pandemic unfolded across the globe and the epicentre moved to Europe, racism and Britain took centre stage. In a whirlwind of daily Boris-led briefings, policy blunders and rising infection and death rates, Britain's Black, Asian and ethnic minority (BAME) populations seemed to be dying at higher rates than their white counterparts. At first, somewhat ironically, racist biological arguments that BAME people were more predisposed to Covid or suffered from a lack of vitamin D were mustered to explain this phenomenon (Busby, 2020). Yet, what really explained these issues were the structural conditions of poverty, overcrowded housing and precarious work that afflict many of Britain's BAME communities.[1] What also became clear was that, from taxi drivers to bus drivers to NHS workers, the backbone of what became seen as 'essential' work in Britain was and is being done by Britain's BAME communities. Quite simply, institutional practises that see BAME people over-represented across poverty indicators and within bad working conditions – the effects of structural and institutional racism[2] – exposed BAME people to the virus more often and, therefore, they died more frequently (Lawrence, 2020).

What went wrong with Britain?

The second moment happened within the first. On 25 May 2020, the murder of George Floyd, a Black American man, by a police officer in Minneapolis, Minnesota, and the release of footage of his arrest and murder, saw a second iteration of the Black Lives Matter (BLM) movement and mass uprisings across the United States. In the UK, the trans-Atlantic diffusion of anti-racism that had once seen Black Power migrate from the Caribbean and US to these shores in the 1960s, and the first iteration of BLM in 2014, happened once more (for more information on how BLM in the UK fits into a wider history of resistance to policing by Britain's Black communities, see Elliott-Cooper, 2021). BLM protests exploded across the UK with the most famous image of such protest being the dumping of Edward Colston's statue into the very Bristol Harbour from which his fortune had been accrued. The reenergising of BLM in the UK during the summer of 2020 highlighted the institutional racism of the police but also racism across employment, education and health. The reality of racism in Britain was again confirmed in the summer of 2024 as orchestrated far-right riots targeted hotels housing asylum seekers, immigration advice centres and mosques. This series of racist and Islamophobic attacks, which had been engendered by state racism and mediatic mainstreaming of hate, saw the far-right appropriate the tragic murders of Bebe King, Elsie Dot Stancombe and Alice da Silva Aguiar, aged 6 to 9, at a Taylor Swift-themed holiday club in Southport, Merseyside.

The second iteration of BLM, and contemporary British anti-racism more generally, has in large part become animated by an abolitionist framework. Policing and prison abolition calls for a recognition that policing and prisons do not safeguard the public but rather exacerbate social problems generated by capitalist social relations. As Adam Elliot-Cooper points out, such abolitionism does not demand the end of the penal system immediately, but rather the realisation that other methods and other institutions – which empower communities to deal with the kind of economic and social inequalities that give rise to the need for such carceral institutions and practices – must be sought (Elliott-Cooper, 2021). Abolitionism – which can and is applied to other facets of social life beyond the penal system – thus rejects a longing for state authority

What happened to all the anti-racists?

through highlighting the links between state violence, capitalist exploitation and the reproduction of racism and patriarchy. The idea is that we must find our future beyond state-controlled organisations – pushing us to imagine non-racist, non-patriarchal, non-transphobic and non-capitalist futures within our communities. Abolition thus conjoins abolishing prisons and borders and defunding the police with building institutions, practices and ways of living that liberate us all (for the US context, see Purnell, 2021; for the UK context see Day and McBean, 2022).

Covid and BLM opened a conversation around the nature of racism in British history and contemporary society. However, one of the largest anti-racist mobilisations in British history was met with a pincer movement between the state and the corporate world. In the face of calls for institutional change came a plethora of half measures where everyone and everything claimed to be an anti-racist. Global banks such HSBC, super-exploitative corporations such as Nike and even England's hyper capitalist Premier League embraced the calls for BLM with corporate statements and plans for equality and diversity, but – as we shall see – without really reckoning with the relationship between race and class needed to make anti-racist change. BLM's new economy of anti-racism engendered entrepreneurial community spokespeople, talking heads and so-called radical authors who now sell products such as self-help books for white people, unconscious bias training and anti-racist workshops for *Guardian* readers.

This was accompanied by an even stronger counter by the British state, which initially had seen the then Prime Minister Boris Johnson recognise the 'incontrovertible, undeniable feeling of injustice, a feeling that people from Black and minority ethnic groups do face discrimination: in education, in employment, in the application of the criminal law' (Stewart, 2020). Johnson had been quick, however, to juxtapose this acknowledgement with a need to also obey the state's Covid rules in order to discourage protests. In the weeks and months that followed, characters such as the then Home Secretary, Priti Patel, criticised the protests and called for a greater extension of police powers; whilst the then Equalities Minister Kemi Badenoch criticised BLM as anti-capitalist and argued that schools that backed it were breaking the statutory duty to be politically impartial. Labour's position, which had initially seen the leader of the opposition take the knee on the date of George Floyd's funeral, now saw Keir Starmer decry that he has no 'truck' with 'nonsense' such as defunding the police and restated his law-and-order credentials as the former Director of Public Prosecutions. A week later, in the face of public criticism of his take on BLM, Starmer claimed he would sign up to unconscious bias training. A promise that seemingly remains unfulfilled as the Labour Party secured a landslide election victory in July 2024 that saw Starmer assume the role of Prime Minister.

The confirmation of the state's closing of ranks over debates about racism was confirmed with the government's creation of the Commission on Race and Ethnic Disparities (CRED) in the wake of BLM – with CRED given the brief of investigating race and ethnic disparities in the UK. The appointment of Munira Mirza, who spent eight years as Boris Johnson's deputy mayor for culture in London, and who criticised what she called its 'culture of grievance' of anti-racism, to set-up CRED was heavily criticised. The subsequent appointment of Tony Sewell, who has cast doubt on the existence of institutional racism, to lead CRED intensified the feeling that the government was attempting to sideline issues of institutional racism. Indeed, the publication of the report in March 2021 denied institutional racism was an issue in Britain (Commission on Race and Ethnic Disparities, 2021). Whilst the report acknowledged issues of structural racism as 'historic' but not contemporary, it pitched some ethnic minorities against others. The report focused on differences between communities, primarily in educational attainment and elite employment, but made no attempt to address common ethnic minority experiences of structural racism within areas such as the criminal justice system, employment and housing. For example, Black Caribbeans were compared with Black Africans, and deemed to have culturally internalised past injustices to the detriment of their own social advancement. As the Institute of Race Relations outlined, the 'report fit neatly with the government's attempts, post-Brexit, to portray the British nation as a beacon of good race relations and a diversity model', in the report's words, for

What happened to all the anti-racists?

'white majority countries across the globe' (Institute of Race Relations, 2021).

In the four years since the eruption of BLM during the summer of Covid, the anti-racist future dreamed of back then feels distant. The institutional statements around BLM are largely unfulfilled, the over-policing of Black communities continues, and the British state has embarked on a culture war against migrants, trans people, climate change activists, anti-racists and just about anybody else that challenges its power and policies. How did we get from BLM and abolition to CRED and the government's gaslighting of contemporary anti-racism? And what are our hopes for an anti-racist future? The next two sections seek to provide answers to these questions. The next section outlines how the history of British anti-racism that emerged in the middle of the twentieth century and the strategy the British state used to contain British anti-racism is key to understanding why those who hit the streets in the cause of BLM were given CRED rather than real change. The final section outlines how the abolitionism of BLM may yet be a key resource for rethinking society in the current crisis of neoliberalism.

The denial of race and class

Modern British anti-racism emerged as post-war British state racism targeted 'coloured' British citizens and new commonwealth migrants from Africa, Asia and the Caribbean. On this basis, a collective 'Black' political subject – which included all non-white migrant communities – was used to create a political identity and praxis. This identity was the foundation for anti-racist cooperation and solidarity between these communities in the pursuit of racial justice and underpinned grassroot community campaigns and institutional initiatives against racist immigration controls, police brutality, racist discrimination in the workplace, housing and education and the threat of racial violence. This approach to anti-racism underpinned iconic anti-racist movements such as British Black Power groups, the Asian Youth Movements and anti-racist Trade Union activity up until the 1980s (Sivanandan, 1981; see also Narayan, 2019).

What went wrong with Britain?

What defined this era of British anti-racism was an appreciation of 'racism' rather than 'racialism'. The latter term, often confused for racism, can be used for everyday personal prejudice, but the former is seen as institutional power. For British anti-racism, racism was primarily animated and diffused into popular racism and institutionalised by the state apparatus, and its relation to capital and imperialism. Racism is thus defined by laws, constitutional conventions, judicial precedents and institutional practices – all of which have the 'imprimatur of the state'. This state racism entrenches discrimination for some and death for others often in the service of economic exploitation:

> In a capitalist state, that power is associated with the power of the capitalist class and racial oppression cannot be disassociated from class exploitation. And it is that symbiosis between race and class that marks the difference between the racial oppressions of the capitalist and pre-capitalist periods. The fight against racism is, therefore, a fight against the state which sanctions and authorises it – even if by default – in the institutions and structures of society and in the behaviour of its public officials. (Sivanandan, 2019)

This anti-racism was not simply focused on divisions of UK class relations but also the global link between race and class and what W.E.B. Du Bois had famously called the problem of the twentieth century: 'the colour-line'. During decolonisation and driven by mass movements and the failures of capitalist development, the 'darker nations' of the 'Third World' were drawn loosely together through a shared history of being the victims of western imperialism and continuing targets of western neo-imperialism. Through organisations such as the Non-Aligned Movement, G77 and the UN Conference on Trade and Development, the so-called Third World nations embarked upon a 'Project' to remodel geo-economic and geopolitical structures towards liberation and justice for those whose subjection had helped create the bounty of capitalist modernity (Prashad, 2007).

British anti-racism thus combined the struggle with minority rights at home with solidarity with the struggles of the global majority abroad and bound anti-racism with anti-imperialism and anti-capitalism. Racialised communities 'over here' were literality taken to be 'Third World' people from 'over there'. This linked the struggles of minoritised communities

What happened to all the anti-racists?

in Britain with the activities of the US Black Panther Party, Australian Aboriginal rights activism, national liberation struggles in Africa and Asia, the post-colonial struggles of the Dalits in India and struggle against settler colonialism in Palestine. This anti-imperialism also allowed anti-racists to move beyond simply embracing binary definitions between First (white) vs Third (Black) World forms of oppression. Anti-racists in the 1960s and 1970s regularly indicted non-white dictators in so-called Third World states and formed solidarity with Irish republicans – who had been kicked out, or rather not yet allowed into, the category of whiteness. In this sense, anti-racism did not make sense without anti-imperialism, and anti-imperialism did not make sense without anti-racism (Narayan, 2019).

In response to British anti-racism, and its idea of racism, the British state offered cultural explanations for the effects of institutional racism – poverty, poor housing, educational disadvantage – on Britain's minority communities. Minority communities were thus simply culturally maladjusted or unable to assimilate into and succeed in the British way of life. This line of reasoning took centre stage in the early 1980s when the neoliberal revolution was accompanied by an emergent form of neoliberal anti-racism, which was embraced by the state and successive governments as a response to militant forms of British anti-racism. As Arun Kundnani points out, neoliberal ideology is based on a tension between the expansion of universal market relations in society and the need to defend market relations from communities, groups and states that would question the ethics and economics of such market relations within and beyond the state. The neoliberal state has therefore used two methods of racialisation to deal with this tension. The first has been to racialise and demonise (e.g., welfare scroungers, Black muggers, illegal immigrants) the very 'surplus populations' (working class, migrants) generated by the neoliberal economy's dispossession and to use such 'deviant' figures to expand policing and securitisation (e.g., policing, border control) of such 'surplus populations'. This helped to bolster and deflect from the effects of the neoliberal market relations – such as deindustrialisation, privatisation, welfare retrenchment and rising inequality (Kundnani, 2023).

What went wrong with Britain?

The second method has been to use such a racialised idea of 'deviancy' to explain away anti-racist questioning of neoliberal ideals. The neoliberal state has thus often used racialised ideas to explain such groups as simply not possessing the correct traits to succeed in a neoliberal society. For example, on the back of the 1981 urban rebellions by communities across Britain against institutional racism and police brutality – most famously in Brixton – the Scarman report centred the definition of racism away from structural and institutional explanations towards cultural and individualist explanations such as Caribbean family values and second-generation minority identities (the political fallout from Scarman's report is discussed in Sivanandan, 2019). The link between state racism, exploitation and global inequality was thus declared ethereal to understanding racism and replaced with static ideas of cultural disadvantage and the need to expand entrepreneurism amongst racially disadvantaged groups.

As Shafi and Nagdee (2021) outline, the state's reaction to British anti-racism in the early 1980s was to usher in a form of 'anti-racism from above' that looked to contain the radical demands of British anti-racism through a form of 'multiculturalism'. This saw minority communities, movements and groups encouraged by the state to disarticulate racisms around distinct and separate ethnic communities and categories (e.g., Black, Asian, Muslim). Instead, communities who suffered from structural and institutional racism were now encouraged to compete with one another as market actors to obtain economic resources and policy attention from the state – even when their goal was to obtain less attention from the state. These processes also saw the state domesticate issues of racism as matters of the nation state. Anti-racism was now infused with ideas of national market correctives and representational equality: Black and Brown faces in state and business offices, across screens and on sports pitches. This neoliberal form of anti-racism was about inclusion into the system – for an emergent minority petit bourgeoise – rather than institutional transformation.

The British state's response to BLM, and through it the CRED report, should be best understood as adhering to this idea of neoliberal anti-racism: the severing of race from class, a focus on culture and representation over institutional or structural issues, and the reducing of racism to the problems of individuals or groups and disaggregating minority groups so that they cannot collectively make claims on the state. The hallmark of this was that contributors to the CRED report were almost all eminent ethnic minorities – being drawn from the world of business and science – but not anti-racism or social research. Whilst the report looked inclusive it lacked the inclusion of people who could have conducted research on institutional racism and thus was rejected, near universally, as unscientific and lacking credibility (Bourne, 2021). Indeed, the very Conservative government that commissioned the report was a mirror image of this neoliberal approach to anti-racism – with the most ethnically diverse Cabinet in British history rejecting the very idea of institutional racism and its links to economic and political forms of inequality.

It should also be clear now why BLM and its abolitionist politics garnered such a reaction from the British state. BLM's abolitionism – which ties anti-racism to anti-capitalism – mirrors elements of Britain's anti-racist movement of the past. Moreover, UK activists took an abolitionist framework – which has its own distinct British history – and applied it to the current UK context. This included rethinking ideas of policing not in a context of the rampant expansion of police budgets – as in the US – but in the context of a decade of austerity, welfare retrenchment and the expansion of policing and surveillance within and beyond the police. For example, Day and McBean (2022) show that abolitionist articulations of the nature of racism as being tied to state violence make it impossible to think through racist policing practises, such as the Met Police's Gangs Matrix, without thinking through how this is linked to Islamophobic state surveillance practices such as Prevent and how such practices draw on old (Empire) and more recent imperial counter insurgency logics (the War on Terror) abroad. The Gang Matrix, which is an intelligence database compiled by the Metropolitan Police to rank individuals by their risk of gang violence, is structured by racist ideas of Black criminality: 78 per cent of the entries are Black – despite Black people making up only 27 per cent of youth violence convictions – and around 35 per cent of those on the list have never committed a serious crime but rather have found themselves on the Matrix by association with peers. The Gang Matrix is eerily similar to the state Prevent programme, which uses institutions such as the school and university to criminalise parts of the Muslim community. What Day and McBean highlight is that both forms of state racism expanded and were operationalised through the wider geo-economics and geo-politics of the War on Terror and the systemic shocks of the global financial crisis of 2008–9.

UK abolitionist analysis more generally links the expansion of state racism and carceral forms of punishment through and within a global economy that super-exploits racialised labour, where arms companies provide the means for authoritarian dictators to maintain power over their people, and states police the victims of such neoliberal globalisation through murderous border policies. Abolition thus rejects the idea that you can simply reform the system: increasing ethnic minority representation in higher income jobs, border and police forces, and government positions or supplying training around 'unconscious bias' is very unlikely to deal with conditions that demand state racism in the first place. What abolition proposes is a series of 'non-reformist reforms' across society rather than revolution. Sarah Lamble provides a great example of one of these 'non-reformist reforms' around policing and mental health, where rather 'than training police to better deal with people in mental distress, non-reformist reforms call for resources to be redirected to non-police-based crisis intervention and prevention services' (Lamble, 2022). Abolition thus calls for the rethinking of the institutions and practices around anti-racist – and by default anti-capitalist – objectives through community empowerment and institution building. And it is abolitionism's twining of economic critique and its belief in the democratic empowerment of communities that have made it so reviled by the state.

Racist or anti-racist futures?

The dismissal of issues raised by BLM and abolitionism by the state is best summed up by then Prime Minster Rishi Sunak's backing of an extension of police powers in light of the 2023 Casey Review's report on

What happened to all the anti-racists?

the Metropolitan Police, which claimed widespread 'racism, misogyny and homophobia' in the UK's biggest police force. The Casey Review had been commissioned following the murder of Sarah Everard in 2021 by a serving Metropolitan police officer. Indeed, such has been the deprioritising of anti-racism that only six months earlier a news channel claimed that a protest march over the police shooting of Chris Kaba, a Black man, was in fact a crowd of people mourning the death of Elizabeth II (Waterson, 2022). Yet, despite this dismissal by the state and media, the march for Chris Kaba also highlighted that despite the reality of an entrenched state and institutional racism, there still existed an agency from below that refused to accept such a reality. What I want to suggest in the close of this piece is that the moment of anti-racism, and ideas of abolition, may yet find their time and space as the crisis of the global economy challenges the very nature of Britain's political economy and its politics.

For some the current global economy is characterised by a crisis. A few commentators, such as George Meadway (2021) and Paolo Gerbaudo (2021), have recently suggested that neoliberalism is dying or in a process of retreat. This crisis hasn't come out of nowhere: the neoliberal global economy has been zombie-like since the 2008 global financial crisis, and not only are the effects of climate change making the economy harder to globalise but profiteering and war have also caused recent inflationary spikes. During the disruption to global commodity chains caused by the COVID-19 pandemic, free market policies that have dominated the global economy for the past forty years appeared to have less purchase. These authors point to a reversion to a national form of capitalism and protectionism, the questioning of globalisation and a return of state intervention in the economy. The causes of this anti-neoliberal turn are located within both right- and left-wing movements against the effects of neoliberalism and the rise of China as a real geopolitical rival to US interests. The prime example here is the Biden regime's approach to the US economy, which has turned to deficit driven social spending, an expansion of union rights and protectionist measures to public procurement. The retreat of neoliberalism this offers is a possible opening – through a critique of globalisation and the return of the state. Here, a rejuvenated politics of the left may be able to avoid the pitfalls of an emergent authoritarian capitalism and launch a new national form of progressive politics around welfare policies (for an overview of the end of neoliberalism discourse see Krhuna and Narayan, 2021).

Britain had appeared more of an outlier to these sea changes in international and national political economy – with the previous Conservative Government laying down plans for another round of austerity rather than state intervention. With the economy stagnant and inflation high there was no surprise that British state racism was mobilised as bread and circus for the country. Hence, the regular briefings from the Home Office about the 'invasion' of asylum seekers and the culture war against the 'woke' and the demonisation of a plethora of agency from below that confronted the state: anti-racists and prison abolitionists (BLM), climate and ecological activists (Extinction Rebellion, Just Stop Oil) and feminist direct-action groups (Sisters Uncut).

This reflected the familiar neoliberal strategy of the state creating deviant figures to deflect from the defectiveness of the economy but also the expansion of real forms of institutional power – as Frances Webber has eloquently highlighted, the British state, through legislation (including the Police, Crime, Sentencing and Courts Bill, the Nationality and Borders Bill, the Overseas Operations Act, the Elections Bill and the Judicial Review and Courts Bill), has been entrenching 'impunity for officials and ministers, while filling prisons and immigration detention centres and further criminalising marginalised communities, dissenters and human rights defenders' (Webber, 2022). For all the rejection of state intervention into the economy – at least in the interest of the majority of its people – the British state expanded the reach of its racialised authoritarianism.

The current Labour government seem intent on shifting some elements of the previous government's approach to the economy – with a focus on capital spending on infrastructure projects to deflect from cuts to welfare and tax rises. But the government's approach to a fallout from the far-right riots of 2024 reveals a continuity with Britian's history of racialised authoritarianism. Keir Starmer was quick to narrate the riots as a law-and-order issue – changing the subject of the riots from the far-right to the more nebulous threat posed by 'criminality' and 'thuggery' and the need for greater integration (Fekete, 2024). This has allowed to the state to separate their own responsibility for engendering and creating a hostile environment for migrants and Muslims in Britian. Thus, on one hand, the Labour government has framed the riots as a community cohesion issue – allocating £15million to fund local authority–voluntary sector partnerships in areas affected by the riots. However, as Runnymede Trust Director, Shabna Begum, has pointed out, community cohesion frameworks that home in on a lack of 'integration' amongst different communities as the cause of 'riotous violence' underplay the role that state racism and austerity have played in fragmenting communities (Begum, 2024).

On the other hand, the framing of the riots as a law-and-order issue has again allowed the state to expand its own powers. Rather than counter anti-migrant discourse, the current government has launched a major new drive in immigration enforcement and returns activity – expanding its Border Security Command to combat people smugglers and smash 'the gangs' – perpetuating anti-migrant government policy. In tandem, prosecutions over the riots have seen the state claim violent thuggery exists on both sides of the political spectrum – with custodial sentences for those who partook in far-right orchestrated rioting and also for those (mainly Muslim) who sought to defend their communities. For example, the fourteen-month prison sentence handed out to Noman Ahmed, who had no previous convictions, for throwing a punch at two white men while attempting, as the judge accepted, to protect a mosque in Middlesbrough that had been targeted by racists. The state's attempt to protect law and order denies any distinction between aggressor and defender, and thus denies the distinction between racist violence and anti-racist self-defence, continuing the approach of demonising progressive agency from below (Institute of Race Relations, 2024).

More hopefully, after decades of trade union acquiescing in the face neoliberal reform, Britain's workers appear to have rediscovered their militancy. Faced with the legacy of under-investment and wage freezes after a decade of austerity and the current cost of living crisis, workers across Britain's quasi-public sector (railway, education, communication and health care workers) have embarked on a scale of industrial action not seen for 40 years. Is this the return of the economic clout of the working class that we thought lost for four decades? It is too early to say yes but what we can say is that there has been a sea change in worker militancy – with more workers prepared to collectively act and, importantly, the public supporting such action. We can also say that this approach has garnered results with the Labour government committing to a number of public-sector pay deals. As Britain faces international (from other states) and domestic pressures (from its workers) against its neoliberal settlement, what I want to suggest is that the generation who declared their support for BLM and abolitionism have a pivotal role to play in such politics.

Conclusion

Writing on the back of the 1981 rebellions of Black youth across Britain in response to the state authoritarianism and racism that underpinned Thatcher's launching of Britain's neoliberal era, the legendary Director of the Institute of Race Relations, Ambalavaner Sivanandan, wrote:

> it is not merely that a free-market economy requires a law-and-order state but that, even in its passing, it leaves only the option of a mixed economy with a corporate state maintained by surveillance. They are but two shades of the same authoritarianism, the one more modern than the other, but neither speaking to the birth of a new society. (Sivanandan, 1981)

What Sivanandan was arguing was that anti-racists could not simply let the supplanting of a neoliberal society be a return to ideas of social democracy and the racism and imperialism that underpinned such a society. Indeed, Sivanandan would argue later in the decade against the idea that anti-racism, feminism and green politics were new social movements divorced from working class politics. Rather, he suggested that the 'richest political seams' of the working class were to be found in such movements, which had the capacity to help steer class politics away from economism and expand the idea of class struggle and the very idea of socialism itself (Sivanandan, 2019).

What happened to all the anti-racists?

The recent return of class politics in Britain offers an opportunity for a new settlement over forms of economic inequality and democracy – but echoing Sivanandan, without the anti-racism of the summer of 2020 this will not be the birth of a new society. If the free market state in Britain and beyond is in trouble, then the role of anti-racism appears to be to help birth a new society that is not simply a return to a securitised form of social democracy that Sivanandan warned us about in the 1980s. This requires that, along with worker demands for higher wages and better working conditions, such a return of class politics demands an end to that super-exploitation of racialised and gendered labour, the end of state violence against women, the end of imprisoning working-class people abandoned by the state and economy, and the dismantling of the border regimes that target those whose worlds have been torn apart by imperialism and the effects of climate change.

Elements of this sort of anti-racist politics can be found in the anti-racist response to the ongoing occupation and military offensive of Israel in Gaza and the wider Middle East, and the UK's far-right riots of 2024. Israel's military assault on Gaza, which has seen 40,000 plus Palestinian deaths (40 per cent being children) and the systematic destruction of Gaza's economic and civil infrastructure in response to the killing of over 800 Israeli civilians on October 7, 2023 has been ruled by the International Court of Justice (ICJ) to possibly fall under the genocide convention. The ICJ ruling in January 2024 that declared that Palestinians in Gaza had plausible rights under the Genocide convention, and its conclusion that they were at risk of irreparable damage, has been replicated in sentiment by anti-racist campaigning and protest in the UK – which has questioned the racist dehumanisation of Palestinian life in the media and in domestic and international politics. This has seen demands for the end of the occupation of Palestinian land and divestment from the arms manufacturers and companies linked to Israel spread across university campuses (with continued solidarity marches across the UK in the hope of achieving a ceasefire); groups conducting direct action against UK arms manufactures who supply components to the Israeli military; and the wider political demand that Britain itself stops commissioning arms licences for arms sales to Israel. The return of an internationalist form of anti-racism that recognises the link between race, class and imperialism can be found across Britain.

Indeed, the far-right's orchestration of riots in the summer of 2024 – which was in part an Islamophobic response to such anti-racist solidarity with Palestine – has also garnered a response and discussion of anti-racist self-defence and progress. This has seen the return of conversations – recovered partly from the 1970s and 1980s and from groups such as the Asian Youth Movement – on how to foster unity against racism and fascism at street level and also tying such anti-racist unity to trade union activity, whether by making sure bosses secure worker safety or the reorientating of divisive debates about migration to issues such as austerity and inequality in Britain.

Along with questioning the neoliberal settlement of the British state, what this anti-racist activism highlights is that people, groups and movements are still raising anti-racist (and, indeed, abolitionist) questions about institutions and practices, such as policing, prisons, bordering and militarisation. Indeed, as the trial of the armed officer for the murder of Chris Kaba resulted in a non-guilty verdict the questions about policing of the Black community and the state's sanctioning of lethal force have been forced back into the public sphere by campaigners and activists. Thus, although seemingly relegated to a eulogy of equality, diversity and inclusion, the summer of BLM – and the promise of a new anti-racist society it heralded – continues to haunt the current crisis of capital and democracy. After reading all of this, and understanding the link between race and class, the only question that remains is: are you still an anti-racist?

Notes

1 For example, approximately under one in five Bangladeshi workers and over one in ten Pakistani workers are paid below the national minimum wage compared to three in one hundred white workers. A quarter of BAME workers, excluding Indian workers, are paying housing costs that are unaffordable, compared with 10 per cent of white workers. Poverty rates among BAME individuals are also much higher than the white British majority – and even more so among

children. Pre-pandemic, more than half (52 per cent) of Bangladeshis, including more than two-thirds of Bangladeshi children (67 per cent), were in poverty after housing costs. For more stats on ethnic inequalities in the UK please see Mirza and Warwick (2022).

2 We can define structural racism as the outcome, here paraphrasing Ruth Wilson Gilmore's (2022) definition of racism, of a 'state-sanctioned and/or extra-legal production and exploitation of group-differentiated vulnerabilities'. Institutional racism here translates into how institutions reproduce racist outcomes that perpetuate structural racism. See also Elliott-Cooper (2023).

References

Begum, S. (2024) 'Community cohesion won't stop the far-right' *Tribune*, 13 September, https://tribunemag.co.uk/2024/09/community-cohesion-wont-stop-the-far-right

Bourne, J. (2021) 'Sewell: A report for neoliberal times', Institute of Race Relations, 20 April, https://.irr.org.uk/article/sewell-a-report-for-neoliberal-times/

Busby, M. (2020) 'UK public health bodies reviewing vitamin D's effects on coronavirus', *Guardian*, 17 June, www.theguardian.com/world/2020/jun/17/uk-ministers-order-urgent-vitamin-d-coronavirus-review

Commission on Race and Ethnic Disparities (2021) 'Commission on Race and Ethnic Disparities: The Report', https://assets.publishing.service.gov.uk/government/uploads/system/uploads/attachment_data/file/974507/20210331_-_CRED_Report_-_FINAL_-_Web_Accessible.pdf

Day, A. S. and McBean, S. O. (2022) *Abolition Revolution*, Pluto Press, London.

Elliott-Cooper, A. (2021) *Black Resistance to British Policing*, Manchester University Press, Manchester.

Elliott-Cooper, A. (2023) 'Abolishing institutional racism', *Race & Class*, 65(1): 100–118.

Fekete, L. (2024) 'Stop changing the subject: The problem is fascism', Institute of Race Relations, 4 August, https://irr.org.uk/article/stop-changing-the-subject-the-problem-is-fascism/

Gerbaudo, P. (2021) *The Great Recoil*, Verso, London.

Gilmore, R. W. (2022) *Abolition Geography: Essays towards Liberation*, Verso, London.

Institute of Race Relations (2021) 'Sewell report seeks to sideline structural factors attached to racism', 31 March, https://irr.org.uk/article/irr-responds-to-commission-race-ethnic-disparities-report/

Institute of Race Relations (2024) 'Combatting the far-right: Different roads can lead to the same destination', 23 August, https://irr.org.uk/article/combatting-the-far-right-different-roads-can-lead-to-the-same-destination/

Krhuna, I. and Narayan, J. (2021) '(After) Neoliberalism? Rethinking the return of the state', *Discover Society: New Series* 1(4), https://discoversociety.org/2021/12/06/after-neoliberalism-rethinking-the-return-of-the-state/

Kundnani, A. (2023) *What is Antiracism? And Why it Means Anticapitalism*, Verso, London.

Lamble, S. (2022) 'Bridging the gap between reformists and abolitionists: Can non-reformist reforms guide the work of prison inspectorates?' Institute for Crime and Public Policy Research, 22 March, www.icpr.org.uk/news-events/2022/bridging-gap-between-reformists-and-abolitionists-can-non-reformist-reforms-guide

Lawrence, D. (2020) 'The Lawrence Review: An avoidable crisis. The disproportionate impact of Covid-19 on Black, Asian and minority ethnic communities', Labour Party, https://uploads-ssl.webflow.com/5f5bdc0f30fe4b120448a029/5f973b076be4cadc5045fad3_An%20Avoidable%20Crisis.pdf

Meadway, J. (2021) 'Neoliberalism is dying – now we must replace it', openDemocracy, 3 September, www.opendemocracy.net/en/oureconomy/neoliberalism-is-dying-now-we-must-replace-it/

Mirza, H. and Warwick, R. (2022) 'Race and ethnicity: IFS Deaton Review of Inequality', The Institute of Fiscal Studies, https://ifs.org.uk/inequality/

Narayan, J. (2019) 'British Black Power: The anti-imperialism of political blackness and the problem of nativist socialism', *The Sociological Review*, 65(5): 945–947.

Prashad, V. (2007) *The Darker Nations: A People's History of the Third World*, The New Press, New York.

Purnell, D. (2021) *Becoming Abolitionists: Police, Protests, and the Pursuit of Freedom*, Verso, London.

Shafi, A. and Nagdee, L. (2021) *Race to the Bottom: Reclaiming Anti-racism*, Pluto Press, London.

Sivanandan, A (1981) 'From resistance to rebellion', *Race & Class*, 23(2/3): 111–52.

Sivanandan, A (2019) 'RAT and the degradation of black struggle', in A. Sivanandan, *Communities of Resistance*, Verso, London.

Stewart, H. (2020) '"I hear you": Boris Johnson to Black Lives Matter protesters', *Guardian*, 8 June, www.theguardian.com/us-news/2020/jun/08/i-hear-you-boris-johnson-to-black-lives-matter-protesters

Waterson (2022) 'Ofcom investigates Sky News over Chris Kaba protest mix-up', *Guardian*, 26 September, www.theguardian.com/media/2022/sep/26/ofcom-investigates-sky-news-over-chris-kaba-protest-mix-up

Webber, F. (2022) 'Impunity entrenched: the erosion of human rights in the UK', *Race & Class*, 63(4): 56–80.

10

Gender, austerity and crisis in an age of catastrophe

Frankie Rogan and Emma Foster

Introduction

From the perspectives of two UK-based academics who were girls and young women in the nineties and noughties, this chapter tells a story about gender politics in Britain over the last thirty years. Like the story of Britain itself, it is a story of decline. Starting from the hopeful 1990s, characterised by the zeitgeist of postfeminism, where young (largely white, cis-gender, middle-class) women looked all set for a bright and fulfilling (economic) future, we trace the erosion of that promise to meet the here and now, in an era of seemingly continual crises. Along the way we demonstrate two things. First, that the non-fulfilment of the postfeminist promise that so heavily characterised the cultural terrain of the 1990s and 2000s is entwined with, and even contributed to, Britain's lack of resilience in the face of various shocks. Second, that on this journey through various crises, individuals who benefitted least from the supposed 'postfeminist' era have felt that decline even harder.

In telling this story, we identify 2010 as a pivotal moment when the Conservative–Liberal Democrat Coalition Government implemented an austerity agenda that entrenched gender, and other, inequalities; derailing any semblance that the objectives of feminism had been satisfied through neoliberal capitalism. This is because, in attempting to protect the socio-economic status quo, austerity measures further entrenched and exacerbated long-standing gendered inequalities. This entrenchment has intensified through more recent crises (Blundell *et al.*, 2020), hindering the country's internal and external capacity to respond, particularly when dealing with acute public health problems (e.g., COVID-19) (Scally *et al.*, 2020; Duncan, 2022), severe budgetary and financial pressures (e.g., the cost of living crisis) (Bailey and Tomlinson, 2022) and the effects of chronic environmental degradation (Crowther *et al.*, 2022).

The following, then, begins by setting the scene between 1997–2007, a decade dominated by discourses of 'girl power', 'choice' and individualised forms of 'gender equality'. We then turn to focus on the pivotal moment when, in 2007–8, the markets crashed and, more crucially, Britain responded with drastic austerity measures that have since become the norm in UK economic policy. At the time of writing, the first few months of a new Labour government has signalled more of the same, as Keir Starmer and Rachel Reeves take every opportunity to prepare the country for more misery in advance of the government's first budget in October 2024. Despite introducing pay rises for public sector workers and vague assertions that public services will be protected under a Labour government, the continual talk of 'tough decisions' and things 'getting worse before they get better' makes it difficult to see any substantial deviation from what has become the norm for many. We frame the beginning of this era of austerity as a 'sliding doors' moment where the postfeminist promise was broken. From this historical juncture we pan out to discuss the wider repercussions of austerity, consequently broadening our own focus to assess how gender, cut across by other intersectional identities, has fared in the context of the so-called culture wars. And finally, we unpack the gendered dynamics of COVID-19 and the cost of living crisis, arguing that the austerity that so heavily impacted on women's lives and shattered the illusion of the 'postfeminist promise' has, relatedly, hobbled Britain politically, culturally and economically.

The promise of postfeminism: Sociocultural gender-based violence

Before the financial crash of 2007–8, women in the UK never had it so good – or so they were told. A heady combination of postfeminism and neoliberalism coalesced in such a way as to construct the popular belief that 'real' gender inequality was a 'thing of the past'. It was repeatedly stated, even as far back as the late 1970s, that the various successes of the second-wave feminist movement meant that feminism was no longer relevant to the lives of a new generation of women, who were now – apparently – operating on an equal playing field to men (Mendes, 2011: 551). After women's legal equality was supposedly secured under legislation such as the Equal Pay Act of 1970 and the Sex Discrimination Act of 1975, feminism was gradually transformed from a radical oppositional movement to an 'institutionalised form of common sense' (Rogan and Budgeon, 2018: 5). This transformation meant that the once political goal(s) of gender equality were depoliticised and individualised through discourses of individual choice. In turn, feminist rhetoric could be (and often was) used to reproduce, rather than challenge, the status quo. Through supposedly granting legal equality, it thereafter became possible to explain away any remaining inequalities in both the public and private spheres as down to individual 'choice' and personal preference. For example, the gender pay gap was – and continues to be – explained through essentialist discourses that suggest women's consolidation in part-time, contingent and low-paid work is down to their 'natural' predilection for particular occupations (such as service and/or care work) and, relatedly, their supposedly biological urge to take on the bulk of (unpaid) domestic and reproductive work. As notions of 'choice' and 'freedom' became ideologically tied to the construction of femininity and increasingly individualised, the development or maintenance of a coherent feminist movement became progressively more difficult. Indeed, within this postfeminist context, unequal relations of power could always be explained away by the need to respect individual 'choice', with no real analysis of the structures that bind, shape or constrain the choices available.

What went wrong with Britain?

The media and popular culture played a key role in producing and disseminating this belief in postfeminism. Becoming particularly pronounced in the 1990s and 2000s, discourses of 'girl power' produced 'new femininities', which rested heavily on neoliberal ideals of 'empowerment', choice, individualism and self-actualisation (Gill and Scharff, 2011). For young women (specifically young, white, middle-class women), these discourses represented the opportunity for new and exciting subjectivities as specific demographics of young women were increasingly encouraged to be self-sufficient, career-driven (within limits) and economically independent. Living in the aftermath of the second-wave feminist movement, British girls, like many girls in the West, were presented as having 'the world at their feet' (Harris, 2004: 13) and became metaphors for the social change and progress that had been witnessed since the 1970s. As such, an obvious shift took place, wherein girls and young women became the primary focus of various public policies, non-governmental programmes and cultural markets (Harris, 2004). Within these contexts, then, young western women were increasingly positioned as key consumers and skilled choice makers, 'the stake upon which the future depends' (McRobbie, 2000: 201). As previously mentioned, these discourses were particularly pronounced and hegemonic during the 'postfeminist decade' of 1997–2007 (McRobbie, 2012).

The end point of this 'postfeminist decade' being pinpointed as 2007 is, of course, important. As detailed in the next section of this chapter, the landscape of Britain post-2007 was changed considerably by a post-recessionary terrain shaped by austerity and increasing precarity, which often disproportionately targeted women (Budgeon, 2018; Pearson, 2019), as well as young people (McDowell, 2012; Ryan, 2019). This contrasted sharply with the images of economic prosperity and neoliberal self-actualisation that were presented to young people – particularly young women – in the 1990s and early-to-mid 2000s. The global financial crash of 2007–8 and the onslaught of austerity measures that followed resulted in a distinctly different economic landscape wherein the 'postfeminist girls' of the 1990s entered the labour market, often to be confronted by precarious, insecure and low-paid regimes of employment, unaffordable housing and few opportunities for the social mobility that they had been promised. These issues cannot be attributed only to the immediate period following the financial crash of 2007–8, as challenges around work, housing and the cost of living have increasingly worsened in the years since and show no signs of impending change.

Austerity and the precarity of the postfeminist promise

This chapter characterises the economic policy decisions of the newly elected Conservative–Liberal Democrat Coalition in 2010 to embark on a programme of punishing spending cuts (Blyth, 2013) as a pivotal moment in recent British history. This acceptance of austerity as the only policy option (Basu, 2019) endured until a global pandemic came along in 2020 (at which point a huge financial stimulus was essential to keep the weak pulse of the economy alive) and looks set to fiercely resume as countries, including the UK, begin to 'recover' and face manifold economic crises in the form of inflationary pressures, labour shortages and hikes in the cost of energy.

Despite the 2010 Coalition's catchphrase 'we're all in it together', austerity was not, by any stretch of the imagination, experienced equally – impacting the most vulnerable in society and disproportionality affecting women, including young women who only three to four years prior had been assured they could 'have it all'. At the time, austerity measures left 'none but the most privileged in the UK ... untouched' (Cooper and Whyte, 2017: 9), exposing how precarious the promising future set out for young women had (perhaps always) been. In other words, in this economic moment, the opportunities that (mostly white, middle-class, university-educated) women had been told to expect in early adulthood were not, in fact, readily available – although access to these opportunities continued to be structured by social class and 'race' (see Allen, 2016). The cultural representation of femininity as a vanguard for optimism and dynamism gave way to a post-recessionary articulation of 'young women's anger, insecurity, anxiety, and misplaced confidence' (Dobson and Kanai, 2019: 771). These conditions exposed the 'cruel optimism' of postfeminism as the promise of the 1990s and 2000s came unstuck and the reality of a grossly unequal world set in (Berlant, 2011).

And what of the reality of a grossly unequal world? Simply speaking, in seeking to reduce public expenditure, austerity usually works to the disadvantage of the most vulnerable in society. The UK, during the initial phases of austerity in the 2010s, saw drastic cuts to public sector services, changes to benefits eligibility, a reduction in state support for third sector services and, subsequently, a growing reliance on the charitable sectors (cutely packaged under the moniker of the 'Big Society'). The legacy of these cuts, as well as the persistence of the austerity project – which was only temporarily interrupted to salvage the economy during the global pandemic – have affected and continue to affect the most vulnerable, where gender intersects with other characteristics – notably class, age, ethnicity, sexuality and disability – to compound the experiences of the hardest hit (Durbin and Conley, 2010). In fact, data from the Women's Budget Group, an independent non-profit network set up in the wake of the 2007–8 financial crisis to promote gender equality in the economy, estimated that while young women may be facing unexpected precarity, it was lone parents, most of whom are women, and women pensioners who felt the biggest reduction in living standards in 2010, with lone parents seeing an 18 per cent reduction to income and women pensioners seeing a 12 per cent reduction (Women's Budget Group in Ginn, 2013: 31).

In terms of job security and family income, it is well documented that the recession following the 2007–8 financial crash initially saw a sharp rise in male unemployment, with male-dominated sectors, such as manufacturing and construction, feeling the brunt of the initial effects (Rubery and Rafferty, 2013: 129). In addition, the austerity policies that were put in place as a response subsequently decimated the public sector jobs market. Given their disproportionate representation in this market, women were primarily affected. Moreover, the generally high levels of men's unemployment at the time increased the importance of women's wages to (nuclear, heterosexual) family income, especially as household finances were squeezed. This found more women, across generations, taking on part-time and precarious work out of necessity rather than choice (Rubery and Rafferty, 2013).

However, this economic violence cannot be reduced to a simple calculation of income and job security equating to positive living standards. The consequences were far more pervasive and acute for many women. For instance, the cuts to the public sector meant that those public sector workers who remained employed, many of whom were and still are women, suffered increasingly challenging working conditions. The reduction in financial assistance from the state for important services, including women's refuges and rape crisis centres, meant that crucial, sometimes lifesaving, support for many women experiencing intimate partner and gender-based violence was severely reduced. And the promise of the Coalition's 'Big Society' project –where the retraction in state provision and support, particularly for health and care, was made on the basis that charities and individuals would address the gap – relied on the unpaid labour of volunteers and individual carers, many of whom were and still are women. As such, beyond a reduction of income, many women saw their experience of everyday life deteriorate due to miserable working conditions, increases in unpaid labour and a reduction in support services (Durbin *et al.*, 2017). The consequences of austerity were thus felt by women both 'in and out of work' (2017: 2). This was due to the double helix of benefits cuts and a reduction in public sector employment resulting in women, who are more likely to be in receipt of benefits or/and work in the public sector, being disproportionately impacted by the economic violence of austerity.

Gender in the crossfire of the culture wars

The austerity agenda in Britain from 2010 put an end to the illusion of the postfeminist dream and worked to entrench gender inequalities – felt by most women, but particularly low-income women and those from other marginalised and minoritised groups (based on age, ethnicity, race, sexuality, disability). Against this backdrop, a renewed cultural and political interest in feminism emerged. As the era of postfeminism was characterised by a focus on women's supposed unfettered choice and individual self-actualisation, 'feminism' as a political goal had fallen out of favour. Indeed, McRobbie notes that the 'ritualistic denunciation of feminism' (2004: 258) amongst girls and young women was common in the 1990s and 2000s, as they instead narrated their lives through discourses of choice and individualisation (Budgeon, 2001). However, in the 2010s, the word 'feminism' returned to the cultural lexicon and, by 2014, experienced something of a revival within popular culture, with a specific form of 'popular feminism' becoming commercially embraced (Banet-Weiser, 2018). However, while also witnessing a new generation of feminists (see Cochrane, 2013), the 2010s set in motion a populist politics in Britain that, too, had serious implications for gender and, indeed, feminism. It is to a discussion of Britain's brand of populist politics that this chapter now turns.

Contemporary British populism is stronger on the right, at least culturally and politically (Inglehart and Norris, 2016). At its core, British populist politics is both nationalist and jingoistic, frequently drawing life-force from stimulating anti-immigration sentiment (Koch, 2017). So much so that the vote to leave the European Union in 2016, and the subsequent Brexit, is regarded by many as the ultimate expression of that sentiment to date (Koch, 2017). Populism operates by way of constructing an idea of 'the people' – people who have been ignored, even injured, by a corrupt establishment and for whom only populist leaders can speak. As such, populism functions through manufacturing a simplistic view of society irreconcilably and antagonistically split in two: 'the people' and 'the corrupt elite' (Mudde, 2014). While populist politics can be found across the political spectrum, right-wing populism (as opposed to left-wing populism that tends to focus its attention on challenging financial elites) is deliberately divisive and antagonistic, pitching certain groups against others (Mouffe, 2022). In Britain, while the corrupt elite and 'the people' are presented as making up the opposing forces in what is commonly described as the culture wars, only some groups are included as 'the people' while others – for instance feminists – are positioned as being in cahoots with the elite. This task was perhaps made easier by the fact the (popular) feminist revival of the 2010s was so heavily shaped by the regular endorsement of wealthy celebrity women. In the 2010s, for example, media outlets often listed their 'top' feminist celebrities (Alter, 2014; Jang, 2017; Najjar, 2015), with women such as Emma Watson, Angelina Jolie and Beyonce hailed for their feminist credentials.

Right-wing in flavour, 'the people' in Britain's populist politics tend to be those who feel aggrieved by multiple, complex socio-economic shifts. These individuals and groups have been attracted to a politics that demonises 'political correctness' (PC); encouraging 'the people' to identify this (which can be read as progressive values or, what's derogatorily termed by the right, as 'wokeness') as the locus of their dissatisfaction. The spectrum of 'progressive' values that constitutes the PC folk devil of the culture wars goes beyond a belief in gender equality and feminism to include anti-racism, pro-migration, trans rights, environmentalism and vegetarianism/veganism (where even 'meat-free-Mondays' can be equated with gratuitous woke-ness). The values that make up the other side (deliberately and provocatively) stand in stark contrast – being the active negation of those principles aligned with 'progressiveness' (McNeill and Harding, 2021) and modernisation (Kerr et al., 2018). These two sides are the battling forces in the so-called culture wars. While there are multiple economic and sociopolitical explanations as to Britain's most recent iterations of populist politics and the related culture wars divided along the lines of the populist right and progressive left/liberals (for a good summary see Clarke and Newman, 2017), ultimately these cleavages find traction in the disenchantment of groups who have felt ignored by the political elite; including low-income groups whose living standards have been decimated through the austerity measures outlined above (Koch, 2017) as well as the middle classes who, while not experiencing impoverishment, acutely perceive a Britain in economic decline (Kurer, 2020). However, rather than locating their disenchantment in the austerity measures that whittled down living standards, right-wing populist political actors have harnessed this distress to aggravate and manufacture a war on progressive values – including values related to gender equality and gender expression. These culture wars, we argue here, have had damaging implications for feminism and gender politics. While the election of a new Labour government in July 2024 suggests that this particular brand of right-wing populism has been electorally defeated in the UK, uncritical optimism in response to this should be tempered. The relative success of Reform UK, led by Nigel Farage, in the 2024 elections demonstrates that right-wing populism continues to resonate with many in the UK. While it is too soon to assess the impact of a new Labour government on these issues, early indications suggest that Labour's failures to resonate with much of the public may well serve as ammunition for further revivals of right-wing populism in future elections.

Highlighted by the disproportionately male support for populist movements, populism is almost invariably male dominated, subscribing to an image of a certain type of masculinity (for an insightful collection of essays on this topic see Löffler et al., 2020). Even where a populist party or group is led by a woman, men tend to make up the majority of supporters (Harteveld et al., 2015). This immediately raises the question of who counts as 'the people' in populist politics, with the male bias in support suggesting that 'the people' is almost certainly equated with men and masculinity. Further, in the UK, this masculinity is mostly associated with the working class; implicitly understood as white and residing outside of London (where the metropolis is a metaphor for the rich). This male support is unsurprising given that men are more likely to feel aggrieved or threatened by progressive changes including gender equality; with white, male, 'indigenous', low-income Brits, in particular, feeling a sense of loss of the status and privilege they believe they are entitled to by virtue of their gender, race and geography (Inglehart and Norris, 2016). That is not to say that, in these culture wars, the middle class or women invariably stand in opposition to the populist right. Taking the issue of trans rights, for instance, resistance is often fronted by middle-class cis-women rather than working-class cis-men (Smith, 2022). Similarly, it is often wealthy men who are seen to be leading other populist frontiers, such as Nigel Farage and Boris Johnson, who ironically became positioned as the voice of 'the people' during the Brexit referendum. Despite this, populism (or more precisely, populist leaders) seems to pro-actively seek out white, working class men in an attempt to make manifest this idea of 'the people'.

In terms of gender dynamics and relations, this has multiple problematic consequences. First, populist politics in Britain, and elsewhere, aggravates and agitates discontent among men and channels that discontent towards women, feminism, values of gender equality, immigrants and people of colour. However, in so doing, the more likely culprits of these men's discontent – for instance, austerity, neoliberalism, individualisation, the unrealistic pursuit of consistently performing an idealised type of masculinity – are not addressed. As such, these men's often painful experiences are not ameliorated in any way through populist politics, which often focuses on superficial wars of identity rather than any real analysis of material conditions. Despite the populist right often positioning itself in opposition to 'identity politics', within populist right discourses specific groups or individuals are often targeted for vilification (e.g., migrants, trans people, women and feminists – often categorised by the catch-all term 'woke lefties'). Through these mechanisms, anger and resentment towards entire groups is cultivated. And, what if you're at the receiving end of this anger and resentment? Well, the second problematic gender-related consequence of populist politics, in Britain and elsewhere, is that it encourages very conservative forms of gender politics and family values that exclude LGBT+ and other non-normative sexuality and gender expressions. Indeed, concerns over the purity of 'the people' and the perception of threat from 'outsiders' is not limited to migrants and often finds expression in anxiety around women, gender and sexuality. Donald Trump's brand of populist politics in the US, for instance, has run hand-in-hand with the erosion of LGBT+ individuals' and women's (reproductive) rights, finding traction with the anti-gay, anti-trans and anti-abortion alt- and religious right. So much so that Sarah Franklin and Faye Ginsberg have noted that '[t]hese distinctly coded signifiers ... structure an overarching grammar of national belonging defined by the preservation of whiteness, biological men and women, heterosexual marriage, and the right to carry one's weapon of choice' (2019: 4).

Franklin and Ginsberg highlight that while Trump's particular brand of populism is in some ways unique to America, there are similarities with the populism of (post-) Brexit Britain, which is also rooted in a nationalist/nativist premise, subsequently seeking 'the reproduction of white ethnic nationalism' and, in so doing, reproducing (hetero)sexist logics and conservative family values (2019: 8). The assertion that this form of conservative politics is often as much about the reproduction and protection of 'whiteness' as it is about the reproduction of gender norms is, of course, epitomised by the fact that 53 per cent of white women in the USA voted for Donald Trump in the 2016 presidential elections. As such, gender politics plays out in complex ways, where white women (even white feminists) are often complicit in the reproduction of 'political whiteness' (Phipps, 2020), even when it means trading off some of their own rights in the process. A (perhaps extreme) example of the ways in which gender traditionalism, conservatism and white nationalism have coalesced in recent years is the rise of the online 'tradwife' movement, wherein (predominantly young, white) women champion the return to 'traditional' gender roles and (white) male dominance. Nancy Love, citing Annie Kelly, argues that 'tradwives' serve to 'soften and normalise white supremacy' by constructing a 'hyperfeminine aesthetic' to 'mask the authoritarianism of their ideology' (Kelly, 2018 cited in Love, 2020: 2).

Finally, alongside the rise of populism there has been a backlash against gender theory/research in the academy. As Isabelle Engeli (2020) has so astutely demonstrated in her review of academic gender and sexuality research, feminism and gender/sexuality research has become the 'bête noire of the populist and radical right'. Recounting multiple examples of hostilities towards gender and sexuality research across Europe and in European universities, Engeli notes that there is a paradox at work between moving towards a more inclusive academy where gender-related research is increasingly institutionalised, and a backlash from the populist and radical right. This is entwined and shares commonalities with the public and political demonisation of Critical Race Theory in the USA and, albeit to a lesser extent, the UK (Schuessler, 2021; Trilling, 2020). Primarily this is related to the reasons outlined above, where gender and racial equality are deemed front-and-centre of any progressive politics and are regarded as having been imposed on 'the people' by the establishment. Gender equality, and feminism, is presented by right-wing populists as something anti-democratic that 'the people' are subjected to and that runs counter to 'the people's' beliefs and interests. 'Gender patches together various dissatisfactions and resentments towards globalization, Europeanization and the current economic order, the political establishment and, more generally, the elites' (Engeli, 2020). The right's obsession with gender and sexuality, and its determination to stifle academic research in the field, seen acutely in places like Hungary (Apperly, 2019), is symptomatic of a wider anti-intellectualism (Engeli, 2020). Populists seek to present the population with 'common-sense' views, to uphold their own authority of speaking for 'the people'. After all, what could be more 'common sense' than biological gender (and, indeed, race)? Academic research on gender and sexuality in the social sciences, then, is either trivialised as academic folly with no 'real world' application or presented as a dangerous trend that seeks to pervert 'our children'.

Keep calm and carry on? (Gendered) vulnerability/resilience in an age of Covid

As noted above, austerity in Britain was achieved, in the main, through reducing the size of the public sector and by relying on the unpaid and often unseen work of volunteers, charity workers and private carers. With major disinvestment in the NHS and social care, Britain saw the loss of jobs commonly done by women (such as nursing and care work), the reduction of services used by many women (such as women's domestic abuse services and reproductive health services) and the non-reimbursement of care labour (again, disproportionately done by women). This recalibration of economies of care meant that at the height of the pandemic, Britain was already at a disadvantage in managing ill-health and mortality related to COVID-19. For example, the experiences of health care workers (HCWs) during the pandemic tells us a lot about the lack of capacity built into the NHS. As Nina Regenold and Cecilia Vindrola-Padros (2021) have shown through their interviews with HCWs in England, nurses, many of whom had been redeployed to intensive care wards, were managing unsustainable nurse-to-patient ratios (with one nurse for every four to six severely ill patients). In general, nurses experienced high levels of stress, aggravated by an inability to do their job properly and long hours wearing PPE. Obviously, this was bad for all nurses, where in the NHS over 80 per cent are women (NHS England, 2021), but more generally this is indicative of the under-investment in feminised care work over a longer period resulting in high COVID-19 mortality and morbidity. Britain saw around 180,000 COVID-19 deaths between February 2020 and July 2022, with higher rates of excess mortality than nearly all high-income comparator countries, with the exception of Spain and Italy (Raleigh, 2022). The experiences of HCWs, the majority of whom are women, during the pandemic and the country's inability to effectively manage COVID-19 are two sides of the same coin. The HCWs' experiences were made worse due to austerity's stripping back of resources. Similarly, the inability to effectively respond to the pandemic was the result of this same stripping back of resources, including the poor pay and working conditions experienced by HCWs. The devaluation of feminised work has been bad for those tasked with that work (mainly women) and has led to a country less able to mitigate a whole range of crises. This lack of resilience is bad for everyone but is felt much more starkly by those from marginalised and minoritised groups, themselves hit harder by austerity, making an intersectional reading of this crisis and other crises essential.

The pandemic, according to authors such as Shahnaz Akhter, Juanita Elias and Shirin Rai (2022), highlighted and exacerbated existing socio-economic inequalities already entrenched through austerity policies in Britain since the financial crisis of 2007–8. This is starkly demonstrated in the considerable disparity in mortality rates between racial and ethnic groups and in areas of high deprivation, with mortality rates being '2.6 times higher in the most deprived than the least deprived tenth of areas', and in the significantly higher risk of infection and death among ethnic minority groups, particularly from Bangladeshi, Pakistani and Black Caribbean communities (Raleigh, 2022). Given that many of the most deprived areas have large ethnic minority populations, this statistic, while shocking, is hardly surprising. Austerity in Britain saw severe and sweeping cuts to the care profession and voluntary sectors, making accessibility much more difficult for vulnerable people, including older and disabled people. For deprived and ethnic minority groups, access to paid and unpaid care is even more difficult, largely as a result of the classed and racialised assumptions that these communities are either too complicated (presenting complex care needs) or too unreachable (resistant to accepting support) for effective intervention (Akhter et al., 2022). For ethnic minority individuals this is further aggravated by the perception that support is being sought in a 'foreign land' and the orientalist[1] construction that in some ethnicities the family is self-sufficient, meaning, therefore, the state is safe to 'turn a blind eye' (Akhter et al., 2022: 1122). But where these communities are hidden or avoided, falling into somewhat of a care gap, it is again usually women's unpaid care work that is called upon to address public sector neglect. These dynamics were well entrenched prior to the pandemic, but COVID-19 saw them intensified, and the oscillating lockdown policies restricted access to familial care networks making the crisis of care ever more acute for these groups.

As well as the disproportionate impact of Covid on ethnic minority groups, mortality rates disaggregated by gender show men to be more likely to die of Covid than women. However, what is often overlooked through this essentialising binary disaggregation is the experience of trans and non-binary individuals. The limited research available on trans and non-binary communities has shown an equally bleak picture, with trans and non-binary people more likely to be exposed to Covid, and to experience severe outcomes. This is because, disproportionately, trans and non-binary people find themselves in precarious working and living conditions, have pre-existing health conditions and are economically disadvantaged (Munro, 2003). In addition, trans and non-binary people are more likely to have a complicated relationship to the healthcare system and the state due to anxieties around transphobia. The especially negative experience of many trans and non-binary people throughout the pandemic has been exacerbated for those trans and non-binary individuals who reside at the marginalising intersections of class, race and age, with poor, non-white and older trans and non-binary people faring the worst (Pearce et al., 2020). Covid exposed the vulnerability of the health service in the UK, with fatal consequences for thousands of already disadvantaged people, but the impact of the pandemic extended to every workplace, not just healthcare settings, and the economic ramifications, in the form of a cost of living crisis, shortly followed (and is where this chapter provides some final reflections).

What now, what next? The cost of living crisis, feminised debt and the spectre of postfeminism

As aforementioned, during the height of the pandemic, job and earnings losses were gendered, having profound implications for economic gender relations. Firstly, these losses were more marked for women, young people, those who were self-employed or who grew up in a poor family (Major et al., 2020). However, the gendered nature of job and income loss goes further than statistically impacting women in uneven ways. Lockdowns and uncertainty shaped the economic reality of the country, job losses were disproportionately felt in some sectors that have traditionally been feminised such as hospitality and retail, while the feminised sectors discussed above, such as care work, healthcare and teaching, were tasked with keeping the country running. As Britain continues to 'recover' from the pandemic, those public sectors hailed as 'heroes' during the crisis were denied a meaningful pay rise, meaning that public sector workers such as nurses were among the rising numbers of workers using food banks in the wake of the pandemic (Butler, 2022). This stagnating pay becomes even more unmanageable in a cost of living crisis, where inflation exceeded 11 per cent in October 2022 (Trading Economics, 2023). While the newly elected Labour Government announced real terms pay rises for many public sector workers in July 2024, this gesture – while welcome – was limited given the fourteen years of pay decline experienced by those working in the public sector. This speaks to a wider disregard for feminised work – and is reminiscent of gendered relations in the private sphere, wherein women's social reproduction is often superficially praised but otherwise entirely uncompensated.

In times of financial hardship, ordinary individual citizens are often rendered responsible for living within their means. Drawing on myths perpetuated by 'handbag economics' (Mellor, 2016), politicians often instruct individuals to 'tighten their belt' in order to 'balance the books' of the country. Most affected are those already disadvantaged. In the same way that austerity hit the poorest hardest, the 'cost-of living' crisis – not unrelatedly – doubles down on financially crippling the most hard up. Marginalised and minoritised groups are disproportionately represented in low-income areas, and within those low-income households women tend to take the biggest financial hit. However, it is unclear how these demands can be reconciled with a wider culture of hyper-consumerism that explicitly encourages people – particularly women – to continue to consume at high rates, even during times of extreme financial hardship. While postfeminism may have been disrupted by austerity, a postfeminist legacy that marketises women's empowerment persists and has even become intimately linked with contemporary types of feminism. For example, a heavily feminised 'self-care'/'wellness' industry, often disseminated by an equally feminised social media 'influencer culture', often presents and promotes lifestyles that much of its audience cannot afford to cultivate – another 'cruel optimism' (Berlant 2011) that obscures the precarity and economic insecurity that structures many women's lives. Online 'buy now, pay later' mechanisms, such as Klarna and Clearpay, have become increasingly available for online shopping in recent years (Rogan, 2022). The use of these schemes is itself gendered, with reports suggesting that 75 per cent of users are women, in part due to their 'strong uptake in the online fashion sector' (Financial Conduct Authority, 2021). And so, as we see a rise in women burdened with personal debt as they navigate the cost of living crisis, so it stands that the economically and culturally aspirational figure of the postfeminist woman remains an unavailable or unachievable category for most women.

What went wrong with Britain?

Conclusion

This chapter has told a story of the transformation of gender relations in Britain since the 1990s. The promise of postfeminism that dominated media and culture in Britain during the 1990s and 2000s told girls and young women that they were the benefactors of a new, more egalitarian world. In the era of 'girl power', young women were encouraged to work hard, make the right choices and consume their way to a 'good life'. While these promises were always contingent, as they rendered invisible the structures of power that continued to entrench class and racial inequality, they became increasingly difficult to uphold after the financial crash of 2007-8 and the related austerity measures from 2010. As public spending was slashed, women's paid and unpaid work became increasingly difficult and services that women disproportionately relied on became harder to access. Simultaneously, and not unrelatedly, Britain has seen the emergence of a right-wing populism with an unhealthy obsession with gender, sexuality, race and ethnicity. This has played out through the regular vilification of feminism (and Critical Race Theory) and a desire to entrench gender norms. So not only do we see economic disadvantage disproportionately affect women, people of colour, trans people and other discriminated groups, but we see an increase in other violences against these groups. Multiple discriminations have deepened through both austerity, where low-income groups have found themselves at the brunt of economic violence, and right-wing populism, where marginalised groups have found themselves further and more violently marginalised. And this deterioration of living standards, felt even by those middle-class women who had once been the darlings of postfeminist empowerment, has had a disastrous effect on Britain's resilience to the pandemic and other crises.

So, in ending this chapter, we will leave the reader with this final reflection. While postfeminist discourses in the 1990s and 2000s promised young women more opportunity, freedom and economic mobility than previous generations of women, it seems impossible to make this promise to the young women of the 2020s, whose formative experiences have been shaped by economic turmoil, environmental degradation and a global pandemic. This broken promise is symptomatic of a wider economic and political breakdown, whose harmful impact is not restricted to gender but cuts across income, race, ethnicity, age, sexuality and so on. Although the promise of a kind of 'postfeminist' gender equality was always illusionary, the precarious landscape of the 2010s and 2020s has revealed what feminists have always known: that gender equality in Britain is far from won. While it would be tempting to equate a new Labour government with the hope and optimism that surrounded (rightly or wrongly) the last Labour landslide of 1997, it seems impossible to do so. The run-up to the 2024 election and the months after it have demonstrated that the early days of Starmer's government are to be characterised by the same 'doom and gloom' that has shaped much of the last fourteen years of Conservative rule. The inability of Starmer's Labour to produce even the illusion of sustained hope and optimism in the UK is indicative of the long-standing consequences of austerity and permacrisis, and the inability of most politicians to imagine a world beyond it.

Note

1 'Orientalism' is an academic term coined by post-colonial scholar Edward Said, which critiques western constructions of 'the East'.

References

Akhter, S., Elias, J. and Rai, S. M. (2022) 'Being cared for in the context of crisis: Austerity, COVID-19, and racialized politics', *Social Politics: International Studies in Gender, State & Society*, 29(4): 1121–1143.

Allen, K. (2016) 'Top girls navigating austere times: Interrogating youth transitions since the "crisis"', *Journal of Youth Studies*, 19(6): 805–820.

Alter, C. (2014) 'Emma Watson is the top celebrity feminist of 2014', *Time*, 19 December, https://time.com/3642115/emma-watson-celebrity-feminist/

Apperly, E. (2019) 'Why Europe's far right is targeting gender studies', *The Atlantic*, 15 June, www.theatlantic.com/international/archive/2019/06/europe-far-right-target-gender-studies/591208/

Bailey, D. and Tomlinson, P. (2022) 'April will be cruel to UK households, but the economy's problems are much longer term, *The Conversation*, 30 March, https://theconversation.com/april-will-be-cruel-to-uk-households-but-the-economys-problems-are-much-longer-term-179526

Banet-Weiser, S. (2018) *Empowered: Popular Feminism and Popular Misogyny*, Duke University Press, Durham NC.

Basu, L. (2019) 'Living within our means: The UK news construction of the austerity frame over time', *Journalism*, 20(2): 313–330.

Berlant, L. (2011) *Cruel Optimism*, Duke University Press, Durham, NC.

Blundell, R., Costa Dias, M., Joyce, R. and Xu, X. (2020) 'COVID-19 and inequalities', *Fiscal Studies*, 41(2): 291–319.

Blyth M. (2013) *Austerity: The History of a Dangerous Idea*, Oxford University Press, Oxford.

Budgeon, S. (2001) 'Emergent feminist(?) identities: Young women and the practice of micropolitics', *European Journal of Women's Studies*, 8(1): 7–28.

Budgeon, S. (2018) 'The resonance of moderate feminism and the gendered relations of austerity', *Gender, Work & Organization*, 26(8): 1138–1155.

Butler, P. (2022) 'Nurses among rising numbers of workers using food banks, research shows', *The Guardian*, 10th November, available at https://www.theguardian.com/society/2022/nov/10/nurses-among-rising-numbers-of-workersusing-food-banks-research-shows [theguardian.com] (accessed 28 March 2025)

Clarke, J. and Newman, J. (2017) '"People in this country have had enough of experts": Brexit and the paradoxes of populism', *Critical Policy Studies*, 11(1): 101–116.

Cochrane, K. (2013) 'All the rebel women: The rise of the fourth wave of feminism', Guardian Books, Kindle edition.

Cooper, V. and Whyte, D. (eds) (2017) *The Violence of Austerity*, Pluto Press, London.

Crowther, A., Petrova, S., Evans, J. and Scott, K. (2022) 'The crises of a crisis: The impact of Covid-19 on localised decarbonisation ambitions in the United Kingdom', *Energy Research and Social Science*, 93: 102838.

Dobson, A. S. and Kanai, A. (2019) 'From "can-do" girls to insecure and angry: Affective dissonances in young women's post-recessional media', *Feminist Media Studies*, 19(6): 771–786.

Duncan, J. (2022) 'The death of neoliberalism? UK responses to the pandemic', *The International Journal of Human Rights*, 26(3): 494–517.

Durbin, S. and Conley, H. (2010) 'Gender, intersectionality and labour process theory', in P. Thompson and C. Smith (eds) *Working Life: Renewing Labour Process Analysis*, Palgrave, London.

Durbin, S., Page, M. and Walby, S. (2017) 'Gender equality and "austerity": Vulnerabilities, resistance and change', *Gender, Work and Organization*, 24(1): 1–6.

Engeli, I. (2020) 'Gender and sexuality research in the age of populism: Lessons for political science', *European Political Science*, 19(2): 226–235.

Financial Conduct Authority (2021) 'The Woolard Review: A review of change and innovation in the unsecured credit market', www.fca.org.uk/publication/corporate/woolard-review-report.pdf

Franklin, S. and Ginsburg, F. (2019) 'Reproductive politics in the age of Trump and Brexit', *Cultural Anthropology*, 34(1): 3–9.

Gill, R. and Scharff, C. (eds) (2011) *New Femininities: Postfeminism, Neoliberalism and Subjectivity*, Palgrave, London.

Ginn, J. (2013) 'Austerity and inequality: Exploring the impact of cuts in the UK by gender and age', *Research on Aging and Social Policy*, 1(1): 28–53.

Harris, A. (2004) *Future Girl: Young Women in the Twenty-First Century*, Routledge, New York.

Harteveld, E., Van Der Brug, W., Dahlberg, S. and Kokkonen, A. (2015) 'The gender gap in populist radical-right voting: Examining the demand side in Western and Eastern Europe', *Patterns of Prejudice*, 49(1–2): 103–134.

Inglehart, R. F. and Norris, P. (2016) 'Trump, Brexit, and the rise of populism: Economic have-nots and cultural backlash', HKS Working Paper, No. RWP16-026. https://papers.ssrn.com/sol3/papers.cfm?abstract_id=2818659#

Jang, M. (2017) 'Emma Watson, Beyonce, 23 more stars on embracing feminism and empowering women', *Hollywood Reporter*, 8 March, www.hollywoodreporter.com/lists/international-womens-day-2017-feminist-quotes-25-celebrities-983702/uzo-aduba-2/

Kelly, A. (2018) 'The housewives of white supremacy', *New York Times*, 1 June, www.nytimes.com/2018/06/01/opinion/sunday/tradwives-women-alt-right.html

Kerr, P., Foster, E., Oaten, A., and Begum, N. (2018) 'Getting back in the DeLorean: Modernization vs. anti-modernization in contemporary British politics', *Policy Studies*, 39(3): 292–309.

Koch, I. (2017) 'What's in a vote? Brexit beyond culture wars', *American Ethnologist*, 44(2): 225–230.

Kurer, T. (2020) 'The declining middle: Occupational change, social status, and the populist right', *Comparative Political Studies*, 53(10–11): 1798–1835.

Löffler, M., Luyt, R. and Starck, K. (2020) 'Political masculinities and populism', *NORMA: International Journal for Masculinity Studies*, 15(1): 1–9.

Love, N. (2020) 'Shield maidens, fashy femmes, and TradWives: Feminism, patriarchy, and right-wing populism', *Frontiers in Sociology*, 5:619572.

Major, L.E., Eyles, A., Machin, S. (2020) 'Generation COVID: Emerging work and education inequalities', available at http://cep.lse.ac.uk/_NEW/publications/abstract.asp?index=7462 [cep.lse.ac.uk] (accessed 28 March 2025)

McDowell, L. (2012) 'Post-crisis, post-Ford and post-gender? Youth identities in an era of austerity', *Journal of Youth Studies*, 15(5): 573–590.

McNeill, K. and Harding, R. (2021) 'Counter culture: How to resist the culture wars and build 21st century solidarity', Fabian Society, https://fabians.org.uk/wp-content/uploads/2021/07/FABJ9000-Fabian-Ideas-pamphlet-210628-WEB.pdf

McRobbie, A. (2000) 'Sweet smell of success? New ways of being young women', in A. McRobbie, *Feminism and Youth Culture*, Macmillan, London.

McRobbie, A. (2004) 'Post-feminism and popular culture', *Feminist Media Studies*, 4(3): 255–264.

McRobbie, A. (2012) 'Angela McRobbie "postfeminism + beyond"', 24 June, www.youtube.com/watch?v=Wk-QIXlx2wk&t=90s

Mellor, M. (2016) '"Handbag economics" and other myths that drive austerity', *Independent*, 27 March, www.independent.co.uk/voices/handbag-economics-and-the-other-myths-that-drive-austerity-a6954851.html

Mendes, K. (2011) '"The lady is a closet feminist!" Discourses of backlash and postfeminism in British and American newspapers', *International Journal of Cultural Studies*, 14(6): 549– 565.

Monro, S. (2003) 'Transgender politics in the UK', *Critical Social Policy*, 23(4): 433–452.

Mouffe, C. (2022) *Towards a Green Democratic Revolution: Left Populism and the Power of Affects*, Verso, London.

Mudde, C. (2014) 'Fighting the system? Populist radical right parties and party system change', *Party Politics*, 20(2): 217–226.

Najjar, C. (2015) '10 of the best celebrity feminist moments of 2015', *Teen Vogue*, 28 December, www.teenvogue.com/gallery/best-feminist-moments-2015

NHS England (2021) 'NHS celebrates the vital role hundreds of thousands of women have played in the pandemic', 8 March, www.england.nhs.uk/2021/03/nhs-celebrates-the-vital-role-hundreds-of-thousands-of-women-have-played-in-the-pandemic/

Pearce, R., Erikainen, S. and Vincent, B. (2020) 'Afterword: TERF wars in the time of COVID-19', *Sociological Review*, 68(4): 882–888.

Pearson, R. (2019) 'A feminist analysis of neoliberalism and austerity policies in the UK', *Soundings*, 71: 28–39.

Phipps, A. (2020) 'White tears, white rage: Victimhood and (as) violence in mainstream feminism', *European Journal of Cultural Studies*, 24(1): 81–93.

Raleigh, V. (2022) 'Deaths from Covid-19 (coronavirus): How are they counted and what do they show?', The King's Fund, 23 August, www.kingsfund.org.uk/publications/deaths-covid-19

Regenold, N. and Vindrola-Padros, C. (2021) 'Gender matters: A gender analysis of healthcare workers' experiences during the first COVID-19 pandemic peak in England', *Social Sciences* 10(2): 43.

Rogan, F. (2022) 'Digital femininities: Visibility, consumption and celebrity in the digital age', *Everyday Society*, 27 October, https://es.britsoc.co.uk/digital-femininities-visibility-consumption-and-celebrity-in-the-digital-age/

Rogan, F. and Budgeon, S. (2018) 'The personal is political: Assessing feminist fundamentals in the digital age', *Social Sciences*, 7(8): 132.

Rubery, J. and Rafferty, A. (2013) 'Gender, recession and austerity in the UK', in M. Karamessini and J. Rubery (eds) *Women and Austerity: The Economic Crisis and the Future of Gender Equality*, Routledge, London.

Ryan, F. (2019) 'Young people like Jess need the safety net. But austerity has destroyed it', *Guardian*, 28 February, www.theguardian.com/commentisfree/2019/feb/28/young-people-safety-net-austerity-cuts

Scally, G., Jacobson, B. and Abbasi, K. (2020) 'The UK's public health response to Covid-19', *British Medical Journal*, 369.

Schuessler, J. (2021) 'Bans on critical race theory threaten free speech, advocacy group says', *New York Times*, 8 November, www.nytimes.com/2021/11/08/arts/critical-race-theory-bans.html

Smith, M. (2022) 'Where does the British public stand on transgender rights in 2022?', YouGov UK, 20 July, https://yougov.co.uk/topics/society/articles-reports/2022/07/20/where-does-british-public-stand-transgender-rights

Trading Economics (2023) 'United Kingdom inflation rate' (May), https://tradingeconomics.com/united-kingdom/inflation-cpi

Trilling, D. (2020) 'Why is the UK government suddenly targeting "critical race theory"?' *Guardian*, 23 October, https://www.theguardian.com/commentisfree/2020/oct/23/uk-critical-race-theory-trump-conservatives-structural-inequality

11
The Conservatives and the climate crisis: Ambition trumping delivery
Neil Carter

Introduction

The planet faces a climate crisis with existential implications: emissions of greenhouse gases (GHGs) from fossil fuel production and combustion, agriculture, waste and other sources have warmed the planet by around 1.0°C above pre-industrial levels. A greater frequency of extreme weather events – droughts, storms and flooding – is already apparent, as are some of the impacts on humanity, which fall disproportionately on vulnerable communities. While all countries must mitigate and adapt to climate change, as the first nation to industrialise, the UK has contributed significantly to anthropogenic climate change and, as one of the richest nations globally, has a moral obligation to help less developed countries to transition to a low carbon future.

Climate change is not an issue that the UK government can, or has, ignored. Since the Climate Change Act (CCA) was passed in 2008 with cross-party support, the UK has been a climate leader in the level of its ambition and in establishing the legal architecture to deliver on that ambition. The UK is committed to achieving net zero GHG emissions by 2050, and an interim 2030 target that is broadly aligned with the aim of the Paris Climate Agreement to limit average increases in global temperature to 1.5°C. However, despite the publication of a 'Net Zero Strategy' in 2021, it has long been apparent – and remains so – that, in the words of the independent Climate Change Committee (CCC), 'tangible progress is lagging the policy ambition' (2022: 14).

This chapter explores this gap between ambition and policy, arguing that the capacity and willingness of successive Conservative governments to deal with the climate crisis was shaped, mostly negatively, by other crises, notably the financial and economic crisis, Brexit, COVID-19, the war in Ukraine and the Conservative Party's own permacrisis, resulting in serious weaknesses in UK climate mitigation policy.

Context: crisis, what crisis?

Prior to 2005–6, UK climate policy – like environmental policy more broadly – was characterised by continuity and complacency, with limited party politicisation of the issue. Low political salience enabled both major parties to pursue preference-accommodation strategies, characterised by a reactive approach to public opinion, but largely resisting competition over the environment (Carter, 2006). During the first two Blair governments, fierce business resistance to Chancellor Gordon Brown's climate change levy and the widespread public opposition to high petrol duties that prompted the fuel protests in 2000 (and a later petition against road pricing) demonstrated some of the political challenges confronting progressive climate measures, which have made all policymakers tread very carefully. However, several factors – including deepening scientific knowledge, extensive media coverage, rising public concern and environmental group campaigning – combined to politicise climate change during 2005–06. A 'competitive consensus' emerged among the major parties, in large part due to the new Conservative leader, David Cameron, making the environment his signature issue. This resulted in a rapid step-change in climate policy that led to the Climate Change Act 2008 and a range of new policy measures (Carter and Jacobs, 2014).

Yet there remained a lingering tension between economic growth and environmental protection that continued to shape Conservative climate policy, and which was exacerbated by the period of economic austerity following the 2008 financial and economic crisis (FEC). Chancellor George Osborne (2010–16), for example, regarded any suggestion of UK leadership on climate change as a threat to economic competitiveness (Carter and Clements, 2015: 215). Although Liberal Democrat ministers protected the broad consensus on climate change during the Coalition Government, in 2015 the newly elected Conservative Government cited public expenditure constraints to justify dismantling several climate policy measures. These included cutting or reducing subsidies for onshore wind, solar and biomass, selling off the Green Investment Bank and withdrawing over £1 billion earmarked to support pilot Carbon Capture, Utilisation and Storage (CCUS) projects. Budget cuts also severely hampered efforts to adapt to climate change. The budget of the Environment Agency, which has a strategic goal to 'create a nation resilient to climate change', was slashed by two thirds from £120 million in 2010 to £40 million in 2021–22 (McGlone, 2021). Its specific budget for flood defence work in 2021–22 was, according to its Chair, £50 million short of what was required to meet its commitments to defend communities.

The Brexit crisis contributed to a marginalisation of environmental issues, alongside many other policy areas, during the referendum campaign and its politically chaotic aftermath. Climate change struggled to secure any bandwidth in a frenzied ongoing state of political crisis.

However, the COVID-19 lockdown resulted in an almost immediate and visible range of environmental benefits. Motor vehicle traffic dropped by 63 per cent during the first 'stay home' period (Department for Transport, 2022a: 3) with a rapid improvement in air pollution levels (National Centre for Atmospheric Science, 2020). Although many of these benefits soon dissipated, one development that has outlasted the lockdown was a transition to hybrid working: many businesses have embraced flexible working patterns enabling staff to work just two or three days a week in the office. Pre-pandemic around 12 per cent of staff worked at home on at least one day per week, rising to up to 40 per cent in early 2023 (Office for National Statistics, 2023). As a consequence, after the lockdowns lifted, traffic levels steadily increased but did not consistently reach pre-pandemic levels: during February to March 2023, weekday motor traffic ranged from 86 to 97 per cent of pre-pandemic levels, rail traffic from 79 to 103 per cent and bus journeys from 75 to 93 per cent (Gov.uk, 2025). The environmental impact of this shift is mixed: the reduction in GHG emissions from fewer commuting journeys is countered by higher domestic energy consumption (but a more limited decline in office energy consumption). The precise balance remains unclear (see Shreedhar et al., 2022).

The Russian invasion of Ukraine in February 2022 led to an immediate energy crisis across Europe that had a major economic impact, fuelling inflation and recession. In 2021, only 4 per cent of the gas used in the UK was imported from Russia (plus 9 per cent of oil and 27 per cent of coal), so energy supplies were less directly disrupted compared to many of its EU neighbours. However, the UK could not avoid the huge spike in gas and oil prices that forced the government to spend around £69 billion subsidising domestic and business energy bills (National Audit Office, 2023: 5). Not surprisingly, energy security shot up the political agenda as the government grappled with the challenge of ensuring energy supplies and prices were protected from current and future shocks.

Finally, after the Brexit referendum, the Conservative Party presided over a seemingly permanent crisis (or permacrisis) of government and governance. Between 2016 and the 2024 general election there were five prime ministers, seven chancellors of the exchequer, and eight secretaries of state with prime responsibility for climate change, with that role transferring across three different departments – Department for Energy and Climate Change (to 2016), Department for Business, Energy and Industrial Strategy (2016–23) and Department for Energy Security and Net Zero (2023–24). This unprecedented political instability inevitably exerted a profound impact on the effectiveness of the government's response to climate change and its net zero strategy.

This chapter argues that the overarching existential crisis of climate change has been neglected because more immediate crises – FEC, Brexit, COVID-19, the war in the Ukraine and the Conservative Party's own permacrisis – drew the government's attention and often deflected it from making effective climate policy.

What went wrong with Britain?

Climate policy ambition

With the groundbreaking CCA, the UK became the first country to make GHG emission reduction targets legally binding. The CCA originally set the then relatively ambitious target of an 80 per cent reduction in GHG emissions below 1990 levels by 2050. To deliver that ambition, the CCA introduced innovative five-yearly carbon budgets. Each carbon budget is set twelve years in advance so there are always three budgets in existence, both to give sufficient long-term incentives for investors and to bind future governments to meeting emissions targets. The Act established a Climate Change Committee consisting of independent experts to provide recommendations on what GHG emissions should be permitted under each carbon budget and to monitor the government's progress in meeting its targets. The government must set out policies to meet the carbon budgets and report regularly to Parliament on progress implementing them (Carter and Jacobs, 2014). A failure to do so can lead to legal action, as illustrated by the High Court finding in 2022 that the government's existing net zero strategy failed to meet its obligations under the CCA to produce detailed climate policies, with the government given eight months to update this strategy (Carbon Brief, 2022).

The UK continued to be a climate leader, prior to Brexit, among those states pushing to strengthen EU climate policy, but its overarching domestic emission reduction targets remained unchanged for a decade. However, by 2019 climate change was ascending the political agenda in response to ever-strengthening scientific evidence about the threat it posed and growing public concern stimulated by environmental protests such as the school strikes led by Greta Thunberg. In May 2019, Parliament passed a symbolic resolution declaring a climate emergency. One month later, Prime Minister Theresa May committed the UK to reaching net zero emissions by 2050. This announcement was part of a government bid to ensure the COP26 annual climate summit, planned for 2020, would be held in the UK – and perhaps May was also considering her legacy before she left office (Gov.uk, 2019).

The Conservatives and the climate crisis

Boris Johnson, although primarily concerned with 'getting Brexit done', did, rather unexpectedly, pick up the gauntlet of climate change. His positive response was initially prompted by the electoral threat posed by the main opposition parties campaigning hard on the environment in the run-up to the December 2019 general election (Carter and Pearson, 2020). However, having won the election, Johnson was clearly determined – for personal and statecraft reasons as much as a commitment to climate action – to make a success of the delayed COP26 summit, which was the first major post-Brexit international summit hosted in the UK. He therefore raised the UK's Nationally Determined Commitment under the UN Paris Climate Agreement to a 68 per cent reduction in GHG emissions by 2030, compared to 1990 levels. In April 2021, he further strengthened the UK's ambition by committing to a 78 per cent reduction in emissions by 2035 (Gov.uk, 2021). In short, the UK's overarching domestic ambition remained strong, although, as discussed below, sectoral targets, policies and delivery often failed to match that ambition.

Delivering climate mitigation

Before the adoption of the net zero target in 2019, the CCC had already questioned whether the UK was on track to meet its existing long-term 80 per cent emissions reduction target. For example, when the long overdue 'Clean Growth Strategy' was published in October 2017, the CCC warned that its decarbonisation policies indicated that the fourth and fifth carbon budgets might not be met (CCC, 2018: 9). Between 2019 and 2021, the sixth carbon budget (2033–37) and a net zero strategy (HM Government 2021) were published, each containing a range of policies designed to meet the 2030 and 2050 targets. Yet still the CCC identified 'significant risks in the plans' for meeting the Nationally Determined Commitment, and the sixth carbon budget (CCC, 2022: 22). Indeed, as noted above, environmental groups won a landmark legal judgement against the government for failing to show that the policies in the sixth carbon budget would deliver the legally binding targets (Client Earth, 2024). In response, a former Conservative minister, Chris Skidmore (2023), was commissioned to write a review of net zero and, as required by the judicial decision, in March 2023 the government published a revised strategy, 'Powering Up Britain: The Net Zero Growth Plan' (HM Government, 2023b), alongside 'Powering Up Britain: Energy Security Plan' (HM Government, 2023a). The common title and joint launch reflected a new willingness since the Russian invasion of Ukraine to frame net zero as integral to achieving energy security. However, with the government admitting that the revised strategy would still not meet the legally enforceable targets, it unsurprisingly met extensive criticism from scientists and environmental groups (BBC, 2023; Carbon Brief, 2023a). A feature of UK climate policy is that while there has been good progress in some sectors, there is worryingly little progress elsewhere.

Energy

On the positive side, the largest emissions reductions have been achieved in electricity generation, notably through the closure of coal-fired power stations, which supplied just 1 per cent of electricity in 2021 compared to around 70 per cent in 1990. Moreover, since the 2000s there has been a huge expansion of renewable energy (RE), which generated over 40 per cent of electricity in 2023, with wind and solar energy leading the way (National Grid, 2024). Currently, just over 50 per cent of electricity comes from low carbon sources (i.e., RE plus nuclear power), but some huge challenges need to be overcome to achieve the UK's ambitious sectoral target of decarbonising electricity generation by 2035.

Although the steady growth in RE has been impressive, it could have been significantly better had the climate crisis not been frequently neglected while the government grappled with more immediate crises. The Renewables Obligation, launched in 2002 by the Labour Government, had kick-started the RE revolution by requiring (and subsidising) energy companies to develop RE sources. This scheme was replaced in 2013 with Contracts for Difference (CfD), which involves auctions that fix prices for low carbon generation in order to encourage private sector investment. CfD has boosted the growth of large-scale offshore wind, although the Cameron government's austerity-driven decision to remove subsidies for onshore wind and slash them for solar energy in 2015 hampered the development of these low-cost forms of electricity generation. Thus, whereas 405 new onshore wind projects came on-line in 2014, just 23 did so in 2019 (Ambrose, 2020). The revised net zero strategy failed to lift the de facto ban on onshore wind even though it is a cheap and quick way to deliver greater energy security (HM Government, 2023b). Moreover, the English planning framework represents a serious obstacle to *all* forms of RE: for example, although an offshore wind farm takes only about three years to build, it currently takes a further three to five years to move through the consenting process before construction can start.

Another major obstacle is the electricity grid system, which is simply not fit for purpose. The grid was designed for a small number of large fossil fuel generators, rather than numerous smaller scale suppliers such as wind and solar farms. This problem was exacerbated by privatisation, which established no proper strategic planning for the grid. Instead, network providers can only build new capacity in response to a specific connection request, rather than in anticipation of expansion. Consequently, a 'first come, first served' approach to grid connections means that large queues of potential new RE projects have developed: over 140 projects were waiting in 2023 with some quoted a connection date of 2036, which has become a major investment disincentive (Gosden, 2023; Plimmer and Dempsey, 2023). These (and other) systemic problems with the grid have had a negative impact on RE investment and development. The revised net zero strategy indicated some awareness of these problems, including plans to reform Ofgem and to speed up the planning process by designating offshore wind as 'critical national infrastructure' (HM Government, 2023b: 30–31). However, there remained an apparent lack of urgency within government about implementing the wide-ranging structural and governance reforms needed to accelerate RE development to meet the 2035 decarbonisation target.

The Conservative government was committed to commissioning a new generation of nuclear power stations. The nuclear sector has been in steady decline over the last two decades, slipping to around 15 per cent of electricity generation in 2021, with four out of the five remaining reactors due to be retired by 2028. A massive reactor at Hinkley Point is under construction, although at an estimated cost of up to £46 billion it is already hugely over budget and repeated delays mean it is unlikely to come on line until at least 2031 (Millard, 2024). The government planned to commission three further reactors by 2030, starting with Sizewell C, with the long-term objective that nuclear power would deliver around 25 per cent of UK electricity by 2050. A non-departmental public body, Great British Nuclear, was established to encourage small modular reactors as a more cost-efficient option. But there is considerable risk in the reliance – endorsed by the new Labour government – on this unproven technology and its optimism that three new reactors will be operating by 2035.

There is continuing debate over the merits of regarding nuclear power as a low-carbon energy source when considering factors, including: huge carbon emissions in construction; the intractable problem of safely disposing of radioactive waste; and ensuring a resilient electricity supply with very low emissions once operating. By contrast, the Conservative government's continued support for oil and gas exploration was unquestionably incompatible with its net zero strategy. Between 2015 and 2022, the UK government gave close to £80 billion in subsidies to fossil fuels compared to £60 billion for renewable energy, with the gap increasing after 2020 (Horton, 2023). Even when Chancellor Rishi Sunak imposed a 25 per cent windfall tax (later raised by Chancellor Jeremy Hunt to 35 per cent and extended to 2028) on oil and gas companies in May 2022 it came with a 91 per cent rebate on investment projects in the North Sea (Graham, 2022). Meanwhile, a licensing round held between October 2022 and January 2023 approved 82 production licences to explore and drill for oil or gas. Sunak subsequently announced legislation to make these licensing rounds an annual event, yet even before the election of a Labour government committed to approving no further licenses, the success of these recently approved licences was under serious threat. After a production licence has been awarded, companies have to obtain development consent before commencing drilling operations. Previously companies only had to provide data on the emissions directly arising from their operations, but following a landmark Supreme Court judgement in June 2024, companies seeking approval for fossil-fuel projects must provide information about the emissions caused by the gas and oil that they will extract (Carbon Brief, 2024). Consequently, the ultimate decision to provide consent in each case now lies with the Labour Secretary of State, Ed Miliband.

It is worth noting that Sunak justified his decision to make these licences a regular event as providing job security for the 200,000 workers in the industry (a sentiment echoed by Scottish National Party politicians). But among other possible explanations for this long-standing sympathetic treatment were the significant financial donations given by climate sceptic and fossil fuel interests to the Conservative Party and its individual MPs, which amounted to £1.3 million between 2019 and 2021, while three (of thirteen) board members of the industry regulator, the Oil and Gas Authority, held significant shareholdings in oil companies (Waitzman, 2022).

This continuing commitment to fossil fuel extraction helps explain the prominent role in the net zero strategy for the engineered removal of carbon emissions. Retrofitted CCUS will ensure the continued use of some gas-fired electricity generation, while some carbon-intensive industries, such as cement production, will be very hard to decarbonise. Yet several previous efforts to subsidise CCUS pilot projects, dating back to the Brown Government, have failed. The strategy promised up to £1 billion per year over twenty years to support CCUS with the objective of capturing 20–30 $MtCO_2$ annually by 2030. The Conservative government announced support for eight CCUS projects in March 2023, yet none would go live before 2027. The Labour government has also pledged to support CCUS, even though considerable weight rests on a technology not yet proven at large scale.

Thus, even in electricity generation, the sector where the greatest progress has been made, the Conservative government still faced significant challenges in meeting its 2035 target to decarbonise electricity generation.

Transport

Elsewhere, pre-pandemic transport emissions had remained broadly static for over two decades so that by 2016, due to lower emissions from electricity generation, transport was the sector responsible for the highest level of GHG emissions. A key problem was that successive ministers made little effort to reduce traffic growth. Policy was shaped by a long-established 'predict and provide' approach: predict traffic growth and build the roads or airports to cater for it. However, the accelerating global transition to electric vehicles (EVs) means that significant reductions in this sector can be anticipated. An initial target set in 2017 to ban the sale of new petrol and diesel vehicles from 2040 was brought forward to 2030 (2035 for hybrid vehicles) in Johnson's 'Ten Point Plan for a Green Industrial Revolution' (Gov.uk, 2020). UK sales of battery EVs have indeed increased rapidly from 15,510 in 2018 to 314,687 in 2023, or 16.5 per cent of all new car registrations, with plug-in hybrid EVs contributing a further 7.4 per cent of registrations (Society of Motor Manufacturers and Traders, 2024).

The EV revolution is hugely important, but they still make up only around 3 per cent of all vehicles on UK roads, with electric van sales notably sluggish. A proposed Zero Emission Vehicle mandate requiring manufacturers to sell a minimum percentage of EVs from their total annual vehicle sales should boost market growth, but significant obstacles to a more extensive take-up of EVs remain (Department for Transport, 2021). EVs are very expensive, more so than equivalent petrol vehicles. Their limited range, while steadily improving, remains a significant disincentive for many consumers. Huge improvements are needed in the charging infrastructure; although the number of charging points has rapidly multiplied, provision remains inadequate on major arteries, in rural areas and for urban on-street residential areas.

While EVs help mitigate the failure of successive governments to reduce road traffic, there is no similar technofix solution to aviation emissions, which increased by 10 per cent between 2010 and 2019. UK aviation emissions per person were 33 per cent higher than the OECD average

(CCC, 2022: 327, 340). The pandemic had a huge impact on aviation: emissions fell by 59 per cent in 2020 and demand in 2022, while growing, had still not returned to pre-pandemic levels. Yet although there may be some long-term reduction in business trips, the pandemic will soon represent a mere blip in the inexorable increase in aviation traffic. The 'Jet Zero Strategy' anticipates passenger numbers increasing by 70 per cent by 2050 (Department for Transport, 2022b), reflected in current plans by the eight biggest UK airports to fly 150 million more passengers annually – equivalent to 300,000 extra jumbo jet flights (Georgiadis, 2023). Indeed, Jet Zero explicitly rejects government intervention to limit aviation growth, relying instead on various untested technologies to deliver emissions cuts. Thus, a central plank of the strategy is that 'sustainable aviation fuels' will make up 10 per cent of aviation fuel by 2030 and 50 per cent by 2050, even though these expensive fuels rely on a technology that has not yet been proven at scale (Carbon Brief, 2022). The strategy also identifies an important role for aircraft fuel-efficiency improvements, but replacing fleets with modern aircraft will take decades, while zero-emission aircrafts remain on the drawing board. Moreover, even if these savings do occur as planned, the strategy concedes that aviation emissions will still be higher in 2050 than in 2019, which would (optimistically) require engineered removal. The decision by the newly elected Labour government in August 2024 to approve London City Airport's expansion of passenger numbers by over one third – ignoring the contrary advice of the CCC – suggests that there will be little change in aviation policy (Pfeifer and Pickard, 2024).

Lastly, one pre-pandemic transport 'success' – the doubling of the annual number of rail passenger journeys over 20 years to peak at 1.8 billion in March 2019 – has stuttered. More people were commuting by rail because of an overall increase in population, a structural shift of employees from factories to offices, and the spatial concentration of jobs and houses in South-East England (Williams and Jahanshahi, 2018). The growth owed little to government policy as austerity meant that between 2010 and 2018 the train operating companies received no subsidies from the government. Unfortunately, the pandemic hit the rail industry hard:

despite the government paying a huge subsidy to keep the rail system running, rail travel was slow to recover with the entire industry beset by industrial unrest and poor performance. Only in 2023-24 did the volume of passenger journeys at 1.6 billion almost return to pre-pandemic levels (Office of Rail and Road, 2024).

Buildings

One of the long-standing weaknesses in Conservative climate policy is its calamitous approach to energy efficiency in buildings. Emissions from buildings were virtually unchanged between 2015 and 2019, largely because, post-FEC, the government substantially reduced the financial support available for energy efficiency improvements, resulting in a collapse in the number of cavity wall and loft insulation installations after 2012 (CCC, 2022: 167). A Green Deal introduced by the Coalition Government allowed consumers to borrow money for energy efficiency improvements with the loan secured against the property, but there was a very low take up and it was scrapped in July 2015 as a cost-saving measure. Later, Chancellor Sunak introduced a 1.5 billion Green Homes Grant scheme in 2020 offering up to £5000 for energy efficiency improvements, but this poorly organised scheme was terminated within months, having reached just 10 per cent of the 600,000 targeted homes (Ambrose, 2021). Even though widespread hybrid working has increased domestic buildings emissions, the revised 2023 net zero strategy failed to significantly strengthen measures or increase spending on energy efficiency measures (HM Government, 2023b).

A further challenge is the necessary transition away from gas as the main source of domestic heating in UK homes. Heat pumps are the most practical, if not perfect, current solution. Yet in early 2023 only around 280,000 heat pumps had been installed, and at just 412 pumps per 100,000, the UK ranked twentieth out of twenty-one European countries, compared to Norway at the top of the list with almost 25,000 pumps per 100,000 and France on 4,586 (Jackman, 2023). A House of Lords inquiry concluded that existing policy was 'seriously failing to deliver on its objectives' with a very poor take-up (Parminter, 2023). Heat pumps are relatively expensive to buy and run, so the government introduced a subsidy – the Boiler Upgrade Scheme, which provides a £7,500 grant for consumers – intended to boost installations and encourage technical improvements and lower prices so that they rapidly reach parity with gas boilers. Phased targets should increase the market, encouraged by proposals to ban gas boilers in new-build homes from 2025 and in all homes by 2035. Another key element is the need to train a new generation of workers – around 200,000 by the mid-2020s – in the skills needed to install and maintain heat pumps. Although installations are slowly increasing it is hard to avoid the conclusion that the target of 600,000 heat pumps installed annually by 2028 looks hopelessly optimistic.

Agriculture and land use

Decarbonisation policies for agriculture and land use are also inadequate. The CCC states that the sector must become a net sink by the mid-2030, yet there has been very little progress in shifting to low-carbon farming. The Environmental Land Management Scheme, the post-Brexit replacement for Common Agricultural Policy funding with financial support for land use that benefits the climate and nature, has been repeatedly delayed. Moreover, voluntary take-up of the scheme remains low. The Conservative government also rejected food policies that would help shift diets away from carbon-intensive meat and dairy consumption, and it had no stated target to reduce livestock numbers, which would reduce methane emissions. Targets for tree planting and the restoration of degraded peatlands, which would enhance carbon storage and sequestration, are not being met (CCC, 2022: 294–297).

Explaining climate policy failure

So how do we explain these gaps between ambition and delivery? The next sections identify three principal characteristics of the Conservative government's approach to climate policy that help to provide an explanation.

Mainstreaming

The Conservative government failed to mainstream climate change across all departments, raising doubts about its commitment to the net zero strategy. One example was the 2019 Conservative election manifesto promise to spend an additional £28.8 billion on road building. Another was the way the government responded to the 2022 energy crisis. It could have used energy security as an opportunity to ramp up investment in RE and supporting infrastructure (relaxing the ban on onshore wind, extending tax breaks on RE investments, grid upgrades and building port facilities for offshore wind turbines) as a green path to domestic energy security, which is relatively cheap and much quicker to bring on stream than other energy sources. Instead, ministers focused on exploiting fossil fuels. Jacob Rees-Mogg, during his brief sojourn as Secretary of State at the Department of Business, Energy and Industrial Strategy, promised to extract 'every cubic inch of gas out of the North Sea' (Horton, 2022), a sentiment implicit in the revised net zero strategy. There was also a brief resurgence of support for fracking – which has long had strong backers in the Conservative Party – although Liz Truss's attempt to force a fracking bill through parliament contributed to her resignation as prime minister. Conversely, the Conservatives rarely emphasised the co-benefits of climate measures, such as the health benefits (and related cost-savings) of cutting meat consumption.

Reliance on market solutions

The Conservative net-zero strategy focused on market-led solutions to climate policy, guided by long-term phase-out target dates for non-zero emissions vehicles and gas boilers designed to stimulate industry investment in EVs and heat pumps. But the strategy contained some very optimistic assumptions about the speed and extent of these and other green transitions. The Conservative government was unwilling to utilise other market mechanisms, such as stringent fuel and energy taxes, or windfall taxes on fossil fuel producers, to provide a financial incentive for consumers to adopt these greener technologies. Nor did it direct sufficient levels of investment into supporting green measures. For example, the cost of the huge tax break for oil and gas companies announced in the May 2022 budget could instead have been used for a domestic energy efficiency programme that would upgrade some 2.1 million homes (Graham, 2022).

Technological vs demand-side solutions

A distinctive feature of the Conservative's net zero strategy was its dependence on technological solutions rather than demand management. The positive aspect of this approach is most apparent in the energy sector, where support for wind and solar energy – alongside governments elsewhere – has enabled renewable energy to become the most cost-effective form of electricity generation. A similar development path is anticipated for EVs to reduce transport sector emissions.

However, considerable weight was placed on some technologies that have not yet been tested at scale. The net zero strategy assumed that at least one new modular nuclear reactor will be operating by 2035, but evidence suggests that the construction of every nuclear reactor overruns – and is hugely over budget – so it seems unlikely that the new modular reactors can avoid similar outcomes. The absence of a viable green propulsion technology and slow development of sustainable aviation fuels means that zero carbon aviation remains a distant dream. CCUS also played a central role in the revised strategy even though large-scale projects do not yet exist. Technologies are central to delivering climate mitigation, but the Conservatives often placed too much emphasis on the wrong technologies and failed to invest sufficiently in the right technologies, such as low-cost wind and solar energy, improving the electricity grid and domestic energy efficiency measures.

The flipside of this focus on technological supply-side solutions was their reluctance to try reducing demand in key sectors. Conservative governments made no serious, sustained attempt to reduce energy demand in buildings. Austerity contributed to the collapse of support for fitting cavity wall and loft insulation, especially in lower income homes: by 2022,

98 per cent fewer homes were insulated with government support compared to 2012 (Carbon Brief, 2023b). Although 80 per cent of the homes that will exist in 2050 are already built, there was no effective policy, for example, to retrofit millions of dwellings without cavity walls where occupiers are currently dissuaded by the cost and disruption associated with fitting internal solid wall insulation and related measures. Elsewhere, there were no policies encouraging the public to consume less meat and dairy products in order to reduce emissions from farming, and despite the absence of any technological solution that could significantly reduce aviation emissions, the Conservatives set no targets to reduce aviation growth.

Conservative politics

Why did successive Conservative governments so often make the wrong choices and fail to introduce the right policies? This section identifies three political factors that have consistently underpinned the weaknesses in their climate policy.

First, some climate measures are regarded as unpopular with the public, and Conservative ministers were clearly dissuaded from adopting more stringent policies on several issues because they feared the political consequences. This reluctance is not peculiar to the Conservatives: most parties tread carefully around measures that impose costs on consumers, such as road pricing or fuel taxes, or interfere in lifestyles by discouraging meat consumption or restricting air travel. These political challenges help explain the Conservative government's emphasis on *technological* solutions – EVs, CCUS, sustainable aviation fuels – that minimise public opposition. They also contribute examples of a failure to *mainstream* climate policy, such as repeated freezing of fuel duties and the halving air passenger duty on domestic flights in 2022. Moreover, Conservative governments were undoubtedly influenced by opinion polls that consistently showed Conservative voters are less concerned about climate change than supporters of other parties (Carter and Pearson, 2024).

Second, the focus of Conservative climate policy on *technological* solutions that often reflect the absence of climate *mainstreaming* was shaped in part by powerful corporate and industrial interests. The imprint of major energy corporations was evident in the continuing financial and regulatory support for the oil and gas industry, and the government's enthusiasm for hydrogen to provide future domestic heating, despite the contrary evidence from independent experts (Parminter, 2023). Corporate lobbying provides the most plausible explanation for Conservative support for fracking (DeSmog, 2017; Hall 2018), which has never been popular with the public and offered no short-term solution to the energy crisis. The construction and house-building industries have encouraged continuing Conservative support for road building and the postponement of the zero-carbon homes commitment. The agricultural lobby – especially powerful in Conservative rural constituencies – has strongly defended the large livestock sector, which contributed around 60 per cent of agricultural production in 2021.

Finally, the permacrisis of political divisions and partisanship that has divided and distracted the Conservative Party for over a decade profoundly affected its approach to climate policy. Within the Brexit-supporting right wing of the parliamentary party there is a residual climate sceptic, or 'climate delayism', sentiment that is anti-regulation, anti-tax, anti-state intervention and, therefore, suspicious of climate policy. During the Cameron Governments these views were manifested in a visceral hatred of onshore wind turbines and disgruntlement about green levies. In an infamous moment, Cameron despairingly asked for someone to rid him of all the 'green crap', while former Environment Secretary Owen Paterson led a vitriolic assault on the 'powerful, self-serving' environmental lobby, or 'Green Blob' as he disparagingly called it and demanded the repeal of the CCA (Carter and Clements, 2015: 217). Since 2021, that critical position has been represented by the Net Zero Scrutiny Group, formed by backbench MPs in 2021 with the aim of pausing or dispensing with the net zero commitment, and questioning the cost of policies associated with it. While it should be noted that there is a (bigger) pro-environment party group, the Conservative Environment Network, the Net Zero Scrutiny Group clearly represents a sizeable – and vocal – minority of Conservative MPs. Indeed, a 2022 poll found that only 33 per cent of Conservative MPs reported that achieving net zero would be a campaign issue for them at the next general election, while a quarter declared that they would campaign *against* a prioritisation of net zero over other issues (Cavendish Consulting, 2022). Widespread criticism of net zero policies is also frequently expressed in the right-wing media, notably the *Spectator* and *Daily Telegraph*, and across the wider party. Conservative members are notably unconvinced by the urgency of addressing climate change: for example, in 2021 two thirds rejected the view that there is a climate emergency (Conservative Home, 2021). Many constituency parties insisted that their MPs and parliamentary candidates pledge to oppose onshore wind farms. Meanwhile, Liz Truss campaigned to be party leader by railing against filling fields with solar panels and promising to scrap green levies. This deep-seated opposition to many climate measures helps explain the Conservative government's reluctance to fully embrace action on climate change and why it adopted several inconsistent positions (see also Carter and Pearson, 2024).

Thus, successive Conservative governments resisted supporting onshore wind despite it being the cheapest form of electricity generation. For example, the 'Energy Security Strategy' (HM Government, 2022) offered no substantial measures to promote onshore wind, yet leaked documents reveal that an earlier version of the strategy included substantial proposals to do so, but these were watered down in response to pressure from Cabinet members and backbench MPs (Waugh, 2022). The response to the energy crisis caused by the war in Ukraine also revealed the tensions within the Conservative Party over the commitment to net zero. Leading advocates of 'climate delayism', such as Craig Mackinlay MP (2022), called for a reappraisal of net zero on the intellectually incoherent grounds that it undermined the 'incontrovertible need for secure and affordable energy supplies', even though fossil fuels had just shot up in price while renewable energy prices had been falling rapidly in recent years and domestically generated renewable energy clearly strengthened UK energy security. Similar incoherent arguments underpinned the ideologically driven resurgence of support for fracking when shale gas could have no significant impact – even long-term – on the price of gas in the UK. Subsequently, when the government published its revised net zero strategy, the original plan to label the launch date as 'green day' was replaced by 'energy security day' because Sunak's advisors feared a Tory backlash (Webber, 2023).

Conclusion

It will not be easy for the UK to meet its net zero target, especially as it is the more intractable challenges that remain, such as shifting away from the use of fossil fuels to heat buildings and slashing aviation emissions. The Conservative government undoubtedly made some progress in recent years, ramping up the ambition, and implementing progressive measures in several sectors. But the persistent and significant gap between ambition and delivery was evidence of serious weaknesses in its approach. Of course, other crises diverted attention for significant periods and impeded effective policy development, with austerity exerting a lingering, negative impact by severely limiting investment in low carbon technologies, and Brexit resulting in several negative consequences for climate policy (Kuzemko et al., 2022). Crucially, the Conservative government ignored an important lesson from the COVID-19 pandemic, which is that during a crisis governments can intervene successfully to educate the public, provide political cues and shape public behaviour. The energy crisis caused by the war in Ukraine provided opportunities to lead public opinion, yet the government struggled to frame energy security positively to justify increased investment in both RE and energy efficiency measures, or to demonstrate how these would also bring cost savings to consumers. Rather, the energy crisis underlined the enduring tensions over net zero within the Conservative Party, where even the attempt to repackage aspects of the net zero agenda as 'energy security' met opposition. Not surprisingly, despite the 2023 Skidmore Review underlining the economic benefits of net zero, the Conservatives failed to embrace the green revolution by matching the massive fiscal stimulus of $369 billion in subsidies through grants, loans and tax credits for investment in green technologies promised in President Biden's Inflation Reduction Act (2022), or even the EU's broader, albeit less financially generous, Green Deal Industrial Plan. On the contrary, in the face of negative opinion polls and growing discontent towards net zero within the vocal right wing of his party, in autumn 2023 Rishi Sunak announced a U-turn by watering down key climate policy measures. Defended as a new 'honest' approach to net zero, he delayed the 2030 ban on the sale of petrol and diesel vehicles by five years, relaxed the 2035 phase-out of new gas boilers and abandoned plans to require landlords to improve the standard of insulation in their rental properties. Together, these U-turns could put the UK carbon budget targets out of reach (Carbon Brief, 2023c). Overall, Conservative governments were consistently unable and unwilling to adopt necessary measures to address the climate challenge effectively, which in turn exemplifies a wider crisis of climate governance.

It remains to be seen whether the Labour government can overcome these challenges. During the election campaign, Labour's manifesto rhetoric certainly trumped that of the Conservatives by asserting that 'the climate and nature crisis is the greatest long-term global challenge that we face' and promising to make the UK 'a clean energy superpower to cut bills, create jobs and deliver security with cheaper, zero-carbon electricity by 2030, accelerating to net zero' (Labour Party, 2024). There are reasons to be cautious, especially given Labour's pre-election decision to slash its (probably undeliverable) promise to spend £28 billion annually on its green prosperity plan to just £4.7 billion annually. Yet Labour appears genuinely committed to ramping up the expansion of renewable energy (including onshore wind) coordinated by the new state company Great British Energy. It will upgrade the electricity grid, issue no new North Sea oil or gas extraction licences, invest in home insulation upgrades and restore the targets prohibiting the sale of petrol and diesel vehicles. If implemented, these policies would undoubtedly help close the gap between ambition and delivery in UK climate policy.

References

Ambrose, J. (2020) 'Just one new onshore windfarm started under current UK policies in 2019', *Guardian*, 13 January, www.theguardian.com/environment/2020/jan/13/just-one-new-onshore-windfarm-started-up-in-uk-in-2019

Ambrose, J. (2021) 'Audit office blames UK government for botched £1.5bn green homes scheme', *Guardian*, 8 September, www.theguardian.com/environment/2021/sep/08/audit-office-blames-uk-government-for-botched-15bn-green-homes-scheme

BBC (2023) 'New UK plan to reach net zero goal faces criticism', 30 March, www.bbc.co.uk/news/science-environment-65107072

Carbon Brief (2022) 'Analysis: UK's 'jet-zero' plan would allow demand for flying to soar 70%', 21 July, www.carbonbrief.org/analysis-uks-jet-zero-plan-would-allow-demand-for-flying-to-soar-70/

Carbon Brief (2023a) 'UK admits revised net-zero strategy will fail to hit emission targets', 31 March, carbonbrief.org/daily-brief/uk-admits-revised-net-zero-strategy-will-fail-to-hit-emission-targets/

Carbon Brief (2023b) 'Energy bill support pushes UK budget deficit to February record', 22 March, www.carbonbrief.org/daily-brief/energy-bill-support-pushes-uk-budget-deficit-to-february-record/

Carbon Brief (2023c) 'What do Rishi Sunak's U-turns mean for UK climate policy?', 22 September, www.carbonbrief.org/in-depth-qa-what-do-rishi-sunaks-u-turns-mean-for-uk-climate-policy/

Carbon Brief (2024) 'Analysis: UK could approve 13 new oil and gas projects despite North Sea pledge', 5 August, www.carbonbrief.org/analysis-uk-could-approve-13-new-oil-and-gas-projects-despite-north-sea-pledge/

Carter, N. (2006) 'Party politicization of the environment in Britain', *Party Politics*, 12(6): 747–767.

Carter, N. and Clements, B. (2015) 'From "greenest government ever" to "get rid of all the green crap": David Cameron, the Conservatives and the environment', *British Politics*, 10(2): 204–225.

Carter, N. and Jacobs, M. (2014) 'Explaining radical policy change: The case of climate change and energy policy under the British Labour government 2006–10', *Public Administration*, 92(1): 125–141.

Carter, N. and Pearson, M. (2020) 'A "climate election": The environment and the Greens in the 2019 UK general election', *Environmental Politics*, 29 (4): 746–751.

Carter, N. and Pearson, M. (2024) 'From green crap to net zero: Conservative climate policy 2015–2022', *British Politics*, 19(1): 154–174.

Cavendish Consulting (2022) 'What politicians think about net zero and the green economy' https://cavendishadvocacy.com/what-politicians-think-about-net-zero-and-the-green-economy/

Client Earth (2024) 'We've won in court against the UK government for the second time' 3 May, www.clientearth.org/latest/latest-updates/news/clientearth-are-suing-the-uk-government-over-its-net-zero-strategy/

Climate Change Committee (2018) 'An independent assessment of the UK's Clean Growth Strategy: From ambition to action', www.theccc.org.uk/wp-content/uploads/2018/01/CCC-Independent-Assessment-of-UKs-Clean-Growth-Strategy-2018.pdf

What went wrong with Britain?

Climate Change Committee (2022) 'Progress in reducing emissions: 2022 report to parliament', www.theccc.org.uk/publication/2022-progress-report-to-parliament/

Conservative Home (2021) 'Our survey. On the environment, Tory members support action but not hysterics about an "emergency"', 2 June, https://conservativehome.com/2021/06/02/our-survey-on-the-environment-tory-members-support-action-but-not-hysterics-about-an-emergency/

Department for Transport (2021) 'Outcome and response to ending the sale of new petrol, diesel and hybrid cars and vans', www.gov.uk/government/consultations/consulting-on-ending-the-sale-of-new-petrol-diesel-and-hybrid-cars-and-vans/outcome/ending-the-sale-of-new-petrol-diesel-and-hybrid-cars-and-vans-government-response

Department for Transport (2022a) 'Road traffic estimates: Great Britain 2021', https://assets.publishing.service.gov.uk/government/uploads/system/uploads/attachment_data/file/1107056/road-traffic-estimates-in-great-britain-2021.pdf

Department for Transport (2022b) 'Jet Zero Strategy: Delivering Net Zero Aviation by 2050', https://assets.publishing.service.gov.uk/government/uploads/system/uploads/attachment_data/file/1095952/jet-zero-strategy.pdf

DeSmog (2017) 'Mapped: How fracking lobbyists from the UK and America have infiltrated Parliament', 26 January, www.desmog.com/2017/01/26/mapped-how-fracking-lobbyists-uk-and-america-infiltrate-parliament

Georgiadis, P. (2023) 'UK's top airports aim to fly 150mn more passengers a year', *Financial Times*, 19 March, www.ft.com/content/52cdd536-103b-4db0-91c5-f1337be47baa?emailId=43758842-e86c-4a22-b33f-ebcbac5cf5f9&segmentId=2f40f9e8-c8d5-af4c-ecdd-78ad0b93926b

Gosden, E. (2023) 'Ofgem to slay zombie projects on National Grid ESO queue', *The Times*, 14 November, https://www.thetimes.com/article/ofgem-to-slay-zombie-projects-on-national-grid-eso-queue-bn2f79jdl

Gov.uk (2019) 'PM Theresa May: We will end UK contribution to climate change by 2050', Prime Minister's Office, 12 June, www.gov.uk/government/news/pm-theresa-may-we-will-end-uk-contribution-to-climate-change-by-2050

Gov.uk (2020) 'The Ten Point Plan for a Green Industrial Revolution', www.gov.uk/government/publications/the-ten-point-plan-for-a-green-industrial-revolution/title#point-7-greener-buildings

Gov.uk (2021) 'UK enshrines new target in law to slash emissions by 78% by 2035', 20 April, www.gov.uk/government/news/uk-enshrines-new-target-in-law-to-slash-emissions-by-78-by-2035

Gov.uk (2025) 'Domestic transport usage by mode', 15 March, www.gov.uk/government/statistics/transport-use-during-the-coronavirus-covid-19-pandemic/domestic-transport-usage-by-mode

Graham, E. (2022) 'Tax relief for oil and gas is trouble for UK bills and energy transition', E3G, 30 May, www.e3g.org/news/tax-relief-oil-gas-trouble-uk-household-bills-energy-transition/

Hall, A. (2018) 'Of Brexit, the fracking lobby and the revolving door', openDemocracy, 28 June, www.opendemocracy.net/en/opendemocracyuk/of-brexit-fracking-lobby-and-revolving-door/

HM Government (2021) 'Net Zero Strategy: Build Back Greener', https://www.gov.uk/government/publications/net-zero-strategy

HM Government (2022) 'British Energy Security Strategy', https://www.gov.uk/government/publications/british-energy-security-strategy/british-energy-security-strategy

HM Government (2023a) 'Powering Up Britain: Energy Security Plan', https://assets.publishing.service.gov.uk/government/uploads/system/uploads/attachment_data/file/1148252/powering-up-britain-energy-security-plan.pdf

HM Government (2023b) 'Powering Up Britain: the Net Zero Growth Plan', https://assets.publishing.service.gov.uk/government/uploads/system/uploads/attachment_data/file/1147457/powering-up-britain-net-zero-growth-plan.pdf

Horton, H. (2022) 'Rees-Mogg: "Britain must get every cubic inch of gas out of North Sea"', *Guardian*, 23 September, www.theguardian.com/politics/2022/sep/23/rees-mogg-tells-staff-britain-must-get-every-cubic-inch-gas-out-of-north-sea

Horton, H. (2023) 'Fossil fuels received £20bn more UK support than renewables since 2015', *Guardian*, 9 March, www.theguardian.com/environment/2023/mar/09/fossil-fuels-more-support-uk-than-renewables-since-2015

Jackman, J. (2023) 'Which countries are winning the European heat pump race?', The Ecoexperts, 26 January, www.theecoexperts.co.uk/heat-pumps/top-countries

Kuzemko, C., Blondeel, M. and Froggatt, A. (2022) 'Brexit implications for sustainable energy policy in the UK', *Policy & Politics*, 50(4): 548–567.

Labour Party (2024) 'Change: Labour Party Manifesto', https://labour.org.uk/change/

Mackinlay, C. (2022) 'Politicians must be honest with the public about the costs of Net Zero', Conservative Home, 2 March, https://conservativehome.com/2022/03/02/craig-mackinlay-politicians-must-be-honest-with-the-public-about-the-costs-of-net-zero/

McGlone, C. (2021) 'Funding cuts have put communities and environment at risk, EA chair tells Eustice', ENDS Report, 22 June, www.endsreport.com/article/1720062/funding-cuts-put-communities-environment-risk-ea-chair-tells-eustice

Millard, R. (2024) 'Hinkley Point C delay deals blow to UK energy strategy', *Financial Times*, 27 January, www.ft.com/content/55ef86b4-f55c-47a9-8121-c6c8cf6b5b18

National Audit Office (2023) 'Energy bills support', Department for Business, Energy and Industrial Strategy, www.nao.org.uk/wp-content/uploads/2023/02/Energy-bills-summary.pdf

National Centre for Atmospheric Science (2020) 'Air pollution falling across UK cities, latest data shows', 31 March, https://ncas.ac.uk/air-pollution-falling-across-uk-cities-latest-data-shows/

National Grid (2024) 'Energy explained', 17 January, www.nationalgrid.com/stories/energy-explained/how-much-uks-energy-renewable

Office for National Statistics (2023) 'Characteristics of homeworkers, Great Britain: September 2022 to January 2023', 13 February, www.ons.gov.uk/employmentandlabourmarket/peopleinwork/employmentandemployeetypes/articles/characteristicsofhomeworkersgreatbritain/september2022tojanuary2023

Office of Rail and Road (2024) 'Passenger rail usage', https://dataportal.orr.gov.uk/statistics/usage/passenger-rail-usage/

Parminter, Baroness (2023) 'The Boiler Upgrade Scheme and the wider transition to low-carbon heat', letter from Chair, House of Lords Environment and Climate Change Committee, 22 February, https://committees.parliament.uk/publications/34006/documents/187196/default/

Pfeifer, J. and Pickard, J. (2024) 'Labour gives green light to London City Airport expansion', *Financial Times*, www.ft.com/content/b1c59fd6-88b8-4643-b5c5-dc35c191ae46

Plimmer, G. and Dempsey, H. (2023) 'Renewables groups sound alarm over UK grid connection delays', *Financial Times*, 6 February, www.ft.com/content/bc200569-cb85-4842-a59a-f04d342805fc

Shreedhar, G. Laffan, K. and Giurge L. (2022) 'Is remote work actually better for the environment?', *Harvard Business Review*, 7 March, https://hbr.org/2022/03/is-remote-work-actually-better-for-the-environment

Skidmore, C. (2023) 'Mission zero: Independent review of net zero', https://assets.publishing.service.gov.uk/government/uploads/system/uploads/attachment_data/file/1128689/mission-zero-independent-review.pdf

Society of Motor Manufacturers and Traders (2024) 'New car market delivers best year since 2019 as fleets fuel growth', 5 January, www.smmt.co.uk/2024/01/new-car-market-delivers-best-year-since-2019-as-fleets-fuel-growth/

Waitzman, E. (2022) 'Oil and gas industry: Outside interests', House of Lords Library, 17 January, https://lordslibrary.parliament.uk/oil-and-gas-industry-outside-interests/

Waugh, P. (2022) 'The energy security strategy shows Boris Johnson is a prisoner of his party and his cabinet', *The I*, 7 April, https://inews.co.uk/opinion/energy-security-strategy-boris-johnson-prisoner-own-cabinet-1562251

Webber, E. (2023) 'It's Rishi Sunak's "green day". Just don't mention net zero', *Politico*, 29 March, www.politico.eu/article/rishi-sunak-cutting-emissions-green-day-net-zero-target-energy-security/

Williams, I. and Jahanshahi, K. (2018) *Wider Factors Affecting the Long-Term Growth in Rail Travel*, Independent Transport Commission, London.

12
The politics of debt and perpetual crisis
Johnna Montgomerie

Introduction

This chapter examines the politics of debt in the United Kingdom as the source of ongoing structural economic crises since 2008. Debt is a concept applied to both the state (public debt) and the individual or household (private debt), represented numerically as a stock of obligations (liabilities) to creditors. The aim of this chapter is to evaluate the character of state interventions in response to episodes of debt-related 'crisis'. Starting from 2008, through austerity in 2010, the referendum vote on leaving the European Union in 2016, and the outbreak of the COVID-19 pandemic in 2020, to the cost of living crisis since 2022, the objective is to analyse the storytelling about debt. Economic storytelling refers to the quasi-scientific (macroeconomic) framing used by UK policymakers and politicians to substitute technocratic solutions for democratic accountability. These narratives are important to analyse because what is *said* and *not said* about the liabilities accumulated by the state and society is about power relations. The argument presented here is that economic storytelling about debt obscures how the state and household balance sheets are interconnected – the state operates the monetary system that households must navigate to survive.

What went wrong with Britain?

The politics of debt is a key aspect of the neoliberal state (Graeber, 2011; Lazzarato, 2012; Soederberg, 2014). During the post-war period (from 1945–70) the way in which the UK government managed public (and private) debt was a key innovation of Keynesian economic policies to promote full employment and social progress (Clarke, 1988; Gamble, 2009). In the 1970s, Keynesian economic policies were criticised for generating unsustainable public debts, which in the 1980s became a moral argument that the public debt was being unjustly passed on to the next generation (Glyn, 2006). The neoliberal turn in British politics from the Conservative (1979–97) and Labour (1997–2010) governments is succinctly articulated by Colin Crouch (2009) as a form of 'privatised' Keynesianism, which denotes the consistent reliance on the state to intervene in markets given the use of private debt to drive domestic economic growth. Abandoning Keynesian employment and welfare policies led to a greater prevalence of macroeconomic insecurity and economic crisis (Konzelmann et al., 2018). With the outbreak of economic crisis in 2008, policy interventions were used to prevent the worsening of conditions rather than the prevention of crisis (Hay, 2011). Austerity was known internationally as 'structural adjustment programs' (SAPs) before it became the policy agenda of the Conservative–Liberal Democrat Coalition Government in 2010, consisting of policy interventions designed to reduce levels of public debt after a crisis in the financial markets. State intervention in response to an outbreak of economic crisis is necessary, and certainly better than nothing. Unless, of course, the impact of the state's response is to prolong the impact of the crisis on society.

This chapter argues that episodes of economic crisis in the UK since 2008 are connected and continuous. Since 2008, the interventions of the UK state have not prevented the worsening of crisis but have substantially escalated the levels of public and private debt, thereby making crises more likely. The politics of debt obscures the power relations at the centre of state interventions. When markets panic the UK state uses public debt freely to restore 'confidence', which bestows new powers on the Bank of England (BoE) to use 'unconventional' means to rescue global corporate balance sheets with liquidity, or government debt. State intervention hinges

The politics of debt and perpetual crisis

on issuing public debt as a guarantee of liquidity (or money). In turn, financial institutions use this liquidity to pass on further debt to private households, mainly as residential mortgages or consumer credit. However, as the stock of private debt mounts, this adds to present (and future) demands on household income. Thus, when the UK state makes public debt freely available, these liabilities flow through global asset markets to the benefit of the already wealthy (and to some extent, middle-class) and affluent regions and metropolitan centres, but at the expense of everyone else.

It is unlikely that the Labour government elected in 2024 under Sir Keir Starmer will take meaningful action to address the economy, as his time in opposition was largely characterised by a lack of campaigning or policy development aimed at improving the conditions of everyday life for ordinary citizens. Instead, it is more probable that Starmer and the new Chancellor, Rachel Reeves, will repackage austerity measures as urgent and necessary interventions to the large public debt caused by austerity – a circular argument that frames the politician as responsible for fiscal management in the face of ongoing economic challenges. Meanwhile, the BoE is likely to continue to be granted broad leeway to manipulate interest rates, prioritising the stability and profit margins of financial institutions over the needs of the average household. As public debt flows into private hands through liquidity provisions, it reinforces a cycle that disproportionately benefits the wealthy and affluent regions, further marginalising those already struggling. Thus, without a substantive shift in policy direction and commitment to equitable economic reform, the Labour government's approach is likely to perpetuate existing inequalities rather than mitigate them.

Economic storytelling and the politics of debt

In the UK, economic storytelling about 'debt' is a tale of two separate realms: the public sphere, where the state collects taxes that it distributes in the form of spending in government departments, and the private sphere where all the paid (employment) and unpaid (care) work come together to drive consumption (final demand) in the household 'sector'. Economic storytelling refers to the quasi-scientific claims made by policymakers when justifying neoliberal state interventions that substitute democratic deliberation with technocratic justifications. Economic policy is storytelling because it relies on 'common sense' understandings of an economy that are false to justify public policy choices that have negative social outcomes. For example, in recent research briefings on the UK's public finances both the Office for National Statistics (2023) and the House of Commons Library (Keep, 2023) describe the national deficit as the shortfall between government taxation and expenditure to frame public policy decisions. Meanwhile, the actual analysis uses the standard measure of the national deficit as 'net government borrowing', or how much sovereign debt the government issued from fiscal one year to the next. A deficit will refer to a year-on-year change in how much the state borrowed, not the difference between taxes and expenditure. The public debt is a stock of liabilities that are paid back (yield) in one, five or ten years. The sum of the bonds sold in a calendar year is measured as the net public sector debt, which excludes the debts of public sector banks and institutions. Both of these measures of debt dominate government, media and policy discussions about economic policy, especially in times of crisis, controlling the frame for when and how intervention takes place.

Common sense accounting principles tell us that a budget deficit is the gap between incomings and outgoings on the balance sheet, but in practical terms this applies only to household accounts, not financial or government accounting. A government's balance sheet does not operate in the same way as a household. Primarily, this is because the state issues its own debt, denominated in its own currency, which generates money in the national economy. In other words, the state does what no household can: increase its income by issuing as much debt as it can sell (it helps that UK gilts are a triple A-rated asset) using taxation as a guarantee to investors that interest payments will be serviced. Therefore, the power struggle over debt is evident in the persistent framing of the state and household balance sheets as the same, while knowing it is factually wrong. What matters is that the economic storytelling about the need for austerity to 'balance the budget' or 'pay down the debt' (frequently referred to as the UK's 'credit card') are no more than simple metaphors to explain state intervention in the economy. Control over the public debt is politically powerful because the Treasury is central to the distribution of state resources.

Economic storytelling about the national deficit, or the build-up of the public debt, is a long-standing battlefield of neoliberal politics. Debates over the national deficit and debt are expressions of moral economy as much as public policy commitments (Roos, 2019). A focus on the national debt serves to focus on the state as the site of reform efforts, whilst remaining silent about the financial institutions in 'crisis' as the site in need of reform. Meanwhile, any discussion of private debt in the UK is muted or considered interference in the functioning of financial markets. This narrative is prevalent throughout the boom years of financialisation as the British economy expanded its government, corporate and household debt stock to such a degree that it became uniquely vulnerable to shocks that generate financial market crisis, as it did in 2008 (Thompson, 2009). The political battle over the story told about the build-up of debt in the run-up to the 2008 crisis culminated in the technocratic justification for austerity.

Austerity: The boom, the bust and the bailout

Debt is at the centre of economic storytelling about austerity. In her review of austerity as a policy agenda, Konzelmann (2014) outlines the political arguments in favour of deficit reduction targets and budget surplus commitments, showing that austerity was presented as urgent and necessary (not a choice) to reduce the government's debt and restore market confidence. However, the outcomes are mixed because austerity often brings economic stagnation. In the UK, austerity was a political tool to reform the state. Stanley (2016) argues that deficit targets are a form of anticipatory action that allow policymakers to control the direction of travel even if they do not actually succeed in meeting the target. It is certainly the case that these targets were missed, and the national debt grew (and continues to do so). Therefore, the politics of debt is about messaging the direction of travel in government departments – 'there will be budget cuts' is a powerful way of curtailing government investment and services. In turn, these ideas become a 'common sense' understanding of austerity. As Berry writes: 'Fiscal consolidation is, at most, a secondary objective of austerity – but the popular notion of austerity as aggregate-level belt-tightening, even if consolidation is never achieved, serves to legitimise the notion that each individual must play their part in fixing the UK's economic problems through labour market participation' (2016: 13). Reducing the national debt is the justification for state intervention, it is not a target or objective of austerity-led reforms. Economic storytelling makes sense of the reality gap created between the political rhetoric of deficit and debt reduction with the actual outcomes of increasing public and private debt levels since 2008.

What is more telling is the contrast between the robust public economic storytelling about the national debt (used to justify state intervention) and the political silence on the increasing size and scope of private debt. In the lead-up to, and long after, the 2008 financial crisis there was very little economic storytelling about the growing private debt stock. Looking at the public and private debt stock side-by-side since 2008, the incoherence of austerity becomes clear. The total stock of UK net public debt (excluding public banks) rose from £750 billion in 2008 to £2,559 billion in 2023 (Office for National Statistics, 2023a/b). Over the same period, the stock of household debt (owed to retail banks and excluding student loans) was £1,388 billion in 2008, and £1,845 billion in 2023 (BoE, 2023). Both are taking on even more debt than in the lead up to 2008, however the private and public balance sheets are moving at very different paces. Households have curtailed taking on debt since 2008, increasing by £500 billion over fifteen years, while the government took on £1.8 trillion of new debt over the same period. What this demonstrates is that prioritising the reduction of public debt while remaining silent on private debt is a very good way of reforming the state while leaving the financial market unmolested.

The politics of debt and perpetual crisis

Brexit: The referendum panic and the transition period mania

The period of austerity under Prime Minister David Cameron ended with the referendum vote in June 2016. He resigned immediately following the outcome because he did not support exiting the European Union. Still, the state intervened immediately via the Bank of England in response to market panic about the vote to leave. The BoE cut interest rates to 0.25 per cent and extended another round of Quantitative Easing (QE) to reassure the markets. The justification was provided by a press release that read: 'Following the UK's vote to leave the European Union, the exchange rate has fallen and the outlook for growth in the short to medium term has weakened ... This is the result of a protracted period of heightened uncertainty that is now in prospect and a higher cost of capital for UK-focused firms' (BoE, 2016: 2). The referendum vote was a self-inflicted crisis and the central bank responded by buying corporate bonds (using government debt) to lessen the negative effects on the domestic economy. State intervention was explicitly designed to manage corporate balance sheets by issuing government debt as liquidity (cash reserves) and for asset purchases (securities) to mitigate against any losses for large corporations, especially those with headquarters in the UK.

One notable change is that the Bank of England imposed 'domestic conditionality' for the first time on its asset purchases in times of crisis. This meant that £10 billion in corporate bonds and £60 billion in gilts were dedicated to domestic firms, or companies that make a 'material contribution' to UK economic activity, by having headquarters and significant employment of workers in the UK (BoE, 2016). Politics brought about the addition of domestic conditionality, suggesting that the Conservative government was more willing to direct market interventions. By the end of 2016, six months after the referendum vote, interventions by the BoE accumulated £435 billion of corporate bond assets held by the UK government – double the amount (£200 billion) committed after the financial crisis in 2008 (BoE, 2016). Holding vast stocks of corporate assets on the public balance sheet is support enough but, in response to the Brexit vote, the BoE began to target strategic industries to shore up the domestic economy. In other words, the Conservative government's established economic storytelling about debt was easily dispensed with to find 'fiscal space' for justifying interventions in the aftermath of the referendum vote.

During the extended 'transition period' from 2016–20, the character of UK state intervention became more interventionist without any concern for increasing public, or private, debt levels. In 2017, the industrial strategy was designed in response to the protracted economic uncertainty caused by the tumultuous political negotiations over the terms of exiting the single market and customs union. What was 'conditionality' in monetary policy became 'strategic sectors' in the industrial strategy to denote eligible transnational corporations: those that contribute to the economy with domestic headquarters and local jobs (Department for Business, Energy and Industrial Strategy, 2017). Indeed, national industrial policy was not permitted in this way when the UK was a member of the European Union. Berry *et al.* (2021) reviewed this revival of UK industrial policy, describing the 2017 initiative as a response to concerns over the underlying weakness of the UK economy, such as low productivity, inequality and regional deprivation. Moreover, when the UK transitioned out of the EU, the 'Build Back Better' strategy for domestic growth furthered the same objectives (HM Treasury, 2021a). There is little evidence that these government policies were of any benefit to strategic sectors or the domestic economy.

COVID-19: The market shock and the lavish bailout

The move between the protracted 'transition' period for leaving the EU (which spanned four years and two prime ministers) and the outbreak of the global pandemic was a matter of weeks. The date for the UK's exit from the EU was set to be 30 January 2020, and the Cabinet was entirely focused on political grandstanding, ignoring the warnings of a deadly virus circulating the globe (Hui, 2023). At the time of writing it is still early in the UK's COVID-19 inquiry, but the inner dysfunctions of the

Conservative government, especially the Cabinet, are clear (*The Economist*, 2023). Most jarring is the lack of concern shown by those working at the heart of the British government. When circumstances demanded effective state intervention to protect society they chose to get drunk instead. The impact of a global pandemic was almost immediately obvious. In early February 2020, the market shock was shown in the FTSE 100 slumping by approximately 8 per cent, or £152 billion (Wearden, 2020). By June 2020, the wider economic crisis became evident in the 19 per cent increase in unemployment levels, reaching 1.6 million people, and a 9.8 per cent contraction in the gross domestic product (HM Treasury, 2021c). These were 'record-breaking' drops in economic activity and the largest decline in the volume of economic activity in all the G7 nations (Dey-Chowdhury et al., 2021).

Such extreme market shock and domestic economic decline compelled the state to intervene to support the global financial system and the national domestic economy, while simultaneously fighting a global pandemic. The BoE was the first to act, reducing interest rates to 0.1 per cent and committing £1.04 trillion to monetary measures. Of that, £129 billion went to loan guarantees via the Contingent Term Repo Facility, the Term Funding Scheme, the COVID Corporate Financing Facility, the Coronavirus Business Interruption Scheme and the Bounce Back Loan Scheme (Bank of England, 2020). Additionally, in the first nine months of the pandemic the BoE purchased assets worth £895 billion, which was considerably more than the response to the crisis of 2008 (Bank of England, 2021). The Bank was estimated to have contributed an equivalent of 19.5 per cent of GDP to national wealth, measured at £756 billion (Office for National Statistics, 2022). Evident from the outset was that the BoE used large-scale monetary interventions compared to the Treasury's carefully crafted fiscal response.

Once again, the contested politics of debt was at the centre of the state's response to the COVID-19 pandemic and market shock. On the one hand, the BoE transferred gilts from the Treasury with the condition being that a portion needed to go to corporations headquartered in the UK. On the other hand, the Treasury restrained the use of automatic stabilisers such as Universal Credit or direct income transfer, which would cause an increase in the national debt. When the economic crisis erupted, the BoE deployed well-worn monetary measures with vigour while the Treasury invented bespoke temporary measures almost from scratch that took months to get up and running. Foremost of these was the Coronavirus Job Retention Scheme or 'furlough', which was reported to have transferred £70 billion to employers to secure the income of workers in the Pay As You Earn (PAYE) taxation system, which excludes zero-hour or temporary workers. Much smaller was the Self-Employed Income Support Scheme, which transferred £28 billion to businesses with a turnover that declined by 30 per cent or more due to the pandemic (HM Treasury, 2021b). Deploying new business subsidy schemes, rather than direct income transfers like the economic stimulus payments made in the US and Canada, was justified as a more efficient way to deliver state welfare to targeted populations, not universally.

Neoliberal statecraft relies on public debt to constrain fiscal, not monetary, policy. Instead of transferring money directly to people (like QE does for banks) the fiscal stabilisers used employers to distribute almost £100 billion in expenditure. The conditions imposed were to full-time employees (pay-as-you-earn on the payroll system) to a maximum of £2,500 per month. The use of employer payroll rather than the public taxation or welfare system was about politics, not costs. According to the Institute for Fiscal Studies, approximately one million people were made redundant between April 2020 and June 2021 compared with 550,000 a year earlier, thereby suggesting that the narrow scope of business subsidies limited their overall effectiveness (Cribb and Salisbury, 2021). Further, relying on employers to distribute fiscal relief led to concentrations of state aid in metropolitan areas and surrounding counties. A report by the Office for National Statistics (2021) reveals that London received 6 per cent of all funds (or 232,700 claims) compared with all other regions and devolved nations (approximately 3 per cent). The next furlough flowed into the Midlands, North Yorkshire and the regions with the lowest uptake – Wales and Scotland. By targeting state support using conditionality, the Conservative government evoked the potential impact on the national debt, sending a clear message that British society could not rely on the government for anything more than emergency relief.

The Universal Credit (UC) and Working Tax Credit (WTC) programmes (flagship Conservative welfare reform initiatives that were justified on the grounds of fiscal probity and moral reform) could have provided widespread relief to people in temporary, zero-hours and part-time employment. Instead, the 'universal' capacity was limited in favour of means-tested schemes. It is reported that £70 billion was spent on additional UC and WTC to provide an emergency 'uplift' of £20 per week until October 2021 (HM Treasury, 2021c). By February 2021, it was reported that five million people received the temporary uplift, but the extent to which that uplift influenced family incomes varied substantially depending on the other benefits to which the household was entitled, as well as by region (Powell and Francis-Devine, 2022). The Institute for Fiscal Studies reports that UC and WTC over the period 2020–21 were most substantial for families with low or no earnings, while a working-age family had no noticeable benefit. However, most increases were temporary (Cribb and Salisbury, 2021). There can be little doubt that fiscal interventions provided much-needed relief, preventing the worsening of economic hardship due to the economic shock of the pandemic. However, state intervention did not reach areas of high deprivation and did not protect them from economic shocks.

Perpetual crisis is the result of worsening inequality

Overall, the pandemic has been as much a driver of wealth gains as it was of deprivation. Globally, estimates put over 100 million people falling into the category of 'living in poverty' due to the pandemic, while $37 trillion US dollars in financial wealth gains amassed to just 0.1 per cent of the world's population (Chancel *et al.*, 2022). A UN report on the pandemic response noted: 'While virtually all asset classes have been inflated by the unprecedented monetary policy responses to the pandemic, global equities have seen the strongest price increases. Major stock indices have been breaking all-time high after all-time high even as many economies were struggling to recover from the crisis' (Rashid et al., 2022: 3). In the UK context, the BoE's ever-expanding balance sheet has direct implications for wealth inequality. In the first year of the pandemic, monetary interventions contributed £756 billion to total national wealth, which is concentrated among the already wealthy. As Leslie and Shah put it: 'the richest households have seen the largest wealth increases in absolute terms, reflecting their larger existing wealth holdings on entering the crisis' (2021: 31).

Economic storytelling eclipses economic indicators in the epistemic politics of neoliberalism. Previous research of the impacts of QE by the BoE (2012) shows that only the top 5 per cent of households in wealth and income percentiles benefited from the QE programme. In their analysis of the post-2008 period, Green and Lavery argue that these are the dynamics of a 'regressive recovery' that will 'further entrench structural weaknesses in Britain's economy in the years ahead' (2015: 896). This argument is advanced further by Montgomerie's (2023) analysis of the COVID-19 responses in the US and UK, which identified the disparity between lavish 'unconventional' monetary policy measures compared to time-limited and budget constrained fiscal automatic stabilisers as the underlying cause of worsening social inequality and deprivation.

The neoliberal politics of debt relies on a simple metaphorical parallel between the public and private balance sheet. The debt story is composed of booming proclamations about the increasing national debt and silence when the same happens to private debt stocks. Both the noise and the silence work together to obscure the distributional realities of debt-led growth. If we take current public and private debt stocks as the cumulative impact of crisis events in 2008, 2016 and 2020, the ongoing 'cost of living' crisis is simply an example of economic crisis 'taking another form'. Economic storytelling about debt is both what is *said* and *not said*. When the Treasury issues more gilts the justification provided is political, whether sovereign debt goes directly to markets or the central bank. What matters most is the unequal distributional outcomes of UK state interventions. Distributional moments occur when the state intervenes to rescue one economic agent over another. What transpired in 2008, 2016 and 2020 were different configurations of economic crisis, which nevertheless all shared a neoliberal state response.

Of course, the trajectory of economic recovery was not a straight line. Both the government and British society (represented at the household level) experienced the Brexit vote and the COVID-19 crash as additional episodes of 'crisis' since 2008. Yet, when the stock of gross debt is measured as a percentage of national GDP, public debt went from 50.5 per cent in 2008-9 to 100.5 per cent in 2022-23 (Office for National Statistics, 2023a/b). Private debt was 105 per cent of GDP and reached its peak at 108.5 per cent in 2010, before falling to 84 per cent in 2023 (CEIC Data, 2023). The ebb and flow of debt is moving at different intensities. The average household has been reducing its debt commitments while the government's doubled over the same period. While the economic storytelling about state intervention since 2008 shifted away from debt as an emotive or moral category in British politics, this only changed the script, not the direction of travel. The overall stock of personal debt at the end of 2008 stood at £1,457 billion, the vast majority of which was for mortgages (£1,228 billion) – the remainder being consumer debt (£230 billion). By 2023, total personal debt reached £1,847 billion, split between mortgages (£1,629 billion) and consumer credit (£217 billion) (The Money Charity, 2008; 2023). The average total debt per household, including mortgages, was £65,756. The figure per adult was £34,716, or 100.4 per cent of average earnings.

Household debt levels during, and since, the COVID-19 pandemic shifted but remain a steadfast feature of the overall finances of the household sector. Research briefings by the House of Commons Library show this as the inverse relationship between types of debt used by the household sector during the pandemic compared to the cost of living crisis (Francis-Devine, 2025). By measuring the change in outstanding levels of debt to individuals, it shows that in the pandemic years 2020-21, there was a marked decrease in unsecured debt levels. Mortgage debt, by contrast, started increasing in September 2020 and in June 2021 reached its highest year-on-year growth since the series began, meanwhile in the current cost of living crisis the opposite happened - mortgage debt decreased while unsecured debt increased (Francis-Devine, 2025: 14).

What has become clearer since 2008 is the interconnections between the public and private balance sheets via the relationships and structures of debt. Having long relied on private debt to drive growth, the long-term impact of increased household borrowing appears to have become unsustainable due to stagnant incomes. Neoliberal policymakers use austerity in the same way the International Monetary Fund uses structural adjustment programs: to privatise losses incurred in financial markets on to national governments, who then download these costs onto the domestic economy of the household by making cuts to government income transfers and public services (Montgomerie and Tepe-Belfrage, 2016), making society the shock-absorber for economic crisis in profoundly unequal ways (Bryan, 2012; see also Elson, 2022; Kabeer et al., 2021). Crises are distributional moments that expose the structural inequities of neoliberal politics. On the one hand, the Treasury makes funds available to expand support into corporate balance sheets; on the other, the Treasury uses the high public debt levels caused by bailouts as justification to cut-back government expenditure on household transfers and public services.

During the COVID-19 shock, the state intervened only to provide emergency support, but what was the alternative: doing nothing? More telling is how rising levels of deprivation can be used as an indicator of the people, communities and regions that were worst hit by COVID-19 (Blundell et al., 2020; Martin, 2021; Sandset, 2021). In the same way, state intervention was a good indicator of the affluent areas and segments of British society, while everyone else held-on to what little they already had before Brexit and COVID-19 hit. These episodes of market panic and shock generated government responses that amplified existing inequality trends (De Henau and Himmelweit, 2020; Macartney et al., 2022). The neoliberal state response to crisis is to bail out markets while imposing market rules on society. Economic storytelling is used to disguise the distributional outcomes of state intervention. However, worsening social inequality remains the primary driver of domestic economic instability and deteriorating living standards: both continue to undermine the credibility of neoliberal economic storytelling.

Conclusion

What went wrong with Britain? The simple answer is the state. Public policy plays a significant role in perpetuating inequality, and the politics of debt make crisis a permanent feature of daily life. State interventions to treat market shock provide windfall wealth gains for corporate balance sheets, but only temporary relief for household balance sheets, perpetuating social inequality and eroding prosperity for as long as politics permits it. This chapter has examined the UK's public and private debt through the lens of the politics and policies of economic storytelling, presenting evidence of the character of state interventions in response to episodes of 'crisis'. Austerity in 2010, the EU referendum vote in 2016 and the outbreak of the COVID-19 pandemic in 2020 show how the UK's interventions in response to episodes of 'crisis' contribute to the permanence of crisis in politics and everyday life.

The brief leadership of Liz Truss and the caretaker role of Rishi Sunak as Conservative Prime Ministers demonstrated a clear commitment to neoliberal politics. Truss, during her brief tenure, promised tax cuts to stimulate growth but quickly faced a backlash from her mini budget, leading to market instability. Such bold neoliberal economic reforms did not go down well in the political realities of public sentiment and financial markets. In contrast, Sunak's leadership revived the 'fiscal' conservative approach, focusing on stabilizing the economy through tailored interventions to support large corporations. However, the legacy of Truss's agenda left lingering challenges that continued to affect public confidence in economic governance.

A closer look at the state of the UK economy in late 2023 shows that conditions had only worsened. Generously funded state interventions in response to crisis had, at best, only mitigated the impacts of pandemic-related disruptions to everyday life. State interventions since the furlough scheme had done little to resolve the underlying causes of persistent economic malaise. If policy interventions to curb deficit spending or the national debt actually worked, then why is the UK's national debt, both public and private, only growing? The ongoing narrative surrounding debt continues to create a sense of optimism among policymakers that conditions will improve in the future, yet ongoing economic challenges continue to shift the political landscapes.

The new Labour government inherits these economic challenges, the ongoing issues of inequality, public and private debt, inflation and public policy interventions in response have intensified since 2010. Starmer's Labour government do not have a coherent economic plan or strategy, which is why public sentiment is cautious and inpatient. But the overall agenda of the Starmer government is unlikely to magically appear. It is not clear if the current UK government has the capacity or ability to implement the changes necessary to foster long-term economic recovery and social equity. The challenge lies not only in addressing the immediate needs of people but in rebuilding credibility and trust in the government's economic policymaking. The storytelling about debt keeps policymakers optimistic that conditions will improve sometime in the future, regardless of the realities of worsening inequality.

References

Bank of England (2012) 'The distributional effects of asset purchases', Q3, Quarterly Bulletin, https://www.bankofengland.co.uk/-/media/boe/files/quarterly-bulletin/2012/the-distributional-effects-of-asset-purchases.pd

Bank of England (2016) 'Corporate Bond Purchase Scheme: Eligibility and sectors', www.bankofengland.co.uk/news/2016/september/corporate-bond-purchase-scheme-eligibility-and-sectors

Bank of England (2020) 'Bank of England measures to respond to the economic shock from Covid-19', www.bankofengland.co.uk/news/2020/march/boe-measures-to-respond-to-the-economic-shock-from-covid-19

Bank of England (2021) 'Our response to coronavirus (Covid)', www.bankofengland.co.uk/coronavirus

Bank of England (2023) 'Total outstanding credit to individuals 1986–2023' (Time Series LPQZ2A; Data Viewer), www.bankofengland.co.uk/boeapps/database/

Berry, C. (2016) *Austerity Politics and UK Economic Policy*, Palgrave, Basingstoke.

Berry, C., Froud, J. and Barker, T. (2021) 'Introduction: The political economy of UK industrial policy', in *The Political Economy of Industrial Strategy in the UK*, Agenda Publishing, London.

Blundell, R., Dias, M. C., Joyce, R. and Xu, X. (2020) 'Covid-19 and inequalities', Institute for Fiscal Studies, https://ifs.org.uk/sites/default/files/output_url_files/Covid-19-and-inequalities-IFS.pdf

Bryan, D. (2012) 'Going forward: The perpetual crisis of finance', *Culture and Organization*, 18(2): 171–176.

CEIC Data (2023) 'UK household debt: % of GDP, 1987–2023', www.ceicdata.com/en/indicator/united-kingdom/household-debt-of-nominal-gdp

Chancel, L., Piketty, T. and Saez, E. (2022) *World Inequality Report 2022*, Harvard University Press, Cambridge, MA.

Clarke, S. (1988) *Keynesianism, Monetarism, and the Crisis of the State*, Edward Elgar, London.

Cribb, J. and Salisbury, A. (2021) 'Employment and the end of the furlough scheme (The Deaton Review)', Institute for Fiscal Studies, https://ifs.org.uk/books/employment-and-end-furlough-scheme

Crouch, C. (2009) 'Privatised Keynesianism: An unacknowledged policy regime', *British Journal of Politics and International Relations*, 11(2): 382–399.

De Henau, D. J. and Himmelweit, S. (2020) 'Crises collide: Women and Covid-19', Women's Budget Group, https://wbg.org.uk/wp-content/uploads/2020/04/FINAL.pdf

Department for Business, Energy and Industrial Strategy (2017) 'Industrial strategy 2017: Building a Britain fit for the future', HM Government, https://assets.publishing.service.gov.uk/government/uploads/system/uploads/attachment_data/file/664563/industrial-strategy-white-paper-web-ready-version.pdf

Dey-Chowdhury, S., McAuley, N. and Walton, A. (2021) 'International comparisons of GDP during the coronavirus (COVID-19) pandemic', Office for National Statistics, www.ons.gov.uk/economy/grossdomesticproductgdp/articles/internationalcomparisonsofgdpduringthecoronaviruscovid19pandemic/2021-02-01

The Economist (2023) 'The covid-19 inquiry exposes chaos in Boris Johnson's government', 1 November, www.economist.com/britain/2023/11/01/the-covid-19-inquiry-exposes-chaos-in-boris-johnsons-government

Elson, D. (2022) 'Equality, resilience and sustainability: Rebalancing commercial rights and economic and social rights to create more equal economies', in P. Arestis and M. Sawyer (eds) *Economic Policies for Sustainability and Resilience*, Springer, London.

Francis-Devine, B. (2025) 'Household debt: Statistics and impact on economy, House of Commons Library, Research Briefing (Number 7584), https://researchbriefings.files.parliament.uk/documents/CBP-7584/CBP-7584.pdf

Gamble, A. (2009) *The Spectre at the Feast: Capitalist Crisis and the Politics of Recession*, Palgrave, Basingstoke.

Glyn, A. (2006) *Capitalism Unleashed: Finance, Globalization, and Welfare*, Oxford University Press, Oxford.

Graeber, D. (2011) *Debt: The First 5000 years*, Melville, New York.

Green, J. and Lavery, S. (2015) 'The regressive recovery: Distribution, inequality and state power in Britain's post-crisis political economy', *New Political Economy* 20(6): 894–923.

Hay, C. (2011) 'Pathology without crisis? The strange demise of the Anglo-Liberal growth model', *Government and Opposition* 46(1): 1–31.

HM Treasury (2021) 'Build Back Better: Our plan for growth', www.gov.uk/government/publications/build-back-better-our-plan-for-growth/build-back-better-our-plan-for-growth-html#global-britain

HM Treasury (2021b) 'Strategic review of the COVID-19 pandemic financial reporting response', https://assets.publishing.service.gov.uk/government/uploads/system/uploads/attachment_data/file/980417/Strategic_review_for_the_COVID-19_pandemic_response.pdf

Hui, S. (2023) 'UK was ill-prepared for pandemic because resources were diverted to Brexit, ex-health chief says', AP News, 27 June, https://apnews.com/article/britain-uk-covid-inquiry-hancock-643c9a9b126de8bbe49b34dd8d382a08

Kabeer, N., Razavi, S. and van der Meulen Rodgers, Y. (2021) 'Feminist economic perspectives on the COVID-19 pandemic', *Feminist Economics*, 27(1–2): 1–29.

Keep, M. (2023) 'Public finances: Key economic indicators', House of Commons Library, https://commonslibrary.parliament.uk/research-briefings/sn02812/

Konzelmann, S. J. (2014) 'The political economics of austerity', *Cambridge Journal of Economics*, 38(4): 701–741.

Konzelmann, S. J., Deakin, S., Fovargue-Davies, M. and Wilkinson, F. (2018) *Labour, Finance and Inequality: The Insecurity Cycle in British Public Policy*, Routledge, London.

Lazzarato, M. (2012) *The Making of the Indebted Man*, Semiotext.

Leslie, J., and Shah, K. (2021) 'The Wealth Gap Year: The Impact of the Coronavirus Crisis on UK Household Wealth', The Resolution Foundation, www.resolutionfoundation.org/app/uploads/2021/07/Wealth-gap-year.pdf

Macartney, H., Montgomerie, J. and Tepe, D. (2022) *The Fault Lines of Inequality: COVID 19 and the Politics of Financialization*, Palgrave Macmillan, Cham.

Martin, R. (2021) 'Rebuilding the economy from the Covid crisis: Time to rethink regional studies?', *Regional Studies, Regional Science*, 8(1): 143–161.

The Money Charity (2008) 'Money statistics: Personal debt 2008 (October)', https://themoneycharity.org.uk/money-statistics/october-2009/

The Money Charity (2023) 'Money statistics: Personal debt 2023 (October)', https://themoneycharity.org.uk/media/October-2023-Money-Statistics.pdf

Montgomerie, J. (2023) 'COVID Keynesianism: Locating inequality in the Anglo-American crisis response', *Cambridge Journal of Regions, Economy and Society*, 16(1): 211–223.

Montgomerie, J. and Tepe-Belfrage, D. (2016) 'Caring for debts: How the household economy exposes the limits of financialisation', *Critical Sociology*, 43(4–5): 653–668.

Office for National Statistics (2021) 'Coronavirus and the impact on UK households and businesses: 2020', www.ons.gov.uk/economy/nationalaccounts/uksectoraccounts/articles/coronavirusandtheimpactonukhouseholdsandbusinesses/2020

Office for National Statistics (2022) 'BoE: Asset purchase facility gilt holdings', Statistical Release, www.ons.gov.uk/economy/governmentpublicsectorandtaxes/publicsectorfinance/timeseries/mex2/pusf

Office for National Statistics (2023a) 'Public Sector Finance', www.ons.gov.uk/economy/governmentpublicsectorandtaxes/publicsectorfinance

Office for National Statistics (2023b) 'Net Debt (Excluding Public Sector Banks) : £bn', www.ons.gov.uk/economy/governmentpublicsectorandtaxes/publicsectorfinance/timeseries/hf6w/pusf

Powell, A. and Francis-Devine, B. (2022) 'Coronavirus: Impact on the labour market', House of Commons Library, Research Briefing (9152), https://commonslibrary.parliament.uk/research-briefings/cbp-8898/

Rashid, H., Pitterle, I. and Huang, Z. (2022) 'The monetary policy response to covid-19: The role of asset purchase programmes', UN Department of Economic and Social Affairs, Policy Briefs, 25 April.

Roos, J. E. (2019) *Why Not Default? The Political Economy of Sovereign Debt*, Princeton University Press, Princeton, NJ.

Sandset, T. (2021) 'The necropolitics of COVID-19: Race, class and slow death in an ongoing pandemic', *Global Public Health*, 16(8–9): 1411–1423.

Soederberg, S. (2014) *Debtfare States and the Poverty Industry: Money, Discipline and the Surplus Population*, Routledge, London.

Stanley, L. (2016) 'Governing austerity in the United Kingdom: Anticipatory fiscal consolidation as a variety of austerity governance', *Economy and Society*, 45(3–4): 303–324.

Thompson, H. (2009) 'The political origins of the financial crisis: The domestic and international politics of Fannie Mae and Freddie Mac', *The Political Quarterly*, 80(1): 17–24.

Wearden, G. (2020) 'US and UK stock markets plunge as coronavirus panic hits shares – as it happened', *Guardian*, 27 February, www.theguardian.com/business/live/2020/feb/27/stock-markets-plunge-ftse-100-dow-correction-trump-coronavirus-investors-business-live

13
Brexit and the crisis of British democracy
Jonathan Hopkin

Introduction

With a hard Brexit, declining population health and the looming prospect of a continued stagnation in living standards, the third decade of the twentieth century has not begun well for the UK. This chapter argues that the current crisis – which manifests itself in a variety of policy failures around the destructive decision to leave the European Union, continued economic decline and the poor management of the COVID-19 pandemic – has many proximate causes but ultimately boils down to the obsolete nature of the UK's constitution. The 'Westminster model' has allowed the government to be captured by a narrow oligarchical elite that has pursued a dysfunctional brand of neoliberalism. This has exacerbated structural problems, such as low investment, low productivity and high inequality, and has created the conditions for a lurch to the right. The Brexit vote, as well being an expression of popular anger at economic decline, was also an elite-led project to push the state in a direction amenable to the global financial elites that have underpinned the Conservative party's domination of British politics for most of the past half-century. The consequences of this are not only short-term disasters like the mismanagement of Covid, but longer-term problems such as rampant inequality, declining political trust and an inability of the UK's political institutions to adequately represent social interests or adapt to a rapidly changing world. The election of a Labour government with a strong parliamentary majority (but with weak electoral support) in 2024 has opened up opportunities for reform, but Starmer's Labour seems to have little interest in addressing the need for more fundamental constitutional change.

The state we're in: The neoliberal roots of Brexit

Britain's daring bid to arrest economic decline by cutting itself off from its main trading partners is one of the great puzzles of contemporary political economy. Of course, the UK was long known as an 'awkward partner' in the EU, with consistently lower levels of support for the European project than most other member states. However, this instinctive Euroscepticism was a necessary but not sufficient condition for Brexit to happen, especially since conflictual relationships between member states and EU institutions have not been confined to the UK. To explain why the UK would leave, we need to understand the motivations not only of the voters that opted for Brexit, but also the elites that put the item on the political menu in the first place.

Brexit as a project sits awkwardly between hostility to globalisation and the apparent (if somewhat confused) commitment of its elite supporters to a turbocharged version of it. The vote for Brexit can plausibly be described as one of many cases of the backlash against economic liberalism after the Global Financial Crisis of the late 2000s (Hopkin, 2017; 2020). Supporters of Brexit were disproportionately likely to be less educated, have lower incomes and live in economically declining regions of England and Wales that had suffered the most from post-crisis austerity (Becker *et al.*, 2017). However, elite support for Brexit, as indicated by the financial backing enjoyed by the Leave campaigns, seemed to come in large part from the financial, insurance and real estate sectors, particularly hedge funds and those with offshore interests (Martin and Payne, 2017). The fact that so many voters have expressed disappointment for the results of Brexit suggests that the interests of the latter group have been prioritised over the promises of improvements to the labour market and access to public services.

These promises were carefully targeted at the main sources of voter dissatisfaction in the aftermath of the financial crisis, which forced the Labour government of Gordon Brown into an extensive bailout of the banking sector (and financial interests more broadly) while paving the way for its successor, the Conservative-led government of David Cameron, to impose a programme of harsh austerity with socially regressive implications. After the banking crash, which shrunk the British economy by 6 per cent between 2008–9 (Office for National Statistics, 2018), real wages declined and remained below their pre-crisis level for a decade (Cribb and Johnson, 2018). Productivity growth languished to around 0.4 per cent a year in this period, implying that living standards fell behind comparator nations such as France and Germany (CEP and Resolution Foundation, 2022). A society that had suffered that kind of economic damage was naturally open to radical changes aimed at a return to prosperity.

Concerns over migration have been privileged in many political science analyses of Brexit as a typical example of the 'populist' backlash against progressive values and increased diversity (Norris and Inglehart, 2019). Anti-migrant attitudes were commonly cited by supporters of Brexit (Goodwin and Milazzo, 2017), and the Brexit campaign, and particularly the Leave.EU campaign, led by Nigel Farage, and its allies in the right-wing press, made much of claims that EU rules on Freedom of Movement (and disingenuously, membership of the European Convention on Human Rights) were hindering Britain's ability to control migration flows. Interpretations of the referendum result as above all a revolt against open borders abounded in the right-wing press in the aftermath. Conveniently, this shifted attention away from the deeper socio-economic roots of disaffection which had been successfully mobilised by the pro-Leave campaigns, and which pointed towards a Brexit which would break more sharply with the neoliberal ideas that had dominated policymaking since the 1980s. The effects of migration on living standards were hard to detect and possibly broadly positive, unlike the consequences of decades of economic policies that had entrenched inequality and disadvantage in Brexit-supporting areas (Portes, 2016).

There is substantial evidence that deep inequalities, exacerbated by post-crisis austerity, underpinned the Brexit vote. First of all, outside Scotland and Northern Ireland, where support for remaining in the European Union was connected to the hostility of large parts of the population to English nationalism, Remain only won decisively in London and prosperous smaller cities such as Oxford, Cambridge, Brighton and Bristol, with large shares of university graduates and high-paying jobs (BBC News, 2016). A granular analysis of house price dynamics showed that Remain performed best in wards where prices had been rising the most in the period prior to the referendum (Ansell and Adler, 2019). The spectacular success of the Leave vote in some of the most economically depressed regions of England and Wales – the 'places that don't matter' as one economic geographer described it (Rodríguez-Pose, 2018) – put Britain's deep regional inequality at the top of the political agenda. The regions most exposed to global trade shocks – mostly the traditional industrial heartlands of northern England, the Midlands and South Wales, which struggled to cope with the rise of China and other industrial competitors – were particularly enthusiastic for Brexit (Colantone and Stanig, 2018).

As well as territorial divides, the EU referendum also highlighted the deep occupational and educational stratification of the UK. Amongst voters in managerial and professional occupations, Remain had a substantial advantage of over 20 percentage points, whilst amongst the self-employed, semi-routine and routine occupations, and lower supervisory and technical occupations, Brexit enjoyed much greater support: between 25–35 per cent more voters in those groups supported Leave than Remain (Swales, 2016). A similar divide could be discerned in educational qualifications, with university degree holders favouring Remain over Leave with a gap of around 45 percentage points, and with voters lacking any educational qualifications swinging the other way even more strongly: Leave had an almost 60 percentage point advantage in that group (Swales, 2016). These dramatic differences in opinion on the EU suggest Brexit appealed particularly to the groups that had gained the least from market openness and a more competitive economy: the so-called 'losers' from globalisation (Rodrik, 2018). This is reinforced in an analysis by NatCen that shows big advantages for Leave from voters who felt that 'Britain has got a lot worse in the last ten years' and those reporting 'finding it quite/very difficult to get by' (Swales, 2016).

In short, for all the emphasis in the public debate on immigration and migrants, the deep roots of Brexit were unmistakably connected to Britain's lurch towards neoliberalism in the late twentieth century. The regions and occupational groups most damaged by the Thatcher reforms were disproportionately likely to opt for Brexit, with some of Britain's poorest and most downtrodden towns and cities (places such as Blackpool, Hull or Great Yarmouth that ranked highly on all indices of deprivation and disadvantage) registering spectacular margins in favour of leaving the European Union, even though they had often been major beneficiaries of European funding.

In response, the Conservative Party, perhaps taken aback by its unexpected reach beyond its traditional base of the Home Counties, adopted 'levelling up' as one of its main discursive themes (Jennings *et al.*, 2021). Three decades after rapid deindustrialisation and the rise of the City of London tore the territorial cohesion of the UK apart, the concentration of economic opportunity around London and a few other small parts of mainly southern England was finally recognised as one of the defining features of British politics. However, this created a deep tension between the objective needs of the Brexit-voting public, and the preferences of elite supporters of leaving the EU.

Populist turn or authoritarian trap? Brexit and the illiberal elite

There is little doubt that the success of the Brexit campaign lay in its ability to connect with a large share of the electorate that felt disconnected from the mainstream political establishment and were enthusiastic for new leadership and new ideas. The Remain campaign, at least in England

and Wales, was backed by the Conservative government, the Bank of England, the City of London and the Confederation of British Industry, and leading figures in the centre and centre-left of British politics (the official Remain campaign, *Britain Stronger in Europe*, was organised by Will Straw, the son of a former Labour minister). This establishment backing opened up a line of attack from Leave supporters that Brexit would allow for a redistribution of power from the elite to ordinary people. According to this argument, the British growth model had been detached from the needs of the population, and Brexit would be a lever for shifting the economy back in favour of working people in the neglected regions outside London.

However, the Leave campaign could hardly be considered a full-on popular revolt. There was little grassroots mobilisation and the campaign, albeit lacking the institutional advantages of the Remain camp, was generously backed by wealthy individuals from the financial and business sectors, such as hedge fund managers Paul Marshall and Crispin Odey, real estate investors such as Michael Freeman, or offshore manufacturers such as Dyson or Lord Bamford (of JCB) (Electoral Commission, 2016), not to mention Arron Banks, an obscure insurance broker who became the biggest donor to the Leave campaign. Although most mainstream politicians in Parliament backed Remain, a significant share of MPs from the governing Conservative Party – 130 out of 330, more than a third, including seventeen government ministers – backed Leave, alongside a handful of parliamentarians from other parties. The former governor of the Bank of England, Mervyn King, was also a Brexiter, alongside an array of influential Tories from previous eras, such as Nigel Lawson, John Redwood and Peter Lilley. The ease with which the vast majority of the Conservative parliamentary party fell into line with the Brexit project after the referendum confirms that leaving the European Union was hardly seen as a threat to the party elite.

Another major plank of elite support for Brexit was the print media. The newspaper industry in the UK is not only very concentrated and politically skewed to the right, but also exhibits an abnormal presence of foreign or offshore ownership. The Media Reform Coalition reported that

What went wrong with Britain?

in 2023, 90 per cent of the national print newspaper market, and 40 per cent of the online market, were in the hands of just three companies: DMG Media, News UK (part of NewsCorp) and Reach (Media Reform Coalition, 2023). Significantly, News UK is owned by Rupert Murdoch, a foreign national who also has extensive media interests in the US, Australia and elsewhere. DMG Media is owned by the 4th Viscount Rothermere, who is not domiciled in the UK for tax purposes. Other major media players are also in overseas hands, such as the *Evening Standard* and the *Independent*, owned by the Russian oligarchs, the Lebedevs, and the Telegraph Group, long owned by the Canadian Hollinger group, and then by the Barclay brothers, born in Britain but residents of tax havens (Monaco and Jersey in the Channel Islands). Although Britain's level of media concentration, and even of conservative press bias, is not itself unusual for a western democracy, the degree of foreign and offshore ownership is.

On top of this, the print media in Britain has exhibited unusual levels of criminal and unethical activity. The phone hacking scandal of the early 2010s culminated in the Leveson Inquiry, whose report detailed a systematic culture of abuses and 'outrageous' behaviour in sections of the press, and a relationship between the press and politicians 'which has not been in the public interest'. The Leveson Inquiry briefly shone a light on the close connections between the tabloid newspapers and the political system – such as Prime Minister David Cameron's appointment of former *News of the World* editor Andy Coulson as his Communications Officer, and frequent socialising with Coulson's successor, Rebekah Brooks – in which 'media executives and party leaders work together to push the same agenda' (in Cameron's own words to the inquiry) (Fenton, 2018). The first Leveson report recommended a reform of press regulation, which Cameron's government failed to enact, and was intended to be followed by a second phase of inquiry, which was first postponed and ultimately abandoned after the Conservatives won a parliamentary majority in the 2015 general election. This press influence over politics was not confined to periods of Conservative government: Tony Blair famously met Rupert Murdoch in secret shortly before the 1997 election, in which NewsCorp backed Labour, and become so close as to become godfather to one of his children.

Brexit and the crisis of British democracy

The 2003 Communications Act, passed in Labour's second term, removed restrictions on media cross ownership – the so-called 'Murdoch clause' – a move Murdoch's NewsCorp had lobbied for in order to combine print media with ventures into terrestrial TV (Barnett, 2014).

Another branch of the Brexit-supporting elite coalition was the array of influential think tanks and lobby groups close to the Conservative Party, often referred to in shorthand by the address some of them share, 55 Tufton Street (a building close to the Houses of Parliament and the Conservative Party headquarters, owned by a Conservative donor). Organisations such as the Taxpayers' Alliance, Business for Britain and the European Foundation, based out of the building and linked to the right-wing lobbying infrastructure in the US, campaigned for a combination of small-state conservatism, free market ideology, climate scepticism and of course hostility to the European Union (Geoghegan, 2020). When the referendum was called, the official Leave campaign group, Vote Leave, was also based out of 55 Tufton Street. Next door at number 57 the Centre for Policy Studies (CPS) is headquartered, a think tank previously close to Thatcher in the 1970s and 1980s, whilst Policy Exchange (close to leading Brexiter Michael Gove), the Adam Smith Institute and the Institute of Economic Affairs (IEA) (the UK's longest established neoliberal think tank), all have their own offices nearby. These groups are registered as 'educational charities', a status which provides generous tax reliefs, and although transparency over their funding is limited, they appear to rely on large donations from wealthy individuals (Mureithi, 2022). These organisations form a tight-knit network, with significant circulation of personnel: for example, Chris Dougherty, the head of the IEA, has also worked for the CPS and the Adam Smith Institute, as well as the Cato Institute in Washington, DC and the Cobden Centre, another free market think tank with ties to the Conservative Party and the Brexit movement.

It is striking that all of the most prominent think tanks close to the Conservative party should have been pro-Brexit, given that Brexit was a minority preference in the Conservative parliamentary party. Their role was not to represent the views of Conservative voters or even party members, but instead to shape them, and introduce new ideas which their backers hoped could influence British politics. These ideas had been circulating for some time in a diffuse network of opinion leaders and right-wing intellectuals connected to long-standing organisations such as the Mont Pelerin Society, one of the standard bearers of international free market thinking. It brought together academic and non-academic voices around the notions of individual economic freedom and a limited role for the state and for democratic decision-making, embedded in a global legal order (Slobodian, 2018). Most recently, a more aggressive form of libertarian thinking has emerged, one that combines free markets with an authoritarian approach to governance – including harsh attitudes towards immigration (particularly Muslim immigration), and minority rights in general – championed by groups such as the Henry Jackson Society or the independent website Conservative Home. Although the funding of these groups is not entirely transparent, wealthy Conservative donors such as the Eurosceptic Conservative donor Michael Ashcroft, a British-Belizean nominated to the House of Lords in 2000 despite not being domiciled by tax purposes in the UK, or Stanley Kalms, former head of Currys plc, are on record as making contributions.

This does not, however, imply that Brexit was the dominant position of the UK financial elite; quite the contrary. The official position of the bodies representing the interests of the financial sector, such as TheCityUK and the British Bankers' Association, was to back Remain, although there was also a pro-Brexit fringe that formed a rival 'City for Britain' group (James and Quaglia, 2017). The Leave–Remain divide appeared to mirror the different interests of large internationally oriented institutions like the big American investment banks, who valued access to the EU single market, and those of the 'non-banking' sector, such as hedge funds who were instead more concerned about possible future expansion of European Union oversight of the UK financial industry in the aftermath of the global financial crisis (James and Quaglia, 2017). Although the Leave-supporting elements were not representative of the City as a whole, they still had deep enough pockets to make a substantial financial contribution to the Leave campaign. On the other hand, the more 'establishment' view may have been pro-Remain, but was unable to influence the outcome of the referendum and was wary of becoming too politically visible, choosing instead to act behind the scenes to secure its preferred outcomes (Thompson, 2017). In practice, although Brexit was not the City's preferred outcome, the evidence up to now is that it has not harmed the financial sector in the UK as much as many predicted, with financial institutions deploying a range of 'workarounds' to keep hold of, and in some cases even increase, its share of the global market for financial services (Kalaitzake, 2021).

The inability of the City to prevent Brexit certainly challenges the validity of claims that the finance industry wields structural power and is able to condition government policies affecting its operations (James and Quaglia, 2019). However, this is not inconsistent with the claim that Brexit was an elite project responding to the interests of wealthy and powerful groups. An array of well-funded and tenacious organisations advocating right-wing politics, associated with wealthy backers, were able to grow their influence by identifying an opportunity in the aftermath of the Global Financial Crisis to exploit voter anger at plummeting living standards, collapsing public services and rising immigration. Europe had never been popular in British public opinion, but EU membership had low salience, at least until the 2016 campaign began. The referendum opened the door for a narrow elite to force through a radical project, and the porous nature of the UK constitution did the rest.

The Westminster model: A political system up for grabs

The UK political system has long been regarded as paradigmatic of a group of well-established democracies with marked 'majoritarian' characteristics (Lijphart, 1999). The so-called 'Westminster model' stands out amongst established democracies for the high degree of centralisation of power, the domination of the executive over the legislature (through the 'fusion' of the two in the institution of the Cabinet (Bagehot, 1966)), the lack of any clear separation of powers, with parliamentary sovereignty unconstrained by any other institution, and the distortions of the electoral system, which usually manufactures a majority in the House of Commons for one of the two main parties. As a result of these characteristics, coalition government – the norm in most democracies – is rare. The central government has relatively few restrictions on its authority over local institutions, and there is no written constitution to restrain parliament, which in principle cannot be bound by any previous legislation. This level of concentration of political power in a democracy is unique, and yet it has generally been accepted that the United Kingdom is a democracy in good standing, with a high score in the usual rankings of political freedom and accountability (Marshall *et al.*, 2017).

Attempts to reform this system during periods of Labour government attenuated these dynamics but left the fundamental logic of the Westminster model untouched. Tony Blair's first government launched a series of striking institutional reforms, most notably devolution to Scotland, Wales and Northern Ireland, and a new London-wide authority with an elected mayor. However a promise to consider electoral reform came to nought, not surprisingly when Labour enjoyed a comfortable majority in the House of Commons for three full legislative terms. The House of Lords was reformed to drastically reduce the voting rights of hereditary peers – a bizarre anomaly in a modern democracy – but did nothing to enhance the Lords' ability to act as a check on executive power and the dominance of the House of Commons. Attempts to extend decentralisation to English regions foundered as a referendum in the North East rejected, by a massive margin, the institution of an elected regional Assembly. This referendum saw the emergence of a talented Conservative think tanker and electoral strategist, Dominic Cummings, who led the North East Says No (NESNO) campaign to victory, arguing that the costs of the Assembly would be better directed at improving the National Health Service (at that time enjoying a spectacular boom in funding under the New Labour government).

The prominent involvement of right-wing think tanks in a series of referendums with constitutional implications continued with the 2011 referendum on electoral reform, which resulted from the deal between the Conservatives and the Liberal Democrats to form the first formal coalition government in Britain since the war. This time it was the transatlantic think tanker and future Leave campaign coordinator, Matthew Elliott, co-founder of the Taxpayers' Alliance. The campaign, named NO2AV, was very similar to Cummings' NESNO operation, claiming that the costs of the new voting system would be better spent on the NHS and other valued public services (Robinson, 2021). The common thread in these referendums was that they were focused on preserving the Westminster model. Stopping English devolution enabled the central government to continue dominating policymaking in England, which accounts for 85 per cent of the British population, and 86 per cent of GDP. Overturning the proposal to change the electoral system to the Alternative Vote model meant that single party governments, most of the time Conservative ones, would continue to predominate. Any shift to a more consensual model of democracy, with a wider range of interests intervening in the policy process, was a threat to a system of power revolving around the Conservative Party, and by extension its wealthy, often offshore, donors and supporters.

Brexit can be seen in a similar light. The constitutional implications of Brexit were clearly to extract the UK from a set of institutional arrangements that pooled sovereignty at the EU level and therefore subjected the UK Parliament to regulatory and policy influences from a supranational source. Although pro-Remain constitutionalists argued that parliamentary sovereignty was consistent with the supremacy of EU law, it remained the case that, ultimately, EU membership meant that Parliament was constrained in a wide range of policy areas, with immigration and financial regulation being two of the most contentious. This also implied that powerful groups in Britain who had the capacity to influence and shape policies made by the UK parliament and government were constrained by a policy process at the EU level which they could not control to any significant degree. Brexit was therefore both a return to the 'pure' form of the Westminster model, in terms of absolute parliamentary sovereignty (with the awkward exception of Northern Ireland), and a closing off of an avenue for a more consensual, negotiated policy process in which a wider range of interests could be involved.

What went wrong with Britain?

Ironically, the chaotic process of determining the way in which Brexit would actually be implemented presented a very different picture. The initial closing of ranks in the Conservative party around a Leave mandate that the majority of MPs had campaigned against, and the alignment of the vast majority of MPs, including notably the opposition Labour Party, around Brexit through the vote to activate Article 50, suggested a very majoritarian, quasi-plebiscitary, form of government. Almost the entire political class closed ranks around the vague notion that 'Brexit means Brexit', as David Cameron's successor Theresa May incanted. Yet the obvious ambiguities and complications of the referendum mandate necessitated a forceful use of executive power which only a large parliamentary majority would allow. Seeing an opportunity in the Conservatives' leap in the opinion polls, May called a snap election, but failed miserably to enhance her majority, ending up instead as the leader of a minority government dependent on the support of Northern Ireland's Democratic Unionists (DUP). Brexit stalled at that point, illustrating how the Westminster model's institutions made cross-party negotiation and consensus-building close to impossible (Ansell, 2023). Attempts by May to push through a Brexit deal which combined border control to cut migration with a trade agreement maintaining the UK in broad regulatory alignment with the EU were rejected by the Eurosceptic faction, the European Research Group. A cross-party coalition around a 'softer' Brexit was a non-starter due to the hostility of both major parties to such a deal.

With the May Government having failed to develop a Brexit project acceptable to the Conservative party and its parliamentary allies, the DUP, the only answer was to attempt once again to bulldoze opposition by purging the Conservative parliamentary party of Remainers and win a renewed mandate in a general election (Bale, 2023). Boris Johnson's elevation to Number 10 to replace Theresa May marked a shift in strategy aimed at bypassing parliamentary constraints, signalled by the prorogation of parliament in September 2019, and then by forcing through a hard Brexit which left Northern Ireland inside the single market whilst establishing only the thinnest of trade agreements for the Great Britain part of the United Kingdom. Johnson then called yet another election to force the deal through, which he won handsomely against a beleaguered Labour Party. In the run-up to the election, high-profile Tory Remainers either announced plans to leave politics or were expelled from the party and were replaced by hardline Brexiters. Alongside the Johnson campaign's unprecedented inroads into Labour territory, which saw the election of a new generation of Brexiters in the Northern 'red wall', the 2019 election completed the transformation of the Conservative Party into a party of the populist Right, focused on national sovereignty, a hardline policy on immigration and a combative and aggressive populist discourse (Alexandre-Collier, 2022).

Brexit derailed: The limits of elite populism

In early 2020 it appeared that British politics had been fundamentally realigned around a durable coalition of elite neoliberals and disgruntled, mostly English, working-class and retired voters outside the major cities. Labour's catastrophic defeat in 2019, following Jeremy Corbyn's unexpectedly strong showing in Theresa May's snap 2017 election, left the party with its worst parliamentary representation since 1935. Likewise, the other main parties (with the exception of the Scottish National Party), the Liberal Democrats and the Brexit Party, were also left on the sidelines as the Conservatives won a spectacular parliamentary majority, a reward for finally delivering on the mandate of the 2016 referendum. Few would have predicted how quickly it would unravel.

In part the failure of the Johnson Government was down to the pure ill fortune of encountering the worst pandemic for a century, which brutally exposed the weaknesses of the British state and the vulnerability of a society still reeling from the consequences of the financial crash and a decade of austerity (Seldon and Newell, 2023). In particular, COVID-19 hit after a long period of rising demand for health and social care, which the succession of post-crisis Conservative-led governments had failed to meet with adequate investment or current spending (Arrieta, 2022). Worse still, deep spending cuts in other areas – in particular, the budgets of local authorities charged with delivering key social services (such as social care for older and disabled people), as well as welfare benefits paid out to the most vulnerable households – undermined state support for the wellbeing of the poorer and less healthy sectors of society (Case and Kraftman, 2022). In addition to this short-term impact of government policy, the longer-term marginalisation of large parts of the population due to persistent economic inequality – across both occupational and educational groups and between regions – meant that many Britons were simply not in good enough health to survive the waves of COVID-19 infection.

It also turned out that the political skills and ideological preconceptions that had facilitated the Conservatives' electoral successes between 2010 and 2019 were entirely unsuited to managing the most complex economic, social and health crisis of modern times. Chief of all, Boris Johnson's remarkable ability to reach large numbers of voters across the political spectrum with a mixture of boosterism, iconoclastic contrarianism and hardline rhetoric was very quickly exposed by the thankless, technocratic graft required to minimise the damage to public health and the economy posed by the virus. Johnson's inability to attend key meetings as the pandemic developed, and the fatal delays in instituting lockdowns whilst hospitals were encouraged to offload infected patients into care homes, pointed to an amateurish and deluded attitude towards a public health threat that killed hundreds of thousands. Ultimately, Johnson's cavalier approach to complying with his own government's rules in his workplace cost him his job, but the deep flaws in the overall management of the pandemic in Britain were only partially offset politically by the achievement of distributing vaccines slightly earlier than other European countries (British Medical Association, 2023).

The pandemic was such an all-consuming shock to daily life that the formal implementation of Brexit passed almost unnoticed, the new arrangements coming into effect in early 2021, during the UK's second lockdown. Fears of logistical chaos at the borders proved unfounded, and the immediate economic consequences of Brexit were hard to disentangle from the effects of the colossal shock of the pandemic and months of restrictions on social and commercial life. But voters struggled to see any economic benefits of leaving the EU: the post-pandemic withdrawal of heavy government support for the economy and financial markets was complicated by the inflation shock caused by difficulties in rebuilding supply chains and the Russian invasion of Ukraine, which sharply increased energy costs, especially for a major net gas importer like the UK. By the time the dust began to settle on these multiple economic shocks, it became clear that Britain's economic decline was anything but reversed. By 2023, real wages had still not grown since 2007 (CEP and Resolution Foundation, 2022) and were projected to remain flat for years to come as living costs and taxes rose, income inequality between individuals and regions remained as high as ever, and the National Health Service, whose funding had been promised by Boris Johnson to improve if Britain left the EU, was facing perhaps the biggest crisis in its history (Freedman, 2023). By late 2023, a large majority of voters saw Brexit as having failed to improve things and a growing share expressed support for rejoining the EU (Smith, 2023).

Although the pandemic and subsequent shocks were not predictable, the failure of Brexit to spark an economic revival certainly was: for reasons amply discussed during the referendum campaign and afterwards, leaving the EU had few obvious economic benefits since the costs it imposed on trading with Britain's biggest markets more than offset any gains from either lower contributions to the EU budget or from trade agreements designed to gain greater access to markets outside the EU (Springford, 2023). But a further, more deeply political, problem undermined attempts to reconcile the results of Brexit with the hopes of its supporters: the fundamental disagreements within the Brexiter elite coalition about which direction to take in building Britain's post-EU economic model. Building a majority in favour of Brexit as an abstract idea was far easier than winning support for a detailed set of policies and institutional changes to exploit the Brexit 'opportunity'. At least three visions could be identified for what Brexit might look like. One of them, often described as 'Lexit' or a left-oriented Brexit, involved using Britain's newfound freedom from EU constraints over state ownership and macroeconomic policy to build a more socialist-oriented economic strategy, a minority position even in the Labour party which was never going to be implemented by a Conservative government. However Conservatives themselves were deeply divided over what Brexit should mean (Woollen, 2022; Xu and Lu, 2022).

Theresa May's strategy was an awkward mix of tight immigration controls to appease the nationalist right wing of the party alongside a trade agreement which accepted some limited pooling of sovereignty through alignment with single market rules. The philosophy underpinning this strategy, outlined in her first conference speech as leader in autumn 2016, was overtly sceptical of globalisation and its failure to deliver for large parts of the British-born population, and was particularly scathing of globally minded 'citizens of nowhere' (Walshe, 2023). This implied a kind of economic nationalist, even protectionist, approach, in which market openness, especially in sectors dependent on free movement of people, should be sacrificed in order to prioritise the interests of native workers threatened by global competition. Boris Johnson, the leader who had most success in reaching the 'red wall', developed these ideas to emphasise 'levelling up', a rhetorical commitment short of policy substance, which aspired to address the deep regional divides of contemporary Britain (Connolly *et al.*, 2021), in particular the divide between the economic dynamism and sociocultural diversity of the capital city (derided as the home of a Remainer 'liberal elite') and the protectionist instincts of some voters in the much poorer regions of the post-industrial North, Midlands and Wales.

The failure to pursue these visions with any real enthusiasm was at least in part down to its incompatibility with the much more 'globalist' and neoliberal agenda pursued by other leading Tories. 'Levelling up' in particular was a difficult concept to square with the fundamental Conservative principles of free markets and a small state. Not surprisingly, therefore, the Johnson Levelling Up agenda had made little progress beyond minor symbolic measures by the time he was toppled and replaced by Liz Truss, a former Remainer very close to the world of Tufton Street think tanks. Truss was selected through a run-off vote amongst Conservative party members, in which she roundly defeated her rival candidate, the Chancellor of the Exchequer, Rishi Sunak, with a campaign invoking the spirit of Margaret Thatcher and strongly supported by the right-wing press. Truss's post-Brexit vision of small state pro-market conservatism was swiftly, indeed recklessly, presented in a catastrophic budget statement that promised sweeping tax cuts, especially for top earners. 'Trussonomics' had its roots in the thinking of a new generation of neoliberal Tory MPs documented in an extraordinary collective publication, *Britannia Unchained*, written by Truss and her Chancellor, Kwasi Kwarteng, amongst others. The publication outlined a radical plan to deregulate the UK economy, cut taxes and slash the welfare state (Kwarteng et al., 2012). These ambitious aims fell at the first hurdle as the decision to gamble on omitting any serious analysis of fiscal sustainability and sidelining the cautious voices in the Treasury proved mistaken, with financial markets very quickly signalling a lack of confidence that brought the Truss Government down in record time.

The fall of the Truss Government, less than three years after the extraordinary electoral landslide of December 2019, plunged the Conservative Party into the deep crisis that led to its dramatic defeat in the 2024 general election. The arrival in Number 10 of the default option of Rishi Sunak, the loser of the 2022 leadership contest, left the government with little direction, and the fiscal emergency opened up by Truss's gamble necessitated a harsh adjustment which made households even poorer in a context of the worst cost of living crisis on record (Elliott and Crerar, 2022). Jeremy Hunt, the new Chancellor, found himself forced to raise taxes to historically high levels to restore market confidence and stabilise the government's fiscal standing. The grim economic situation that ensued – compounded by the spike in energy prices after Russia's invasion of Ukraine – and which necessitated further massive public expenditure to cushion household energy costs, left the Conservatives deeply unpopular. Disastrous opinion polls undermined Sunak's authority, accentuating the party's internal divisions and lack of programmatic coherence. The elixir of Brexit, which in 2019 brought Conservatives their best electoral performance for almost thirty years, had lost its potency, leaving a disgruntled country to look for another solution to its deep-seated problems.

What went wrong with Britain?

Conclusion

Poor leadership and bad luck certainly had a part to play in the derailing of Brexit, but its failure ultimately boiled down to its superficial and confused analysis of Britain's economic problems and the inability of the Conservative party to match its electoral campaigning talents with any serious conception of how to institute a policy programme that could shape a future for the UK outside the European Union. This is a party political failure, but also, more fundamentally, a constitutional one. The referendum placed a great deal of power into the hands of a narrow elite disconnected from much of civil society and the representatives of productive forces in Britain, and overly influenced by short-term political ambitions and the opaque machinations of donors, lobbyists and newspaper owners. Brexit was a magnificent tool for realigning the party system in the Conservatives' favour, but it was quickly revealed to be an at best incoherent, and at worse entirely deluded, project in policy terms.

The lessons of the Brexit process therefore go much further than the limitations of the Conservative Party or of the suitability of neoliberal thinking for addressing Britain's economic problems. It is hard to imagine anything similar in any other major European Union member state: domestic constitutional constraints and elite alignment with the European orientations of key economic interest groups ensure that, for all their Eurosceptic parties may win substantial numbers of votes, the obstacles in the path of, say, France or Italy ever leaving are enormous. Yet in Britain, a combination of constitutional flexibility – usually touted as a strength – and a confused mix of globalist and protectionist thinking in its most historically successful political party made an act of serious economic self-harm with deeply disruptive political consequences not only possible but indeed impossible to stop. Moving towards a more consensual and inclusive form of government, typical of not only most EU member states, but also the modus operandi of the EU institutions themselves, would not solve all of Britain's problems, but it would at least avoid creating entirely new ones.

It is difficult to see much movement in this direction under the new Labour government, whose outsized parliamentary majority on a historically narrow advantage in terms of votes makes it one of the biggest beneficiaries in British history of the Westminster model's distortions. Timid moves in the direction of greater devolution to regional authorities in England, and the elimination of the voting power of the hereditary peers in the House of Lords, are steps in the right direction but the core of the Westminster model – the outsized power of central government, especially the Treasury, and the wildly unrepresentative composition of the House of Commons – is set to remain firmly entrenched.

References

Alexandre-Collier, A. (2022) 'David Cameron, Boris Johnson and the "populist hypothesis" in the British Conservative Party', *Comparative European Politics* 20(5): 527–543.
Ansell, B. (2023) *Why Politics Fails*, Viking, London.
Ansell, B. and Adler, D. (2019) 'Brexit and the politics of housing in Britain', *Political Quarterly*, 90(S2): 105–116.
Arrieta, T. (2022) 'Austerity in the United Kingdom and its legacy: Lessons from the COVID-19 pandemic', *Economic and Labour Relations Review*, 33(2): 238–255.
Bagehot, W. (1966) *The English Constitution*, Cornell University Press, Ithaca.
BBC News (2016) 'EU referendum local results', www.bbc.co.uk/news/politics/eu_referendum/results/local/
Bale, T. (2023) *The Conservative Party After Brexit: Turmoil and Transformation*, Wiley, London.
Barnett, S. (2014) 'Murdoch and media power – déjà vu all over again?', Media@LSE, 30 January, https://blogs.lse.ac.uk/medialse/2014/01/30/murdoch-and-media-power-deja-vu-all-over-again/
Becker, S.O., Fetzer, T. and Novy, D. (2017) 'Who voted for Brexit? A comprehensive district-level analysis', *Economic Policy*, 32(92): 601–650.
British Medical Association (2023) 'Boris Johnson's covid inquiry evidence was "a masterclass in double-speak", says BMA', BMA Media Centre, 7 December, www.bma.org.uk/bma-media-centre/boris-johnson-s-covid-inquiry-evidence-was-a-masterclass-in-double-speak-says-bma
Case, A. and Kraftman, L. (2022) 'Health inequalities', IFS Deaton Review of Inequalities, Institute of Fiscal Studies.
CEP and Resolution Foundation (2022) 'Britain, a services superpower sinking into stagnation', LSE Business Review, 5 August, https://blogs.lse.ac.uk/

businessreview/2022/08/05/britain-a-services-superpower-sinking-into-stagnation/
Colantone, I. and Stanig, P. (2018) 'Global competition and Brexit', *American Political Science Review*, 112(2): 201–218.
Connolly, J., Pyper, R. and van der Zwet, A. (2021) 'Governing "levelling-up" in the UK: challenges and prospects', *Contemporary Social Science*, 16(5): 523–537.
Cribb, J. and Johnson, P. (2018) '10 years on – have we recovered from the financial crisis?', Institute for Fiscal Studies, 12 September, https://ifs.org.uk/articles/10-years-have-we-recovered-financial-crisis
Elliott, L. and Crerar, P. (2022) 'Biggest hit to living standards on record as Hunt lays out autumn statement', *Guardian*, 17 November, www.theguardian.com/uk-news/2022/nov/17/biggest-hit-to-living-standards-on-record-as-jeremy-hunt-lays-out-autumn-statement
Fenton, N. (2018) 'Regulation is freedom: Phone hacking, press regulation and the Leveson Inquiry – the story so far', *Communication Law*, 23(3).
Freedman, S. (2023) 'How bad does the NHS crisis need to get?' Institute for Government, 14 June, www.instituteforgovernment.org.uk/comment/how-bad-nhs-crisis
Geoghegan, P. (2020) *Democracy for Sale*, Head of Zeus, London.
Goodwin, M. and Milazzo, C. (2017) 'Taking back control? Investigating the role of immigration in the 2016 vote for Brexit', *British Journal of Politics and International Relations*, 19(3): 450–464.
Hopkin, J. (2017) 'When Polanyi met Farage: Market fundamentalism, economic nationalism, and Britain's exit from the European Union', *British Journal of Politics and International Relations*, 19(3): 465–478.
Hopkin, J. (2020) *Anti-System Politics: The Crisis of Market Liberalism in Rich Democracies*, Oxford University Press, Oxford.
James, S. and Quaglia, L. (2017) 'Brexit and the limits of financial power in the UK', GEG Working Paper, No. 129, University of Oxford.
James, S. and Quaglia, L. (2019) 'Brexit, the City and the contingent power of finance', *New Political Economy*, 24(2): 258–271.
Jennings, W., McKay, L. and Stoker, G. (2021) 'The politics of levelling up', *Political Quarterly*, 92(2): 302–311.
Kalaitzake, M. (2021) 'Brexit for finance? Structural interdependence as a source of financial political power within UK-EU withdrawal negotiations', *Review of International Political Economy*, 28(3): 479–504.
Kwarteng, K., Patel, P., Raab, D., Skidmore, C. and Truss, E. (2012) *Britannia Unchained*, Palgrave, London.
Lijphart, A. (1999) *Patterns of Democracy: Government Forms and Performance in Thirty-Six Countries*, Yale University Press, London.
Marshall, M.G., Gurr, T.R. and Jaggers, K. (2017) 'POLITY IV Project: Political Regime Characteristics and Transitions, 1800–2016', Center for Systemic Peace, www.systemicpeace.org

Martin, W. and Payne, A. (2017), 'The 21 biggest donors to the Brexit campaign', Business Insider, 9 May, https://www.businessinsider.com/twenty-one-biggest-donors-to-the-leave-brexit-campaign-2017-5

Media Reform Coalition (2023) 'New report: Who owns the UK media?', https://www.mediareform.org.uk/wp-content/uploads/2023/10/Who-Owns-the-UK-Media-2023.pdf

Mureithi, A. (2022) 'UK's most secretive think tanks bank £14.3m from mystery donors', openDemocracy, 17 December, www.opendemocracy.net/en/dark-money-investigations/think-tanks-transparency-funding-who-funds-you/

Norris, P. and Inglehart, R. (2019) *Cultural Backlash: Trump, Brexit, and Authoritarian Populism*, Cambridge University Press, Cambridge.

Office for National Statistics (2018) 'The 2008 recession 10 years on', 30 April, www.ons.gov.uk/economy/grossdomesticproductgdp/articles/the2008recession10yearson/2018-04-30

Portes, J. (2016) 'Immigration, free movement and the EU referendum', *National Institute Economic Review*, 236(1): 14–22.

Robinson, R. (2021) 'A dry run for Brexit: The 2011 Alternative Vote referendum ten years on', *Byline Times*, 29 March, https://bylinetimes.com/2021/03/29/a-dry-run-for-brexit-the-2011-alternative-vote-referendum-ten-years-on/

Rodríguez-Pose, A. (2018) 'The revenge of the places that don't matter (and what to do about it)', *Cambridge Journal of Regions, Economy and Society*, 11(1): 189–209.

Rodrik, D. (2018) 'Populism and the economics of globalization', *Journal of International Business Policy*, 1(1): 12–33.

Seldon, A. and Newell, R. (2023) *Johnson at 10*, Atlantic Books, London.

Slobodian, Q. (2018) *Globalists: The End of Empire and the Birth of Neoliberalism*, Harvard University Press, Cambridge, MA.

Smith, M. (2023) 'Britons would vote to rejoin the EU', YouGov, 18 July, https://yougov.co.uk/politics/articles/45910-britons-would-vote-rejoin-eu

Springford, J. (2023) 'Are the costs of Brexit big or small?', Centre for European Reform, 9 May, https://www.cer.eu/insights/are-costs-brexit-big-or-small

Swales, K. (2016) *Understanding the Leave Vote*, NatCen Social Research, London.

Thompson, H. (2017) 'How the City of London lost at Brexit: A historical perspective', *Economy and Society*, 46(2): 211–228.

Walshe, G. (2023) 'Putting lipstick on a bigotry', *Foreign Policy*, 18 December.

Woollen, C. (2022) 'The space between leave and remain: Archetypal positions of British parliamentarians on Brexit', *British Politics*, 17(1): 97–116.

Xu, R. and Lu, Y. (2022) 'Intra-party dissent over Brexit in the British Conservative Party', *British Politics*, 17(3): 274–297.

14
Fighting back? Britain's shifting capitalism and its discontents
David J. Bailey

Introduction

Britain's model of capitalism is shifting. It relies on a starkly unequal, de-industrialised, de-unionised and increasingly precarious workforce. It is fuelled by financial speculation, a seemingly endless drive to privatise whatever remains of the welfare state and an over-inflated housing market that perennially teeters on the edge. Under the Conservative Government it was led by a strange hybrid nationalist-neoliberal elite, with populist-dystopian dreams of sending migrants to Rwanda and scant regard for the country's physical, social or ecological health. This shift, however, has not been without its discontents. The 2010s was a decade of anti-austerity, national riots, student revolts, housing activism, anti-fracking, school strikes and new precarious workers' movements.

This growing dissent did not go unnoticed. Government responses throughout the period saw a combination of limited concessions in order to address the most visible expressions of dissent, creeping authoritarianism designed to stem the opportunities for further expressions of dissent, and nationalist rhetoric designed to offset any further opposition. Faced with managing the pandemic, and in the light of the growing social panic that accompanied it, we saw a continuation of this escalating cycle of discontent, and reactionary efforts to thwart it. The Johnson Government

Fighting back?

was forced to abandon its goal of 'herd immunity' and instead spend billions on furloughing much of Britain's workforce. The Truss Government was brought down following a reckless attempt to cut taxes, whilst at the same time committing to fund the Energy Price Guarantee in order to support the public with rising fuel costs; a combination of measures considered implausible both by the public and international financial markets. As Truss was replaced by Sunak as Prime Minister the Conservative Government entered a period where defeat at the next general election seemed inevitable, turning increasingly to authoritarian measures in a desperate attempt to rule out all forms of dissent, and relying on an ever-growing anti-immigration stance to increase its popularity. The Public Order Act 2023 further criminalised protest, the Strikes (Minimum Service Levels) Act 2023 forced trade unions to ensure some of their members would continue to work on days when they took strike action, and the Safety of Rwanda (Asylum and Immigration) Act 2024 declared the so-called Rwanda Plan to be both safe and legal, overturning the earlier contrary verdict of the Supreme Court.

At the same time, new instances of 'mutual aid' sprang up across the country both during and after the pandemic. Teachers' unions forced the government into multiple U-turns on plans to open schools during the pandemic; the Black Lives Matter movement exposed the racist roots of British capitalism; and the cost of living crisis witnessed an emergent 'Don't Pay' campaign and a wave of strike action as wages failed to keep up with inflation. The only attempt to actually use the measures introduced in the Strikes (Minimum Service Levels) Act saw a rapid climbdown by rail company LNER when it was faced with a retaliatory additional five days of strike action by the train drivers' union, ASLEF.

Whereas many accounts of Britain's neoliberal decline present an (accurate) account of the damaging trends that afflict the country's socio-economy, we also need to consider how those who inhabit and suffer British capitalism are also fighting back. This chapter offers an assessment of those trajectories of dissent and the way in which they shaped Britain's decaying model of capitalism during the period of Tory rule. This will similarly be a key challenge facing Starmer's Labour Government, as it seeks to identify new opportunities for economic growth whilst at the same time seeking to contain the potential for expressions of social discontent that became so visible under the Conservatives.

Britain's shifting model of capitalism

The problems and pathologies of the UK's model of capitalism have been well documented across the comparative and critical political economy literature (Lavery 2019; Christophers 2020; Clift and McDaniel, 2021). Perhaps the most common observation is that the UK, along with the US, represents one of the most liberalised of the advanced capitalist democracies, including a highly open and liberal financial and trade regime, and relatively low levels of labour market protection coupled with legislation designed to inhibit trade union activity (Lavery 2019: 21–28). This is a model of capitalism that was imposed through a series of measures, introduced from the 1980s onwards, that sought to address the declining profitability of the British economy and high levels of strike activity, both of which were diagnosed as fundamental problems facing British capitalism during the 1970s (Glyn 2006; Copley 2022). This process of liberalisation was especially associated with a corresponding growth in importance of the financial sector within the British economy, as banks and other financial corporations took advantage of the liberalising measures adopted by the British government and the advantages accrued to the City of London as a major international financial centre (Norfield, 2017). This, in turn, is associated with high levels of wage inequality, as high levels of pay and bonuses in the financial sector contribute to very high levels of pay at the top end of the pay scale, alongside declining wages for lower paid workers due to the erosion of union bargaining power, diminished labour market protections and the fragmentation of the workforce as a result of the outsourcing and contracting-out of work (Christophers, 2020; Clift and McDaniel, 2021). The deprioritisation of welfare spending and a relative decline in welfare generosity have been viewed as a way to incentivise participants in the labour market in order to minimise any unemployment caused by moving away from manufacturing, placing responsibility for

Fighting back?

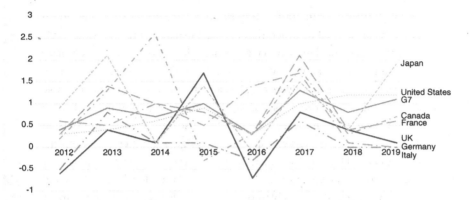

Figure 14.1 Labour productivity growth, total economy (GDP per hour worked, average annual growth rate)
Source: OECD, 2020

unemployment on the shoulders of the unemployed themselves (Hay, 2013: 31).

The shifting nature of the UK's model of capitalism became most visible in the fallout from the 2008 global financial crisis. As Lepper *et al.* describe, the 'UK was affected immediately because of its importance as an international financial centre' (2016: 84). Productivity growth dramatically fell as the shock of the 2008 global financial crisis significantly discouraged investment (Crafts and Mills 2020). This has seen the UK become increasingly uncompetitive, with average productivity growth lagging behind all G7 countries except for Italy (OECD, 2020) (Figure 14.1, UK represented by the solid black line, G7 represented by a solid grey line).

In an attempt to respond to this experience of decline, the Conservative-led government, in power since 2010, resorted to a number of somewhat desperate measures that amounted to a reinforcing of the neoliberal tendencies introduced from the 1980s, largely worsening the problem. These neoliberal stimulus measures included further attempts to reduce welfare generosity and public services, legitimated by deploying the idea of 'austerity' as a form of common sense that applies to all households seeking to balance the books (Stanley 2014). This included a 49 per cent cut in central government funding for local authorities (National Audit Office, 2018) as well as draconian measures such as the 'bedroom tax';[1] a 'workfare' scheme designed to force benefit claimants to take up voluntary work;[2] a massive hike in student fees to fund an equally large reduction in public spending on universities; and a further curtailing of the principle of universal welfare provision through the introduction of means testing for the receipt of childcare benefits. We also saw further attempts to liberalise the labour market, especially through a number of key attacks on workers and trade unions, including the further removal of employment protections by increasing the threshold for claims for unfair dismissal (from one year to two) and by introducing fees for access to employment tribunals (a move which was subsequently reversed following a successful legal challenge), alongside the introduction of new balloting rules under the Trade Union Act 2016, making it more difficult still for trade unions to engage in collective action. Arguably the most important stimulus measure introduced during this period was the very large reduction in interest rates that took the form of quantitative easing. This represented a continuation of the boom-bust policy approach adopted in the 1980s, using monetary policy as a means through which to stimulate a financialised socio-economy in a way that creates growth through financial and asset bubbles (which eventually burst) (Oren and Blyth, 2019). Indeed, quantitative easing targeted support on asset holders, and especially the key socio-economic (and electoral) group of homeowners, as a central pillar of neoliberal hegemony in Britain.

As a result of the austerity measures introduced by the Conservatives, the 2010s saw declining real wages and growing inequality.[3] This, in turn, created a legitimacy issue for the Conservative-led Government. Public opinion increasingly turned against the idea that austerity was necessary, with those agreeing that there was a need for public service spending to be cut in order to pay off the national debt falling from 59 per cent of those surveyed in 2010 to 22 per cent in 2017 (Deloitte and Reform, 2017). Similarly, by 2016 responses to the British Social Attitudes survey found, for the first time since the 2007–8 global economic crisis, that more people wanted taxation increased to allow greater spending, rather than wanting

Fighting back?

tax and spend levels to stay as they were (Clery *et al.*, 2017). Despite this shift in opinion, the Labour Party under Ed Miliband proved unable to capitalise on any anti-austerity sentiment, as did the Liberal Democrats who were complicit with the austerity imposed between 2010 and 2015. By the time of the 2015 general election, therefore, only the right-wing UK Independence Party (UKIP) had proven able to mobilise any resentment in British society into an electoral programme that would challenge the Conservatives, channelling that resentment into a xenophobic campaign against the European Union and migrants (Evans and Mellon, 2016). As a result, the outright victory for the Conservatives in 2015 was ultimately underpinned by its manifesto offer of a referendum on the UK's membership of the European Union, in an attempt to fend off the growing popularity of UKIP (which nevertheless won an impressive 12.6 per cent of the overall vote), and to appease a growing proportion of right-wing Conservatives who took a similar view to UKIP (Bailey, 2018).

The surprising outcome of the 2016 Brexit referendum was, at least in part, a direct result of the austerity measures introduced by the Cameron Government, as support for Brexit increased amongst those hit hardest by austerity (Fetzer, 2019). This right-wing expression of dissent proved sufficient to prevent the election of the now more left-wing Labour Party under Jeremy Corbyn's leadership, with the 2019 general election witnessing potential Labour supporters shift support *both* to the Conservatives on the grounds that Corbyn was insufficiently pro-Brexit *and* to the Liberal Democrats on the grounds that he was insufficiently opposed to Brexit (Cutts *et al.*, 2020). By this time, the right wing of the Conservative Party, including Prime Minister Boris Johnson, had successfully re-defined Brexit along both highly nationalist and free market/libertarian lines, in which 'no deal' was considered better than any negotiated exit from the European Union (Kettell and Kerr, 2020).

As Britain entered the pandemic, therefore, it was governed by a pro-Brexit right-wing Conservative Party under Boris Johnson, which combined a commitment to further liberalisation of Britain's economy with a xenophobic commitment to Brexit (Worth 2016). The libertarian elements of this dangerous mix became apparent as the pandemic started, with an ongoing reluctance by the Johnson Government to impose restrictions on social interaction in the early stages of the outbreak. Even once a lockdown had been accepted as necessary, the government was frequently willing, in private, to contravene the rules it had set itself (Ryder, 2022). The pro-business tendencies of the government were also clearly on display during the pandemic, most obviously in the use of private contracts and outsourcing to private firms with direct political connections to the government, highlighting the cronyism that marks Britain's model of neoliberal capitalism (Wood et al., 2022).[4] Government measures were also put in place to support the housing market, prompting yet another round of over-heating, to the benefit of homeowners and the detriment of those who do not own a home (Inman 2021). Perhaps unsurprisingly, therefore, Covid exacerbated the deep-rooted inequalities that already characterised neoliberal Britain (Macartney et al., 2022).

As Britain emerged from the pandemic it faced inflationary pressures arising from bottlenecks in the supply chain and a glut of savings accrued by those on moderate and higher incomes during the lockdowns. Yet some of the core problems of British neoliberal capitalism remained. The Bank of England predicted (in August 2022) that Britain would face both rising interest rates (in an effort to control inflation), and a prolonged recession throughout 2023 (Bank of England, 2022). The key mechanisms that have driven growth throughout the post-2008 period – especially quantitative easing and ultra-low interest rates – appeared to have reached their limit, posing the very real prospect of a period of stagflation marked by real terms wage cuts and extremely low levels of growth.

In July 2022, Boris Johnson was forced to resign from office following one misleading statement to the public too many – this time having wrongly denied that he knew his deputy chief whip, Chris Pincher, had a track record of sexual misconduct allegations against him. He was replaced by Liz Truss, whose short-lived time in office was perhaps the most disastrous prime ministership in Britain's history. Elected as Conservative Party leader on a promise to dramatically cut taxes and put into place a hyper-neoliberal programme of growth-led reforms, the global financial markets instead took the view that hers was a reckless economic programme

Fighting back?

and speculated heavily against it, quickly prompting her resignation from office. As she was subsequently replaced by Rishi Sunak and his seemingly more sober governorship of the British socio-economy, nevertheless his priorities remained a commitment to maintaining fiscal conservatism, further attacks on organised labour in the form of the new Strikes (Minimum Service Levels) Act 2023 and more xenophobia with the Illegal Migration Act 2023 and Safety of Rwanda (Asylum and Immigration) Act 2024.

Discontent: Where's the opposition?

Much of the foregoing analysis, highlighting the neoliberal nature of the British model of capitalism, especially under the Conservative Government, is widely established within the comparative and critical political economy literature (for a recent development of this analysis, see Berry 2022). Far less often remarked upon in discussions such as these are the expressions of discontent and resistance that have emerged in opposition to this shifting neoliberal socio-economy. Indeed, many of the most insightful commentaries on the plights of the British model of capitalism have failed to highlight any acts of resistance at all (see, for instance, Clift and McDaniel, 2021 and Hofman and Aalbers, 2019). Grassroots opposition, refusal and resistance are otherwise absent from much of the literature on the UK's neoliberal model of capitalism.

In focusing only on the ways in which inequality has worsened, and hardship has increased (which of course it has), many of the critical and comparative political economy accounts of the UK's model of neoliberal capitalism consolidate the view that no resistance occurred, or indeed *could have occurred*, and that therefore the imposition and consolidation of neoliberalisation has been a relatively smooth process achieved at the whim of those elites who promote such changes, and in the face of passivity by those most harmed by them. This paints a picture in which resistance is either absent or futile, with little or no scope for agency on the part of those who suffer from neoliberal restructuring. Yet rather than meekly acquiescing to the ongoing attacks launched over the past decade, Britain has witnessed a vibrant mobilisation of resistance that has posed a number of challenges to those in power (Bailey, 2020). This includes contestation of, and resistance to, austerity, the housing crisis generated by Britain's rising housing prices, core features of financialisation, the ecological destruction associated with the neoliberal model of capitalism, the growing racism and xenophobia being propagated by Britain's right-wing political elite, and the ongoing assaults on working people and workers' capacity for collective action. In each case, the outcome of these different forms of resistance has been to prompt *both* concessions, as those in power seek to pacify resistance, *and* repressive measures designed to thwart the capacity to resist.

In 2010, as the newly elected Conservative-led Government announced a swathe of public spending cuts, it was the announcement of the tripling of university tuition fees that sparked a dramatic upswell of opposition, as students took to the streets outside parliament on several occasions between October and December 2010, occupying Conservative Party headquarters in Millbank, and also staging occupations of university buildings across the country (Myers, 2017). The tuition fee rise went ahead, and the protests were met with repressive measures that included enclosing protesters in a confined space on Westminster Bridge for several hours. Nevertheless, the concessions extracted from the government saw an indexing of the salary threshold at which fees would need to be repaid. This indexing subsequently ensured that large amounts of student debt would never be repaid, resulting in £3 billion of student debt written off in 2014, and the Institute for Fiscal Studies estimating total savings for the public purse of only 5 per cent following the fee regime change (for more details see the online materials that accompany Bailey and Shibata, 2019). This salary threshold was raised further in 2017, in part due to fear that votes were being lost to the Labour Party, which was becoming increasingly popular amongst younger voters under Jeremy Corbyn's leadership (Adams and Mason, 2017). Further, in 2018, a re-categorisation of tuition fee debt resulted in a one-third increase in the annual public deficit, highlighting the impact that the new regime (and its policy of write-downs) was having on the government coffers (McGettigan, 2019).

The student tuition fee protests contributed to the formation in 2010 of UK Uncut, a new direct action movement, with many of the same participants in the student tuition fee protests. UK Uncut occupied, blockaded and disrupted a number of high-profile firms that stood accused of tax avoidance. In doing so, it sought to highlight an alternative way to reduce the fiscal deficit, which the government had claimed underpinned the need for austerity measures to be put in place. Again, UK Uncut met with serious forms of repression, which peaked in March 2011 when several protesters were arrested and charged with aggravated trespass following the occupation of the Fortnum & Mason store during a national trade union march. Nevertheless, despite this repression, UK Uncut went a considerable way to politicise the issue of tax avoidance, which had become a central feature of the UK financial sector, and its close links to offshore financial centres such as the Cayman Islands. This saw the Chancellor, George Osborne, announce a series of measures between 2013 and 2015 designed to tackle tax avoidance and evasion (Bailey *et al.*, 2018: 131–137).

Britain's shifting neoliberalism would face similar challenges throughout the 2010s. The trade union, Unison, launched a successful legal challenge against the introduction of a £1,200 charge for employment tribunals. In addition, precarious workers – a group which had grown in size, and precarity, as a result of over three decades of neoliberal reforms – began to successfully organise in smaller 'indie unions', such as United Voices of the World and Independent Workers' Union of Great Britain, resulting in a number of successful campaigns to improve the employment rights of platform workers such as Uber drivers, and the wages of low paid (often mainly migrant) workers (Smith, 2021; Tassinari and Maccarrone, 2020; Weghmann, 2022). A wave of protests and resistance to the housing crisis emerged in 2015, with groups such as the E15 Mothers organising a number of occupations, demonstrations and protest events to oppose the practice of re-housing residents in distant locations (Gillespie *et al.*, 2018).

The government and energy companies sought to consolidate the dependence upon fossil fuel extraction, including a move towards fracking as a new source of extraction (on fuel extraction as a key feature of UK neoliberalism, see Christophers, 2020). This, however, was met with such a scale of opposition that drilling was almost entirely prevented from going ahead. Near-permanent camps at the site in Preston New Road combined with public opposition to prevent the drilling from proceeding. Similar events occurred at Balcombe, with the local authority refusing to grant permission for drilling (Garland *et al.*, 2022). Similarly, considerable pressure was placed on financial institutions which continued to support the carbon fuel sector. This included a sustained campaign against the Royal Bank of Scotland in opposition to its role as a major funder of the oil industry and tar sands. Protests included blocking access to its buildings and demonstrations outside several AGMs (Lander, 2018). Due in part to the heightened publicity and exposure for the bank, in 2018 it announced a new commitment to stop financing new coal projects worldwide, as well as ending its support for the tar sands sector (Louvel, 2018). Despite (or, rather, because of) these successful instances of resistance, environmentalism in the UK has also received considerable repression. This is perhaps most apparent in the passing of the Public Order Act 2023 that restricted 'locking on' as a protest strategy (which is often used by environmentalists) as well as criminalising protests that target important national infrastructure.

The growing racism and xenophobia propagated by Britain's right-wing political elite also came under attack from popular protest throughout the 2010s. The anti-migrant detention centre Yarl's Wood saw more than 3,000 hunger strikes conducted by migrants detained in the centre between 2015 and 2019 (Hill, 2019). In addition, the Goldsmiths Anti-Racist Action occupation of Deptford Town Hall in London lasted for 137 days in 2019, successfully winning a range of commitments by the university to tackle institutional racism. 2017 also saw a wave of protest across the UK in opposition to the racist policies of Donald Trump following his 'Muslim ban' on entry into the United States, signalling a broader unwillingness to endorse the most extreme forms of right-wing populism.

Fighting back?

Resistance and austerity during the pandemic

In the context outlined above, it is perhaps unsurprising that the Johnson Government's approach to the pandemic was met with a wave of resistance. The initial response of the government to the pandemic suggested that the aim would be to achieve 'herd immunity' and simply allow the infection to 'move through the population'. This response was later found to be a 'serious early error' (House of Commons 2021). It saw a rapid growth in concern and confusion as people increasingly lost confidence in (and comprehension of) the message that the government was sending (Cooper and Furlong, 2020).

Eventually the government was moved to impose a lockdown in March 2020, amid moves by organisations and individuals to independently avoid social settings, witnessing high absence rates, for instance, amongst both staff and pupils at schools, immediately prior to the latter's closure (BBC 2020; Adams and Stewart, 2020). Likewise, the government was left with no option other than to introduce a furlough scheme to protect the wages of those who were unable to work, at a cost of £70 billion (Francis-Devine *et al.*, 2021).

Grassroots initiatives emerged across the country as a form of 'mutual aid' that would seek to fill the gaps left by Britain's under-resourced welfare system (Firth, 2020). Trade unions and community activist groups also sought to find ways to mobilise, despite the restrictions created by the lockdown. The teachers' union National Education Union (NEU) was especially successful in challenging government policy, forcing the government into a U-turn on the question of re-opening primary schools in both summer 2020 (Weale, 2020), and again in January 2021 when the NEU issued legal advice to its members advising that they should not return to schools (Ferguson, 2021). Many 'key workers' also successfully mobilised action, typically around the question of health and safety. As Gregor Gall (2020) describes, 'in Royal Mail, in meat processing plants, on construction sites, at distribution hubs and in fulfilment centres (warehouses) along with refuse workers, council library workers and local government workers have gone on strike unofficially'. Cleaners at the

What went wrong with Britain?

Ministry of Justice downed tools and staged a wildcat strike due to concerns over health and safety. School pupils also successfully protested in opposition to their exam grades, prompting another government U-turn in the face of popular protest (Weale and Stewart, 2020). University students rallied against the corporatised university system, protesting accommodation costs and conditions and their de facto detention as a result of the pandemic, witnessing rent strikes, and considerable damage to the reputation of university leaders, especially in the case of Manchester (Robson, 2021). As a result, rent rebates were eventually provided by many universities, in some cases in a direct attempt to address the reputational damage suffered, amounting to a total cost to universities of £140 million (Shaw, 2021; for a summary of the fallout from the University of Manchester debacle, where the cost of the rent rebate reached £21 million, see University of Manchester, 2021). Finally, as the Black Lives Matter protests spread from the United States to the United Kingdom, in the wake of the outrage at the killing of George Floyd, protesters sought to highlight the disproportionate impact that the pandemic was having on minorities within the UK, with Black Lives Matter becoming perhaps the most prominent protest movement in the UK of 2020.

On exiting the pandemic, many of the pre-Covid neoliberal tendencies re-asserted themselves, again witnessing a combination of repression and concessions in response to the ongoing contestation of these different forms of inequality and hardship. The housing crisis, exacerbated by the stamp duty holiday put in place during the pandemic, fuelled another rapid rise in house prices. Inflation also climbed throughout 2022 and, further exacerbated by the effect of the Ukraine War, began to create a cost of living crisis as the UK's largely de-unionised workforce was unable to ensure that wages kept up with prices, especially of energy and food, resulting in a real terms annual rate of decline in total pay between September and November 2022 of 2.6 per cent (a rate of decline not seen since the immediate aftermath of the global economic crisis in 2009) (Office for National Statistics, 2023a). In an attempt to limit the right to protest, and partly in response to the success of movements such as Extinction Rebellion and Black Lives Matter, the government announced

Fighting back?

proposals for a new anti-protest law, the Police, Crime, Sentencing and Courts Bill, which sparked a national wave of protests, and in the case of Bristol a series of riots, seeking to 'Kill the Bill'. The post-lockdown period also saw the government step up its scapegoating of migrants, introducing the 'Rwanda Plan' which threatened to deport asylum seekers for processing in Rwanda.

Each of these developments were also the subject of considerable contestation. Campaigning around the housing crisis by groups such as the direct action tenants union, Acorn, prompted a series of housing sector reforms, and a proposal to end the so-called 'no fault' evictions of tenants, as part of the government's Renters Reform Bill announced in 2022 (Butler, 2022). Insulate Britain, a spin-off group from Extinction Rebellion, successfully forced the energy crisis and climate crisis onto the political agenda through the use of direct action road blockades. Migrant support networks, such as Stop Deportations, successfully prevented deportations and detentions of migrants through the use of a direct action strategy in which supporters prevented deportations and detentions by blocking the roadway, for instance in Peckham and Glasgow, and by causing considerable disruption to the first attempt to deport migrants to Rwanda (which was subsequently prevented as a result of an interim legal challenge) (Taylor *et al.*, 2022). The cost of living crisis sparked a wave of protests by both workers and consumers, with a significant upturn in industrial action, including a successful six-month strike by the Coventry bin drivers that resulted in a 12.9 per cent pay rise; strike action by railway workers and train drivers that gained considerable popular support; a successful dispute by the independent union, United Voices of the World, to 'in-source' workers at Great Ormond Street Hospital; and an impromptu walkout by Amazon workers. In an attempt to stymie such actions, the government announced it would move to allow temporary agency workers to be hired in order to break strike action, which had up until that point been prohibited, and which would represent an attempt to make collective trade union action more restricted still. As the new Truss Government came into office a 'Don't Pay' campaign looked set to put further pressure on the government to respond to the rising fuel price crisis. In doing so, however, the commitment to further reductions in taxation, alongside increased spending to support households with the cost of the fuel price rises, combined to turn the financial markets against the government, prompting Truss's ousting after just forty-nine days in office.

As Rishi Sunak replaced Truss as the leader of the Conservative Party and Prime Minister, he faced a growing wave of strike action across the workforce, and especially in the public sector, which was mobilised around a rallying call that doubled as the name for a new trade union-backed campaign initiative: Enough is Enough. By early 2023 strike action was either being (or about to be) staged, or had recently been, by nurses, teachers, university employees, barristers, railway workers, postal workers, junior doctors and civil servants in one of the biggest waves of strike action that the UK had witnessed since the 1980s. This created a growing sense that Sunak was the head of a government which had almost entirely lost the confidence of its workforce. Whilst almost all of these industrial disputes prompted at least some form of increase in the pay offer being presented to the unions representing the striking workers, perhaps predictably the responses also included a further attack on trade union rights, in the form of the Strikes (Minimum Service Levels) Act 2023, which was introduced to limit strike action which had the potential to impinge on public service delivery. Yet even this minimum services legislation proved unable to successfully quell the new strike wave, as the only attempt to use the legislation to force workers to continue to work during a planned strike action, by rail company LNER, was met with the threat of an additional five days of strike action by the train drivers' union, ASLEF, prompting LNER to back down.

Conclusion

Britain's model of capitalism is shifting. It is marked by seemingly ever-growing inequality, hardship and insecurity for a growing section of the population. This inequality and hardship are direct results of the anti-trade union measures, outsourcing, low wages, and minimal and draconian

Fighting back?

welfare provisions that characterise the UK's model of neoliberal capitalism, alongside a privileged financial sector and a systemic prioritisation of homeowners. Under the Conservative Government, efforts at legitimation increasingly depended on a xenophobic anti-migrant agenda that sought to create scapegoats on racialised lines. To return to the question of this volume – *What went wrong with Britain?* – clearly there was quite a lot. The establishment of a nationalist-neoliberal capitalism, built on its imperialist past, was clearly rooted in Britain's historical claim to being the place where capitalist social relations first emerged. These capitalist relations depended (and continue to depend) upon exploitation, (neo-)colonialism and extractivism. Britain has since entered a prolonged period of decline, as the country has long since been overtaken as the leading global capitalist power. Between 2010 and 2024 this decline was largely responded to through measures by the Conservative-led Government that sought to further the neoliberal tendencies which caused the very problems they sought to address, predictably making matters considerably worse. As this chapter has sought to show, however, during the same period, each of the core elements of Britain's decaying neoliberal model of capitalism have also been subjected to considerable dissent and resistance. Whilst it would clearly have been better had the austerity and hardship which prompted the acts of contestation charted in this chapter not been pursued in the first place, the absence of such reports of resistance in many of the accounts of neoliberal Britain represents a failure to make visible the capacity for (and the actualisation of) the different forms of agency 'from below' that continue to be both possible and prevalent. Rather than the straightforward imposition of ever intensifying neoliberalisation, instead we have seen ongoing instances of contestation across British society, opposing, refusing and disrupting efforts at neoliberal restructuring. These forms of resistance regularly extracted considerable concessions and modifications of neoliberal reforms, highlighting the difficulties which Britain's political and economic elite are required to manage, and which they also often seek to do through a range of different forms of repression. As one cycle of resistance–restructuring–concessions–repression comes to an end, another quickly arises, and will continue to do so. Indeed, Britain's decaying model of neoliberal capitalism will only be free of the crises, contestation and instability that comprises it once this deeply divisive, harmful and unequal socio-economic system is replaced – i.e., when there ceases to be (neoliberalism) capitalism. All of this obviously raises the question of how Starmer's incoming Labour Government will fare, as it faces the dual challenge of putting in place a recovery programme that seeks a return to a more sustainable form of economic growth, and in doing so must navigate the (ever present) potential for social conflict and dissent to occur. Regarding some of the key sources of social tension during the period of Tory rule, there appears to be a willingness by the incoming Labour Government to introduce concessions that might help reduce levels of social conflict. A series of above-inflation public sector pay deals introduced soon after entering office helped to ease relations with public sector workers and trade unions. The government is also committed to repealing both the Trade Union Act 2016 and the Minimum Services Act, both of which were key sources of tension between government and the trade unions under the Conservatives. Likewise, the introduction of a new Renters' Rights Bill promises to introduce a number of measures to ameliorate the housing crisis for tenants. There does not appear, however, to be any move to reverse the anti-protest legislation introduced towards the end of the Conservative's period of rule, and indeed Starmer was already on record in 2022 declaring his support for tough sentences for environmentalists using disruptive protest tactics (Gayle, 2022). The austerity-focused approach to macroeconomic management also appears set to continue, with Labour committing itself since before the election to fiscal constraints that would see it continue the efforts of the preceding government to reduce public spending; a sentiment which has seemingly underpinned the decision in the early stages of the government both to vote against attempts to remove the two-child cap on social benefits, and to reject calls to keep the winter fuel allowance for pensioners. The question of whether, and to what extent, the new Labour Government will continue its predecessors' socially divisive approach to policymaking – and to thereby continue to prompt ongoing rounds of protest, concessions and/or repression –remains to be seen.

Fighting back?

Notes

1 The 'bedroom tax' is the name colloquially given to what the government termed the 'removal of the spare room subsidy' and consisted of a reduction in housing benefit for any claimants living in social housing with any spare bedroom.
2 Whilst 'workfare' was a scheme initially launched under the Major Government in the 1990s, and was subsequently extended in the form of 'welfare-to-work' under the Blair Government, under the Cameron Government this was substantially extended through the introduction of a series of sanctions imposed upon unemployed people claiming benefits who were considered to be insufficiently striving to find employment (for a discussion, see MacLeavy, 2011).
3 In real terms, average total pay fell throughout much of the first half of the 2010s, declining by an average of 0.9 per cent per year between the beginning of 2010 and the end of 2014. Whilst real pay began to increase for the second half of the 2010s, for the decade as a whole the average real total pay rose by an average of only 0.1 per cent per year (Office for National Statistics, 2023a). Disposable income inequality (which includes the effects of state benefits) rose throughout the period from 2013 to 2022, especially inequality between retired households. Similarly, the S80/S20 ratio, which is the ratio of the total income received by the richest 20 per cent of people to that received by the poorest 20 per cent, rose from 5.3 in 2010/11 to 6.3 in 2021/22 (see Office for National Statistics, 2023b).
4 Whilst Boris Johnson's populist rhetoric included his infamous 'fuck business' remark when Foreign Secretary in 2018, this nevertheless transformed into a more cosy (crony) relationship with those businesses with close contacts with the government during the pandemic.

References

Adams, R. and Mason, R. (2017) 'Tuition fee repayment earnings threshold to rise to £25,000', *Guardian*, 1 October, www.theguardian.com/education/2017/oct/01/tuition-fee-repayment-earnings-threshold-rise-to-25000

Adams, R. and Stewart, H. (2020) 'UK schools to be closed indefinitely and exams cancelled', *Guardian*, 18 March, https://www.theguardian.com/world/2020/mar/18/coronavirus-uk-schools-to-be-closed-indefinitely-and-exams-cancelled

Bailey, D. J. (2018) 'Misperceiving matters, again: stagnating neoliberalism, Brexit and the pathological responses of Britain's political elite', *British Politics* 13(1): 48–64.

Bailey, D. J. (2020) 'Decade of dissent: how protest is shaking the UK and why it's likely to continue', The Conversation, 3 January, https://theconversation.com/decade-of-dissent-how-protest-is-shaking-the-uk-and-why-its-likely-to-continue-125843

Bailey, D. J., Clua-Losada, M., Huke, N. and Ribera-Almandoz, O. (2018) *Beyond Defeat and Austerity: Disrupting (the Critical Political Economy of) Neoliberal Europe*, London: Routledge.

Bailey, D. J. and Shibata, S. (2019) 'Austerity and anti-austerity: The political economy of refusal in "low-resistance" models of capitalism', *British Journal of Political Science* 49(2): 683–709.

Bank of England (2022) 'Monetary policy report: August 2022', www.bankofengland.co.uk/-/media/boe/files/monetary-policy-report/2022/august/monetary-policy-report-august-2022.pdf

BBC (2020) 'Coronavirus: West End shuts down as Boris Johnson's advice sparks anger', BBC News, 17 March, www.bbc.co.uk/news/entertainment-arts-51906370

Berry, C. (2022) 'The substitutive state? Neoliberal state interventionism across industrial, housing and private pensions policy in the UK', *Competition & Change* 26(2): 242–265.

Butler, P. (2022) 'No-fault evictions and barring tenants on benefits to be outlawed in England', *Guardian*, 15 June, www.theguardian.com/money/2022/jun/15/white-paper-to-tackle-unfair-evictions-and-bad-landlords-in-england

Christophers, B. (2020) *Rentier Capitalism: Who Owns the Economy and Who Pays for It?*, Verso, London.

Clery, E., Curtice, J. and Harding, R (2017) *British Social Attitudes: 34th Report*, NatCen Social Research, London, www.bsa.natcen.ac.uk/media/39196/bsa34_full-report_fin.pdf

Clift, B. and McDaniel, S. (2021) 'The politics of the British model of capitalism's flatlining productivity and anaemic growth: Lessons for the growth models perspective', *The British Journal of Politics and International Relations*, 24(4): 631–648.

Cooper, C. and Furlong, A. (2020) 'Going viral: Boris Johnson grapples to control coronavirus message', *Politico*, 16 March, www.politico.eu/article/going-viral-british-prime-minister-boris-johnson-grapples-to-control-coronavirus-covid19-message/

Copley, J. (2022) *Governing Financialization: The Tangled Politics of Financial Liberalization in Britain*, Oxford University Press, Oxford.

Crafts, N. and Mills, T. C. (2020) 'Is the UK productivity slowdown unprecedented?' *National Institute Economic Review*, 251: R47–R53.

Cutts, D., Goodwin, M., Heath, O. and Surridge, P. (2020) 'Brexit, the 2019 general election and the realignment of British politics', *The Political Quarterly*, 91: 7–23.

Deloitte and Reform (2017) 'Citizens, government and business: The state of the state 2017–18', Deloitte LLP, London, www2.deloitte.com/content/dam/Deloitte/uk/Documents/public-sector/deloitte-uk-the-state-of-the-state-report-2017.pdf

Evans, G. and Mellon, J. (2016) 'Working class votes and Conservative losses: Solving the UKIP puzzle', *Parliamentary Affairs*, 69(2): 464–479.

Ferguson, D. (2021) 'Covid fears spark revolt by unions over return to school in England', *Guardian*, 2 January, www.theguardian.com/world/2021/jan/02/

government-faces-major-revolt-on-schools-reopening-in-england-over-covid-fears

Fetzer, T. (2019) 'Did austerity cause Brexit?', *American Economic Review*, 109 (11): 3849–86.

Firth, R. (2020) 'Mutual aid, anarchist preparedness and COVID-19', in J. Preston and R. Firth (eds) *Coronavirus, Class and Mutual Aid in the United Kingdom*, London: Palgrave.

Francis-Devine, B., Powell, A. and Clark, H. (2021) 'Coronavirus Job Retention Scheme: statistics', House of Commons Library, No. 9152, https://researchbriefings.files.parliament.uk/documents/CBP-9152/CBP-9152.pdf

Gall, G. (2020) 'Britain's coronavirus wildcat strikes', *Tribune*, 1 May, https://tribunemag.co.uk/2020/05/britains-coronavirus-wildcat-strikes

Garland, J., Saunders, C., Olcese, C. and Tedesco, D. (2022) 'Anti-fracking campaigns in the United Kingdom: The influence of local opportunity structures on protest', *Social Movement Studies*, 22(2): 211–231.

Gayle, D., 2022, 'Keir Starmer backs stiff sentences for climate protesters who block roads', *The Guardian* 24 October, www.theguardian.com/politics/2022/oct/24/keir-starmer-backs-stiff-sentences-for-climate-protesters-who-block-roads

Gillespie, T., Hardy, K. and Watt, P. (2018). 'Austerity urbanism and Olympic counter-legacies: Gendering, defending and expanding the urban commons in East London', *Environment and Planning D: Society and Space*, 36(5): 812–830.

Glyn, A. (2006) *Capitalism Unleashed: Finance, Globalization, and Welfare*, Oxford University Press, Oxford.

Hay, C. (2013) *The Failure of Anglo-Liberal Capitalism*, Palgrave, Basingstoke.

Hill, A. (2019) 'More than 3,000 hunger strikes at immigration centres in UK since 2015', *Guardian*, 15 August, www.theguardian.com/uk-news/2019/aug/15/more-than-3000-hunger-strikes-at-immigration-centres-in-uk-since-2015

Hofman, A. and Aalbers, M.B. (2019) 'A finance-and real estate-driven regime in the United Kingdom', *Geoforum*, 100: 89–100.

House of Commons (2021) 'Coronavirus – Lessons learned to date: Sixth report of the Health and Social Care Committee and third report of the Science and Technology Committee of session 2021-22', House of Commons (HC 92), https://committees.parliament.uk/publications/7496/documents/78687/default/

Inman, P. (2021) 'UK housing market is on fire, warns Bank of England chief economist', *Guardian*, 8 June, www.theguardian.com/business/2021/jun/08/uk-housing-market-is-on-fire-warns-bank-of-england-chief-economist

Kettell, S. and Kerr, P. (2020) 'From eating cake to crashing out: constructing the myth of a no-deal Brexit', *Comparative European Politics*, 18(4): 590–608.

Lander, R. (2018) 'Royal Bank of Scotland: 10 years of climate campaigning', Friends of the Earth Scotland, 14 September, https://foe.scot/royal-bank-scotland-10-years-climate-campaigning/

Lavery, S. (2019) *British Capitalism After the Crisis*, Palgrave, London.

Lepper, J., Shabani, M., Toporowski, J. and Tyson, J. (2016) 'Monetary adjustment and inflation of financial claims in the UK after 1980', in E. Hein, D. Detzer and N. Dodig (eds.), *Financialisation and the Financial and Economic Crises: Country Studies*, Edward Elgar, Cheltenham.

Louvel, Y. (2018) 'RBS moves on coal and tar sands and takes the lead of UK banks', Bank Track, 30 May, www.banktrack.org/news/rbs_moves_on_coal_and_tar_sands_and_takes_the_lead_of_uk_banks

McGettigan, A. (2019) 'ONS confirms: loan sales now affect the deficit', Critical Education blog, https://andrewmcgettigan.org/2019/09/25/ons-confirms-loan-sales-now-affect-the-deficit/

Macartney, H., Montgomerie, J. and Tepe, D. (2022) *The Fault Lines of Inequality: COVID 19 and the Politics of Financialization*, Palgrave, London.

MacLeavy, J. (2011) 'A "new politics" of austerity, workfare and gender? The UK coalition government's welfare reform proposals', *Cambridge Journal of Regions, Economy and Society* 4(3): 355–367.

Myers, M. (2017) *Student Revolt: Voices of the Austerity Generation*, Pluto Press, London.

National Audit Office (2018) 'Financial sustainability of local authorities 2018', 5 March, www.nao.org.uk/wp-content/uploads/2018/03/Financial-sustainabilty-of-local-authorites-2018.pdf

Norfield, T. (2017) *The City: London and the Global Power of Finance*, London: Verso Books.

OECD (2020) 'Labour productivity growth, total economy: GDP per hour worked, average annual growth rate', www.oecd-ilibrary.org/sites/501c137c-en/index.html?itemId=/content/component/501c137c-en

Office for National Statistics (2023a) 'Statistical bulletin: Average weekly earnings in Great Britain: November 2022', www.ons.gov.uk/employmentandlabourmarket/peopleinwork/employmentandemployeetypes/bulletins/averageweeklyearningsingreatbritain/january2023

Office for National Statistics (2023b) 'Statistical bulletin: Household income inequality, UK: Financial year ending 2022', www.ons.gov.uk/peoplepopulationandcommunity/personalandhouseholdfinances/incomeandwealth/bulletins/householdincomeinequalityfinancial/financialyearending2022

Oren, T. and Blyth, M. (2019) 'From big bang to big crash: The early origins of the UK's finance-led growth model and the persistence of bad policy ideas', *New Political Economy*, 24(5): 605–622.

Robson, S. (2021) 'University of Manchester students occupy building in fresh protest over rent and tuition fees', *Manchester Evening News*, 25 April, https://www.manchestereveningnews.co.uk/news/greater-manchester-news/university-manchester-students-occupy-building-20464006

Ryder, A. (2022) 'Boris Johnson, Brexit, and the decline of public standards', LSE blog: EUROPP – European Politics and Policy, 21 January, https://blogs.

lse.ac.uk/europpblog/2022/01/21/boris-johnson-brexit-and-the-decline-of-public-standards/

Shaw, D. (2021) 'Exclusive: Students were given £140m in rent refunds last academic year', *The Tab*, 2 November, https://thetab.com/uk/2021/11/02/exclusive-students-were-given-140m-in-rent-refunds-last-academic-year-227450

Smith, H. (2021) 'The "indie unions" and the UK labour movement: Towards a community of practice', *Economic and Industrial Democracy*, 43(3): 1369–1390.

Stanley, L. (2014) '"We're reaping what we sowed": Everyday crisis narratives and acquiescence to the age of austerity', *New Political Economy*, 19(6): 895–917.

Tassinari, A. and Maccarrone, V. (2020) 'Riders on the storm: Workplace solidarity among gig economy couriers in Italy and the UK', *Work, Employment and Society*, 34(1): 35–54.

Taylor, D., Syal, R. and Sinmaz, E. (2022), 'Rwanda asylum flight cancelled after 11th-hour ECHR intervention', *Guardian*, 14 June, www.theguardian.com/uk-news/2022/jun/14/european-court-humam-right-makes-11th-hour-intervention-in-rwanda-asylum-seeker-plan

University of Manchester (2021) 'Board of Governors minutes', 20 January, https://documents.manchester.ac.uk/display.aspx?DocID=55029

Weale, S. (2020) 'Reopening schools: What is happening in England?' *Guardian*, 9 June, www.theguardian.com/education/2020/jun/09/reopening-schools-what-is-happening-in-england

Weale, S. and Stewart, H. (2020) 'A-level and GCSE results in England to be based on teacher assessments in U-turn', *Guardian*, 17 August, https://www.theguardian.com/education/2020/aug/17/a-levels-gcse-results-england-based-teacher-assessments-government-u-turn

Weghmann, V. (2022) 'Theorising practice: independent trade unions in the UK', *Work in the Global Economy* 2(1): 132–147.

Wood, G. T., Onali, E., Grosman, A. and Haider, Z.A. (2022) 'A very British state capitalism: Variegation, political connections and bailouts during the COVID-19 crisis', *Environment and Planning A: Economy and Space*, 55(3): 673–696.

Worth, O. (2016) 'Reviving Hayek's dream', *Globalizations*, 14(1): 104–109.

15

Security in Britain today
Lee Jarvis and Michael Lister

Introduction

In this chapter, we argue that the British approach to security suffers from significant and recurrent failings. This matters because the idea of security carries a lot of political weight. Politicians often see national security as their primary responsibility, which is why it gets invoked when cuts to civil liberties, for instance, are being explained or justified. Many of the most contentious political issues – energy, migration, terrorism, climate change and so on – take on extra urgency when they are discussed in the language of security. Yet, it is also important to remember that security means very different things to different people. Do CCTV cameras, nuclear weapons, armed police, hostile environments, gated communities and so on make 'you' – or 'us' – more secure? Or do they leave 'us' (or some of 'us') more anxious, more fearful, more insecure?

Our main claim in this chapter is that the dominant way in which British politicians think about (national) security is problematic because it focuses on dramatic rather than everyday harms; on external threats rather than internal dangers; and on immediate rather than longer-term risks. Taking examples from counter-terrorism policy, the politics of austerity and the COVID-19 pandemic, we argue that this approach to security is doubly disempowering for minoritised or other disadvantaged

Security in Britain today

populations. On the one hand, more mundane threats that disproportionately affect such communities are treated less seriously than those where the risk of harm is more evenly distributed across the wider population. And, on the other, because the 'costs' of security policies that are implemented by national government and others tend to be weighted more heavily towards disadvantaged communities.

This disadvantaging is compounded, we argue, by more parochial temptations within the British approach to security, such as groupthink and cronyism, which cloud the government's ability to develop security policies that benefit the entire UK citizenry. Taken together, these conceptual and political failings all contribute to a politics of security that is frequently wasteful, often counterproductive and typically removed from the needs of the least secure within – and beyond – the UK. The new Labour government's efforts to position itself as 'the' party of national security – including through commitments to nuclear deterrence and increasing defence spending – highlight just how difficult it is to change established ways of thinking, doing and communicating 'security' (Adu, 2024).

Imagining national security

Security is a variable and fluid concept, the meaning of which changes depending on where, when, how and by whom it is used. This fluidity matters more than we might think because it gives a lot of flexibility to governments when they go about the work of designating, prioritising and responding to particular threats. The UK's most recent 'Integrated Review of Security, Defence, Development and Foreign Policy' (HM Government, 2021) – refreshed and extended in 2023 to take account of changes in the interim, such as Russia's invasion of Ukraine (HM Government, 2023a) – positions security next to sovereignty and prosperity as one of the three most important interests of the British people. The Strategy defines the term in the following way:

> Security: the protection of our people, territory, CNI [Critical National Infrastructure], democratic institutions and way of life. Ensuring security in today's world involves a growing range of activities: from tackling threats

from states and non-state actors such as terrorists and organised crime groups; to building societal resilience so that we are better able to withstand risks and unexpected shocks, including future environmental and global health emergencies. (HM Government, 2021: 13)

In this official definition, security is seen as a many-faced and ever-changing phenomenon. In this, the Strategy echoes the approach set out in the UK government's National Risk Registers – essentially, published catalogues of potential future dangers – the most recent of which is organised around nine primary risk themes: terrorism; cyber; state threats; geographic and diplomatic; accidents and systems failures; natural and environmental hazards; human, animal and plant health; societal; conflict and instability (HM Government, 2023b: 6). Such statements, at first glance, imply a broad – and perhaps inclusive – understanding of security that takes into consideration the wide range of dangers encountered by different individuals and groups. In this they build on earlier UK frameworks such as its first ever 'National Security Strategy' released in 2008 under Labour Prime Minister Gordon Brown (see McCormack, 2015: 501–502). They also resonate with recent academic efforts to widen our understanding of security by shifting focus from the needs of the state to the needs of the human (e.g., United Nations Development Programme, 1994) or by attempting to link security to goals such as emancipation or freedom instead of its older association with order and stability (e.g., Booth, 2007).

These broad understandings are important because they take security away from traditional 'guns and bombs' understandings of this word. They are also often seen as politically progressive because they encourage us to seek security in new and creative ways, not only through the lens of military power. If we look a little more closely, however, the expansive approach to security that is taken within official frameworks of the British government (such as those above) is not without problems. In the first instance, by widening the range of harms that can be seen as *security* issues, the attention of security powers (e.g., laws and policies), technologies (e.g., body scanners or cameras) and professionals (e.g., police or security guards) is inevitably directed towards an increasing range of places, interactions and behaviours. Threats to national security are now monitored, measured and policed throughout the whole of the UK: from airports to doctors' surgeries, from classrooms to children's nurseries, and from social media platforms to sportsgrounds. In the process, the employees and citizens who inhabit those places are increasingly asked to act as 'detectives' (Vaughan-Williams, 2008) or 'stakeholders' (Jarvis and Lister, 2010) with a responsibility to help deliver national security by surveilling, recording and responding to possible risks. And, in practice, of course, it is threats associated with dangerous or foreign 'others', such as terrorism, extremism or 'illicit' migration, that tend to receive this treatment, rather than other harms such as, for instance, food scarcity or energy poverty.

Second, the British security framework is also based on a series of important and powerful exclusions. Although a number of issues that were not traditionally thought of as security are now often treated as such, other causes of harm are rarely afforded this treatment. This matters, in part, because it introduces hierarchies of priority between risks, dangers and threats: hierarchies that may not reflect the actual human toll of particular sources of harm. The 2008 'National Security Strategy', to illustrate, contains no mention at all of gendered violences (Cabinet Office, 2008), despite official estimates that 2.3 million adults experienced domestic abuse in the year ending March 2020 (Office for National Statistics, 2021). Indeed, the word 'gender' does not appear at all in the current Risk Register (HM Government, 2023b) although pregnant women are identified as a potentially vulnerable community. Although the 2021 'Integrated Review of Security, Defence, Development and Foreign Policy' does better here by noting the importance of discrimination, violence and inequality against women, these are all seen as problems that exist *elsewhere* – beyond the UK – and that are the concern, therefore, of aid and diplomatic activities in low- and middle-income countries (Cabinet Office, 2021).[1]

Third, the expansion of the UK's security agenda that follows recognition of a wide range of dangers is also potentially misleading because so-called 'traditional' security threats are still prioritised therein. Militaristic dangers, for instance, account for three of the four 'Tier One' Priority Risks in the 2008 'National Security Strategy': international terrorism; hostile attacks upon UK cyberspace; and an international military crisis (Cabinet Office,

2008: 27). The 2021 'Integrated Review' has a similar feel to it, with its focus on a military alliance – NATO; a great power rival – Russia; and 'a range of transnational state threats, radicalisation and terrorism, SOC [Serious and Organised Crime] and weapons proliferation' (HM Government, 2021: 18). A similar emphasis on the military threat of other states is evident, too, in the 2023 refresh of that review with its identification of four main trends in the international environment: 'shifts in the distribution of global power; inter-state, "systemic" competition over the nature of the international order; rapid technological change; and worsening transnational challenges' (HM Government 2023a: 7).

To summarise, governments around the world have some flexibility in how they imagine national security and the main threats towards it. Although the UK's approach, on first reading, seems to be a broad one that recognises a wide range of dangers, a more careful look reveals it to be closer to a more traditional approach emphasising the importance of militaristic dangers.

Dealing with risks

The priority given to traditional, military security threats in the UK approach reflects a particular national security imaginary: a particular way of thinking and 'doing' security. This imaginary is one that shuffles political attention towards dramatic rather than everyday threats; that prioritises external rather than internal dangers; and that focuses on urgent rather than gradual causes of harm. It is an imaginary underpinned, fundamentally, by continuing faith in the armed forces as a provider of (national) security, as evident in the commitments of Conservative *and* Labour governments to increases in defence spending to cement 'the UK's position as the largest defence spender in Europe and the second largest in NATO' (Prime Minister's Office, 2020). The imaginary also, of course, shapes Britain's posturing on the global stage: consider, for instance, Boris Johnson's eagerness to play the global statesman in response to Russia's 2022 war in Ukraine: a performance that, ultimately, did little to protect him from those demanding his defenestration (Selwood, 2022).

The militaristic emphasis of the UK's security imaginary connects to a widely held view of the UK as one of the international community's great powers. This identity has short-term value for political leaders keen to cement the international standing of themselves or their government. But it also speaks to more localised interests within the UK's defence and military establishments, not least within the UK's vast defence and aerospace industry. And yet, whatever the value of military power, we would do well to remember that its resources often translate poorly for addressing less dramatic – but arguably more pronounced – security challenges. As Edward Newman argued of the COVID-19 pandemic with reference to the UK and US: 'Military preparedness and relative strength – a key measure of security and state capacity according to traditional thinking – did not positively correlate to effectiveness in being prepared for, or addressing, the Covid-19 coronavirus' (2022: 439). Indeed, according to the government's own statistics relating to the pandemic, the UK experienced over 137,000 excess deaths due to all causes in the period between March 2020 and June 2022 (Office for National Statistics, 2022). *The Economist* (2021), puts the figure far higher, noting over 175,000 excess deaths to 19 August 2022, with the UK's COVID-19 death toll of 205,450 being the sixth highest globally.

The emphasis on dramatic, 'external' threats in the UK approach to national security also helps to explain the continuing prioritisation of dangers such as terrorism. Although almost everyone recognises that it is impossible to prevent all terrorist attacks, the continuing belief that no deaths from terrorism are ever acceptable (or, perhaps, ever 'allowable') feeds into a zero-risk approach to this threat aimed at bringing its death-toll as close as possible to zero. This approach, combined with worst-case-scenario planning, leads to a stark precautionary logic that underpins countless counter-terrorist activities and the harm that they cause, from indefinite detention to shoot-to-kill policies that became prominent in the UK and beyond in the post-9/11 period (Aradau and van Munster, 2007: 102–107).

The UK's precautionary approach to threats like terrorism – where action must be taken irrespective of a threat's probability – is illuminating precisely because it is not in keeping with how Britain approaches other harms – such as those experienced by women and minorities – where, as noted above, tolerance or acceptance of risk appears much higher. Consider, again, the COVID-19 pandemic, which saw political (perhaps even public) tolerance of weekly death tolls stretching into the thousands that were disproportionately higher in areas already suffering socio-economic deprivation (Marmot *et al.*, 2020). Consider also the tolerance towards other deaths that are clearly relatable, if indirectly, to political decisions. Recent estimates suggest that problems in emergency care within the UK's National Health Service, for instance, may be responsible for up to 500 'excess deaths' a week (Burn-Murdoch, 2022): deaths that are over and above the expected mortality of a population. Here, a toxic combination of treatment backlogs due to the COVID-19 pandemic and 'a decade of flatlining funds for social care' have created blockages within Accident and Emergency departments, such that a lack of places for patients has meant urgent cases cannot be seen in a timely fashion (Burn-Murdoch, 2022). With one coroner in Cornwall recently linking ambulance delays to deaths (*The Times*, 2022), the Chair of the British Medical Association Council, Professor Philip Banfield, has starkly stated of the problems in emergency care: 'This is a political choice and patients are dying unnecessarily because of that choice' (*Guardian*, 2023).

Problems such as these are not, importantly, unique to the tragedy of the COVID-19 pandemic. The series of spending cuts in the name of 'austerity' introduced by the Conservative–Liberal Democrat Coalition Government in 2010, for instance, is estimated to have reduced UK spending on welfare, housing subsidies and social services by somewhere in the region of £30 billion (Mueller, 2019). This neoliberal appetite for austerity has, again, been linked directly to excess deaths within the British population: deaths of over 330,000 people, in this case. And, as with the examples considered above, the victims here are disproportionately drawn from poorer, more vulnerable populations (Walsh *et al.*, 2022).

Clearly the issues here are complex, and the link between political decisions and avoidable deaths is not straightforward, monocausal or necessarily deliberate. One might even argue that governments should prioritise the threat posed by hostile actors such as terrorists or rival states because the harm that they cause is deliberate rather than accidental (compare Byman, 2005 and Mueller, 2005). And yet, how governments choose (not) to spend public finances, clearly, has life or death consequences. In 2019, Defence Secretary Ben Wallace stated that the UK government had spent £15 billion on countering terrorism between 2015 and 2020 (Hansard, 2019). This is roughly half of the total amount cut from social spending during austerity. Given that since 1970 there have been around 3,500 deaths due to terrorism in the UK (Kirk, 2017) – around 70 per year – would we have seen fewer excess deaths had that money been allocated elsewhere? Even if that spending had been able to reduce excess deaths from austerity by 10 per cent between 2015 and 2020, this would have equated to 33,000 lives saved. The point we are making, in short, is that government decisions to (i) reduce spending overall during austerity and (ii) spend money on specific threats, such as terrorism, almost certainly led to the deaths of some people who would otherwise have lived. If security is, at some level, about the preservation of life, then, the differences between, say, terrorism and pandemics within government spending decisions might be thought of as differences of degree, rather than kind.

Evaluating risks and their costs

In our discussion so far, we have focused on the direct benefits (e.g., how many lives are saved) and indirect costs (e.g., lives that were not saved) of national security decisions. It is, though, important to add in a third factor here: the direct costs *of* security policies. However inhumane it sounds, when deciding which threats to prioritise, governments also have to consider whether the immediate and potential costs of enhancing security are worth their hoped-for benefits (Mueller and Stewart, 2011: 1). Throughout the UK's COVID-19 pandemic, for instance, there was ongoing debate over whether measures such as national or local lockdowns were justifiable given their negative impact on things from mental health to education, the economy, and so forth. Yet such questions – difficult, but important – are often conspicuous by their absence in other security areas. This absence appears especially pronounced where the 'costs' of security policies – which are not only financial – are disproportionately borne by minority groups, or where a threat is more likely to target more privileged sections of society.

Consider, again, counterterrorism measures that – aside from their shared financial burden – have an unquestionably uneven impact on individuals from different ethnic and religious communities. In this post-9/11 period, Muslims have been disproportionately singled out for counterterrorism actions, becoming thought of as members of 'suspect communities' or 'the enemy within' upon which government attention should focus (Pantazis and Pemberton, 2009). The UK's counter-radicalisation programme, Prevent, continues to suffer from accusations of racism and Islamophobia, with one former senior police officer prominently describing the strategy as a 'toxic brand' (Halliday and Dodd, 2015), while a recent (controversial) independent review led by the Lord Shawcross argued the strategy needed to refocus its attention on Islamist extremism (see Macdonald *et al.*, 2024). In a broader context, official statistics show that Black people in England and Wales are nine times more likely than white people to be stopped and searched by police (Dodd, 2020). Examples such as these matter because they show how disadvantaged communities are presented as a *threat to* security and are, therefore, disproportionately targeted by security professionals. Given this, it is, perhaps, unsurprising that members of white communities in countries like the UK often see security measures as abstract and distant from their own lives and citizenship (Jarvis and Lister, 2013; 2015).

We have, then, a situation in which the costs of security policy in relation to something like counterterrorism are borne by minority – often disadvantaged – communities, and perhaps, therefore, seen as a price worth paying. Much of the cost of the politics of austerity, relatedly, was borne by members of lower income, vulnerable groups (McCartney *et al.*, 2022). In this sense, British security politics appears not only to be geared towards 'spectacular' low probability risks associated with external organisations determined to cause 'us' harm – it is also a politics in which the costs, frustrations and what we might call the 'negative externalities' are borne disproportionately by minority groups. Of relevance here may be the class narrowness of the British political elite. A report from the Commission on Social Mobility and Child Poverty (2019), for instance, found that 75 per cent of senior judges, 59 per cent of the Cabinet and 24 per cent of MPs attended independent schools, compared to 7 per cent of the population as a whole. A 2017 *Guardian* and Operation Black Vote report, relatedly, found 97 per cent of Britain's most powerful elite to be white, with only 36 of the 1000-person sample of political, financial, judicial, cultural and security figures being from a minority ethnic background (Duncan, 2017). However we explain this, though, the outcome for Britain is a turning of attention away from mundane, yet higher probability, risks to life – especially where these are experienced disproportionately by disadvantaged groups. Put more starkly: the UK experiences of austerity, COVID-19 and counterterrorism do not demonstrate attention to the greatest harms to the UK population as a whole, or to those harms posing greatest risk to marginal or vulnerable individuals. Rather, these experiences point to a politics of security that is heavily skewed around – and reproduces – racialised, class-based, gendered and other inequalities.

A wider politics of security

There is a temptation – amongst academics and others – to see politics and security as somehow separate from one another (Neal, 2018: 71; Lister, 2019: 419). Politicians are keen not to be accused of 'playing politics' with matters of national security, with the latter's importance somehow shielding issues from the pejorative connotations of 'the political' (Hay, 2007: 1). If we look at government efforts to ban terrorist groups within the UK, for example, these are *always* supported by the political opposition – irrespective of the group being banned, or the government in power (Jarvis and Legrand, 2020). And yet this separation of politics and security is, fundamentally, a fiction: national security decisions and the policies they produce are deeply political. They are political in a fundamental sense, because, as we have seen, national security involves mobilising political power to make, to communicate and to justify decisions that could have been otherwise: from caps on migration limits to nuclear weapons decision-making (see Doyle, 2017). National security is also, however, political in a much more immediate, pejorative sense in which politics is associated with the self-interest and other failings of its participants, such as short-termism, cronyism and groupthink.

In the first instance, decisions around national security unquestionably fall prey to the short-termism that is incentivised by democratic political life. The reasons for this short-termism might not be nefarious: addressing political challenges is difficult, and governments have limited amounts of time, resources and goodwill with which to work. As Former Labour Home Secretary Charles Clarke argues, a lot needs to be in place for an issue to avoid relegation to the 'too difficult box' (2014: 3–4): realistic solutions must be identified, vested interests must be defeated or placated, legal and international contexts must be managed, and the domestic political process must be travelled with all of the staying power and creativity this requires. These contexts mean political priorities are frequently chosen because they will resonate with particular constituencies, and – in the process – help politicians to meet their own aspirations. Such constituencies may be very narrow ones such as party donors or international allies. Or they may be far broader, where political decisions are guided by perceptions of what will sit well with public opinion at a particular moment.

Examples of short-termism in British security politics include the frequent rushing of counter-terrorism legislation through parliament in reaction to extraordinary tragedies (Neal, 2012). We might also put in this category the pervasiveness of 'dog-whistle' politics and the scapegoating or demonisation of minority groups and communities. The effort to make Britain a 'hostile environment' for undocumented migrants under the premierships of David Cameron and Theresa May, for example, spoke to long-standing public concern over immigration, delivering, in the words of human rights organisation Liberty, a series of 'brutal policies [which] prevent people from accessing housing, healthcare, education, work, bank accounts, benefits and even drivers' licences' (2019: 6). Such brutality has, if anything, become only more pronounced against a backdrop of right-wing policies and rhetoric, such as: the UK's extensive, yet ultimately failed, efforts to deport asylum-seekers to Rwanda – described as a 'dream' and an 'obsession' by then Home Secretary Suella Braverman (Dearden 2022); the political space given to anti-immigration slogans such as Rishi Sunak's 'Stop the Boats'; the rise of right-wing political parties and media organisations such as Reform UK and GB News; and the dozens of deaths of asylum-seekers within the UK (Purkiss et al., 2022) and at its borders. In examples such as these, the long-term consequences – for effectiveness as well as ethical – often take a back seat to the short-term gains for policymakers whose priorities are organised, in no small part, by the demands of electoral cycles and calendars.

Important here, too, is the privileging of established networks, people and partners in the design and implementation of security politics. Lord Butler's post-Iraq War *Review of Intelligence on Weapons of Mass Destruction*, for instance, noted that intelligence assessments often reflect a 'prevailing wisdom' of over-cautious, worst-case estimates (2004: 112). Groupthink – in which dissenting views are silenced or self-silenced – militated, in that case, against alternative views including that the threat posed by Saddam Hussein's regime was exaggerated, with disastrous consequences for citizens' lives in Iraq and beyond. Groupthink in the intelligence community and its relations with politicians was a problem, too, in quietening apprehensions around the 2011 intervention in Libya (Parker, 2020: 995–996). Although organisational changes to the foreign policy and security communities may have alleviated some of this tendency (Williams, 2004: 917; Daddow and Schnapper, 2013: 345), a recent report by the Joint Committee on the National Security Strategy (2021) noted that a lack of diversity within Whitehall's national security community, and a lack of engagement with external experts, means it remains an ongoing concern.

More disturbing, finally, are prominent allegations of cronyism in the politics of security. Connections between politicians and those with material interests relating to the delivery of security policy are, of course, nothing new. Over sixty years ago, President Eisenhower famously used his Farewell Address to warn of the growing influence of the military and arms producers in shaping US security policy, arguing: 'In the councils of government, we must guard against the acquisition of unwarranted influence, whether sought or unsought, by the military-industrial complex'. Similar concerns have long surrounded the 'terrorism industry', both before and after the 9/11 attacks (e.g., Herman and O'Sullivan, 1989; Mueller, 2006).

Such worries, though, have become increasingly pronounced in the UK's recent experience, especially in relation to the management of the COVID-19 crisis. A 2021 report by the anti-corruption organisation Transparency International found that over £3.7 billion worth of questionable COVID-19 contracts *between February and November 2020 alone* merited further investigation, with at least £1.6 billion of these going to established connections with the Conservative Party that was then in government (2021: 4–5).[2] The figures in a 2020 *New York Times* report are even more stark, with the revelation that of the $22 billion awarded via UK central government contracts and made public, $11 billion 'went to companies with political connections, no prior experience or histories of controversy' (Bradley *et al.*, 2020). The ongoing case of Lady Mone – a former government minister and member of the House of Lords, on leave of absence from the latter at the time of writing who is alleged to have personally benefited to the tune of tens of millions of pounds for a COVID-19 contract that supplied substandard and unusable personal protective equipment (PPE) – has served to compound such concerns amongst critics (Conn, 2022).

The cronyism revealed by the COVID-19 pandemic has attracted considerable – and well-justified – public attention. Its importance for this chapter is the weight it adds to our understanding of British security policy as a fundamentally partial enterprise. Partial because it is based, as we have seen, on the neglect or outright omission of issues and considerations that could have been taken far more seriously. It is also partial, moreover, because it disproportionately benefits the partisan interests of already privileged individuals and groups – whether intentionally or otherwise.

Conclusion

In this chapter, we have argued that the UK approach to risk and danger suffers from a series of significant problems with profound implications for security policy. Security threats, we have suggested, are not given; they are made. They are constructed or created in the language of political elites, in the laws and policies they introduce, in the actions of security professionals such as border guards or police officers, and in the technologies and algorithms that are called upon to designate risks. Yet, as we have seen, not all threats are constructed equally. In the first instance, the British security imaginary continues to prioritise 'traditional' issues such as the military threat posed by hostile states, or the risk of terrorist attacks. Because of this it is less equipped to respond to non-traditional issues, as patently evident in its disastrous response to the COVID-19 pandemic. Moreover, the temptation towards a populist, short-termist approach to national security that is closed to outsiders and focused on spectacular rather than quotidian or everyday threats helps to reinforce and reproduce these injustices, inequalities and biases.

Although the UK's growing concern with threats to the security of people – rather than the country as a whole – might be seen as a progressive move, we suggested that this development, too, has been both limited and parochial. It has been limited because a number of prominent sources of harm – such as violences against women – remain unrecognised as issues *of security* and therefore lack the attention and resources necessary to be adequately addressed. It is parochial because there is a privileging of violences that can be cast in a general, rather than particular, register constructed around an imagined 'typical' citizen. This register, of course, suffers from the gendered, racialised and other biases inherent to all universal constructions of personhood. As a result, violences against – or costs borne by – 'the citizen' appear to be taken far more seriously when that citizen benefits from deeply embedded structural privileges. The continuation of ethnic, gender and socio-economic inequalities in the British political and wider 'establishment' (see Jones, 2015) is no doubt a key part of this.

Whether these dynamics will change under Keir Starmer's new Labour government remains an open question. Although some of the most egregious actions of the preceding Conservative administrations have been jettisoned – most obviously the anticipated deportations to

Rwanda – Starmer's self-styling as a 'pragmatist' means other security options, including the offshore processing of asylum seekers, remain on the table (Stacey and O'Carroll, 2024). Despite the move away from populist slogans such as 'Stop the Boats', his government remains committed to key planks of its predecessor's security ambitions such as the UK Protect Duty, which will dramatically expand counter-terrorism responsibilities to retail, entertainment and other venues. Recent controversies around important personnel decisions – not least Starmer's search for a new national security advisor – return us, too, to uncomfortable questions around groupthink and cronyism that besieged his Conservative forebears. And the willingness to cut universal benefits such as winter fuel payments of pensioners points, perhaps, to a willingness to discount the real implications of government spending for everyday life and security within the UK. Only time will tell, therefore, whether the new Labour government is able adequately to serve the interests of British security in the more expansive and less elitist sense argued for, and advocated, above.

Notes

1 One might also question the framing of 'poverty, inequality, and poor governance' as problems with the UK in the 2008 'National Security Strategy' (Cabinet Office 2008: 19).
2 For an interactive visualisation of cronyism allegations in this crisis, see Sophie E. Hill's (n.d.) My Little Crony website, www.sophie-e-hill.com/post/my-little-crony/

References

Adu, A. (2024) 'Keir Starmer to declare Labour as "party of national security"', *Guardian*, 2 June, www.theguardian.com/politics/article/2024/jun/02/keir-starmer-to-declare-labour-as-party-of-national-security

Aradau, C. and van Munster, R. (2007) 'Governing terrorism through risk: Taking precautions, (un)knowing the future', *European Journal of International Relations*, 13(1): 89–115.

Booth, K. (2007) *Theory of World Security*, Cambridge University Press, Cambridge.

Bradley, J., Gebrekidan, S. and McCann, A. (2020) 'Waste, negligence and cronyism: Inside Britain's pandemic spending', *New York Times*, 17 December, www.nytimes.com/interactive/2020/12/17/world/europe/britain-covid-contracts.html

Byman, D. (2005) 'A corrective that goes too far?', *Terrorism and Political Violence*, 17(4): 511–516.

Burn-Murdoch, J. (2022) 'The NHS is being squeezed in a vice' *Financial Times*, 11 August, www.ft.com/content/f36c5daa-9c14-4a92-9136-19b26508b9d2

Cabinet Office (2008) 'The National Security Strategy of the United Kingdom: Security in an Interdependent World', https://assets.publishing.service.gov.uk/government/uploads/system/uploads/attachment_data/file/228539/7291.pdf

Cabinet Office (2021) 'Global Britain in a Competitive Age: The Integrated Review of Security, Defence, Development and Foreign Policy', www.gov.uk/government/publications/global-britain-in-a-competitive-age-the-integrated-review-of-security-defence-development-and-foreign-policy/global-britain-in-a-competitive-age-the-integrated-review-of-security-defence-development-and-foreign-policy

Clarke, C. (2014) 'Introduction', in C. Clarke (ed.) *The Too Difficult Box: The Big Issues Politicians Can't Crack*, Biteback Publishing, London.

Commission on Social Mobility and Child Poverty (2019) 'Elitist Britain?', https://assets.publishing.service.gov.uk/government/uploads/system/uploads/attachment_data/file/347915/Elitist_Britain_-_Final.pdf

Conn, D. (2022) 'Revealed: Tory peer Michelle Mone secretly received £29m from 'VIP lane' PPE firm', *Guardian*, 23 November, www.theguardian.com/uk-news/2022/nov/23/revealed-tory-peer-michelle-mone-secretly-received-29m-from-vip-lane-ppe-firm

Daddow, O. and Schnapper, P. (2013) 'Liberal intervention in the foreign policy thinking of Tony Blair and David Cameron', *Cambridge Review of International Affairs*, 26(2): 330–349.

Dearden, L. (2022) 'Suella Braverman says it is her "dream" and "obsession" to see a flight take asylum seekers to Rwanda', *Independent*, 5 October, www.independent.co.uk/news/uk/politics/suella-braverman-rwanda-dream-obsession-b2195296.html

Dodd, V. (2020) 'Black people nine times more likely to face stop and search than white people', *Guardian*, 27 October, www.theguardian.com/uk-news/2020/oct/27/black-people-nine-times-more-likely-to-face-stop-and-search-than-white-people

Doyle, S. (2017) 'A foregone conclusion? The United States, Britain and the Trident D5 Agreement', *Journal of Strategic Studies*, 40(6): 867–894.

Duncan, P. (2017) 'Revealed: Britain's most powerful elite is 97% white', *Guardian*, 24 September, www.theguardian.com/inequality/2017/sep/24/revealed-britains-most-powerful-elite-is-97-white

The Economist (2021) 'Tracking Covid-19 excess deaths across countries', 20 October, www.economist.com/graphic-detail/coronavirus-excess-deaths-tracker

Guardian (2023) 'BMA condemns "political choice" not to tackle "intolerable" pressure on NHS', 2 January, www.theguardian.com/society/2023/jan/02/nhs-under-intolerable-and-unsustainable-pressure-say-medics

Hay, C. (2007) *Why We Hate Politics*, Polity, Cambridge.

Halliday, J. and Dodd, V. (2015) 'UK anti-radicalisation Prevent strategy a "toxic brand"', *Guardian*, 9 March, www.theguardian.com/uk-news/2015/mar/09/anti-radicalisation-prevent-strategy-a-toxic-brand

Hansard (2019) 'House of Commons Debates', Vol. 657, 1 April, Col. 794.

Herman, E. S. and O'Sullivan, G. (1989) *The Terrorism Industry: The Experts and Institutions That Shape our View of Terror*, Pantheon Books, New York.

Hill, S. E. (n.d.) 'An interactive visualization of the links between Tory politicians and firms winning government contracts', My Little Crony, www.sophie-e-hill.com/slides/my-little-crony/

HM Government (2021) 'Global Britain in a Competitive Age: The Integrated Review of Security, Defence, Development and Foreign Policy', https://assets.publishing.service.gov.uk/government/uploads/system/uploads/attachment_data/file/975077/Global_Britain_in_a_Competitive_Age-_the_Integrated_Review_of_Security__Defence__Development_and_Foreign_Policy.pdf

HM Government (2023a) 'Integrated Review Refresh 2023: Responding to a More Contested and Volatile World', https://assets.publishing.service.gov.uk/media/641d72f45155a2000c6ad5d5/11857435_NS_IR_Refresh_2023_Supply_AllPages_Revision_7_WEB_PDF.pdf

HM Government (2023b) 'National risk register, 2023 edition', https://assets.publishing.service.gov.uk/media/64ca1dfe19f5622669f3c1b1/2023_NATIONAL_RISK_REGISTER_NRR.pdf

Jarvis, L. and Legrand, T. (2020) *Banning Them, Securing Us? Terrorism, Parliament and the Ritual of Proscription*, Manchester University Press, Manchester.

Jarvis, L. and Lister, M. (2010) 'Stakeholder security: The new western way of counter-terrorism?', *Contemporary Politics*, 16(2): 173–188.

Jarvis, L. and Lister, M. (2013) 'Disconnected citizenship? The impacts of anti-terrorism policy on citizenship in the UK', *Political Studies*, 61(3): 656–675.

Jarvis, L. and Lister, M. (2015) *Anti-Terrorism, Citizenship and Security: In Anti-Terrorism, Citizenship and Security*, Manchester University Press, Manchester.

Joint Committee on the National Security Strategy (2021) 'The UK's national security machinery: First report of session 2021–22', HC132, HL68, https://committees.parliament.uk/publications/7375/documents/77226/default/

Jones, O. (2015) *The Establishment and How They Get Away with It*, Penguin, London.

Kirk, A. (2017) 'How many people are killed by terrorist attacks in the UK?', *Daily Telegraph*, 17 October, www.telegraph.co.uk/news/0/many-people-killed-terrorist-attacks-uk/

Liberty (2019) 'Guide to the hostile environment', www.libertyhumanrights.org.uk/issue/report-a-guide-to-the-hostile-environment/

Lister, M. (2019) 'Explaining counter terrorism in the UK: Normal politics, securitised politics or performativity of the neo-liberal state?', *Critical Studies on Terrorism*, 12(3): 416–439.

Macdonald, S., Whiting, A. and Jarvis, L. (2024) 'Evidence and ideology in the independent review of Prevent', *Journal for Deradicalization*, 39: 40–76.

McCartney, G., Walsh, D., Fenton, L. and Devine, R. (2022) 'Resetting the course for population health: Evidence and recommendations to address stalled mortality improvements in Scotland and the rest of the UK', Glasgow Centre for Population Health/University of Glasgow, Glasgow.

McCormack, T. (2015) 'The British national security strategy: Security after representation', *The British Journal of Politics and International Relations*, 17(3): 494–511.

Marmot, M., et al. (2020) 'Build Back Fairer: The COVID-19 Marmot Review', UCL Institute of Health Equity/the Health Foundation, www.health.org.uk/publications/build-back-fairer-the-covid-19-marmot-review

Mueller, B. (2019) 'What is austerity and how has it affected British society?', *New York Times*, 24 February, www.nytimes.com/2019/02/24/world/europe/britain-austerity-may-budget.html

Mueller, J. (2005) 'Six rather unusual propositions about terrorism', *Terrorism and Political Violence*, 17(4): 487–505.

Mueller, J. E. (2006) *Overblown: How Politicians and the Terrorism Industry Inflate National Security Threats, and Why We Believe Them*, Simon and Schuster, New York.

Meuller, J. and Stewart, M. G. (2011) *Terror, Security, and Money: Balancing the Risks, Benefits, and Costs of Homeland Security*, Oxford University Press, Oxford.

Neal, A. W. (2012) 'Normalization and legislative exceptionalism: Counterterrorist lawmaking and the changing times of security emergencies', *International Political Sociology*, 6(3): 260–276.

Neal, A. W. (2018) 'Parliamentary security politics as politicisation by volume', *European Review of International Studies*, 5(3): 70–93.

Newman, E. (2022) 'Covid-19: A human security analysis', *Global Society*, 36(4): 431–454.

Office for National Statistics (2021) 'Domestic abuse prevalence and trends, England and Wales: Year ending March 2021', www.ons.gov.uk/peoplepopulationandcommunity/crimeandjustice/articles/domesticabuseprevalenceandtrendsenglandandwales/yearendingmarch2021

Office for National Statistics (2022) 'Coronavirus (COVID-19) latest insights: Deaths, 23 November 2022', www.ons.gov.uk/peoplepopulationandcommunity/healthandsocialcare/conditionsanddiseases/articles/coronaviruscovid19latestinsights/deaths#excess-deaths

Pantazis, C. and Pemberton, S. (2009) 'From the "old" to the "new" suspect community: Examining the impacts of recent UK counter-terrorist legislation', *The British Journal of Criminology*, 49(5): 646–666.

Parker, C. G. (2020) 'The UK national security council and misuse of intelligence by policy makers: Reducing the risk?', *Intelligence and National Security*, 35(7): 990–1006.

Prime Minister's Office (2020) 'Press Release: PM to announce largest military investment in 30 years', 19 November, www.gov.uk/government/news/pm-to-announce-largest-military-investment-in-30-years

Purkiss, J., Walawalkar, A., Gidda, M., Rose, E. and Townsend, M. (2022) 'Revealed: Dozens of vulnerable asylum seekers have died in Home Office housing since 2020', *Guardian*, 25 June, www.theguardian.com/uk-news/2022/jun/25/asylum-seekers-deaths-home-office-housing-data

Butler, Lord (2004) *Review of Intelligence on Weapons of Mass Destruction, Report of a Committee of Privy Councillors*, HC898, HMSO, London.

Selwood, D. (2022) 'The Ukraine war is an ugly excuse for keeping Boris Johnson in power', *New Statesman*, 13 April, www.newstatesman.com/quickfire/2022/04/the-ukraine-war-is-an-ugly-excuse-for-keeping-boris-johnson-in-power

Stacey, K. and O'Carroll, L. (2024) 'Keir Starmer says he is open to processing asylum seekers offshore', *Guardian*, 18 July, www.theguardian.com/uk-news/article/2024/jul/18/keir-starmer-says-he-is-open-to-processing-asylum-seekers-offshore

Transparency International (2021) 'Track and trace: Identifying corruption risks in UK public procurement for the COVID-19 pandemic', Transparency International, London.

The Times (2022) 'One dogged coroner, four needless deaths and a stark conclusion: The NHS is broken', 19 November, www.thetimes.co.uk/article/one-dogged-coroner-four-needless-deaths-and-a-stark-conclusion-the-nhs-is-broken-6zgz6tflk

United Nations Development Programme (1994) *Human Development Report: New Dimensions of Human Security*, Oxford University Press, Oxford and New York.

Vaughan-Williams, N. (2008) 'Borderwork beyond inside/outside? Frontex, the citizen–detective and the war on terror', *Space and Polity*, 12(1): 63–79.

Walsh, D., Dundas, R., McCartney, G., Gibson, M. and Seaman, R. (2022) 'Bearing the burden of austerity: How do changing mortality rates in the UK compare between men and women?', *Journal of Epidemiology & Community Health*, 76(12): 1027–1033.

Williams, P. (2004) 'Who's making UK foreign policy?', *International Affairs*, 80(5): 911–929.

16

What went wrong with Britain and what did Britain have to do with it?

Colin Hay

There is no time in the political history of the last sixty years in which a book entitled *What went wrong with Britain?* would not have seemed timely. But there is also no time during that period in which a book like this has been *more* timely. There is, it seems, no time like the present.

That is alarming. And alarm oozes from every chapter, page, paragraph and carefully honed phrase of this collection. Yet it is far from being the only emotion – nor perhaps the most raw or visceral. This is quite a rare academic work in any number of respects. But not the least of these is the directness of the emotional attachment of each and every contributor to the object of her analysis that it displays. This is nowhere more clearly expressed than in the poignancy of the possessive adjective in the title of chapter five – 'the crisis in *our* National Health Service'.

This, then, is a book, variously, of soul-searching, grief, outrage, indignation, exasperation, betrayal and, at times, anger. It gets close at times, too, to outright dejection but it never embraces such fatalism, clinging – sometimes rather tenuously – to the, at least implicit, thought that if things have gone wrong they can get better, above all following a decisive swing of the electoral pendulum.

My task in this concluding chapter is a tricky one. It is to try to piece together the various diagnoses of our current affliction that the preceding chapters offer in the hope that, by so doing, I might contribute to a credible sense of what it would take for Britain to turn the corner.

What went wrong with Britain?

To be clear from the outset, though, this is not the book that I imagined when the project was first described to me by the editors. Let me disclose here a little secret. The working title for the still prospective project at the time contained an expletive (and it does not take much to infer both the identity of the offending word and the then prospective title from that alone). That is relevant because, although I don't think of myself as easily shocked (at least in that respect), it did perhaps contribute to my misunderstanding of what was being proposed.

For I imagined, in the expletive deleted version of the collection that arrived in my inbox a few weeks ago, something rather different to what I found. I was anticipating a book comprised of a series of separate and discrete diagnoses – individual answers to the question 'what went wrong with Britain?'. What I found, instead, was a detailed, delineated and above all disaggregated domain-by-domain mapping and description of the condition – the plight, the plights – afflicting Britain socially, politically, economically and culturally.

There are advantages and disadvantages to writing a book like this in that way, just as there are occupational hazards in posing questions of the kind 'what went wrong with Britain?'. It might be good to start by exploring what they are.

Let's start with the positives; we'll come to the negatives and the occupational hazards presently. By writing an edited collection of this kind in an almost layered, domain-by-chapter kind of a way, we build a much stronger sense of a shared collective analytic task leading to a single, if rather complex, diagnosis of Britain's current plight and the pre-history of its benighted present. The place of each chapter is clear and the product is greater than the sum of its parts.

But there is a downside. For the answer to the question 'what went wrong with Britain?' is likely to remain at best implicit. And that is where I start to struggle a little more. After reading the chapters of the collection I find that I have learned a great deal about what has gone wrong in Britain over a significant (if variable) period of time. I have a sense of how I might gauge what has gone wrong in a variety of domains and even to track its evolution over time. I feel well-placed – and certainly

What did Britain have to do with it?

better placed – to offer a description of Britain's current plight and to identify at least some of the factors that have contributed to the severity of that plight and, indeed, its distributional consequences. But I do not feel that I have a clear answer to the question that ostensibly motivates the writing of the book. I see some common factors which I might use to make sense of Britain's trajectory, but I have little sense of their relative significance, nor of what might credibly be done today to ensure that what has gone wrong is rapidly put right – nor even, really, if that is possible.

Part of that is undoubtedly due to the structure of the book. But part of it is also due to the very posing of the question that the book, collectively, seeks to answer – the occupational hazard. To ask what went wrong with Britain is, implicitly at least, to assume that what is wrong with Britain (what has gone wrong in Britain) is, in a sense, Britain's fault – or is, at the very least, Britain-specific. It is to assume that the wrong is (or has been) made in Britain.

That may not be a bad premise. But not many things are made in Britain these days – and this might be one of them. The point is that the premise warrants discussion and defence *as* a premise – a discussion and a defence that the book seems to lack and that requires, I would contend, a more comparative perspective than is found in almost all of its constituent chapters. The book, to be fair, is not entirely devoid of comparative claims. But they are rare, far from systematic and invariably implicit.

Indeed, I think we can go further. Most of the factors pointed to that might credibly account for Britain's precarious position and alarming trajectory are not at all specific to Britain, even if they are specifically British in the form they take. They are not exclusively British even if they have a specifically British expression. That is important, above when it comes to the question of what is to be done.

To be clear, the call for a more comparative perspective – or at least a more consciously comparative contextualisation of Britain's position and predicament – does not come from any sense on my part that things are any better in Britain today than the authors of this book imply. Indeed, there is very little at all in their, frankly bleak, assessment of the situation that I do not agree with. That is not my problem, much though I wish it were.

My point is a rather different one. It is that if we are to get what is currently wrong *right*, as it were – above all, as a means to gauge what it would take to *put it right* – we need to distinguish between what is Britain-specific and what is not.

In fact, as a moment's further reflection suggests, it is a little more complicated than even that implies. More useful here, I suggest, is a three-fold distinction between factors that are genuinely specific to Britain; factors that are far from specific to Britain but to which Britain is either particularly exposed or which pose to it a particular challenge; and factors to which Britain is exposed to much like any of its current or (more likely) former (comparative) peers. Yet even that is something of a simplification. For it is also possible to imagine a tragic combination of interaction effects by which, for instance, a certain combination of factors (whether specific or non-specific to Britain) generate, through their case-specific interaction, a series of specifically British pathologies or, more simply, outcomes that are particularly pathological. Brexit itself, as we will come to presently, might well be seen as an example of precisely such a tragic succession of interaction effects of this kind (see also Hay, 2020).

The point is that if, as seems very credibly the case, things are particularly bad in Britain today (so self-evidently so, in fact, that a comparative analysis is not required to demonstrate it), it does not follow that the factors producing this are specific to Britain. Indeed, I would suggest, a comparative analysis – and even a simple comparative *contextualisation* – would show that they are not.

We'll come to the details presently. But why is this important? Very simply, because if the principal factors responsible for Britain's current plight (either directly or through their interaction effects) are not specifically British then a specifically British response to them may well not be adequate. And to see how, in what ways and to what extent it would not be adequate requires a comparative contextualisation. In short, to see the solution to Britain's plight as arising from an answer to the question 'what went

What did Britain have to do with it?

wrong with Britain?' may well be to fall into an analytic trap – a kind of epistemic (if not necessarily methodological) nationalism.

To be fair, I strongly suspect that the editors and the chapter authors of this collection, too, share a common view that Britain's plight is worse than that of its familiar comparators (its former peers) and that, even if aspects of its current predicament are shared, its experience and exposure to such factors is both specific and worse than that of such peers for reasons that are largely domestic in origin. I don't disagree. But I do think that the collective argument of the book and the political implications of that argument would be clearer and more easily drawn if a distinction were explicitly to be made between those factors seen as narrowly domestic and those seen as shared. There is much to learn about each in this volume.

Boris Johnson – the symptom or the condition?

Matthew Watson's fabulously impassioned character assassination of Boris Johnson that sets the tone for the entire volume is a case in point and a good place to start. It is a chapter oozing with frustration, indignation, exasperation, regret and, above all, moral outrage – here, most specifically, with the conduct, duplicity and comportment of Boris Johnson and those immediately surrounding him. It is a cathartic read, a brilliant piece of writing and I agree with almost every sentiment it contains. But it leaves me frustrated in a way that encapsulates well my wider frustration with the book itself. For in its agent-focused detail and in its forensic search for culpability it lavishes perhaps too much attention on the perpetrator, the staging, the script and the performance of the offence and not enough on the conditions of existence of the crime itself. It is, in this respect, distracted by Boris Johnson. As a consequence, it fails to see both his comportment and the very fact that he could be deemed legitimate to govern as symptoms of a wider – and far from narrowly British – condition.

As that perhaps suggests, the most important task here is not necessarily to document as best possible and in the greatest detail the sordid pursuits and sins of a recent Prime Minister. Rather it is to establish how it could come to be that someone 'like Johnson' could come to hold – and indeed to continue to hold for some significant time – high office. Boris Johnson, as I am sure Matthew Watson would be the first to agree, is a symptom of a Britain that *has gone wrong*. But it is not because of Boris Johnson – nor the sins Watson describes – that Britain is where it is today.

Hindsight suggests that Britain would be better off today had Johnson remained a minor TV celebrity, voted Remain rather than Leave, never contested the Conservative leadership, never become Britain's Prime Minister and never made the country of origin of COVID-19 vaccines an index of national pride. But it is not clear what any of that means when it comes to making Britain, if not 'great again', then better in the years to come than it might otherwise be.

Clearly the answer to that question – *the* question in a volume like this – depends much on what Boris Johnson is seen to be symptomatic of. And that remains far from clear. But there are, I think, plenty of suggestions and, indeed, plenty of material to work with in other chapters. Let me venture an answer, or at least begin to identify some of the parameters of one.

Boris Johnson's leadership (at least in the depiction of Watson's chapter) is symptomatic, I would suggest, of a wider set of phenomena recognisable in most of what are usually termed liberal democracies, but with a specifically British-inflected presence – namely, the rise of a new and distinctive nationalist populism. This type of populism is well-described by Owen Worth, who sees the presence of such a populism in Britain as itself symptomatic of British decline (a point to which we will return presently).

But Johnson's brand of nationalist populism is nonetheless highly distinctive. Yes, it is recognisably nationalist, recognisably populist and recognisably nationalist in its populism (and, indeed, populist in its nationalism) in ways that signal its family resemblances to other contemporary populist nationalisms – most notably, perhaps, those of Donald Trump, Giorgia Meloni and perhaps even Jair Bolsonaro. And, yes, in these family resemblances, intriguingly, it is also rather different from the authoritarian populism of, say, Margaret Thatcher (see Hall *et al.*, 1978; Hall, 1979).

What did Britain have to do with it?

Table 16.1: *Populist nationalism and its 'others'*

What it embraces: normative populist nationalism	What it rejects: normalised (neo) liberal multilateralism
'Positional' and oppositional (divisive) politics (politicisation)	'Valence' politics: credibility and competence (depoliticisation)
Plebiscitary democracy	Professional, depoliticised governance
Direct expression of endogenous political preferences	Expert adjudication of exogenous economic necessities
Primacy of politics (governance by choice)	Primacy of economics (governance by economic imperative)
Protectionist and mercantilist	Ricardian and liberal
National sovereigntism	Need for multi-lateral and global governance
Authoritarian populism	Inclusive republicanism
Moral conservatism	Social liberalism and liberal multiculturalism
Populist 'entryism' (government *by* the people)	Elite governance (government *for* the people)
Welfare 'chauvinism'	Welfare conditionality (reward for economic success)
Turnout elevating	Turnout suppressing

Indeed, if political ideologies are characterised, above all today, as much by what they oppose than by what they embrace, then Johnson's brand of nationalist populism looks both very contemporary and, by contemporary standards, rather conventional – as Table 16.1 suggests.

But it is nonetheless very British in its accent, its articulation and its inflection – and, of course, in its almost intimate association with Brexit.

That final point is crucial. For, as Jonathan Hopkin's chapter reminds us, we used to think that the majoritarian and (invariably) bipartisan character of Britain's political institutions and constitutional settlement insulated the polity from populism (since the barriers to entry were so high). The result is that Britain's populist nationalism was incubated outside of the formal political system, significantly in Nigel Farage's UKIP, and was brought to it, in effect, only through the Trojan horse of what was to become Brexit. For it was the fear of the split of the Conservative Party, through the defection of MPs and voters alike to UKIP, that led Cameron to commit to a referendum on continued membership of the EU in an election he thought himself unlikely to win (Hay, 2020). The resulting referendum campaign gave populist nationalists – Farage and ultimately Johnson too – the stage and the audience that the constitution had previously denied them. The rest, as they say, is history – albeit very contemporary history!

To suggest that Johnson is symptomatic of the wider rise of populist nationalism is not, however, to suggest that he is symptomatic only of the rise of populist nationalism. Symptomatology is, after all, what we make of it – in the sense that to see X as symptomatic of Y is to resolve an interpretive ambiguity ('of what is Y symptomatic?') and to make an argument for resolving it in a particular way ('it is symptomatic of X not Z'). The chapters of the present collection provide plenty of resources for resolving that ambiguity in a variety of different, if still largely complementary, ways.

So whilst populist nationalism is perhaps the closest to being the unifying theme and implicit *via media* in this collection it is not the only credible one. Indeed, drawing on other aspects of Watson's character assassination, we might well wish to challenge the idea that Johnson can even be seen as a populist. We might do so on the simple grounds that it is difficult to imagine anyone less credibly capable of passing themselves off as 'of the people' than he. That said, the history of populism has often proved somewhat paradoxical, and not the least paradoxical of its most familiar themes is the capacity of various members of assorted elites at different points in time to pass themselves (and arguably their perceived interests) off as those of the people. For if to be a populist is to be 'in and of the people', then Trump, Johnson, Farage, Gove and Rees-Mogg are, in this respect at least, merely the latest in a long line of somewhat unlikely populists.

The paradoxes of neoliberalism

If the paradoxical character of the populism that defines our age (in Britain, but not just in Britain) is a near constant, if often implicit, theme in this collection, then so too is the scarcely less paradoxical character of neoliberalism (again, in Britain, but not just in Britain).

Here, if anything, the individual chapters of the collection provide an even richer resource to account for the plight and predicament of Britain today. Particularly notable here are the chapters of Morrison, Thompson *et al.* and Narayan on the staggering disregard of systemic and accelerating poverty of income and, above all, wealth associated with both economic neoliberalism and the (im)moral political economy of individual responsibility that it has spawned. This, too, is a theme whose substantive implications are explored in at times graphic and poignant detail in the chapters by Pollock *et al.* (on the underfunding and internal disintegration of the NHS in the context of Covid adversity), Elias *et al.* and Bowers-Brown *et al.* (on social care) and Rogan and Foster (on the betrayal of the intergenerational gender contract that many assumed had been constructed by at least the 1990s and that it was hoped would progressively reduce the salience of gender as an axis of inequality). How naïve such an expectation now seems. No less poignant is Bradbury's eloquent account of the disintegration of the ties that once bound the Union since Brexit.

These chapters make for difficult reading precisely because the image they present of Britain today is so credible, so bleak and, especially, so much bleaker than that which might have been presented even a decade ago.

Crucial to each, and perhaps the defining theme of the volume taken as a whole, is the cultural and institutional normalisation of Anglo-liberal and neoliberal values normatively. This is present in a radical individualisation of perceived responsibility for poverty to the extent that ever-widening levels of inequality now pass increasingly without collective concern, politicisation or public commentary, an ever more pervasive distrust of public institutions, public authority and public good provision more generally and an almost complete disavowal of governed solutions in favour of the law of the market and market innovation (in which, as in Carter's chapter, questions of climate change mitigation are simply left to the vagaries of market-driven solutions alone).

But it is precisely here, where neoliberalism seems so ascendant as to have become profoundly institutionalised, morally normalised and culturally embedded that the interaction with nationalist populism is arguably so crucial.

It is here important to recall that neoliberalism, above all in its initial Thatcherite incarnation, never existed on its own (see Gamble, 1988; Levitas, 1986). It was buttressed and supported by a rather different form of (authoritarian) populism, which at the time tended simply to be called neo-conservatism. They came together – often in a rather tense interdependence (Farrall and Hay, 2014). The same is arguably true today.

Indeed, the rise – initially in the context of the Brexit debate – of nationalist populism in Britain has arguably contributed to a re-composition of the space within which electoral competition takes place, with important implications for the politicisation and depoliticization of neoliberalism. In the process, populist motifs have increasingly been taken up by mainstream parties, particularly (but by no means exclusively) the Conservatives. The effect has been to breathe new life and political salience into *positional* (as distinct from valence) issues which were always highly divisive but of low electoral significance since the parties sought consciously to depoliticise them. Membership of the EU and migration are perhaps the most obvious examples, but the recent electoral weaponisation by Rishi Sunak of environmental commitments is another.

This new contentious politics, mobilised by positional populism, has reconfigured the space of electoral competition, displacing from the heart of the agenda and serving further to depoliticise and entrench an increasingly institutionalised neoliberal economic and social policy orthodoxy. The result is an effective insulation from scrutiny of neoliberal austerity and the monetary policy innovation that has come to be seen as the condition of the restoration of the asset-appreciation dynamics on which growth in Britain is reliant (as Montgomerie and Bailey's excellent analyses makes clear; see also Hay, 2024). In effect, the tables have been turned. What was once low salience is now high salience and what was once high salience is low salience.

Our politics has become more visceral, more divisive and more ugly in the process. Ironically, perhaps, it has also become more normative. But the distributional effects and consequences of 'austeritarian' neoliberalism

What did Britain have to do with it?

and the political economy of growth based on asset-appreciation and wealth inflation have never been, and are not likely to become, part of that debate.

Conclusion

I began these reflections by suggesting that, even if there is no time like the present, then there has never been a moment, during my lifetime at least, when it would not have seemed both pertinent and timely to ask, 'What went wrong with Britain?'.

But what strikes me is that the various answers, both explicit and implicit, offered in this collection are rather different in kind to those provided in the similarly anxious reflections of the not too distant past. I have suggested that some of that is due to the very direct manner in which the editors of this collection have posed the question to their authors today – and the specific terms in which they have framed that question. But there is something else at work here too.

The most obvious comparison here is with the literature on British decline (see, most famously, Gamble, 1994). To be fair, much if not all of that literature was focused on the more narrow question of British *economic* decline – but really only because economic decline was viewed as the source of a wider decline requiring a political solution. Re-reading that literature today, above all in the light cast by this collection, one discovers a much more structural analysis, one seemingly much less interested in identifying and naming the guilty culprits. That is at least in part because Britain's decline is cast, in much of this literature, as an unfortunate if almost inevitable consequence of its earlier success. Having industrialised first and most systematically, Britain was always likely to be caught and, indeed, overtaken (Gershenkron, 1962), just as the relative absence of the need for wholesale post-war reconstruction delayed its second industrial revolution until it was too late (Tomlinson 1991, 1994).

A third factor, crucial to the more recent literature on British economic decline, has been the role played by the infamous 'City–Bank–Treasury' nexus (Ingham, 1984) in ensuring a set of macroeconomic policies consistently favouring financial service providers in the City over the wider economy – with the resulting, typically punitive, comparative cost of capital in Britain being a drain on both innovation and investment.

Such arguments are largely absent from the present volume, reinforcing perhaps the impression that long-standing systemic frailties are not sufficient to explain the extent to which, post-global financial crisis, post-Brexit and post-Covid, Britain's relative economic decline has become something rather more absolute.

But they do have their relevance, above all, if we look from the present to the future. This is a book which concerns itself, rightly and understandably, with Britain's present and its recent past. But it does not reflect much on its immediate future. Yet it is that, above all, that worries me. And it is here that the rather longer story of Britain's relative and perhaps now absolute political and economic decline becomes important. For the message, long story short, of that literature is that Britain has never been good at transitions.

It has never been good at transitions for two principal reasons. First, because it has tended to leave them to the market and the market has lacked access to capital on competitive terms. Second, and relatedly, Britain's pervasive Anglo-liberal antipathy to the state as a guardian of the public good has never allowed it the capacity to lead any transition that might matter. That is especially troubling today, for we do not live in benign times.

To look at our immediate future is surely to recognise that we are entering, if we have not already entered, a new phase in the Anthropocene – an age of Anthropocenic environmental catastrophism as I have suggested elsewhere (Hay, 2023). If such a claim is warranted then things look a lot bleaker for all of us, but above all for Britain, than even the most pessimistic of these chapters implies. In times like the present, the future comes quickly. It is likely to prove a brutal and exhaustive test of one's institutions, one's political culture and one's governing capacity. Judging by the analysis of this volume, it is a test for which Britain alas seems singularly ill-prepared.

What did Britain have to do with it?

References

Farrall, S. and Hay, C. (eds.) (2014) *The Legacy of Thatcherism*, Oxford University Press, Oxford.

Gamble, A. (1988) *The Free Economy and the Strong State*, Macmillan, Basingstoke.

Gamble, A. (1994) *Britain in Decline*, Fourth Edition, Macmillan, Basingstoke.

Gershenkron, A. (1962) *Economic Backwardness in Historical Perspective*, Harvard University Press, Cambridge, MA.

Hall, S., Critcher, C., Jefferson, T., Clarke, J. and Roberts, B. (1978) *Policing the Crisis: Mugging, The State and Law and Order*, Bloomsbury, London.

Hall, S. (1979) 'The Great Moving Right Show', *Marxism Today*, 23 (1): 14–20.

Hay, C. (2020) 'Brexistential angst and the paradoxes of populism: On the contingency, predictability and intelligibility of seismic shifts', *Political Studies*, 68 (1): 187–206.

Hay, C. (2023) 'The New Orleans effect: The future of the welfare state as collective insurance against uninsurable risk', *Renewal*, 31 (3): 63–81.

Hay, C. (2024) '"Asset-based welfare": The social policy corollary of the Anglo-liberal growth model?', *British Journal of Politics & International Relations*, 26 (2): 299–324, https://journals.sagepub.com/doi/10.1177/13691481231218666

Ingham, G. (1984) *Capitalism Divided? The City and Industry in British Social Development*, Macmillan, Basingstoke.

Levitas, R. (ed.) (1986) *The Ideology of the New Right*, Polity, Cambridge.

Tomlinson, J. (1991) 'A missed opportunity? Labour and the productivity problem, 1945–51', in G. Jones and M. Kirby (eds.), *Competitiveness and the State: Government and Business in Twentieth Century Britain*, Manchester University Press, Manchester.

Tomlinson, J. (1994) *Government and the Enterprise Since 1900*, Oxford University Press, Oxford.

Contributors

David J. Bailey is Associate Professor of Politics at the University of Birmingham. His research and teaching focus on different forms of protest and dissent in contemporary capitalism. He is the convenor of the Critical Political Economy Research Network (CPERN), on the editorial board of the journals *Capital & Class* and *Global Political Economy*, and has recent publications in *Work, Employment and Society* and *Environmental Politics*.

Tamsin Bowers-Brown is founding Director of the Office for Institutional Equity at Leeds Trinity University. As a sociologist of education, Tamsin is passionate about tackling inequality in all its forms and is actively working to instigate and embed collaborative approaches across the University and in partnership with organisations across the region to address structural change and highlight inequity.

Jonathan Bradbury is Professor of Politics at Swansea University. He is currently the Associate Dean for Research Innovation and Impact in Humanities and Social Sciences. His research covers territorial politics, devolution, parties, public policy and local government in the UK. He is the author of *Constitutional Policy and Territorial Politics in the UK Vol 1: Union and Devolution, 1997–2007* (Bristol University Press, 2021) and recent

Contributors

articles in *Regional and Federal Studies*, *Political Quarterly* and *National Institute Economic Review*.

Andrew Brierley is Senior Lecturer in Criminology at Leeds Trinity University. He is the author of three books on crime and justice. His expertise includes project management, risk assessment and family intervention services for at-risk youth.

Neil Carter is Professor of Politics at the University of York. His book, *The Politics of the Environment: Ideas, Activism, Policy* (Cambridge University Press, 2018), is in its third edition, and he has a particular interest in green parties, the party politics of the environment and UK climate policy.

Juanita Elias is Professor of International Political Economy at the University of Warwick. She is a feminist political economist and has undertaken research in both the UK and in Southeast Asia on a range of issues including domestic worker migration, paid and unpaid care labour, and the gendered nature of state policy making. Recent books include *Gender Politics and the Pursuit of Economic Competitiveness in Malaysia: Women on Board* (Routledge, 2020), and, with James Brassett, Ben Richardson and Lena Rethel, *I-PEEL: The International Political Economy of Everyday Life* (Oxford University Press, 2022).

Emma Foster is Associate Professor of International Politics at the University of Birmingham. Her research interests include gender and sexuality studies, (de)politicisation and anti-politics, international sustainable development policy and development studies more broadly.

Laura Hamilton is a Research Fellow at the University of Hertfordshire. Her research uses an interdisciplinary mixed-methods approach, exploring women's and adolescents' food practices in relation to poverty, social security and school food policy. Laura's doctorate was linked to the multinational European Research Council-funded 'Families and Food in Hard Times' study at UCL.

Contributors

Louisa Harding-Edgar is a GP in Edinburgh. She trained and has worked largely in practices serving socio-economically deprived areas. Previously an academic clinical fellow in primary care at the University of Glasgow, she also has a Master's in Public Health from Harvard.

Colin Hay is Professor and Director of Doctoral Studies in Political Science at Sciences Po, Paris, and founding Director of the Sheffield Political Economy Research Institute (SPERI) at the University of Sheffield. He is lead editor of *New Political Economy* and founding co-editor of *Comparative European Politics* and *British Politics*. He is a Fellow of the UK Academy of Social Science and, until recently, President of the European University Institute's Research Council. He is the author or editor of many books including, most recently, *The State* (Bloomsbury, 2024, with Michael Lister and David Marsh) and *Crisis and Politicisation* (Routledge, 2022, with Benedetta Voltolini and Michal Natorski).

Jonathan Hopkin is Professor of Comparative Politics in the European Institute and the Department of Government at the London School of Economics. He is the author of *Party Formation and Democratic Transition in Spain* (Macmillan, 1999) and *Anti-System Politics* (Oxford University Press, 2020), and co-editor of *Coalition Britain* (Manchester University Press, 2012). He has published widely on the party politics and political economy of Europe, with a particular focus on inequality and political polarisation.

Lee Jarvis is Professor of International Politics at Loughborough University. He is author or editor of sixteen books and over fifty articles on the politics of security, including, most recently, *Radicalisation, Counter-Radicalisation and Prevent: A Vernacular Approach* (Manchester University Press, 2024, with Stuart Macdonald and Andrew Whiting). Lee's work has been funded by the ESRC, AHRC, Australian Research Council, NATO and others.

Peter Kerr is Associate Professor in the Department of Political Science and International Studies at the University of Birmingham. His main research interests lie in the areas of UK party politics, public policy and governance. He is the co-founder and co-senior editor of the journal *British Politics*. His recent published work includes studies of the UK government's management of the COVID-19 pandemic, and party leadership and change within the Conservative party.

Steven Kettell is a Reader in Politics and International Studies at the University of Warwick. His research interests are centred on British politics, the politics of secularism, non-religion and the role of religion in the public sphere. He is the co-founder and executive editor of the journal *British Politics*.

James Lancaster is an Associate Researcher at Newcastle University. His research interests are in the areas of history and health policy.

Michael Lister is Professor of Politics in the School of Law and Social Sciences, Oxford Brookes University. He is the author or editor of six books, including, most recently, *Public Opinion and Counterterrorism: Security and Politics in the UK* (Routledge, 2023) and *The State: Theories and Issues 2nd Edition* (Bloomsbury, 2022, with Colin Hay and David Marsh).

Johnna Montgomerie is Professor at the University of British Columbia (UBC). She is a political economist focusing on understanding money, debt and inequality, particularly in the United Kingdom, the United States and other English-speaking countries of the Anglosphere. Her research looks at the close connection between debt, power and inequality, which she publishes in various articles in respected journals, books, teaching materials, handbooks and accessible resources for wider audiences. Her work remains important because of the increasing levels of government and personal debt and the significant challenges posed by inequality, which she incorporates into her teaching, community organisations and social justice initiatives.

James Morrison is Associate Professor of Journalism Studies at the University of Stirling. A former national newspaper journalist, his research focuses on media and political discourses around marginalised groups and the relationship between popular narratives, lived experience and public attitudes towards them. His books include *Scroungers: Moral Panics and Media Myths* (Bloomsbury, 2019), *Familiar Strangers, Juvenile Panic and the British Press* (Springer, 2016) and *The Left Behind: Reimagining Britain's Socially Excluded* (Pluto, 2022).

John Narayan is Senior Lecturer in European and International Studies at King's College London and an anti-racist scholar of globalisation and inequality. John's most recent publications have focused on Black Power and the political economy theories generated by groups like The Black Panther Party and Black Power groups based in the UK. His current research centres on anti-racism, abolitionism and international political economy, and the political economy of the influential anti-racist scholar Ambalavaner Sivanandan. He is Chair of the Council of the Institute of Race Relations and a member of the *Race & Class* Editorial Working Committee.

Alexander Nunn is Dean of Research and Professor of Political Economy and Social Policy at Leeds Trinity University and Visiting Research Fellow in the Faculty of Humanities at the University of Johannesburg. His research focuses on the political economy of inequality and the role of social policy in mitigating or enhancing inequality, with a particular focus on labour market policy. Current projects include a focus on labour market policy implementation globally and in the Latin American and Caribbean region in particular. Recent publications appear in *Social Politics*, *British Journal of Criminology*, *Review of International Studies* and *New Political Economy*.

Ruth Pearson is Emeritus Professor of International Development at the University of Leeds. Her research interests include gender and work in the global economy, home-based work, the gendered analysis of production, migrant workers' identities, gender and economic transitions, microcredit, community currencies and gender-sensitive development policies. Recent research projects include studies of Burmese migrant workers in Thailand (*Thailand's Hidden Workforce*, Bloomsbury, 2012, with Kyoko Kusakabe), Asian industrial workers in the UK from Grunwick to Gate Gourmet Striking Women (www.striking-women.org) and a UN Pathfinders commissioned study on care and Covid ('Learning from Covid: How to Make Care Central to Economic Policy Around the World', with Eva Neitzert). She is a Trustee of the Women's Budget Group (www.wbg.org.uk).

Allyson M. Pollock trained in medicine and is a public health physician and academic scholar. She is Professor of Public Health and was Director of the Institute for Health & Society and of the Newcastle University Centre of Excellence in Regulatory Science. She has previously worked at University College London, the University of Edinburgh and Queen Mary University of London, and was Director of Research and Development at University College London Hospitals NHS Foundation Trust from 1998 to 2005. Allyson's research interests are in access to medicines and appropriate medicines use, and pharmaceutical regulation and regulatory science; the epidemiology of child and sports injury; public–private partnerships and health systems; and long-term care. She is well known for her active commitment, spanning over three decades, to promoting universal public health care in the UK, and her expertise on marketisation and other aspects of health service reform.

Shirin M. Rai is Distinguished Research Professor of Politics and International Relations, SOAS, and a Fellow of the British Academy. Her extensive body of work focuses on gender, governance, development and the intersection of gender with political institutions.

Frankie Rogan is Associate Professor of Sociology at the University of Birmingham, UK. Her research focuses on the role of digital cultures in producing contemporary gendered identities, and her recent monograph, *Digital Femininities* (Routledge, 2023), explores the role of social media platforms in constructing cultural and political identities amongst girls and young women in England.

Contributors

Dianna Smith is Associate Professor of Health Geography at the University of Southampton, where she is Co-Director of Centre for the South, a policy think tank. Her research explores social and health inequalities, particularly around diet, in collaboration with local government and third-sector colleagues.

Daniela Tepe is Senior Lecturer in Political Economy at the University of Liverpool. Her work focuses on gender, social policy and inequality with an empirical focus on British politics and the UK. She sees herself as working between disciplines and interdisciplinary, thus her work has been published in a diverse range of journals including *RIPE, Critical Sociology, Public Administration* and *The British Journal of Criminology*. Her most recent book is *The Fault Lines of Inequality* (Palgrave, 2003), co-authored with Johnna Montgomerie and Huw MacCartney.

Claire Thompson is a Reader in Food, Inequalities and Health and the University of Hertfordshire. She is a qualitative researcher with interests in food poverty, food environments and interventions to address dietary health inequalities.

Matthew Watson is Professor of Political Economy in the Department of Politics and International Studies at the University of Warwick. From 2013 to 2019 he was also a UK Economic and Social Research Council Professorial Fellow.

Owen Worth is Head of the Department of Politics and Public Administration at the University of Limerick, Ireland. He publishes in the areas of hegemony, class, resistance and populism in the fields of Politics and International Relations. He is the author of *Morbid Symptoms: The Global Rise of the Far Right* (Zed, 2019), *Rethinking Hegemony* (Palgrave, 2015), *Resistance in the Age of Austerity* (Zed, 2013) and *Hegemony, International Political Economy and Post Communist Russia* (Ashgate, 2005).

List of acronyms

ACE	adverse childhood experiences
BAME	Black, Asian and ethnic minority
BoE	Bank of England
BLM	Black Lives Matter
BNP	British National Party
CCA	Climate Change Act (2008)
CCC	Climate Change Committee
CCUS	Carbon Capture, Utilisation and Storage projects
CRED	Commission on Race and Ethnic Disparities
DUP	Democratic Unionist Party (Northern Ireland)
EV	electric vehicle
FEC	2008 financial economic crisis
FSM	free school meal
GDP	gross domestic product
GHG	greenhouse gas
HCW	health care worker
HPA	Health Protection Agency
IFS	Institute for Fiscal Studies
OECD	Organisation for Economic Co-operation and Development
OFSTED	Office for Standards in Education, Children's Services and Skills

Acronyms

PHLS	Public Health Laboratory Service
PPE	personal protective equipment
QE	Quantitative Easing
RE	renewable energy
SAGE	Scientific Advisory Group for Emergencies
SNP	Scottish National Party
UKHSA	UK Health Security Agency
UKIP	UK Independence Party
YJB	Youth Justice Board

Index

abolitionism 182–183, 185, 189–181, 194, 196
Acheson, D. (1926–2010) 111–112
Action for Children 147–148
Adam Smith Institute 273
Adult Social Care Committee 124, 136
Age UK 126
All-Party Parliamentary Group for Ending Homelessness 146
Anderson, L. (19??–?) 68
Andrews, Baroness 123, 134
anti-austerity 288, 297
anti-fracking 288, 298
anti-immigration 57, 65, 72
anti-imperialism 186–187
anti-racism 14, 185–189, 194–196, 207, 298
Ashcroft, M. (1946–) 274
Asian Youth Movements 185, 196
Associated Society of Locomotive Engineers and Firemen (ASLEF) 289, 302
Association of Directors of Children's Services (ADCS) 147
AstraZeneca 116
asylum seekers 182, 192, 320–321, 324

Attlee, C. (1883–1967) 36
austerity 2, 6, 9, 10–12, 37–39, 43, 122–125, 129–130, 165–167, 172, 199–205, 211–217, 248–253, 260–261, 267–269, 279, 291–293, 296–297, 303–304, 310, 316–319
aviation 232–233, 237–238, 241

Badenoch, K. (1980–?) 68, 69, 72, 183
BAME (Black, Asian and Minority Ethnic) people 34, 181, 196
Bank of England (BoE) 248–249, 253–256, 258, 271, 294
Banks, A. (1966–?) 57, 66, 73, 271
BBC 35, 45, 48, 150
Become 149–150
'bedroom tax' 41, 292, 305
Belfast Agreement 90
benefits 33–48, 164–166, 170, 187, 189, 192, 204–205, 290–292, 299, 303, 305
Better Together campaign 78
Bevan, A. (1897–1960) 104
Biden, J. (1942–) 241
Big Society 166, 204–205
Black, Asian and ethnic minority (BAME) people, *see* BAME

351

Index

Black Lives Matter (BLM) 9, 11, 68, 182–185, 188–191, 194, 196, 289, 300–301
Blair, A. (1953–) 223, 272, 276, 305
see also Labour government
BMA, *see* British Medical Association
Boiler Upgrade Scheme 235
Bolsonaro, J. (1955–) 334
Border Security Command 193
Brady, G. (1967–?) 61
Braverman, S. (1980–?) 67–68, 321
breakfast clubs 172, 174
Brexit 3, 6–12, 16–17, 21–22, 53–72, 77–84, 87, 90–93, 96–99, 206, 208, 210, 223–227, 235, 239, 241, 253–254, 260–261, 266–284, 293–295, 303, 331–340
Brexit Party 279
Britannia Unchained 283
British Bankers' Association 274
British exceptionalism 7, 17, 22, 23, 25, 29, 63
British history 23–28
British Medical Association (BMA) 104, 165, 280, 316
British National Party (BNP) 55, 57
Brown, G. (1951–?) 100, 134, 223, 231, 268, 312
Build Back Better strategy 254
Business for Britain 273

Cameron, D. (1966–?) 26, 36, 55, 71, 166, 223, 229, 239, 253, 268, 272, 278, 293, 305, 320, 335
Carbon Brief 226–228, 231, 233, 238, 242
Carbon Capture, Utilisation and Storage (CCUS) 224, 231, 237–238
care 8–9, 102, 106–109, 117, 122–131, 130–136, 141–142, 145–156, 211
care leavers 146, 149, 154–155
care homes 107–109, 124, 127, 130

Care Quality Commission 109
Care Review 142, 152
Care Stability Index 149
care work 201, 205, 211–214
care workers 124–126, 130–133
Carers UK 132
Casey Review 190–191
CEIC Data 259
Centre for Communicable Disease Control 112
Centre for Policy Studies (CPS) 273
Centre Point 150
Channel 5 44, 46
charities 163–167, 170–173, 204, 211
child benefit 41, 172
child hunger 163, 172–175
child poverty 34, 39, 48, 145–146, 156, 172–173
Child Poverty Unit 40
Child Protection Plan 145–146
childcare benefits 292
children 163–165, 170–175
Children and Families Act 145
Children's Commissioner 148–150
Children's Social Care 142, 152
City of London 270–271, 274–275, 290
City-Bank-Treasury nexus 339–340
Civil Contingencies Committee 17
class 183, 186, 188, 194–196, 318, 319
'Clean Growth Strategy' 227
climate change 10, 14, 222–227, 233–241, 288, 299, 337
Climate Change Act (CCA) 222–223, 226, 239
Climate Change Committee (CCC) 223, 226–227, 233, 234–235
Coalition government 33, 39, 41, 43, 48, 55, 127, 165–166, 199, 203–205, 224, 234, 248, 268, 279, 293
Colston, E. 182
Commission on Race and Ethnic Disparities (CRED) 184–185, 188–189

Index

Commission on Social Mobility and Child Poverty 319
Common Sense Group 26–27
communicable disease control 102–103, 110–113, 116–117
Confederation of British Industry 271
Conservative Environment Network 239
Conservative-Liberal Democrat Coalition, see Coalition government
Contracts for Difference (CfD) 228
COP26 annual climate summit 226–227
Corbyn, J. (1949–?) 55–56, 70–71, 279, 293, 296
Coronavirus Act 109
Coronavirus Business Interruption Scheme 255
Coronavirus Job Retention Scheme 256
cost of living crisis 33, 35, 37, 43–44, 47–4, 126, 129, 136, 147, 163, 165, 169, 174–175, 200, 203, 214–215, 289, 300–301
Coulson, A. (1968–) 272
counter-terrorism 310, 315–320, 323–324
COVID Corporate Financing Facility 255
Critical Race Theory 210, 216
criminal justice system 142–143, 149, 154–155
cronyism 11, 294, 305, 311, 319–324
culture war 14, 26, 64–68, 72, 97, 200, 205–208
Cummings, D. (1971–?) 57, 61, 66, 276–277

Daily Express 27, 73
Daily Mail 36, 73
Daily Mirror 63
Daily Telegraph 36, 73, 240, 272

debt 10, 247–262
 economic storytelling 248–52, 254, 258–261
 household 250, 252, 259–260
 national 250–252, 256, 262
 private 247–252, 254, 258–262
 public 247–252, 254, 258–262
defence 311–317
Democratic Unionist Party (DUP) 89–94, 278
Department for Business, Energy and Industrial Strategy 225, 236
Department for Education 149, 153
Department for Energy and Climate Change 225
Department for Energy Security and Net Zero 225
Department for Levelling Up 125
Department for Transport 224, 232–233
Department for Work and Pensions 37, 146
Department of Health 111, 113–114
devolution 8, 27, 77–84, 94–99, 285
Dilnot Review 127
Disability Law Service 109
disabled people 35–40, 42, 48
domestic abuse 147, 151, 313, 323
Donaldson, J. (1962–?) 91
'Don't Pay' campaign 289, 301
Dowden, O. (1978–?) 26
Drakeford, M. (1954–?) 54, 64–65, 84–85, 88

EEA (European Economic Area) 58, 73
economic crisis 247–248, 255–262
Education Act 164
Eisenhower, D. D. (1890–1969) 321
Electoral Commission 271
energy 310, 313
 crisis 225, 236, 239–241
 efficiency 234, 237, 241

Index

nuclear power 230, 228–230, 237, 242
renewable energy (RE) 228–230, 236, 240–242
security 225, 229, 236, 240–241
wind energy 224, 228–229, 236–242
Energy Price Guarantee 289
'Energy Security Strategy' 240
English Parliament 95–97
Englishness 63–65
Enough is Enough 302
Environmental Land Management Scheme 235
Equal Pay Act 201
Equality Act 153
Equality and Human Rights Commission 125, 132
EU (European Union) 3, 11, 21–23, 55–59, 62, 65, 68–70, 78–80, 83, 90–91, 97, 104, 126, 225–226, 241, 253–254, 261, 266–278, 281, 284, 293, 334–335, 338
European Convention on Human Rights 23, 268
European Court of Human Rights 69, 73
European Economic Area, *see* EEA
European Research Group 278
European Union, *see* EU
Evening Standard 272
EVs *see* vehicles: electric
exceptionalism, *see* British exceptionalism
Extinction Rebellion 192, 300–301

Fabian Society 134–135
Farage, N. (1964–?) 53–57, 64–67, 208, 268, 335–336
FareShare 171
feminism 200–201, 205–207, 209–211, 216
Fianna Fáil 90, 93

financial crisis 2, 4, 147, 190–191, 201–204, 216, 223–225, 234, 247–248, 251–253, 255, 258–259, 267, 274, 291–292, 300
Financial Conduct Authority 215
financial sector 290, 292, 297, 303
financialisation 288, 291–292, 294, 296, 303
Fine Gael 90
Floyd, G. 182, 184, 300
food
  aid 163, 167–171
  banks 1–2, 39, 41, 163, 165–168, 171–175
  insecurity 9, 35, 163–175, 167, 169–172
foreign policy 311, 313, 321
Foster, A. (1970–?) 89–91
foster care 145, 149–150, 155
fracking 236, 239–240
free school meals (FSMs) 169–174

Galbraith, N. S. (19??–?) 112
Gangs Matrix 189–190
GB News 69, 321
gender 199–200, 204–217, 313, 319, 323, 337
  equality 200–201, 204, 207–209, 211, 217
  violence 313, 323
  inequalities 123–126, 133, 136
Gething, V. (1974–?) 88
Givan, P. (19??–?) 90–91
global financial crisis, *see* financial crisis
globalisation 4, 164, 190–191, 267, 270, 282, 284
Good Friday Agreement 65
Gove, M. (1967–?) 26–29, 57, 66, 147, 273, 336
Government of Wales Act (GOWA) 82
Great British Nuclear 230, 242

Index

Greater London Authority 94
Green Deal 234
Green Homes Grant 234
Green Party 90
greenhouse gases (GHGs) 222, 225–227, 232
Griffin, N. (1959–?) 57

Hannan, D. (1971–?) 28
Health and Social Care Act 114
Health and Social Care White Paper 133
Health Foundation 41
Health Protection Agency (HPA) 111–114
'herd immunity' 289, 299
historians 23–29
Holyrood, *see* Scottish Parliament
Home Office 21, 155, 192
homelessness 146, 147, 150
'hostile environment' 310, 320
House of Commons Committee of Public Accounts 20
housing 181, 184–185, 187, 202–203, 288, 294, 296–297, 300–301, 304
Howard League 155
Hunt, J. (1966–?) 58, 95, 125, 230, 283

Illegal Migration Act 2023 295
Immigration 182, 185, 192–193, 268–269, 277, 279, 282
Independent (newspaper) 45, 272
Independent Food Aid Network 166
Independent Review of Children's Social Care 142, 152
Independent Workers' Union of Great Britain 297, 301
industrial action, *see* strike action
inequality 1, 4, 6–7, 9, 10–12, 32–34, 38, 40–43, 143, 146–148, 153, 156, 164–167, 169–170, 174, 199–201, 204–205, 212, 216, 249, 254, 257–262, 290, 292, 294–295, 300, 302–303, 313, 316, 319, 323, 337

Infected Blood Inquiry 102, 110
Institute for Fiscal Studies (IFS) 39, 44, 47, 256–257
Institute of Economic Affairs (IEA) 273
Institute of Race Relations 184–185, 193–194
Insulate Britain 301
Internal Market Act 79, 84
International Court of Justice (ICJ) 195
International Monetary Fund 260
Ireland 77, 89–90, 92–93
Irish general election 90
Islamophobia 68, 182, 189, 196, 318

Javid, S. (1969–?) 130
'Jet Zero Strategy' 233
Johnson, B. (1964–?) 3, 6–8, 12, 14–29, 44–47, 53–71, 80, 91, 96, 99, 122, 124, 126–127, 133, 208, 227, 232, 278–282, 288–289, 293–294, 299, 305–306, 314, 333–336
Joint Committee on the National Security Strategy 321
Joseph Rowntree Foundation 34, 43, 83

Kendall, L. (1971–?) 34, 48
King, M. (1948–) 271
Kwarteng, K. (1975–?) 67, 283

Laming Review 155
Lawrence Review 181
Lawson, N. (1932–2023) 271
Leadsom, A. (1963–?) 28
Leave.EU 57, 65–66, 268
Leveson Inquiry 272
levelling up 43, 59, 98, 100, 123, 174, 270, 282
Levelling Up and Regeneration Act 94
LGBT+ 209

Index

Liberal Democrat Coalition Government, *see* Coalition government
Liberal Democrats 55, 276, 279, 293
Liberty 320
Lilley, P. (1943–2023) 271
living standards 204–207, 216, 266–268, 274, 280–281
local authorities 147–148, 164–166, 168–172, 175
Local Education Authority 153
local government 107–108, 125, 128–129
Local Government Act 164
London Mayor 174
London North Eastern Railway (LNER) 289, 302
Looked After Children 141–142, 145, 149, 152, 155

May, T. (1956–?) 58, 64, 71, 122, 128, 226, 278–279, 282
media 7, 32–39, 42–49, 268, 271–273, 283
Meloni, G. (1977–) 334
metro mayors 94–97
Metropolitan Police 189, 191
migrants 293, 298–299, 301, 303, 310, 313, 320, 338
Miliband, E. (1969–?) 48, 96, 231, 293
military 312–315, 321, 323
Miller Judgement 79, 83
Minimum Services Act 304
Ministry of Justice 155
Monday Club 57, 59, 72
Mone, M. (1971–) 322
Money Charity 259
multiculturalism 9, 55, 57, 64–65, 188, 335
Murdoch, R. (1931–) 55, 72, 272–273
Muslims 188, 190, 193, 318

National Assembly for Wales 82, 87 *see also* Welsh Parliament

National Audit Office 20, 108, 110, 116, 144, 291–292
National Care Service 134
National Food Strategy 170, 175
National Front 57, 59
National Health Service (NHS) 1, 8, 32, 102–106, 109–117, 122–125, 128, 136, 164, 165, 169, 211–212, 276, 281, 316, 329, 337
National Insurance 45, 127
National Risk Registers 312–313
national riots 288
national security 310–320, 323–324
nationalism 3, 7–8, 12, 53–54, 54, 64–65, 77, 96, 333–338
Nationality and Borders Bill 192
NATO 314
Net Zero Scrutiny Group 239
Net Zero Strategy 222, 225–233, 236–237, 240
net zero targets 81
neoliberalism 11–12, 35, 37, 40, 185–196, 200–202, 206, 209, 266–270, 276, 279, 281, 283–284, 289–291, 294–298, 300, 303–304, 336–338
News Corp 272–273
News of the World 272
NHS, *see* National Health Service
non-binary people 213–214
Northern Ireland 269, 276–278
Northern Ireland protocol 21, 65, 90–91, 93
nuclear power 228–230, 237
Nuclear weapons 310, 320

O'Neill, M. (1977–?) 90–91, 93
OECD, *see* Organisation for Economic Co-operation and Development
Office for National Statistics 108, 124, 268, 300, 302, 313, 315
Office for Statistics Regulation 16

356

Index

OFSTED 149
Organisation for Economic Co-operation and Development (OECD) 40, 232, 291
Osborne, G. (1971–) 224, 297
Overseas Operations Act 192
Oxfam 135

Palestine 187, 195–196
pandemic, see COVID-19
Paris Climate Agreement 222, 227
'Partygate' 63, 66
Patel, P. (1972–?) 67–68, 183
pay 164–170, 173, 200, 212, 214–215, 290, 292, 300–305
   see also gender pay gap
pensioners 35–36, 41, 70, 127, 204, 304, 324
PHE, see Public Health England
Pincher, C. (1969–?) 66, 294
Plaid Cymru 83–88
Police, Crime, Sentencing and Courts Bill 192, 301
populism 8, 10, 12, 53–72, 206–211, 216, 333–338
   authoritarian 334, 338
   empty 55–56, 59, 63, 66, 70–72
   left-wing 55–56, 70–71
   nationalist 8, 53, 333–338
   neoliberal 66, 68, 72
   right-wing 54–57, 69
postfeminism 199–206, 214–217
poverty 1–2, 4, 6–7, 9, 12, 32–35, 38–48, 143–147, 181, 187, 196, 313, 324, 337
   see also child poverty, food poverty
Prevent programme 189–190, 318
Price, A. (1968–?) 83, 86
protest 288, 296–304
Public Accounts Committee 108
Public Health England (PHE) 114, 132, 169, 174

Public Health Laboratory Service 112–113
Public Order Act 2023 289, 298

Quantitative Easing (QE) 253, 256, 258, 292, 294

'race' 183–188, 187–188, 196, 203, 205–208, 210–216
racial inequalities 123–125, 132, 136
racism 9–10, 181–190, 193–197, 296, 298, 303, 318
   see also anti-racism
radicalisation 314, 318
red wall 123, 130
Redwood, J. (1951–) 271
Rees-Mogg, J. (1969–?) 23, 28–29, 236, 336
Reeves, R. (1979–?) 41, 249
referendum 7, 78–82, 85. 267–272, 275–277, 279–281, 284, 335–336
Reform Party 53, 56, 68–69, 72, 88, 208, 321
renewable energy (RE) 228–230, 236, 240–242
Renters Reform Bill 301
Renters' Rights Bill 304
Resolution Foundation 40, 109
Rothermere, 4th Viscount (1967–) 272
Royal Historical Society 26
Runnymede Trust 193
Russia 225, 271, 311, 314
   invasion of Ukraine 225, 228, 281, 283, 311, 314
Rwanda deportation plan 21, 23, 67, 288, 289, 295, 301, 310, 321

SAGE (Scientific Advisory Group for Emergencies) 61–62, 71
Salmond, A. (1954–?) 96
Sandford, M. (19??–?) 95
Scarman report 188

Index

school strikes 288, 299
Scotland 63–66, 68–69, 77–85, 94–5, 98
Scotland Act 78
Scottish Greens 79, 81
Scottish independence 8, 77–81, 85–87, 96
Scottish National Party (SNP) 64, 77–83, 87, 96, 231
Scottish Parliament 78–82, 86, 88, 310–324
Serious and Organised Crime 314
Senedd Cymru, *see* Welsh Parliament
Sex Discrimination Act 201
sexuality 204–205, 209–211, 216–217
Shelter 146
Sinn Féin 77, 89, 90–94
Skidmore, C. 228
Skills for Care 109, 132
SNP, *see* Scottish National Party
social care, *see* care
social harm 141–143, 146, 148–150, 153–154
social security, *see* benefits
Social services 316
solar energy 224, 228–229, 237, 240
Spectator, The 240
Starmer, K. (1962–?) 34, 40, 67–71, 98, 100, 133–136, 174, 184, 192, 200, 217, 249, 262, 267, 289, 304, 323–324
Staying Put 144, 145, 150
'Stop the Boats' 321, 323
Streeting, W. (1983–?) 104, 134
strike action 11, 288–290, 295, 299–302
Strikes (Minimum Service Levels) Act 2023 289, 295, 302
student revolts 288, 296–297
Sturgeon, N. (1970–?) 54, 78–81
Sun (newspaper) 73
Sunak, R. (1980–?) 14–16, 22–23, 33–37, 47, 53, 63, 65–71, 98, 127, 190, 230–231, 234, 241–242, 261, 283, 289, 295, 302, 321
Supreme Court 79, 231, 289, 291
Sustain 166
Swinney, J. (1964–?) 81

Taxpayers' Alliance 273, 277
terrorism 310–318, 322
Thatcher, M. (1925–2013) 24, 46, 53, 59, 61, 66, 113, 270, 273, 283, 334, 338
TheCityUK 274
think tanks 273, 276–277, 282–283
Thunberg, G. (2003–) 226
Times (newspaper) 73
Trade Union Act 2016 292, 304
trade unions 11, 37, 48, 185, 193, 196, 289–290, 292, 297, 299, 301–302, 304
transgender people 14, 81, 207–209, 213–216
Trump, D. (1946–) 209–210, 298, 334, 336
Truss, L. (1975–?) 8, 15, 33, 35, 43, 54, 60, 66–67, 71, 125, 127, 236, 240, 261, 282–283, 289, 294, 301–302
Trussell Trust 166–168, 175
tuition fees 296–297

UK Health Security Agency (UKHSA) 111, 114–116
UK Independence Party (UKIP) 55–57, 66, 293
UK Uncut 11, 297
Ukraine 4, 10, 20–21, 163, 223, 225, 228, 240–241, 281, 283, 300–301, 311, 314
Ulster Unionist Party 90
UN (United Nations) 2, 146
UN Conference on Trade and Development 186
unemployed 35–37, 39–42, 48
Unionist 89–94

Index

United Nations Development Programme 312
United States (US) 65, 69, 182–183, 189, 191, 209–210, 256, 258, 290–291, 298, 300, 321
United Voices of the World 297, 301
Universal Credit (UC) 33–34, 37, 39, 44–47, 165–166, 170, 173, 256–257
unpaid carers 123–124, 129–132

Vallance, P. (1960–?) 19
vehicles 232, 236–237, 242
violence 143, 147, 151, 313, 323
Vote Leave 16–17, 21, 28, 57, 65, 66

wages, *see* pay
Wales 63–68
Wallace, B. (1970–) 317
War on Terror 189–190
welfare, *see* benefits
Welsh Assembly. *see* Welsh Parliament
Welsh Government 83–87

Welsh independence 77, 83–87
Welsh Labour 77, 83–88
Welsh nationalism 8, 77
Welsh Parliament 82, 85–88
West Lothian Question 95
Westminster 53, 54, 64, 78–80, 84
'Westminster model' 266, 275–278, 285
Whitty, C. (1966–?) 19
windfall tax 230, 236
Windsor Framework 65, 91, 93
'woke' 192, 207
Women's Budget Group 125, 133, 135, 204
Working Tax Credit (WTC) 257
World Bank 38
World Health Organisation 103, 112

Yarl's Wood 298
Yes Cymru 64, 83–85
YJB (Youth Justice Board) 149, 155
Yousaf, H. (1985–?) 81

zero-hours contracts 109, 131–132

EU authorised representative for GPSR:
Easy Access System Europe, Mustamäe tee 50,
10621 Tallinn, Estonia
gpsr.requests@easproject.com

www.ingramcontent.com/pod-product-compliance
Lightning Source LLC
LaVergne TN
LVHW040825250725
817018LV00048B/1261